MW01628899

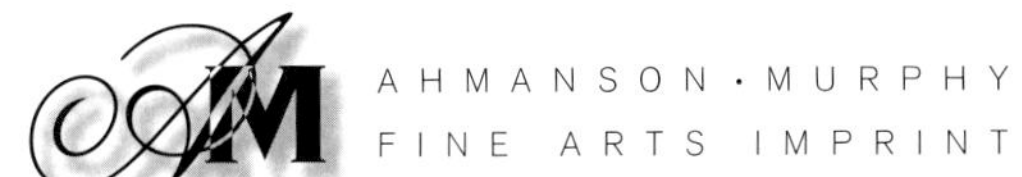

THE AHMANSON FOUNDATION
has endowed this imprint
to honor the memory of
FRANKLIN D. MURPHY
who for half a century
served arts and letters,
beauty and learning, in
equal measure by shaping
with a brilliant devotion
those institutions upon
which they rely.

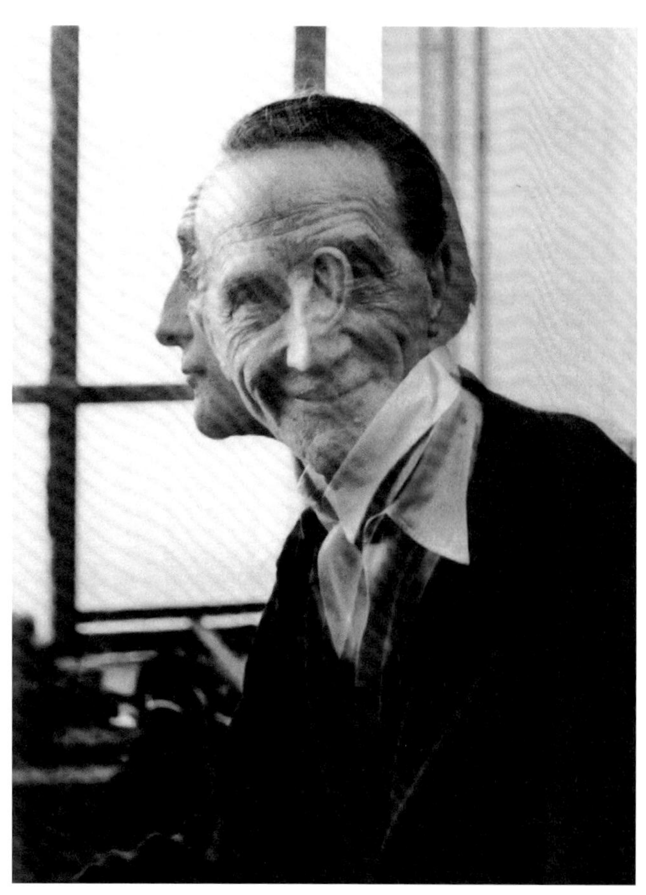

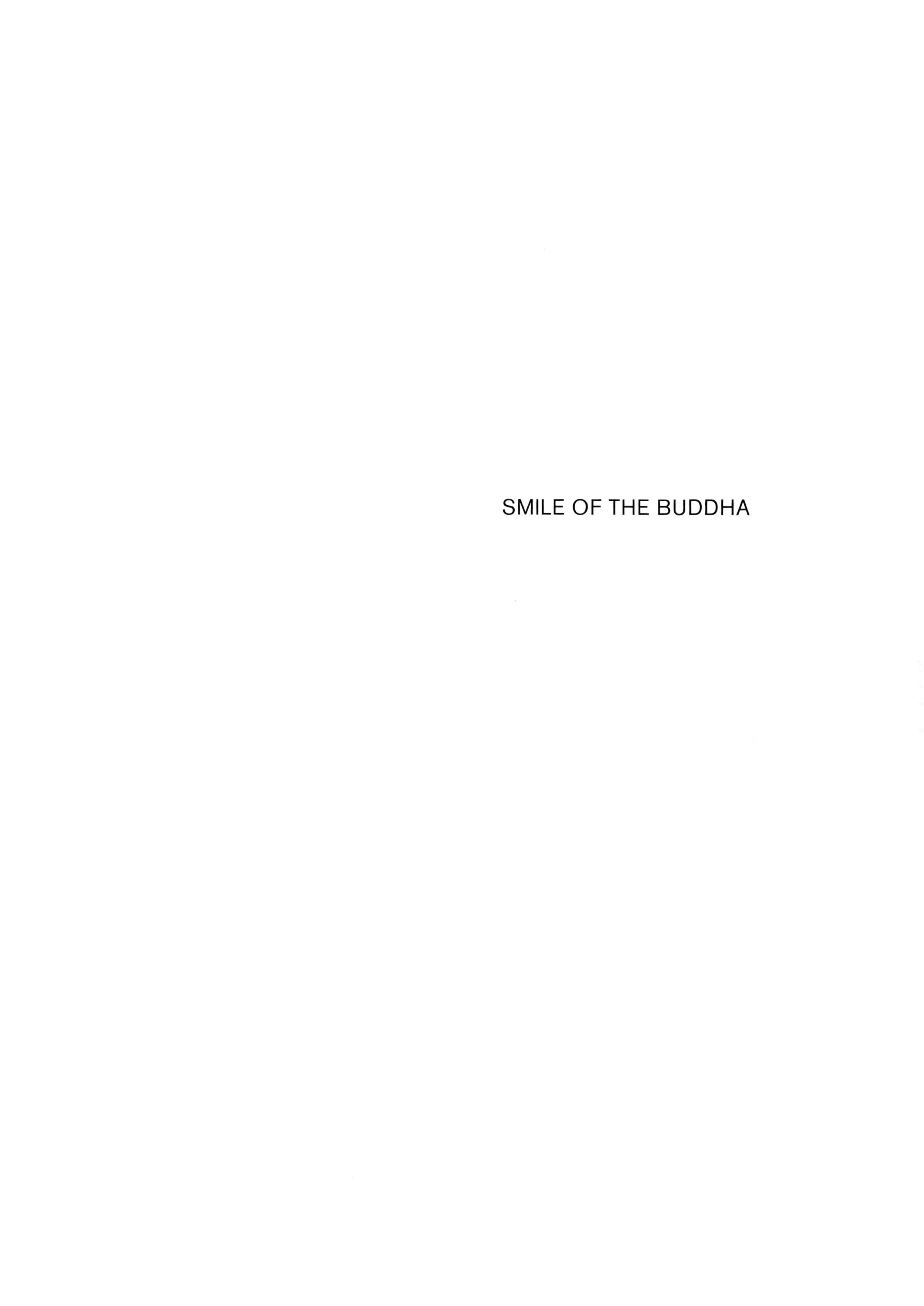

SMILE OF THE BUDDHA

SMILE OF THE BUDDHA

EASTERN PHILOSOPHY AND WESTERN ART
FROM MONET TO TODAY

JACQUELYNN BAAS
FOREWORD BY ROBERT A.F. THURMAN

UNIVERSITY OF CALIFORNIA PRESS BERKELEY LOS ANGELES LONDON

Frontispiece: Victor Obsatz, Portrait of Marcel Duchamp, 1953, gelatin silver print, 13½ x 10½ in. Copyright © Victor Obsatz 2005/Achim Moeller Fine Art, Ltd.

University of California Press
Berkeley and Los Angeles, California

University of California Press, Ltd.
London, England

Wassily Kandinsky's poem "Why?" is quoted by permission from his *Sounds,* translated by Elizabeth R. Napier (New Haven: Yale University Press, © 1981).

Library of Congress Cataloging-in-Publication Data

Baas, Jacquelynn
Smile of the Buddha : Eastern philosophy and Western art from Monet to today / Jacquelynn Baas ; foreword by Robert A.F. Thurman.
p. cm.
Includes bibliographical references and index.
ISBN 0-520-24208-4 (cloth : alk. paper)
1. Arts, Modern—20th century. 2. Arts, Modern—Buddhist influences. 3. Art and philosophy—Europe. 4. Art and philosophy—United States. I. Title.
NX456.B25 2005
709'.04—dc22 2005006293

Manufactured in Canada

14 13 12 11 10 09 08 07 06 05
10 9 8 7 6 5 4 3 2 1

The paper used in this publication meets the minimum requirements of ANSI/NISO Z39.48-1992 (R 1997) (*Permanence of Paper*).

SPONSORING EDITOR
Deborah Kirshman
ASSISTANT ACQUISITIONS EDITORS
Erin Marietta, Sigi Nacson
PROJECT EDITOR
Sue Heinemann
EDITORIAL ASSISTANT
Lynn Meinhardt
INDEXER
Ruth Elwell
DESIGNER
Jessica Grunwald
PRODUCTION COORDINATOR
John Cronin
TEXT
10.5/16 Scala
DISPLAY
Akzidenz Grotesk
COMPOSITOR
Integrated Composition Systems
PRINTER AND BINDER
Friesens

The publisher gratefully acknowledges the following individuals and organizations for their generous support of this book:

BENEFACTORS

Robert L. Elder

Furthermore: A Program of the J. M. Kaplan Fund

The Art Endowment Fund of the University of California Press Associates, which is supported by a major gift from the Ahmanson Foundation

CHAIRMAN'S CIRCLE OF THE UNIVERSITY OF CALIFORNIA PRESS ASSOCIATES

Anonymous

Jeanne Falk Adams

John M. and Jola Anderson

Jacqueline and Clarence Avant

Phyllis K. Friedman

Jean Gold Friedman

Adele M. Hayutin

Barbara S. Isgur

Beth and Fred Karren

Lata Krishnan and Ajay Shah

John Lescroart and Lisa Sawyer

Michael McCone

James and Carlin Naify

Elvira E. Nishkian

Kenneth and Frances Reid

Lisa See and Richard Kendall

Susan Stone

Judith and William Timken

Peter Booth Wiley and Valerie Barth

SUPPORTERS

Barbro Osher Pro Suecia Foundation

Frances and Ed Barlow

Judy and Paul Cortese

John R. and Earlene Taylor

Alta Tingle

THIS BOOK IS DEDICATED TO MY TEACHER YVONNE RAND

Standing on a mountain with his disciples around him, the Buddha did not on this occasion resort to words. He simply held aloft a golden lotus. No one understood the meaning of this eloquent gesture save Mahakasyapa, whose quiet smile indicat[ed] that he had gotten the point.

HUSTON SMITH AND PHILIP NOVAK, *BUDDHISM*

Our best sculpture expresses the effort of thought—one might be tempted to say its impotence—by a tensing of the entire body, from the forehead to the toes. But the thought that the Oriental figure conveys through the serenity of the Buddhist smile is thought released, freed from the flesh. It doesn't search; it neither strives nor tires. It contemplates.

JACQUES BACOT, INTRODUCTION TO *LE POÈTE TIBÉTAIN MILARÉPA,*
BRANCUSI'S FAVORITE BOOK

CONTENTS

FOREWORD

AS I GROW OLDER, I MORE AND MORE THINK TO MYSELF, "How incredibly fortunate that the Buddha smiled!" Upon attaining unexcelled enlightenment, supposed to be the perfect knowledge of the true nature of reality, might one not rather comment, "Oh, no! How awful!"? If the final reality were misery, suffering, an unhappy fate for oneself and other beings, why would one smile? But our Buddha perceived a reality of happiness, felt bliss within himself to the full, and saw both nirvana as immanent for all beings and the way to help them realize nirvana for themselves. His radiant smile was a first step in his ceaseless gift of that help. It has been celebrated for millennia throughout the lands of Asia touched more or less deeply by the Buddha, and it has been central to the profound and magnificent arts of those lands.

How wonderful that Jacquelynn Baas has seen the light of the Buddha's smile shining from faraway Asia into the realm of the art of modern times in what we think of as the West! How amazing that some of the great artists whose works move us so, who have opened our eyes to the shimmering beauties and deeper dimensions of our world, might themselves have been inspired by the enlightenment arts emanating from Asia through the imperialist economy into the museums and bazaars of Europe! This is not to depreciate the achievements of these creative giants, but to pay tribute to their vision of the world, which was broader than that generally available in the theistic and militaristic West, and to appreciate how artists can be inspired with enthusiasm for the higher evolutionary opportunity for human beings that the horizon of enlightenment affords.

When the Buddha walked upon this earth, in ancient India or in mythic reality, he was often recorded as smiling at auspicious moments. His dazzling smile was revered for its wondrous healing and liberating powers. Typical is a lovely story in the *Ashokāvadāna (Legend of King Ashoka)*.[1] The Buddha, having just entered a large city on his morning almsround, meets a small boy playing in a sandbox. The boy feels a strong urge to give something to the Buddha, but he has nothing special. So he imagines giving the Buddha a handful of barley-meal, and with that thought he places a handful of sand in the Buddha's bowl, making with all his might the childish prayer, "In the future may I be king of the whole earth and then I will truly pay homage and serve the Blissful Lord!" Knowing that in a future life this boy would become the great all-Indian emperor Ashoka the Truth-Upholder, the Buddha smiled. The text describes his smile in lavish detail:

> Then the Enlightened One smiled. It is the rule that when the Blissful Buddhas smile, at that time blue, yellow, red, and white rays, and rays which are of the color of madder, crystal, and silver issue forth from their mouths. Some go upwards and some go downwards.
>
> Those which go downwards go to the hells . . . becoming cold they descend into the eight hot hells . . . and becoming hot they descend into the cold hells. Because of this the various torments suffered by the beings who dwell in these hells come to an end, and the thought arises in their minds, "Sirs, have our various torments come to an end because we have passed out from this state of existence and have been reborn in some other place?" In order to inspire them with faith, the Enlightened One sends forth a miraculous likeness of himself. Beholding this, the thought arises in their minds, "Sirs, we have not passed out from this state of existence, we have not been reborn in some other place. This is some being the like of whom we have never seen before. Because of his supernatural power our various torments have come to an end." They conceive faith in that apparition, and after they have exhausted the evolutionary momentum which caused their experience in the hells, they take rebirth among humans and gods where they become recipients of the teachings. The rays which go upwards go to the six desire heavens . . . and the seventeen pure form heavenly planes of the [gods], and there in all of them they proclaim loudly "Impermanence, suffering, voidness, and selflessness." And the rays recite two stanzas: "Rouse yourselves! Renounce this worldly life! Apply yourselves to the teachings of the buddhas! Destroy the army of death as an elephant destroys a hut of reeds! One who will walk without heedlessness in this Teaching and this Discipline will free herself or himself from involuntary rebirth and will put a final end to suffering."
>
> Then these rays, after they have traversed this great universe, return and go following along close behind the Enlightened One. . . . At that time those rays passed clockwise three times around the Enlightened One and disappeared into the palm of his left hand. Then the venerable Ananda joined his hands in reverence and recited a stanza.

> "Not without reason, not without cause,
> The Buddhas are without levity of mind,
> Are free from madness and pride,
> And cause the supreme sainthood in the world.
> Not without reason do the victorious Buddhas
> manifest their smile, white as conch or lotus petal."

When Ananda, the Buddha's attendant, asks the Buddha why he smiled, the Buddha prophesies that this boy will become, by the power of his offering and vow, the Emperor Ashoka, the famous conqueror who in midlife repented his youthful military conquests. Ashoka invented what he called nonviolent "truth-conquest," becoming a major patron of all spiritual people and the Buddhist schools in particular. He left a record of his remarkable realization and transformation in edicts inscribed on stone pillars whose lion and wheel capitals are emblazoned on the flag of modern India.

The Buddha's smile relieves the beings who are tormented in hells, giving them a moment of respite and an inspiration that helps them find eventual rebirth in a vastly better situation. The light rays of his smile rouse the gods from their meaningless shallow pleasures, inspiring them to take advantage of their leisure and intelligence to achieve the higher happiness of freedom and enlightenment. One might say that, whether literary or real, this act of smiling is an original piece of performance art. Like an artist, a buddha sees beauty in the world. His or her delight naturally flows into an expression that automatically shares that vision and delight with others.

The Buddha's great discovery was the third noble truth, the higher reality of nirvana, our true reality of freedom from suffering and enjoyment of bliss, to which we can quite easily awaken. Once his own inner bliss was released, as expressed in his magnificent smile, the Buddha did everything he could to school us all in the teachings and disciplines we can use to come to our own awakening. He worked for forty-five years to provide us with every possible means to critique our habitual delusion of alienated selfhood and free ourselves from the prison of egotism and its stressful and futile struggle against the overwhelming universe of other beings and things. The Buddha did not seek to release us from our habitual prison of self-centeredness only to lock us into some new prison called either the "Buddhist religion" or "ideology." He cannot force us to awaken, or inject us with buddhahood, so to speak; he can only stimulate our imagination so that we may become inspired to employ appropriate methods of wisdom and compassion to accelerate our evolution toward enlightenment.

How do the liberating light rays of the Buddha's smile described in the *Ashokāvadāna* link to Jacquelynn Baas's insightful discernment of both the obvious and the subtle influences of Buddhism in artworks and art trends of the modern West? The colors and reflections celebrated by Claude Monet or the exquisite shapes carved and polished by Constantin Brancusi give us relief from our habitual dissatisfied perceptions of objects in the world. The disturbing conjunctions and disruptions of Marcel Duchamp or John Cage jolt us into a deeper probing of our experience and open us to a more satisfying appreciation of the meaningful aspects of our existence. Baas has carefully untangled history and delicately displayed patterns of connection and influence in avant-garde culture. Her work reveals how some of our most influential artists explored and expressed the sophisticated perceptions and joyful energy emanating from the realm of Buddhist Asia. Theirs was a subversive activity, for this trend got its start at a time when the dominant Western culture was still obsessed with imperialism and colonialism, convinced of its unassailable superiority in all domains—aesthetic and philosophical, as well as religious, technological, and, perhaps above all, military.

This book is part of a courageous and encouraging new trend of a postcolonial scholarship that faces the finding that creativity and sensitivity flourish better in a climate of gentleness and peacefulness than in one of imperialistic expansiveness, militancy, and violence. It is courageous because it bucks the dominant culture of self-seeking scholars, who flatter conventional wisdom by assenting to our ethnocentric pretensions of unquestioned superiority. It is encouraging because it is part of a civilizing cultural evolution. Only when we can begin to see that the gentle conquered are often more developed than the violent conquerors, only when we can face our own need for ethical and spiritual progress, will we begin to learn the things we need to know to have a better life. We are the underdeveloped. We need to develop ourselves in the arts of life: in the life of art, ethics, and even science, especially the science of the mind and heart. Only with such development will our frustrated superpower savagery transform into the peace of mind, gentleness, altruism, and satisfaction that are the signs of true human civilization.

With its well-informed vision and sophisticated insight, I am honored to welcome this delightful book. I enthusiastically salute Baas's meticulously presented revelation of these interconnections between the world's great cultures. May the Buddha smile once more upon this work, and may the rays of that smile open each of our hearts a little more to the blessings of great art, which can move us to the reality of hope for all and the presence of our own true freedom and joy!

ROBERT A. F. THURMAN
Jey Tsong Khapa Professor of Buddhist Studies
Columbia University

ACKNOWLEDGMENTS

MY OWN INTRODUCTION TO A BUDDHIST PERSPECTIVE was seeing Thornton Wilder's play *Our Town* when I was in my early teens. For an unhappy Dutch Calvinist girl in Grand Rapids, Michigan, Wilder's dramatic insistence on the importance of the everyday—so-called ordinary experience—was a Saul-on-the-road-to-Damascus moment. It must have been around the same time that I wrote a book report on J. D. Salinger's *The Catcher in the Rye* for what I now realize was an unusually tolerant ninth-grade English teacher at Oakdale Christian School. I dearly wish I still had that paper. But at that time and in that place, there was no intellectual framework available to me within which these Buddhist-influenced insights could blossom. That came some twenty years later, when I began to research the influence of Buddhism on the work of Paul Gauguin. This book is one of the results.

Another result was an arts consortium entitled "Awake: Art, Buddhism, and the Dimensions of Consciousness," which I developed with Mary Jane Jacob in 1999. Mary Jane's companionship and insights have been key factors in the writing and editing of this book. I want to acknowledge the good supporters of Awake, especially Charles Halpern and the Nathan Cummings Foundation, Melanie Beene and The James Irvine Foundation, and Agnes Bourne. I also owe a deep debt of gratitude to four people who lovingly coached and corrected me during the writing and editing of this book: Rob Elder, Stuart Horwitz, Yvonne Rand, and William Sterling.

Others who have been generous with their time and knowledge include Stephen Addiss, Laurie Anderson, Linda Bamber, Frances Hill Barlow, Reva Basch, Victor Bonfilio, Ramsay Breslin, Derrick Cartwright, Douglas Druick, Linda Duke, Alan Elms, Marilyn Fabe, Gary Gach, Lanier Graham, Louise Gund, Marjorie Harth, Helen and Joel Isaacson, Claire Kahane, Betty Klausner, Kay Larson, Steven Leiber, John Listopad, Mardi Louisell, Tano Maida, Lu and Peter Martin, Wendy Martin, Thomas McEvilley, Forrest McGill, Geneviève Monnier, Martin Muller, Alexandra Munroe, Victoria Nelson, Morton Paley, Barry Pateman, Andrew Pekarick, Hilary Rand, Larry Rinder, Rena Rosenwasser, Mac Runyan, Riet Samuels, Patricia Sanders, Jerry Schifman, Peter Selz, Catherine Shear, Jordan Simmons, Norah and Norman Stone, Charles Stuckey, Sharon Takeda, Martha Tedeschi, Robert Thurman, Marc Treib, Richard Tuttle, Thomas Tweed, Stephen Walrod, Darren Waterston, John Zurier, and Nina Hubbs Zurier.

Special thanks are due to my acquiring editor at the University of California Press, Deborah Kirshman, and to Erin Marietta in her office; to my skillful editor at the University of California Press, Sue Heinemann; to my agent, Amy Rennert; to the wonderful staff in Interlibrary Loan at the University of California, Berkeley; and to Carol Wolf, who managed the illustration program for me with intelligence and patience.

Buddhism is a growth. The diamond-throne of the original enlightenment is now difficult indeed to discover, surrounded as it is by the labyrinth of gigantic pillars and elaborate porticos which successive architects have erected, as each added his portion to the edifice of faith. For there has been no generation that did not bring its own stones and tiles to widen the great roof that, like the bodhi-tree itself, offers every day a broader shelter to mankind.... Yet it is this very power of adaptation and growth that constitutes the greatness of that system.

KAKUZO OKAKURA

The forms of Buddhism must change so that the essence of Buddhism remains unchanged. This essence consists of living principles that cannot bear any specific formulation.

THICH NHAT HANH

INTRODUCTION

THE IMPACT OF ASIAN PHILOSOPHIES on European and American culture is a huge topic that has been addressed by a number of fine writers. One aspect, however—the impact of the teachings of the Buddha on modern artists in the West—remains relatively unexplored. My goal in this book is simply to foreground possible Buddhist perspectives within the art of twenty European and American artists from the last quarter of the nineteenth century to the present. *Smile of the Buddha* is not intended to be comprehensive, but rather to provide a new lens through which to perceive and interpret the art of the recent past.

What the Buddha offered, and what those who followed him elaborated, is an articulated path to freedom from mental and emotional conditioning. Unlike Judaism, Christianity, or Islam, Buddhism is not a revealed religion. It is a realized religion—realized from within. It consists of experiential practices based on a body of accumulated knowledge about the human mind that emphasizes the inevitability of change and the interdependence of all existence. The teaching unique to later Buddhism is "emptiness": all things are empty of "inherent self-existence"; nothing exists separately or permanently. While people throughout human history have observed and analyzed this aspect of existence in various ways, it was Siddhartha Gautama who, in a disciplined search for a solution to the problem of suffering, most notably perceived and conveyed this fundamental understanding of reality. His teachings, referred to by the Sanskrit word *dharma,* earned him the Sanskrit title *Buddha*—"awakened." Being "awake" is not about transcendence; it is about seeing things as they actually are, realizing and accepting what is so. The freedom offered by Buddhism is freedom from suffering, which is how the Pali word *dukkha* is usually translated. The literal meaning of *dukkha* refers to an off-center axle and thus a life that feels awry, bumpy, and generally unsatisfactory.

The Buddha's insights grew out of a patient testing and removal of false views through meditation, the method of his day. Knowledge was understood to be the result of inner transformation—what remains when false beliefs are removed. For example, a man may be frightened by a piece of rope he mistakes for a snake. Once he sees it for what it is, his fear dissipates. "The answer to the question, 'what shall I do about the snake?' is 'Nothing.' Instead, you must learn to see it for what it is."[1] (Marcel Duchamp's version of this riddle was: "There is no solution because there is no problem."[2]) Though simple, this perspective is so different from the way in which Westerners have been conditioned to perceive the world that achieving it usually requires considerable training of the mind through meditation. The Buddha perfected a penetrative form of meditation that he taught to others, urging them to test his theories for themselves.

The Buddha lived in northern India five centuries before Christ, during a time of spiritual uncertainty. From the pantheon of gods contained in the *Vedas,* the creative spirit had, by the time of the *Upanishads* (800–500 BCE), become increasingly identified with the *atman,* or "self." The temporal world of the senses was dismissed, and the goal became escape from the cycle of rebirth and death through positive *karma,* or "deeds," which were associated with sacrifice. By the fifth century BCE, dissatisfaction with elaborate sacrificial rituals requiring the services of Brahmin priests and an increasingly rigid caste system generated numerous alternative spiritual practices. Two have survived; both are ethical philosophies of everyday life. Jainism, founded by Mahavira, who became known as the *Jina,* or Victor, continues to be an important religion in western India. Buddhism, founded by Siddhartha Gautama, spread first in India and then to China, Tibet, Korea, Japan, and Southeast Asia.

We know little for certain about Siddhartha's life. Tradition says he was born into a warrior caste tribe, the Shakyas, who lived on the border of India and Nepal. According to legend, when Siddhartha was born, a sage from the Himalayas told his father the baby would rule the world as a conqueror—unless he became a religious mendicant, in which case he would rule by conquering the human mind. Preferring the former, Siddhartha's father sequestered him at home, surrounded by comforts designed to keep him there. But, disturbed by the suffering associated with illness, old age, and death, and observing that indulgence provided no escape from suffering, Siddhartha embarked on the ascetic's path to seek an answer to his existential questions. He studied with several religious leaders, learned meditation, and practiced austerities, including fasting, but after six years felt he understood suffering no better than anyone else. He then took nourishment and entered a deep meditative state.

When he emerged, his mind was clear and he perceived the interdependence of all things and what are called the four noble truths:

- Our experience of life as unsatisfactory is inevitable.
- The reason for this is that we want what we don't have and want to hang onto what we do have.
- It is possible to escape this cycle of wanting and dissatisfaction.
- This happens by cultivating attitudes and behaviors consistent with the perception of the interrelatedness of all beings—the so-called middle way between indulgence and asceticism.

What the Buddha "woke up" to was not a how-to list for overcoming suffering, but a unified realization of how the mind works. As the Scottish Buddhist scholar Stephen Batchelor puts it, "Understanding anguish leads to letting go of craving, which leads to realizing its cessation, which leads to cultivating the path. These are not four separate activities but four phases within the process of awakening itself."[3] Similarly, the fourth truth, known as the noble eightfold path, is not about stages in perfecting the mind, but rather about eight interrelated attitudes and behaviors: right view of life as it is, which is cultivated through right thought, right speech, and right conduct, which in turn constitute right living, pursued with right effort and right mindfulness generated by right contemplation. These mental tools are both descriptive and prescriptive for how one lives and behaves if one is "awake." The goal is liberation of the mind: *nirvana,* the cessation of suffering.

The Buddha's view of existence emerged as an insight that was complete but hardly sudden. It was an insight about the nature of reality so basic that it seemed obvious to him, although not easy to convey in words. The Buddha was a teacher. His teachings were conveyed orally for generations; only 250 years after his death did they begin to be written down. They were not translated into European languages for over two millennia. During this span of time Buddhism evolved from Siddhartha Gautama's simple but hard-earned "awakening" into various systematized sets of observations and behaviors, an evolution that is still going on. In the places where it has developed, including the Buddha's own India, Buddhism has taken forms that incorporate preexisting beliefs and practices of the local region. Its manifestations thus range from the austerity of Zen Buddhism to the visual and aural complexity of Tibetan Buddhism. Similarly, in the United States, where Buddhism has spread both through immigration and through texts and teachings, its various forms have been adapted and integrated with local cultural and spiritual phenomena ranging from pragmatism to Judaism and Christianity to psychology.

A Western scholar of Buddhism named Christmas Humphreys offered the wheel as a usefully nonhierarchical metaphor for understanding the development of Buddhism.[4] The hub of the wheel is Theravada, a basic form of Buddhism emphasizing the four noble truths and the eightfold path; it developed in India and spread to Burma, Thailand, and Sri Lanka. From this central focus on personal liberation the various spokes of the Mahayana traditions, which emphasize compassion, developed in northern India, Mongolia, Sikkim, Bhutan, Tibet, Nepal, Vietnam, Cambodia, China, Korea, and Japan. Two of these "spokes" have been particularly influential in Western art. The first is the Taoist-influenced, intuition-oriented Ch'an Buddhism—Zen in Japanese—which is what most Americans think of when they think of Buddhism. (Lao Tzu, originator of Taoism in China, was a contemporary of the Buddha who taught that happiness depends on living in harmony with the Tao—the void from which reality emerges.) The second is the esoteric tradition known as Vajrayana or Tantrayana, based on the Mahayana view that *nirvana* and *samsara*, or the phenomenal world, are one. Tantrayana absorbed elements of Hindu yoga (concentration on an internal, numinous object), developing it into a system of rituals and visualizations for transforming anything, including what is unwholesome, into wisdom and compassion.

In response to a request from his foster-mother for the "Dharma in a nutshell," the Buddha offered the following criteria: "These teachings lead to dispassion, not to passion; to freedom from bondage, not to bondage; to decrease [in possessions], not to increase; to few desires, not to many; to contentment, not to discontent; to solitude, not to socializing; to exertion, not to indolence; to ease in maintaining oneself, not to difficulty—indeed, you may consider this is the Dharma."[5] The American Buddhist scholar Jan Nattier points out that the Buddha's reply "offers a set of general guidelines for evaluating anything that purports to be the Dharma, while simultaneously undercutting the all-too-human tendency to grasp at any particular formulation of the Dharma to the exclusion of others."[6]

THE SPREAD OF BUDDHISM TO THE WEST

The Buddha died four centuries before Jesus was born. In the West, we count time backward and forward from Christ's birth: the Buddha's death date is now thought to have been around 400 BCE—"before the Christian era." It could, though, be argued that the

Christian era didn't really begin until 313, when the Roman emperor Constantine the Great established toleration for Christianity with his Edict of Milan. Christianity turned out not to be a particularly tolerant religion. Christian Europe regarded Buddhism as paganism or—worse—idolatry. Its followers were to be converted for the sake of their souls and the consolidation of Western power, in which the church and the state were closely allied. The situation would begin to change only in the 1700s, with the development of that period of relatively open-minded rationalism known as the Enlightenment.

Cultural exchange between East and West goes back several millennia. Caravan roads crossed the lands between China and Europe in the north via the Caspian and Black Seas, and in the south via Iran and Syria, a route that eventually became known as the Silk Road. Information was traded along with goods, information that included stories of the life of the Buddha. These stories were Christianized and, by the 600s, written down in Greek as the legend of the Indian saints Barlaam and Josaphat. Translations into Latin and European languages followed, and the story became popular in medieval Europe. Ironically, in the 1500s the story was translated into Japanese and used by Jesuit missionaries to convert Japanese Buddhists to Christianity; another version was brought to China by the Jesuits in the 1600s.

The Barlaam and Josaphat story and its parables correspond to accounts of the life of Buddha and Indian Buddhist parables, as they were elaborated through oral tradition and eventually written down. The life of the Buddha was relayed to Europeans more directly by Marco Polo. An early editor of Marco's work noticed the resemblance between his account and the legend of Barlaam and Josaphat, glossing the text with the comment: "This is like the life of Saint Iosafat who was son of the king Avenir of those parts of Indie, and was converted to the Christian faith by the means of Barlam." But the connection was not widely noted until around 1860, when a French and a German scholar independently published their research linking Josaphat with the Buddha.[7]

The son and nephew of merchants, Marco Polo traveled through East Asia from 1271 to 1295. His accounts of his travels were translated into many languages over many centuries. They conveyed information about not only the life of the Buddha, but also, less reliably, Himalayan Buddhism, which was the predominant religion of the tolerant court of the Tartar Khans. Marco also related Chinese Buddhist beliefs, including reincarnation and karma:

> Their view of the immortality of the soul is after this fashion. They believe that as soon as a man dies, his soul enters into another body, going from a good to a better, or from a bad to a worse, according as he hath conducted himself well or ill. That is to say, a poor man, if he have passed through life good and sober, shall be born again of a gen-

> tlewoman, and shall be a gentleman; and on a second occasion shall be born of a princess and shall be a prince, and so on, always rising, till he be absorbed into the Deity.[8]

The one-hundred-year reign of the Mongols in China, from 1260 to 1368, allowed for considerable spread of information about Buddhism from East to West. One year after the Mongols were overthrown, however, Christians were expelled from China. Subsequently, Islam resumed its expansion, and communication between West and East was cut off until the Christian Jesuit missionaries began their forays with Francis Xavier's expedition to Japan in 1549.

In 1592 the Italian Matteo Ricci arrived in China, where he would remain until his death eighteen years later. Ricci's efforts to Christianize China were unsuccessful. A Chinese Buddhist monk wrote of Ricci and his colleagues:

> They cling to the idea that the Master of Heaven is the Master of Heaven, that the Buddha is the Buddha, that beings are beings . . . they resort to distinctions between the self and others, this and that, yes and no. . . . If they were not so attached to the idea of a Master of Heaven, they would not be attached to the idea of a Buddha either . . . and then they would begin to understand the profound thought of our Buddhism and the meaning of the expression "to save all beings."[9]

The European colonial and missionary enterprises that began having an impact on the East in the second half of the 1500s affected Europe as well. Samples of nature and culture brought or sent back to Europe by explorers and the Jesuits helped generate an explosion of knowledge and instigated a shift toward the organized, rational approach to life that became known as the Enlightenment. The principles of reason developed by the French philosopher and scientist René Descartes in the second quarter of the 1600s became the new paradigm. Supplanting authoritarian Christian versions of divine revelation, the Age of Reason created a climate of questioning and tolerance in which alternative religious and philosophical traditions could be studied and analyzed.

The term "Buddhism," which appeared in the written English language only after 1800, emerged from this context. The word has no meaning in Asia, where those who follow the teachings of the Buddha as interpreted through various traditions are recognized by appropriately specific language. The academic study of Buddhism in the West began with an English civil servant, Brian Houghton Hodgson, who was posted first to India and then, for reasons of his health, to Katmandu, Nepal, in 1821. This was something of a demotion. To bolster his reputation, Hodgson began sending manuscripts and antiquities to the Asiatic Society in Calcutta and publishing essays on a number of manuscripts, which he subsequently sent to other scholarly organizations in Europe. Hodgson was no fan of

Buddhism, explaining: "I had no purpose, nor have I, to meddle with the interminable sheer absurdities of the Bauddha philosophy or religion; and, had I not been called upon for proofs of the numerous novel statements my two essays contained, I should not probably have recurred at all to the topic."[10]

The Buddhist manuscripts Hodgson sent to Europe lay untouched until the French scholar Eugène Burnouf began translating and elucidating them some fifteen years later. Burnouf was eminently more qualified than Hodgson to take on this task. The son of the French classicist Jean-Louis Burnouf, Eugène had studied Sanskrit and Pali, eventually assuming the chair in Sanskrit at the Collège de France. Around 1840 Burnouf translated what he considered the most representative of the manuscripts to which he had access—the Lotus Sutra—into French. Before publishing it, however, he sought to develop his market by publishing in 1844 a general work on the history of Buddhism in India, his influential *Introduction à l'histoire du buddhism indien (Introduction to the History of Indian Buddhism).*

Burnouf, who died prematurely in 1852 (the year his *Le Lotus de la bonne loi* was published), focused on the Sanskrit texts of later, Mahayana Buddhism. Unfortunately, his successors tended to become confused by the complexities of Mahayana traditions, entangled in philosophical questions, and defeated by the baffling (to the Western mind) concepts of nirvana and emptiness—which they equated with annihilation and nihilism. In England in 1853 the missionary R. Spence Hardy published *A Manual of Buddhism,* based on Pali texts from the older, simpler Theravadan tradition. Hardy was hopeful that his readers could easily understand the "general outline of the system; as, although its literature is elaborate, its elementary principles are few."[11] Hardy's work was translated into French and German, new scholarship appeared that took into account both traditions, and by the early 1870s a more balanced, complex assessment of Buddhism was beginning to emerge in the West.

Among the admirers of Hardy's work was the German philosopher Arthur Schopenhauer. In Buddhism's focus on desire as the cause of suffering, Schopenhauer found a parallel for his own concept of will as the desire for existence, a desire that is not particularly responsive to our rational mind and is never satisfied. Schopenhauer may have arrived at the same conclusion as the Buddha regarding the cause of suffering, but, unlike the Buddha, he did not believe that happiness is attainable in this world, and he offered little practical guidance for dealing with our willful minds beyond suggesting that we develop compassion. Schopenhauer did believe, however, that the contemplation of great art can provide a way to transcend the will and achieve an experience of reality beyond desire. Schopenhauer's theories were popular among nineteenth-century European intellectuals, a popularity whose beginnings coincided with the increasing excitement about Buddhism that followed the publication of Burnouf's and Hardy's work around mid-century and reached its height from about 1880 through the first two decades of the twentieth century.

The earliest Western translators of Buddhist texts were philologists or missionaries. As pedants and as Christians, many of them had a hard time with the Buddhist concepts of emptiness, which they translated as nothingness, and nirvana—which in early Buddhism meant release from the cycle of rebirth, and in later Buddhism freedom from attachment to desire and delusion, but which they interpreted as annihilation. Certain Western artists, on the other hand, intuitively grasped the philosophical implications contained in the Asian art they saw. Some, like Vincent van Gogh and Paul Gauguin, read up on Buddhism, reaching the sophisticated level of understanding conveyed in Gauguin's manuscript "Diverses choses":

> Buddha, a simple mortal who neither conceived nor comprehended God, but who conceived and comprehended fully the intelligence of the human heart, reached that eternal bliss, Nirvana—the last stage of the soul in its progressive movement through the ages—All people, by virtue of the attainment of this wisdom, are able to become Buddhas.[12]

This is not to say Gauguin was a Buddhist. But knowledge of the teachings of the Buddha did inform Gauguin's life-view and thus his art. Buddhism is essentially experiential. If art, as the American philosopher John Dewey believed, is a distillation of experience, then works of art will be significant transmitters of Buddhism from one culture to another. And one place to look for influences of Buddhism in the West is in the work of Western artists.

This book begins with Claude Monet, whose early career around 1870 coincided with the period during which the complexities of Buddhism began to come into focus for Western intellectuals. Certain people served as points of contact—for example, the collector Henri Cernuschi, who traveled in Asia with Théodore Duret in 1871; Emile Guimet, who showed his collection of Buddhist art from India, Japan, and China at the Paris world's fair in 1878 and the following year opened his Musée Guimet as a "museum of religions";[13] the Japanese art dealer Tadamasa Hayashi, who settled permanently in Paris in 1878; and the well-connected scholar of Asian art Ernest Fenollosa, who lived in Japan from 1878 to 1889 and received the precepts of Tendai Buddhism in 1885. Buddhist perspectives were transmitted to European and American artists through books and articles by Western scholars and through Asian devotional art, along with more general forms of Asian cultural expression, such as garden design and Japanese prints. The philosophical content of these cultural products is related to but distinct from their style—the characteristics of their visual appearance. The style of a work of art is the form its content takes, a form that is determined by the culture in which it was made, in much the same way that religious forms of Buddhism were influenced by the cultures in which they developed.

Much has been written about the stylistic influences of Asian art on Western art—for instance, the well-documented influence of Japanese woodblock prints on French nineteenth-century artists. It is important to remember that the game of sources has no beginning and no end, and Western art has been influencing Asian art for as long as Asian art has been influencing the art of the West. In this book, content is emphasized over style and even, at times, over subject matter. A Western form of artistic expression that has been influenced by Buddhism may not "look" Buddhist, in terms of either its subject matter or its style. The criteria will include whether the artist had the possibility of contact with Buddhism through texts, artistic expression, or other information, and whether the content or effect of the work is in keeping with the psychological and philosophical perspectives of the Buddha.

The largely unseen influences I describe should never be construed as the only factor at work in the creation of a work of art. Wherever it has gone, Buddhism has been part of a rich cultural mix. Human beings are social animals, creatures of their culture as well as of their own personal histories. Works of art are complex products of complex minds, and this makes the search for the sources of inspiration that lie behind them cumulative and endless.

A word about the East/West dichotomy implied by the title of this book: any account like the one I am attempting is a history, and history has its conventions. One convention is the use of language that may not be particularly relevant for describing the present moment, but is helpful for clear and efficient discourse about the past. Thus, while today Buddhism has become a world religion and it makes little sense to speak of our globe in terms of East and West (particularly with regard to the relationship of East Asia to the West Coast of the United States), these terms nevertheless do convey very real *historical* cultural differences. Their relevance fades after World War II, when the work of Asian American artists like Isamu Noguchi, Nam June Paik, and Yoko Ono became a vital part of European and American culture.

In the last quarter of the twentieth century, a trend of thought emerged that critically dubbed the Western fascination with things Eastern as "orientalism": a combination of knowledge and fantasy about the East that allowed the West to define itself by means of contrast with its irrational, weak, sensual "other." This self-serving perspective is hard to miss in letters, reports, and other historical documents that have come down to us from the Middle Ages onward. More recently, disenchantment with Western materialism has been construed as fueling fantasies of the East as an exotic, ideal realm of spirituality and union with nature. Buddhism, with its focus on the interdependence of all beings and its promise of liberation from suffering—not to mention the exotic containers in which it is often encountered—is a favored example of Western escapism.

This later view is too superficial, however. J. J. Clarke, in his *Oriental Enlightenment: The Encounter between Asian and Western Thought,* puts it this way:

> The hypothesis that orientalism is fundamentally an escapist strategy ignores a number of important factors . . . which will underline the extent to which orientalist activities have been closely integrated within central Western intellectual concerns in the modern period, and which will imply that orientalism is to be seen not as an escape, an avoidance, but as a means of confronting some of the West's most pressing and immediate problems.[14]

For the artists in this book, Buddhist perspectives provided a means to confront and engage both personal issues and the issues of their time—the issues of the modern and the current global eras. This book is not intended to create a new category: Western Buddhist art. The process of searching out and following this important strand in the tapestry of modern culture is intended as a process of enrichment that will allow new complexities to emerge.

Rather than writing a survey, I have chosen twenty artists to discuss in some depth. For a few of them—John Cage being the most notable example—Buddhism virtually defined their artistic practice. For a few others, such as Claude Monet, Wassily Kandinsky, and Marcel Duchamp, the evidence for Buddhism's influence is implicit rather than explicit. I confess to having made some imaginative leaps, but only where viewing the work through the lens of Buddhism seems to significantly enhance its interpretation. Art comes from and is realized in a place before language, outside of the discursive mind. It shares this place, the place of emptiness, with Buddhist meditation practice. This is one reason why a consideration of the relationship between art and Buddhism turns out to be so rewarding.

The literary theorist Eve Kosofsky Sedgwick has pointed out that, in contrast to current academic practice, "in Buddhist pedagogical thought . . . the apparent tautology of learning what you already know does not seem to constitute a paradox, nor an impasse, nor a scandal. It is not even a problem. If anything, it is a deliberate and defining practice."[15] The appeal of the Buddhist perspective for artists is just this: like art, Buddhism challenges thinking as a path to knowing. And what both the creation and the perception of art share with Buddhist meditation practice is that they allow us to forget ourselves and thus realize ourselves. They are parallel practices. This is, perhaps, what the American painter Ad Reinhardt meant when he wrote, "The fine artist need not sit cross-legged."[16]

I THE INFINITE MOMENT

THE MODERN ERA IN WESTERN ART EMERGED from the Romantic attitude toward life that developed over the course of the 1700s. Romanticism was, on the one hand, a revival of a medieval impulse that valued feeling and the bonds of love over the intellect and moral standards and, on the other, a reaction against the rationalism of the Enlightenment. A number of elements were part of this overall shift of emphasis from intellect to feeling within the culture of the 1700s: a growing nostalgia for the past, an increasing fondness for that carefully contrived casualness of composition known as the "picturesque," a yearning for the experience of awe tinged with terror and exaltation that artists referred to as "the sublime," and a sense of the transitoriness of human life newly understood as an expression of nature rather than of God.

One element in this sense of transitoriness was the Taoist-Buddhist perspective that came packaged with Chinese garden design, taken up with enthusiasm by certain eighteenth-century European landscape designers, especially in England. When Westerners think of Asian influences on garden design, we tend to envision the exquisitely aesthetic Japanese Zen garden. Almost three centuries ago, however, Chinese Taoist and Buddhist concepts of landscape design played a role in changing the character of European gardens from Classical order to Romantic disorder.

The designed landscape in seventeenth-century England imitated formal, symmetrical Italian and French gardens formed by the Renaissance passion for classical order and by the yearning for grandeur that was an expression of the Baroque period of the late 1500s and early 1600s. European writers and philosophers were impressed by what they were learning about Chinese social organization and its Confucian underpinnings of orderliness and duty. The concept of government by philosophers, which is how European intellectuals understood Chinese society to be organized, was exhilarating to contemplate. By the early 1600s, Europeans regarded the Chinese as masters of the pragmatic art of government and, for that matter, of living.

One enthusiast for things Chinese was the English statesman and author Sir William Temple. A passionate lover of gardens, Temple published an essay in 1692 in which he wrote:

> Among us, the beauty of building and planting is placed chiefly in some certain proportions, symmetries, or uniformities; our walks and our trees ranged so as to answer one another, and at exact distances. The Chinese scorn this way of planting . . . their greatest reach of imagination is employed in contriving figures, where the beauty shall be great, and strike the eye, but without any order or disposition of parts that shall be commonly or easily observed: and though we have hardly any notion of this sort of beauty, yet they have a particular word to express it, and, where they find it hit their eye at first sight, they say the sharawadgi is fine or admirable. . . . And whoever observes the work upon . . . their best screens or porcelains, will find their beauty is all of this kind (that is) without order.[1]

Temple's word *sharawadgi,* which seems to mean a sense of beauty without order, remains something of a mystery. In his 1948 essay "The Chinese Origin of a Romanticism," Arthur O. Lovejoy noted that "Mr. Y. Z. Chang, who has considered the problem at my request, finds the probable original of the word in the syllables *sa-ro-(k) wai-chi,* which may have the meaning, 'the quality of being impressive or surprising through careless or unorderly grace.'"[2] The word calls to mind the Japanese Zen expression *wabi-sabi:* simple beauty that evokes a sense of the transience of life. Whatever the word's meaning, the principle of sharawadgi, or sharawaggi, as it was also spelled, was very different from the Western way of ordering nature.

What most caught the attention of Westerners was the Chinese garden's emphasis on constant change. According to the English architect Sir William Chambers, the experience of moving through a Chinese garden was one of shifting perspective. Chambers, who had visited China as a youth and was a tireless propagandist for the Chinese garden, wrote in 1757: "Nature is their pattern and their aim is to imitate her in all her beautiful irregularities. . . . The whole ground is laid out in a variety of scenes and you are led, by winding passages cut in the groves, to the different points of view, each of which is marked by a seat, a building, or some other object."[3] Unlike formal European gardens, which were intended to convey a sense of man's mastery of nature, Chinese gardens were, according to Chambers, calculated to engender a spirit of humble, even melancholic, contemplation of our place in the natural cycle:

> The plantations of their autumnal scenes consist of many sorts of oak, beech, and other deciduous trees that are retentive of the leaf, and afford in their decline a rich variegated colouring. . . . The buildings with which these scenes are decorated, are generally such as indicate decay, being intended as mementos to the passenger . . . to indicate the debility, the disappointments, and the dissolution of humanity; which, by co-operating with the dreary aspect of autumnal nature, and the inclement temperature of the air, fill the mind with melancholy, and incline it to serious reflections.[4]

Chambers's remarks appeared in his 1772 *Dissertation on Oriental Gardening,* which, though more polemical than descriptively accurate, reached a wide audience on the Continent as well as in England.

The *Dissertation* was not illustrated, and though there were a number of published descriptions of Chinese gardens, it is hard to know what people had as visual examples during the 1700s. Temple referred his readers to textiles and painted porcelains and screens. Another source would have been Chinese landscape painting, which was closely linked with garden design. By the last quarter of the eighteenth century, woodcut views of famous Chinese gardens known as the "Forty Scenes" were published in France.[5] But it was the *concept* of impermanence, rather than any particular visual model, that caught the eighteenth-century imagination. This way of understanding the phenomenal world was only one of many shifting perspectives that combined to create the modern era. But its effect on the way humans experienced nature, and thus themselves, was significant.

Romanticism in art, exemplified by the turbulent paintings of Eugène Delacroix, peaked around 1830. It was eclipsed in France by Realism and then Impressionism, but artists' interest in the concept of impermanence continued. The Impressionists pursued the positivist agenda of Realist painters such as Théodore Rousseau and Gustave Courbet in seeking to convey the experience of reality through paint—the "sensation" of existence in the physical world. This increasing interest in the material world was paralleled by Charles Darwin's *On the Origin of Species by Means of Natural Selection,* which appeared in 1859. By the second half of the nineteenth century a significant number of educated people no longer believed in God. The two major available thought systems that eliminated the need for a concept of God were science and Buddhism.

From the middle of the nineteenth century, increasingly, a key issue was the relationship between observable, scientific knowledge and intuitive understanding, between the empirical and the subjective. The debate is often framed as one between "realists," who believed that objects exist independent of human perception, and "idealists," who held that body and mind, universe and idea, are inseparable. Cast in these terms, Buddhism, with its assumption of the interdependence of all things, bolstered the idealist argument. But the Buddha also advocated patient testing of his theory of the mind against actual experience, an attitude that is fundamentally empirical. Buddhism thus offered a solution to the dilemma of satisfying spiritual yearnings in a self-consciously scientific era.

Buddhism was a new kind of threat to Christianity, for science and Buddhism were seen as compatible. In 1886 the Abbé Paul de Broglie wrote, "The appearance of this little known religion on the terrain of science has produced a profound surprise. It seems to destroy the entire basis of Christian apologetics, and even some of the proofs for the existence of God."[6] Two years later, Eugène Burnouf's nephew Emile published a long article on Buddhism in the West in the *Revue des deux mondes*. The article ended with a diatribe favoring Buddhism over Theosophy:

> Pure Buddhism has the amplitude required of a teaching at once religious and scientific. Its tolerance means that it takes umbrage at no one. Basically, it is only the proclamation of the supremacy of reason and its empire over the animal instincts, of which it is the regulator and the check. It finally can be summarized in two words that excellently express human law: science and virtue.[7]

To the prolific late-nineteenth-century publisher Paul Carus, the Buddha's teachings supported the evolutionary theories of Herbert Spencer and Charles Darwin. Carus quoted the Buddha's view on karma in his book *The Gospel of Buddha:*

> Is not this individuality of mine a combination, material as well as mental? Is it not made up of qualities that sprang into being by a gradual evolution? . . . Those who have used the same sense-organs, and have thought the same ideas before I was composed into this individuality of mine are my previous existences; they are my ancestors as much as the I of yesterday is the father of the I of today, and the karma of my past deeds conditions the fate of my present existence.[8]

By the late 1880s Romanticism had begun resurfacing as Symbolism—the attempt to evoke through art a spiritual reality paralleling physical reality. Symbolist art was fueled in part by syncretism, a melding of religious beliefs and symbols from a variety of sources, including Asia. Many a Symbolist artist created a personal profession of faith in pictures that included both Christ and the Buddha. Theosophy ("divine wisdom"), as promulgated by Emanuel Swedenborg and Helena Blavatsky, is often cited as the source of this tendency. But syncretist theory was also informed by European scholars of Buddhism, who were prone to point out the parallels between the lives of Siddhartha and Jesus. In 1888, for example, Emile Burnouf wrote:

> If, by the time of Constantine, the multiple origins of Christianity had not been lost sight of . . . one would perhaps have recognized that the Buddhist view better reflected reality, that Jesus Christ was in fact the second savior, perhaps Maitreya [the buddha of the future] . . . [and] one would not have closed so quickly the series of incarnations.[9]

These ideas registered in the art of the last quarter of the nineteenth century in different ways. For the Impressionist Claude Monet, the evidence of Buddhist influence is largely circumstantial. What evidence there is, however, points to the impact of Buddhism's emphasis on the present moment on the development of his mature style. The Symbolist artist Odilon Redon was Monet's exact contemporary. Although Buddhist imagery was part of his exotic pantheon, Redon seems to have absorbed the Buddha's message only toward the end of his career, when it may have helped him integrate psychological issues from his childhood. Redon viewed his own psychologically evocative art as diametrically opposed to everything Monet stood for. Yet the two artists shared a fundamental view of the function of art: to convey the experience of existence.

Vincent van Gogh considered himself an Impressionist, an heir of Monet. They shared an interest in perception—capturing visual appearance in all its physicality. Over time, however, and with exposure to the increasingly Symbolist attitudes of his friend Paul Gauguin (who also began his artistic career as an Impressionist), van Gogh shifted his emphasis toward the expression of feelings elicited by the natural world. Gauguin's intense emotional bond with van Gogh survived their separation and even van Gogh's death in 1890. Both artists shared an interest in Buddhism, which informed their art in different ways. For van Gogh, the Buddha provided a personal model for how life as an artist might be lived—how artistic practice could be a compassionate practice. For Gauguin, the Buddhist concept of desire as the cause of suffering was a factor in his struggle to sort out internal philosophical and psychological issues, while Buddhist imagery supplied a symbolic language for communicating these issues in his work.

To the extent that Buddhism contributed to the intellectual ferment of the early modern era, it affected the cultural expression of the period. Visual artists were inspired not only directly by Buddhist ideas but secondarily, through the Buddhist-influenced theories of such nineteenth-century musicians and writers as Richard Wagner and Leo Tolstoy. By focusing on the direct influence of Buddhist philosophy on late-nineteenth-century European painters, however, I believe we can enrich our understanding of the art of this period, without denying other religious, philosophical, sociological, and psychological influences.

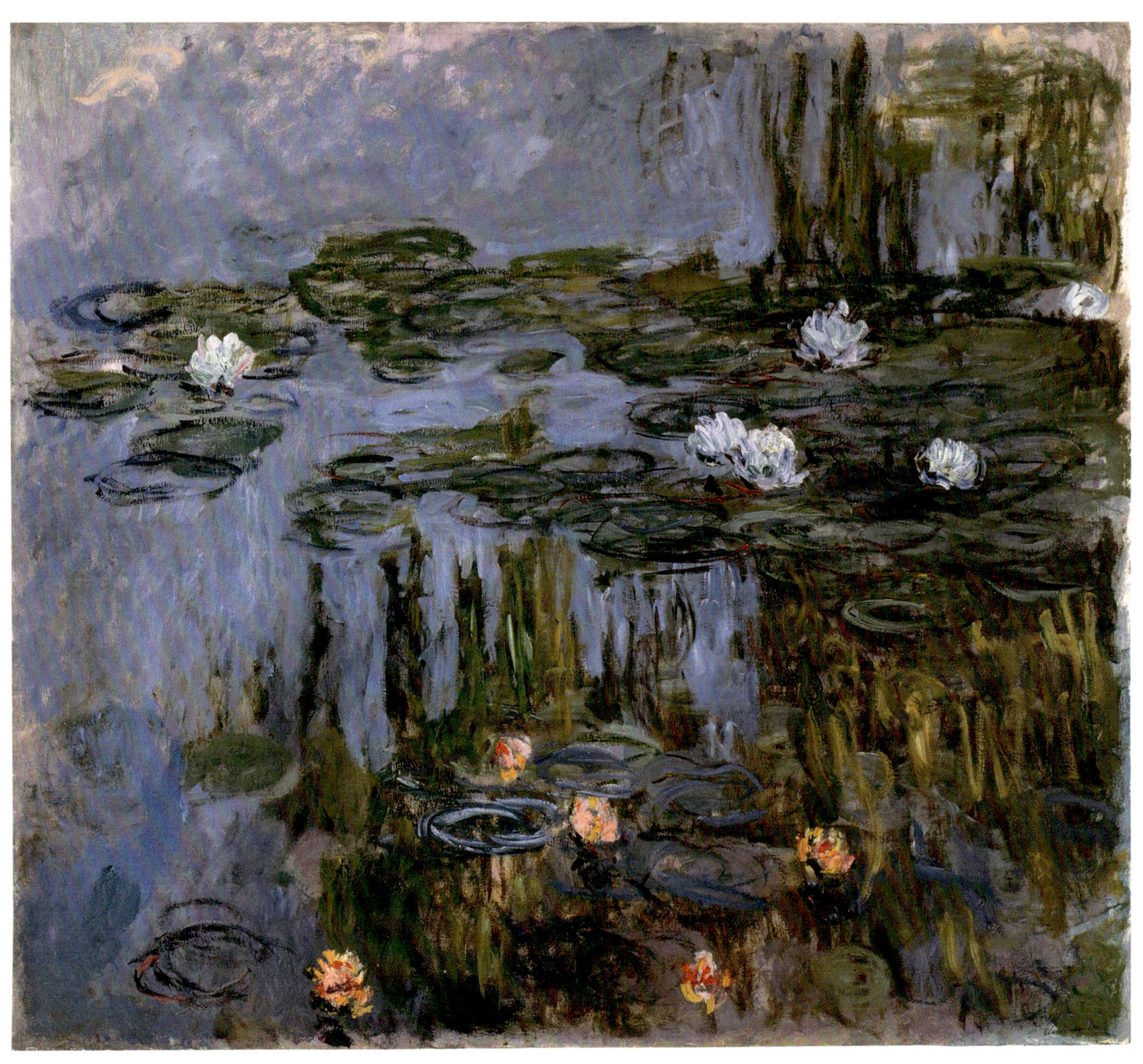

Claude Monet, *Water Lilies,* about 1914, oil on canvas, 61 x 75 in. Portland Art Museum, Portland, Oregon, Ayer Fund Purchase. © 2005 Artists Rights Society (ARS), New York/ADAGP, Paris.

CLAUDE MONET 1840–1926

CLAUDE MONET WAS A PAINTER OF THE MOMENT. In a late painting like his *Water Lilies* in Portland, Oregon, there's something about the color, the internal light, that threatens to bring tears to your eyes. To me, this came as a surprise, as I didn't think I particularly liked late Monet paintings; I considered these blue and pink paintings a bit bland compared with his crisp early work and his vibrant paintings of the 1870s. But this rectangle of tangled paint on canvas suddenly overwhelms me with emotion. What emotion? Sadness . . . no, nostalgia. Intense nostalgia. Still, the sadness is there, too, weaving through the nostalgia like silver strands through my mother's hair. The painting seems to contain a moment or—better—a totality of moments in deep summer, when the greens go dark and the water reflects a bottomless sky. The sensation of a moment I wasn't even aware of losing is suddenly mine again. Or maybe what the painting embodies is change itself, and the awareness is an awareness of time and the losses that time brings.

Claude Monet was one of the first artists to articulate a meditative state of mind in the process of creation. Although it is impossible to know whether this was a cause or a result of his attraction to Japanese art, a contemporary critic, Claude Roger-Marx, emphasized the parallels in an imaginary conversation with the artist:

> People who hold forth on my painting conclude that I have arrived at the ultimate degree of abstraction and imagination that can be found in reality. I should much prefer to have them acknowledge the gift, my total absorption in my work. . . . Perhaps my originality boils down to being a hypersensitive receptor, and to the expediency of a shorthand by means of which I project on a canvas, as if on a screen, impressions registered on my retina. If you absolutely must find an affiliation for me, select the Japanese of olden times: their rarefied taste has always appealed to me; and I sanction the implications of their esthetic that evokes a presence by means of a shadow and the whole by means of a fragment.[1]

Monet's first inkling of the Buddhist philosophy of life probably came through Japanese Ukiyo-e: luminous woodcuts of the "floating world"—moments rescued from passing time. Late in his life, Monet recalled first seeing Japanese prints at the age of sixteen in his hometown of Le Havre, an important port for goods from the East. He also recalled purchasing Japanese woodcuts during a trip to Holland in May 1871, when he was thirty years old. A year or two later he painted *Impression: Sunrise,* a painting that, so the story goes, gave Impressionism its name.

The stylistic influence of Japanese prints on *Impression: Sunrise* and other paintings by Monet from around this time was obvious to the critic Armand Silvestre, who wrote in 1873, "He loves to juxtapose, on lightly wind-ruffled water, the multicolored reflections of the setting sun. . . . This effect, which is completely true, has been borrowed from Japanese pictures."[2] But a statement Monet made to an interviewer in the 1920s about a print by Hokusai suggests that his interest in Japanese Ukiyo-e went beyond style and included content: "How powerful his work is. Look at this butterfly which is struggling against the wind, the flowers which are bending. And nothing useless. Sobriety of life."[3] Monet's comments echo the Buddha's basic message about suffering: like Hokusai's peonies, those who are able to absorb change, to bend with it, will have an easier time than those who resist.

The early 1870s was a time of change for Monet, not only in his painting style but also in his philosophy of life. France had declared war on Germany in July 1870, twelve days after the death of the artist's Aunt Sophie, who had paid to release him from military obligation. In April his paintings had been rejected by the Paris Salon for the second year in a row. In September the impoverished artist moved to London with his wife and small son to escape the war and the German siege of Paris. Two months later, his fellow painter and studio-mate Frédéric Bazille was killed in action. This loss was followed in January 1871 by the death of Monet's father, from whom he was estranged, and by the March revolt of the Paris Commune and its bloody suppression in May. That same month, Monet left London for Holland, finally returning to Paris in the fall.

According to a contemporary biographer, Arsène Alexandre, it was his flight to London in 1870 that "led Monet to examine himself seriously, and to seek something else (in the

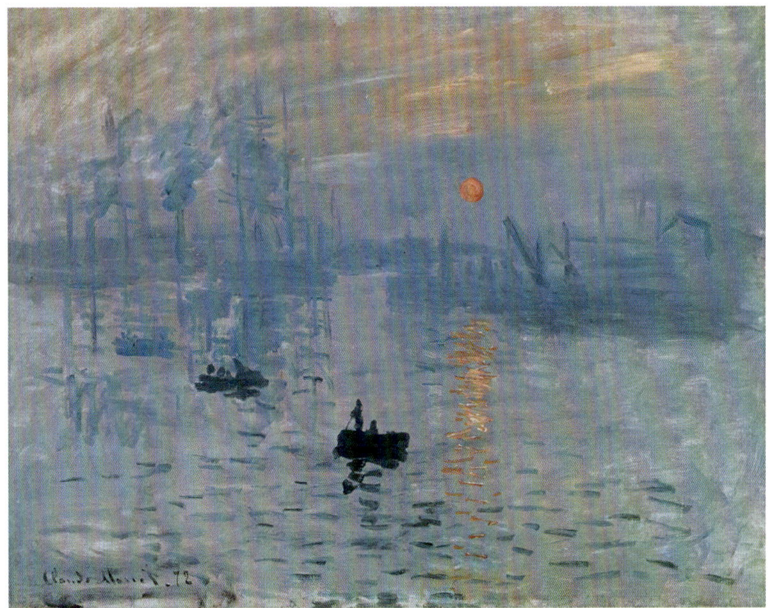

Claude Monet, *Impression: Sunrise, Le Havre,* 1873, oil on canvas, 18¾ x 24½ in. Musée Marmottan, Paris/Grandor/Bridgman Art Library. © 2005 Artists Rights Society (ARS), New York/ADAGP, Paris.

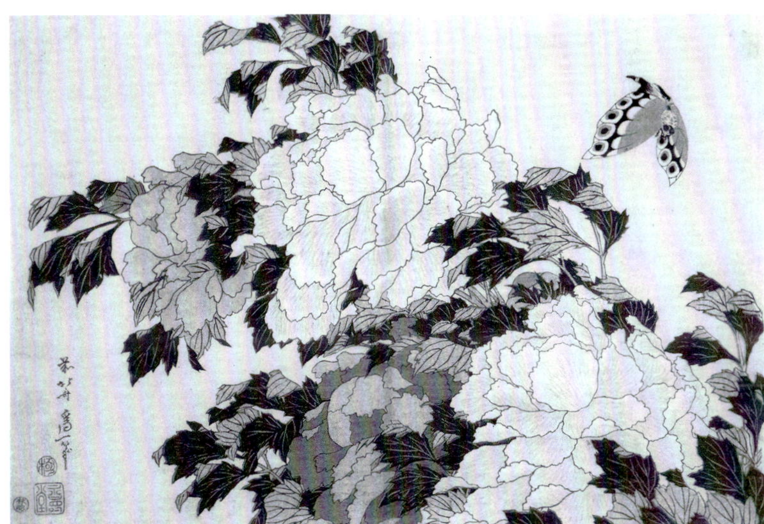

Katsushika Hokusai, *Peonies and Butterfly,* about 1832, color woodcut, 9¾ x 14½ in. National Gallery of Australia, Canberra. © National Gallery of Australia.

sense of his true nature)."[4] A number of books where Monet could have found some "something else" were published around that time. In Paris in 1870, Léon Feer published a book on the Four Truths and Philippe Foucaux put out a book on the *Lalitavistara* (life of the Buddha). In London, Max Müller's translation of the *Buddha's Dhammapada, or "Path of Virtue,"* appeared in 1870; two books published in 1871 were the popular epic poem *The Story of Gautama Buddha and His Creed,* by Richard Phillips, and Henry Yule's new translation of Marco Polo's thirteenth-century account, *Concerning the Kingdoms and Marvels of the East,* which included detailed accounts of the Buddha's life by both Marco and Yule. In a footnote to Marco's passage on Buddhism in China, Yule included excerpts from an 1846 German article, "Land of Enlightenment," that evoke the future water garden of Claude Monet: "a lake of immeasurable expanse, overspread with innumerable red and white lotus flowers, of various sizes, some blooming, some fading."[5]

Some of Monet's contemporaries were searching for "something else" as well. Immediately after the fall of the Commune, the critic Théodore Duret went to India and the Far East with the collector Henri Cernuschi. They returned in January 1873 with a huge collection of Buddhist sculpture and sutras, along with Japanese paintings and prints. That May, Monet met Duret, who had advised Monet's friend Manet that Cernuschi's Buddhist bronzes "will knock you out."[6] Cernuschi's collection was on public view at the Palais de l'Industrie in 1873–74, after which he put it on permanent public display at his Paris mansion. Surely Monet, so interested in Japanese prints, would have familiarized himself with this collection, the focal point of which was a large Japanese sculpture of the Buddha. Duret described this piece (and others) in his 1874 book, *Voyage en Asie:*

> He is seated . . . on a lotus flower. . . . His features convey absolute calm, the absence of passion and of desire, and the stamp of this type of ecstasy particular to Buddha, who, detached from everything and freed from life, has achieved the dissolution of his own feelings, even of his personality; that is to say, all that buddhist metaphysicians and theologians could conceive or dream, the artist has here realized in bronze.[7]

For anyone interested in the cultural content of the Japanese "floating world" and Buddha images, the best source in French would have been a long essay entitled "Le Bouddhisme" that the influential French critic and historian Hippolyte Taine had published in 1865. Here, Taine summarized for the French reading public the results of twenty years of German scholarship on Buddhism. Several passages in Taine's essay resonate with the mature work of Monet and its focus on impermanence, on the infinite moment:

> Nature is . . . an infinite chain of causes from effects and effects from causes, an infinite progeny into the past and the future of decompositions and recompositions with no beginning and no end. Such is the view of the whole to which [Buddhists] are led, on the one hand, by their main theme of nothingness and, on the other, by the spectacle of things incessantly changing. Having suppressed fixed causes, there remains only the series of changing effects. Thereupon, the imagination comes alive.[8]
>
> There is nothing real; there is no existence; everything is empty. And thus the different Buddhist philosophies, each going further than the other, admit—some, that objects only exist during the time one perceives them; others, that nothing exists except interior

> sensation; and finally others, that these sensations have no existence, and that within as outside of ourselves there is only pure nothingness and absolute emptiness. On this emptiness floats a dissolving view of appearances; at bottom, a great calm blackness; above, a childish play of colors and vacillating forms: whosoever fathoms this truth finds no more meaning in the words, youth, death, light, darkness, form, grandeur, time, space; all conceptions, all ordinary judgments are for him only a superficial dream.[9]

Monet did not, however, need to rely only on secondary sources of information. He was friends with the Japanese art dealer Tadamasa Hayashi, who was knowledgeable not just about Ukiyo-e, but about the Buddhist philosophy that lay behind these images. Hayashi had arrived in Paris to help with the Japanese exhibitions at the 1878 Exposition Universelle and had stayed. He saw it as his mission to educate French collectors about the cultural history and meaning of the Japanese art he sold them. One collector, a friend of Monet's, recalled that Hayashi gave French connoisseurs "some of the most profound sensations of art that they ever experienced."[10]

In his book *Les petites religions de Paris* of 1894, Jules Bois listed Monet's friend and biographer, the statesman Georges Clemenceau, as part of a group of Parisian intellectuals attracted to Buddhism. Bois claimed that "the Buddha counts in Paris more than one hundred thousand friends and at least ten thousand adepts. . . . Look around: artists, writers, boulevardiers are Buddhists. . . . M. Clemenceau, free thinker, collects with love religious marvels which come to us from Japan."[11]

Although Clemenceau and Monet shared a passion for Japanese art, they differed in their attitudes toward its underlying philosophy. Clemenceau considered himself an empiricist, ascribing to the philosophy of science that holds all knowledge is derived from experience. Monet's attitude, however, was closer to Taine's "dissolving view of appearances," in which the finite world floats on an infinite experience of emptiness. "While you philosophically seek the world in itself," Monet reportedly told Clemenceau,

> I simply expend my efforts upon a maximum of appearances, in rigorous correlation with unknown realities. When one is on the plane of concordant appearances, one cannot be very far from reality, or at least from what we can know of it. . . . Your error is to wish to reduce the world to your measure, whereas if you increase your knowledge of things, you will find your knowledge of yourself will expand.[12]

At the close of his own memoir, published in 1929, Clemenceau concluded:

> The day is coming, arduous but inevitable, on which by the simple evolution of knowledge will occur that most beautiful and complete phase of human development which will entitle us to take part in the work that the Cosmos requires. We need only renounce

> the heavenly mirages of a divinely personified energy in order to put man, at once fragile and strong, into full possession of that actual power or knowledge which alone can perfect him. "Master," the disciple cries, "who is that God, robed in dazzling majesty, whom I discern yonder above the clouds? Methinks he seems to call me. Didst thou not see?" And, smiling, Buddha replies: "It is thyself whom thou seest, O my son!"[13]

By 1890 Monet was successful enough to purchase the home in Giverny he had been renting. He proceeded with major expansions of his garden there, including the creation of a water garden. The Paris Exposition Universelle of 1889 had included three of Monet's paintings and had also featured a display of water lilies hybridized by Joseph Bory Latour-Marliac in an attempt to produce a plant combining the native hardiness of the *Nymphaea alba* with the intense color of tropical water lilies—lotuses—the Buddhist symbol of clarity of consciousness arising from the mud of ignorance (Taine's "at bottom, a great calm blackness; above, a childish play of colors").

Around the time he was developing his water garden, Claude Monet was obsessed with the theme of impermanence. He had been painting, for example, the same haystack, over and over again: in sunlight at different times of day, through sunlit mist, at sunset, in the snow under a gray sky. With his water garden, Monet joined his theme of impermanence with the theme of regeneration. The life cycle of the water lily is a cycle of renewal. Rising from the mud to the surface of the water, water lilies open to the sun during the day. Every evening the luminous blossoms are pulled back beneath the water, reemerging the next morning to open once more. After fertilization, the flower stays underwater, where the seeds ripen and are released. The seed pods float back to the surface, where they drift until they settle down into the mud to regenerate in another place.

Monet may have had the life cycle of his water lilies in mind when he told his biographer Gustave Geffroy, "I would like, when I die, to be buried in a buoy."[14] Water became Monet's favorite subject. In paintings of his water garden, he combined the fleetingness of light and clouds reflected in water with the glowing colors of water lilies. Entitled "Last Reverie before the Water Garden," the final chapter of Geffroy's monograph on Monet begins: "This is the supreme significance of Monet's art: his adoration of the universe, ending in a pantheistic and Buddhist contemplation . . . pursuing his dream of form and color almost to the annihilation of his individuality in the eternal nirvana of things at once changing and immutable."[15] The book pleased Monet, who wrote Geffroy after reading it, "I have no need to tell you how touched I am, all modesty apart, by the good you say concerning my works and myself."[16]

Geffroy was not the only contemporary writer to perceive Buddhism in the art of Claude Monet. The art historian Louis Gillet wrote soon after Monet's death: "It is perhaps

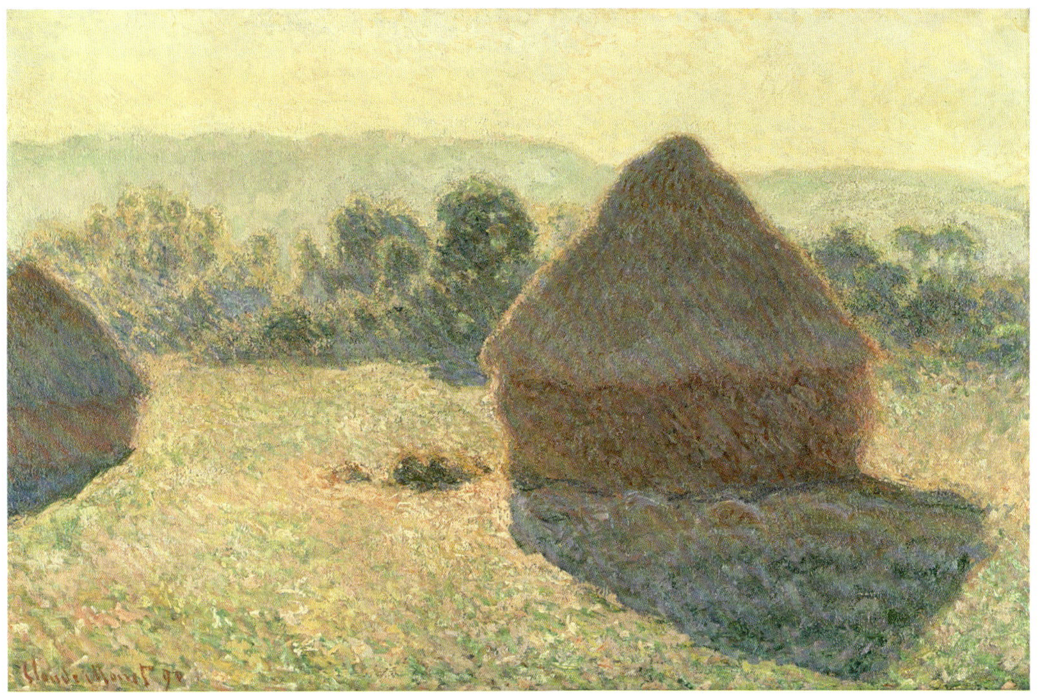

Claude Monet, *Haystacks, Midday,* 1890, oil on canvas, 25½ x 39¼ in. National Gallery of Australia, Canberra.

necessary to see in [Monet's art] the sole European work which is truly related to Chinese thought, to the vague hymns of the Far East on the waters and the mists and the passing of things, on detachment, on nirvana, on the religion of the Lotus."[17] Although this perspective on Monet and his work has been lost today, the paintings of Claude Monet may yet be the most eloquent Western expression of the Buddhist concepts of impermanence and the interdependence of all things, concepts that proved so troublesome to his more scholarly contemporaries.

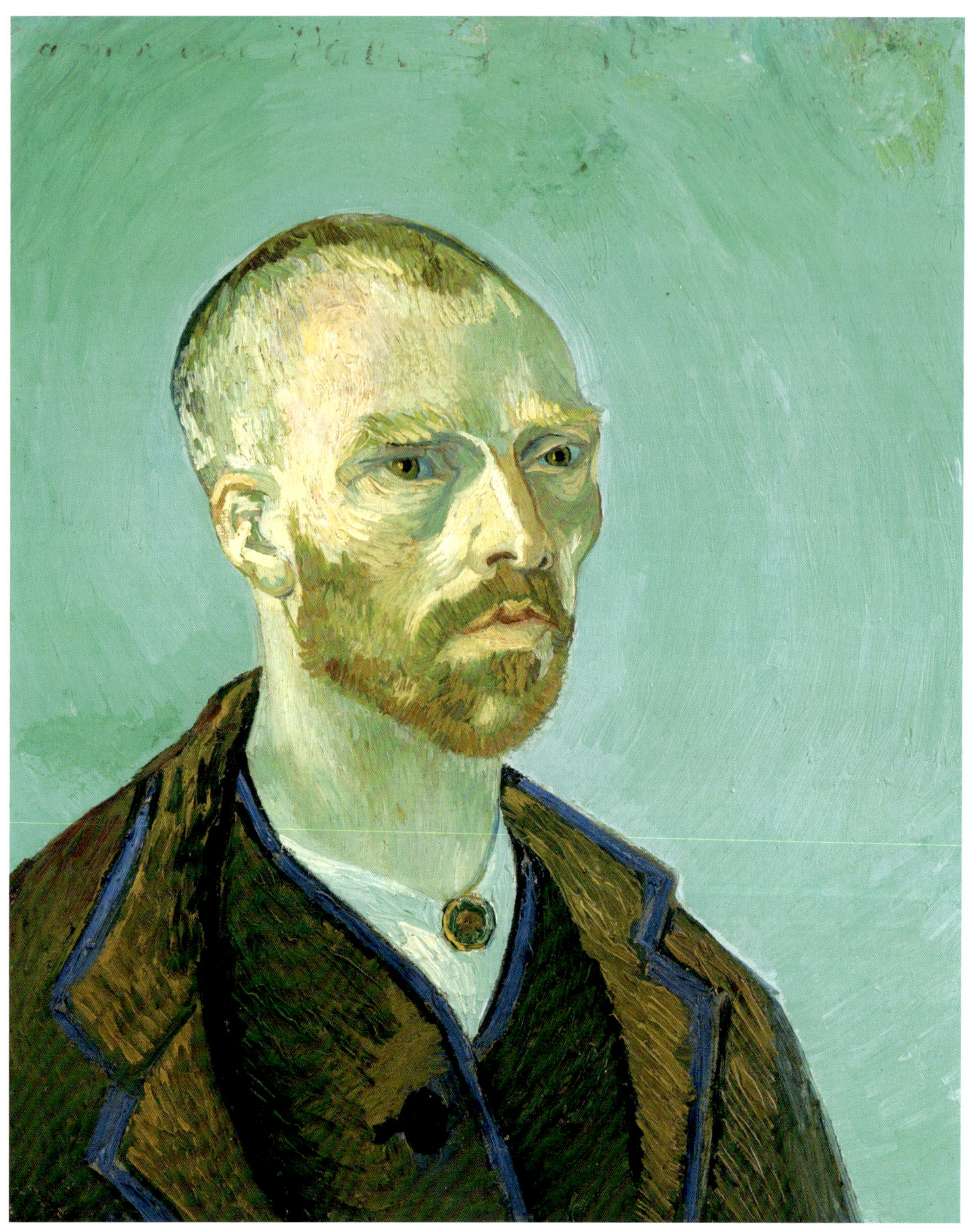

Vincent van Gogh, *Self-Portrait Dedicated to Paul Gauguin,* 1888, oil on canvas, $23\frac{5}{8}$ x $19\frac{5}{8}$ in. Courtesy of the Fogg Art Museum, Harvard University Art Museums, Bequest from the collection of Maurice Wertheim, Class of 1906. Image © 2005 President and Fellows of Harvard College (photo: David Mathews).

VINCENT VAN GOGH 1853–1890

FOR THE FAILED CHRISTIAN EVANGELIST Vincent van Gogh, art was more effective than religion in conveying his deeply felt compassion for humankind. In September 1888 he wrote his painter-friend Paul Gauguin about a self-portrait he intended to give Gauguin:

> I have a portrait of myself, all ash-colored. . . . But I also exaggerate my personality; I have in the first place aimed at the character of a simple bonze worshipping the Eternal Buddha. . . . I think that if, from now on, you begin to feel like the head of the studio, which we shall try to turn into a refuge for many . . . then you will feel more or less comforted after the present miseries of poverty and illness, taking into consideration that probably we shall be giving our lives for a generation of painters.[1]

One eye of this self-sacrificing "bonze," or Japanese monk, is fixed on you, the other on the distance, one might even say: the future. It was the future on which Vincent van Gogh obsessively focused, not on the present or his troubled past.

Van Gogh was a sensitive, deeply spiritual man haunted by a shadow: a brother named Vincent who had been born on March 30, 1852—exactly one year before his own birth—and had died soon afterward. Vincent saw the grave in the churchyard every week when he went with his family to church. The son of a pastor and the nephew of three art dealers, he went to work at the age of sixteen as an apprentice in the Hague office of an international art firm, Goupil and Company, in which his uncle, also named Vincent, was a partner. He was promoted to the London office of the firm when he was twenty. There, rejected in love by the daughter of his landlord, he turned to literature and philosophy in an attempt to assuage his increasingly troubled heart.

Eventually, van Gogh's obsessive Bible-reading and obvious distaste for the social values of the art world led to his dismissal by Goupil. He studied for entrance to a London theological seminary but came to believe that the dogma of institutionalized religion was the opposite of what people needed. In 1878 he joined an evangelical ministry working with coal miners in a depressed area of Belgium. The extremes of his selflessness—giving away his possessions to destitute members of his congregation and going into their cottages rather than waiting for them to come to church—so alarmed his superiors (and perhaps his flock) that his annual contract was not renewed. He broke with his family at this time as well; only his younger brother Theo, who was also employed by Goupil, stood by him.

At the age of twenty-seven, van Gogh decided to become an artist. He began by copying Millet's images of laborers. Drawing the objects of his compassion with the dual goals of expressing his empathy and winning them sympathy proved so satisfying that he conceived a career creating visual parables. *Pear Tree in Blossom,* from April 1888, is such a visual parable. Like Monet, van Gogh was an enthusiastic collector of Japanese prints. The previous summer he had painted his own version of a Hiroshige woodcut of a plum orchard in bloom. *Pear Tree* shows the influence of Japanese prints in its flat, frontal style, but, unlike his "Hiroshige" painting, it has metaphorical content. Next to the blooming pear tree is the stump of another pear tree that has been cut down; a butterfly painted in the same yellow color as the stump hovers amid the blossoms of the blooming tree.

We know from van Gogh's letters that many elements of his paintings, including the colors, were intended to convey a message. In the case of *Pear Tree in Blossom,* the yellow butterfly and the yellow stump juxtaposed with the blooming tree suggest metamorphosis and regeneration. "I have little confidence," he wrote his sister around the time he painted *Pear Tree,* "in the correctness of our human concepts of a future life. We are as little able to judge of our own metamorphoses without bias and prematureness as the white salad grubs can of theirs, for the very cogent reason that the salad worms ought to eat salad roots in the very interest of their higher development. In the same way I think that a painter ought to paint pictures; possibly something may come after that."[2]

To his young painter-friend Emile Bernard, van Gogh wrote of the spiritual development of prostitutes: "Where will this butterfly emerge from the chrysalis? This butterfly that was a sated caterpillar, this cockchafer that was a white grub? Well, this is where I have got to in my study of old whores. I too should like to know approximately what I am the larva of myself, perhaps."[3] The idea of reincarnation fascinated van Gogh. In June 1888 he wrote Emile Bernard:

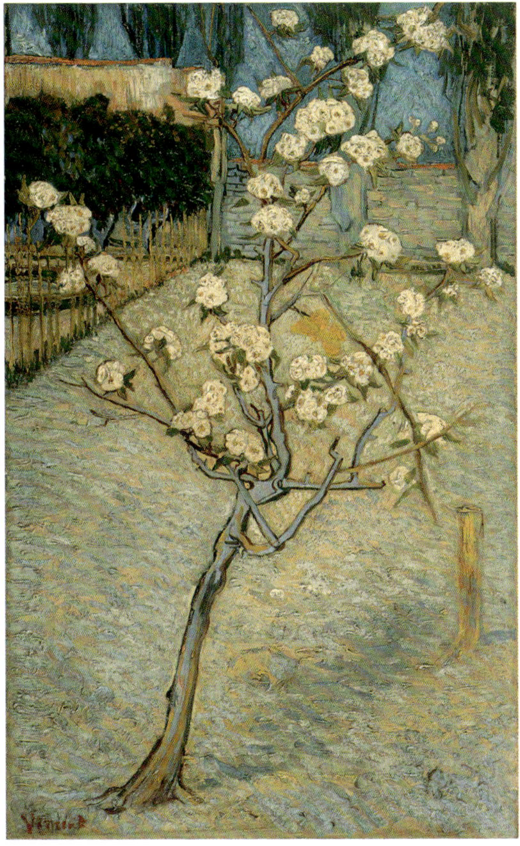

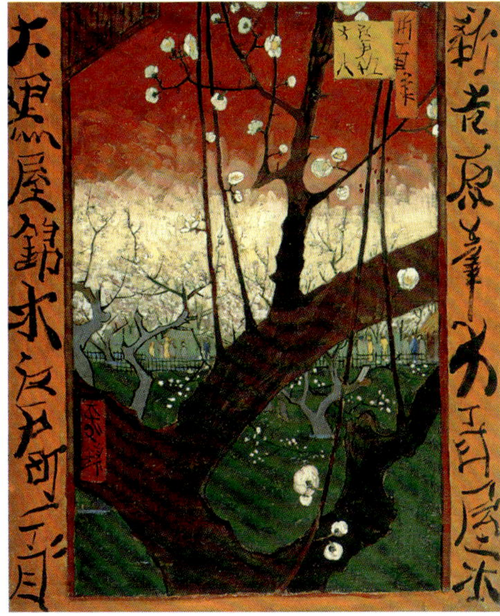

(left) Vincent van Gogh, *Pear Tree in Blossom,* 1888, oil on canvas, 73 x 46 in. Van Gogh Museum, Amsterdam.

(above) Vincent van Gogh, *Flowering Plum Tree (after Hiroshige),* 1887, oil on canvas, 21½ x 18 in. Van Gogh Museum, Amsterdam.

> Science—scientific reasoning—seems to me an instrument that will lag far, far behind. For look here: the earth has been thought to be flat. . . . Which, however, does not prevent science from proving that the earth is principally round. Which no one contradicts nowadays. But notwithstanding this, they persist nowadays in believing that life is flat and runs from birth to death. However, life too is probably round, and very superior in extent and capacity to the hemisphere we know at present.[4]

The art historians Douglas Druick and Peter Zegers recently identified a source for van Gogh's references to metamorphosis: Frederik van Eeden's metaphysical fairy tale *Little Johannes,* published in Dutch in 1887. They do not mention, however, what must have been one of the most appealing elements of the book for the compassionate van Gogh: the bodhisattva-like figure who emerges at the end of the story to point Johannes away from the false light of easy happiness toward the "Great Light." Pointing to the "dark East," this figure declares, "'There you would yourself be what you long to know. *There!* . . . where human nature and its sorrows are, there lies my way.'"[5]

Van Gogh was also interested in the thinking of Richard Wagner and Leo Tolstoy, both of whom were influenced by Buddhism. To his brother Theo, Vincent wrote:

> I have read another article on Wagner—"Love in Music" . . . How one needs the same thing in painting. It seems that in the book *My Religion,* Tolstoy implies that whatever happens in the way of violent revolution, there will also be a private and secret revolution in men, from which a new religion will be born, or rather something altogether new, which will have no name, but which will have the same effect of comforting, of making life possible, which the Christian religion used to have.[6]

What else might van Gogh have read to inform his developing concept of "something altogether new," something that was not a religion but would "have the same effect of comforting, of making life possible"?

It is known that van Gogh read Emile Burnouf's article on "Buddhism in the West," which appeared in the July 15, 1888, issue of *Revue des deux mondes.*[7] He was probably also aware of some of the other publications on Buddhism that were available. In 1885, for example, the *Revue des deux mondes* featured a lengthy article by Edouard Schuré entitled "The Buddha and His Legend," in which Schuré, who was hardly an expert on Buddhism, attempted to analyze seven books published over the previous couple of decades.[8]

Another possible source of information for van Gogh was the fourth edition, in 1886, of Hippolyte Taine's *New Essays of Criticism and History,* featuring this popular historian's fine essay on Buddhism—already mentioned in connection with Monet. In van Gogh's June 1888 letter to Emile Bernard he wrote, "Seeing that nothing opposes it—supposing that there are also lines and forms as well as colors on the other innumerable planets and suns—it would remain praiseworthy of us to maintain a certain serenity with regard to the possibilities of painting under superior and changed conditions of existence."[9] Van Gogh's imaginings about "lines and forms as well as colors on the other innumerable planets and suns" could have been inspired by Taine's descriptions of the "infinite numbers of infinite worlds" envisioned by imaginations set free from belief in a fixed cause. About our unhappy world, Taine wrote:

> human life oscillates, according to the degree of vice or virtue of men. . . . We are, at this moment, in one of the saddest periods. Thus turns "the great wheel" of being, and when, from this little narrow piece where we cling as to an isthmus, we contemplate on either side the two bottomless pits of time, and, completely surrounding us, the stupendous abyss of space, we cannot be aware of all the parts inexhaustibly regenerating in the eternal evolution.[10]

Taine's "great wheel of being" parallels van Gogh's statement to Bernard that "life too is probably round." And van Gogh would surely have identified with Taine's description of the Buddha's teaching methods:

> There were among his listeners street sweepers, the impoverished, beggars, the elderly abandoned by their kin, the feeble-minded, cripples, used-up courtesans, homeless girls sleeping on dung-heaps, even thieves and murderers. All the dishonored or oppressed came to him for guidance to attain spiritual renewal. And his teachings were appropriate to each listener. . . . No theory, no philosophy, no liturgy. . . . He wanted humankind to dream, not of the wrongs of others, but of themselves.[11]

Perhaps the likeliest source, however, is one of van Gogh's favorite writers: the philosopher, historian, and scholar of religion Ernest Renan, author of *The Life of Jesus,* which van Gogh read in the mid-1870s. *The Life of Jesus* was the first installment of Renan's *Studies in Religious History,* published in 1857. In 1884 Renan published his *New Studies in Religious History,* featuring a long essay entitled "First Works on Buddhism." As Renan explained in his preface, he had originally written it for the *Revue des deux mondes* in 1852, during the last months of life of his teacher Eugène Burnouf. The then-editor of the *Revue,* whom Renan described as "the least Buddhist of men," refused to publish the piece, asserting that "it is not possible that there are people as stupid as that."[12] If accepted, "First Works on Buddhism" would have been Renan's first published essay, a fact that helps to explain his rather Buddhist analysis of the divinity of Jesus in *The Life of Jesus:* "the son of God; but all men are so or may become so in diverse degrees."[13]

Van Gogh's assertion to Bernard that "life too is probably round" is reminiscent of the cycle of rebirth described not only by Taine but also Renan: "Beings revolve thus through all the stages of the universe, until the moment they arrive at full mastery of themselves; this is the state of the bodhisattva, the last which one traverses before attaining nothingness."[14] The Mahayana Buddhist concept of a bodhisattva as a person who, having attained enough sanctity to escape rebirth, has nevertheless chosen to remain on earth and help his fellow sufferers, would have appealed to van Gogh. The Buddhist virtue of compassion was central to his personal philosophy. As Renan explained:

> The supreme name for virtue in Buddhism, "maitri," cannot really be translated as "charity." Self-sacrifice impelled him almost to suicide; heroic charity is the basis of almost all the legends of Çakya-Mouni. . . . It was because of his compassion for all creatures that he had accepted one last time the human condition. He ceaselessly repeated this maxim: "Released, release; arrived at the other side, cause others to arrive; consoled, console; having attained complete nirvana, help others attain it."[15]

Shakyamuni became Buddha at the age of thirty-five years. Thirty-five was Vincent van Gogh's age at the time he read Burnouf's essay. By fall 1888 van Gogh had come to see the ideal artist's life as that of a kind of bodhisattva, dwelling austerely and serenely with his compatriots and devoting himself to the expression of compassion through the creation of works of art that evoke the connections between all levels of existence. In life as in art, the Japanese became his models. In the same letter to his brother in which he spoke of Wagner and Tolstoy, van Gogh wrote:

> If we study Japanese art, we see a man who is undoubtedly wise, philosophic and intelligent, who spends his time doing what? In studying the distance between the earth and the moon? No. In studying Bismarck's policy? No. He studies a single blade of grass. But this blade of grass leads him to draw every plant and then the seasons, the wide aspects of the countryside, then animals, then the human figure. So he passes his life, and life is too short to do the whole. Come now, isn't it almost a true religion which these simple Japanese teach us, who live in nature as though they themselves were flowers?[16]

His dream was to develop a "studio of the South" in Arles: a brotherhood of artists who would live in monklike austerity and produce spiritual art. Bernard was one candidate for membership; Gauguin was another. Van Gogh proposed that the three of them exchange self-portraits.

> For a long time I have thought it touching that the Japanese artists used to exchange works among themselves very often. It certainly proves that they liked and upheld each other, and that there reigned a certain harmony among them; and that they were really living in some sort of fraternal community, quite naturally, and not in intrigues.[17]

In September 1888 Vincent painted the portrait of himself as a Japanese Buddhist monk, which he gave to Gauguin, inscribing it, "To my friend Paul Gauguin."

Van Gogh's visual source for his self-portrait appears to have been Pierre Loti's vivid 1887 novel, *Madame Chrysanthème,* which he mentioned often in his letters. An illustration to a passage about a funeral procession shows a cluster of sober Buddhist monks with shaved heads and dressed in dark robes over white V-necked garments. About the same time that he read Loti's novel—mid-June 1888—van Gogh shaved his hair and beard. In the painting, they are just beginning to grow back. Here, van Gogh's attire, very short hair, and the exaggerated slant of his eyes emphasize his monklike appearance, while the circular brushstrokes around his head in the luminous blue-green background give him the aureole of a bodhisattva. In a letter to Gauguin from early October 1888, van Gogh wrote of the spiritual discipline that would be necessary to live up to the ambitions of his self-portrait:

> It has cost me a lot of trouble, yet I shall have to do it all over again if I want to succeed in expressing what I mean. It will even be necessary for me to recover somewhat more from the stultifying influence of our so-called state of civilization in order to have a better model for a better picture.[18]

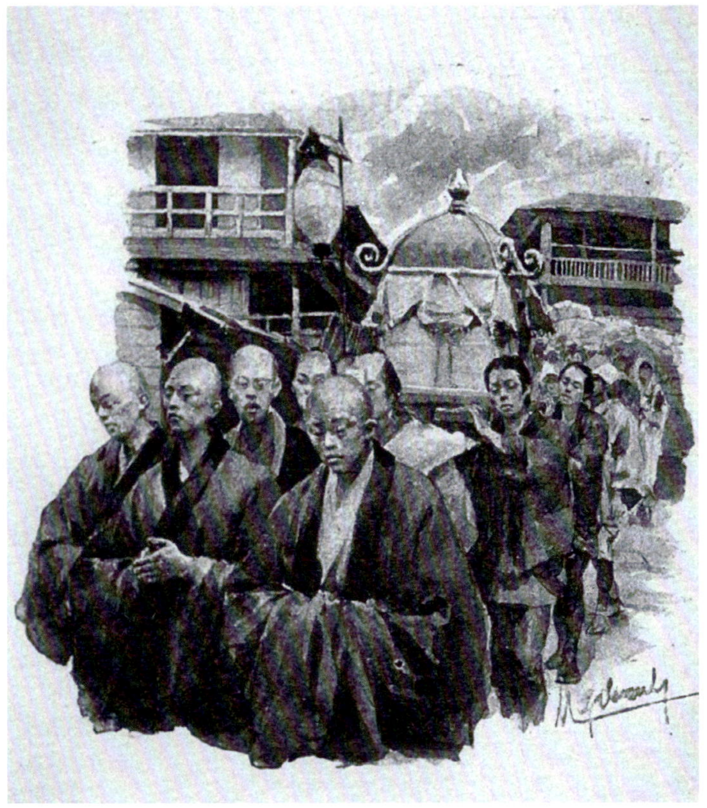

Félicien de Myrbach-Rheinfeld, *Japanese Buddhist Monks Leading a Funeral Procession,* illustration in Pierre Loti, *Madame Chrysanthème* (Paris, 1887), 126.

Clearly, van Gogh felt he had a long way to go in achieving the serene state of mind he wanted to depict in this self-portrait.

The truth of his self-assessment is borne out by the effaced dedication to Gauguin at the top of the painting. It seems likely that van Gogh attacked it during his episode of madness at the end of December 1888 when, according to Gauguin, he threatened his friend with a straight razor and later cut off part of his own ear.[19] The following April a depressed Vincent wrote Theo, "Under the name of optimism we are falling back once more into a religion which looks to me like the tail end of a kind of Buddhism. No harm in that; on the contrary, if you like."[20] Over the next eighteen months, van Gogh lived in fear of his mental "attacks," fought depression, and, after several attempts, succeeded in taking his own life in July 1890.

When he learned of van Gogh's death the following month, Gauguin wrote their mutual friend Emile Bernard: "To die at this time is a great happiness for him, for it puts an end to his suffering, and if he returns in another life he will harvest the fruit of his fine conduct in this world, according to the law of Buddha."[21]

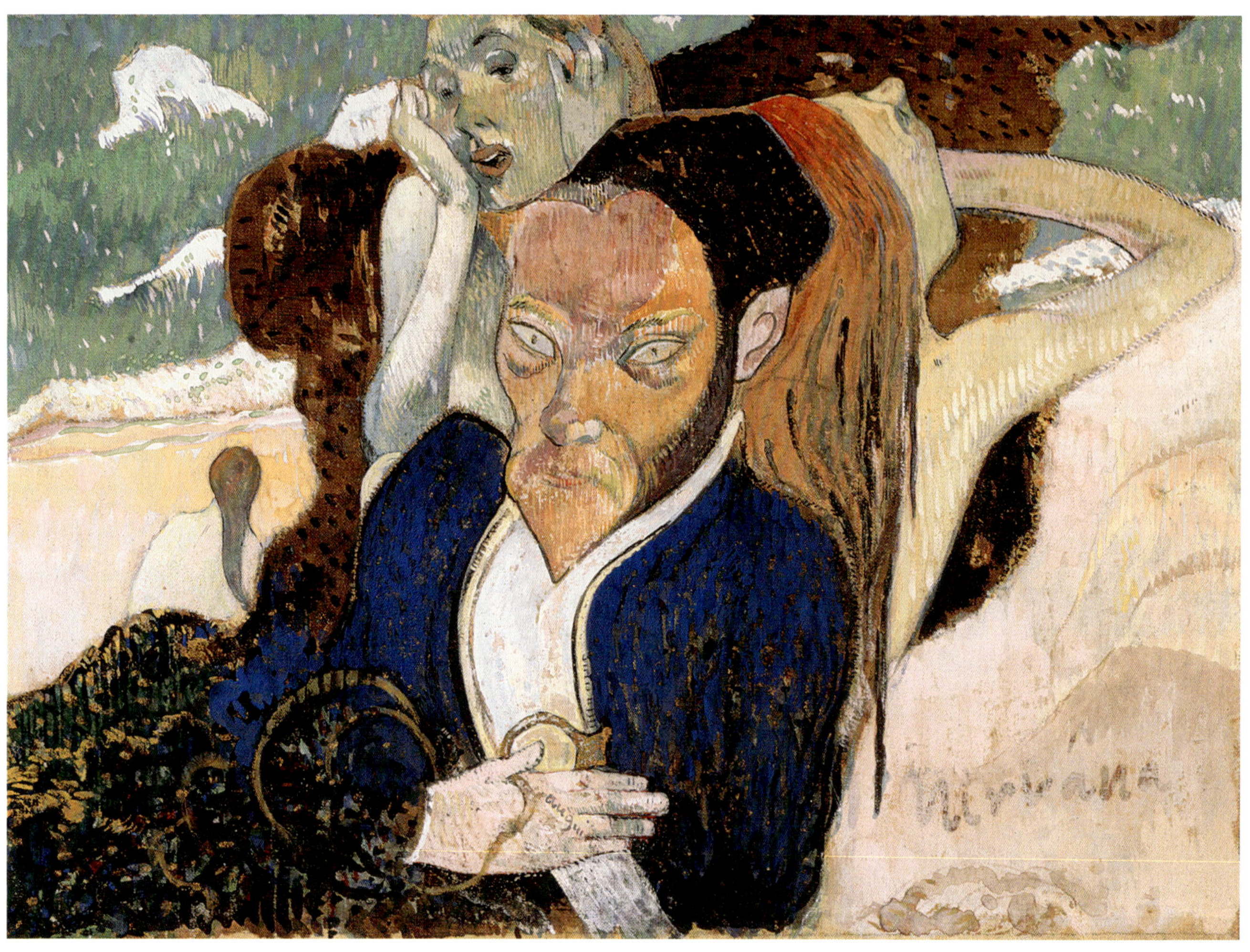

Paul Gauguin, *Nirvana,* 1889–90, gouache with gold on cotton, 8¼ x 11⅜ in. Wadsworth Atheneum, Hartford, The Ella Gallup Sumner and Mary Catlin Sumner Collection Fund.

PAUL GAUGUIN 1848–1903

IN BUDDHISM, PAUL GAUGUIN SOUGHT RELEASE from desire—the source of human misery, according to the Buddha. To be freed from desire is to experience nirvana, the title of a jewel-like painting by Gauguin inscribed "nirvana" in its bottom right corner. The painting presents us with an image of Gauguin's friend Meyer de Haan wearing a vivid blue and white robe. His right hand, which he holds in front of him in a *mudra*-like pose, is wrapped with a golden, tendril-like, diamond-headed snake. De Haan's ears are pointed and his eyes slanted; his pinpoint pupils indicate a trancelike state. Behind him we see rocks, a beach, a green ocean with white waves, and three naked female figures representing three stages of desire—longing, enactment, and loss. The red-haired woman on the right, who flings herself toward the water while apparently stuffing her hand into her mouth, forms a two-sided Janus figure with the black-hatted head and congenitally deformed body of de Haan. Together, they suggest the two sides of desire: abandonment to it and freedom from it—"nirvana."

Gauguin's interest in Buddhism is hard to miss: its imagery shows up regularly in his art from 1888 on. What is difficult is sorting out the meaning of these complex, deeply psychological works. Gauguin experienced a tumultuous childhood. His maternal grandmother was the writer and political activist Flora Tristan. His father, an unemployed former editor of a radical, antigovernment newspaper, died on board ship while the family was fleeing

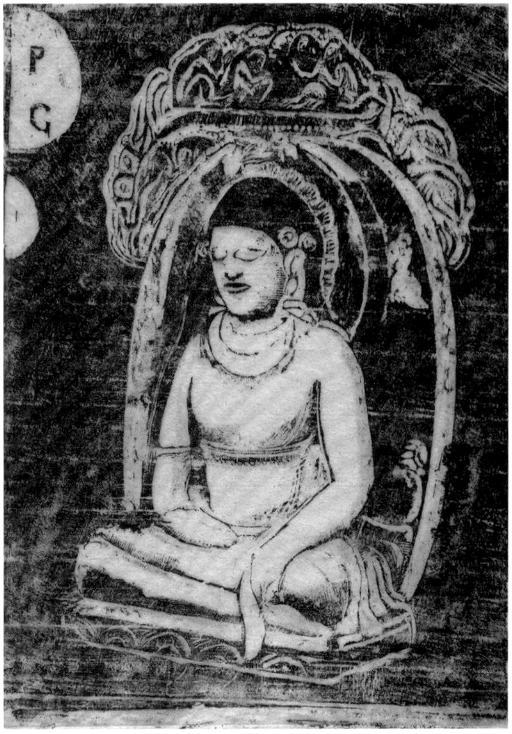
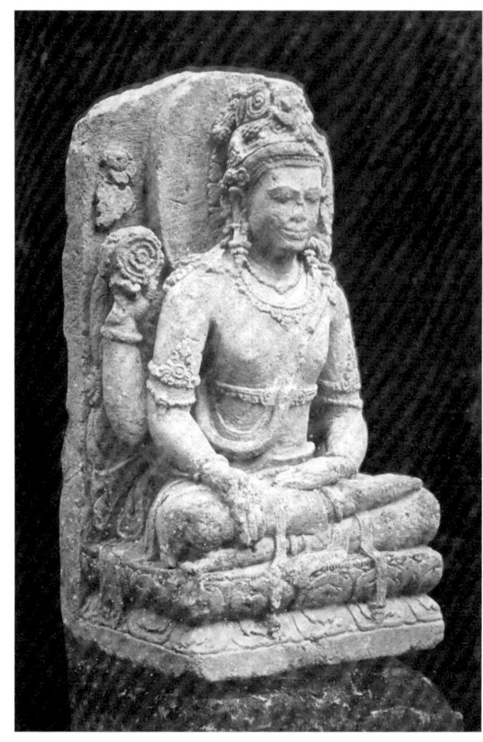

(left) Paul Gauguin, *Buddha,* 1898–99, woodcut, 11½ x 8⅝ in. The Art Institute of Chicago, Print Sales Miscellaneous Fund, 1947.687. Image © The Art Institute of Chicago.

(right) Four-armed Shiva from Wonosobo, Central Java, 8th–10th century. Published in 1872 in Isidore van Kinsbergen, *Oudheden van Java.* Courtesy Kern Institute, Leiden. Kern inventory no. P-044171.

Paris for Peru, where his pretty young mother, Aline, had family connections. Gauguin, who was one and a half at the time, lived in the upper-class Lima household of his great-uncle with his mother and older sister until he was almost seven years old. After their return to Paris, his mother first supported the family as a seamstress and then seems to have become something of a kept woman. Her protector was Gustave Arosa, a collector whose family had business connections in Peru. At the age of seventeen Gauguin joined the merchant marine. He learned of his mother's death on a stopover in India, when he was barely nineteen. Gauguin probably knew that his grandmother, in her divorce proceedings against his grandfather, an artist, had accused him of molesting Aline. Her likeness, preserved in a photograph Gauguin kept with him until his death, made frequent appearances in his art in the guise of Eve and other tempted or violated females.

Gauguin's views on love and sex and his relationships with women can fairly be described as tortured: he gave one of his most important works the ironic title *Be in Love and You Will*

Be Happy. Douglas Druick and Peter Zegers have suggested that the puzzling thumb-at-the-mouth gesture of Gauguin's self-portrait in this wood relief sculpture was borrowed from a relief on the eighth-century Buddhist monument of Borobudur.[1] The Javanese panel depicts the temptation of Buddha by Mara and his minions, a subject appropriate to the theme of *Be in Love,* for which Gauguin adapted not only the gesture, but also the barely compressed physicality of the Borobudur relief.

Druick and Zegers argue that Gauguin's extensive visual knowledge of Borobudur came from photographs inherited in 1883 from his guardian, Gustave Arosa, who collected Latin American and Asian art. But Gauguin had plenty of other visual sources to feed his exotic imagination. In addition to the Cernuschi collection (see p. 22), there was the Museum of Khmer Art, whose collections went on view in Paris in 1878; the Musée Ethnographique, which also opened in 1878; and the Musée Indochinois, which opened in 1882. A large Exposition Universelle opened in Paris in May 1889 featuring a Javanese village complete with dancers, pavilions displaying the art and culture of the French colonies Annam-Tonkin and Cochin China, and a "Pagoda of Great Tranquillity"—a copy of one of the towers at the Cambodian Buddhist temple of Angkor Wat. The Musée Guimet, founded and promoted as a "museum of religions," was probably another important source of visual imagery and information for Gauguin. Located from 1879 through December 1888 in Lyons (through which Gauguin passed on his way to and from Arles to stay with van Gogh), it reopened in Paris with great fanfare in November 1889. Photographs of its galleries from this period show an abundant mix of Buddhist sculpture and paintings from Japan, China, India, Afghanistan, and the Himalayas.

Buddhist iconography was ubiquitous in Gauguin's art from the late 1880s onward. In addition to borrowing Buddhist poses and motifs, Gauguin gave his art an edge by utilizing the double meanings, Western and Eastern, of such Buddhist symbols as the rooster, the snake, and the pig, symbolizing lust, hate, and delusion (the "three poisons" at the center of the Tibetan Buddhist "wheel of life"); peacocks, which are nourished by poisonous plants; and the *vajra*—the masculine symbol of power—in its form of a stylized fleur-de-lis.

Gauguin's interest in the Buddha's teachings probably dates to the fall of 1888, when he went to live with the better-read Vincent van Gogh. Just before his move from Pont-Aven to Arles, the forty-year-old Gauguin experienced unrequited love for Emile Bernard's seventeen-year-old sister Madeleine, who spent the months of August and September with her brother in Pont-Aven, accompanied by her mother. Madeleine, a beautiful, intellectual, "mystical" (her brother's word) girl with an interest in ethnic culture, must have thrilled Gauguin when, like himself, she adopted local Breton costume. But, given the age difference and the fact that Gauguin was married with four children (his family was in his wife's home country of Denmark), he was hardly in a position to press his suit. He wrote Madeleine a letter after her return to

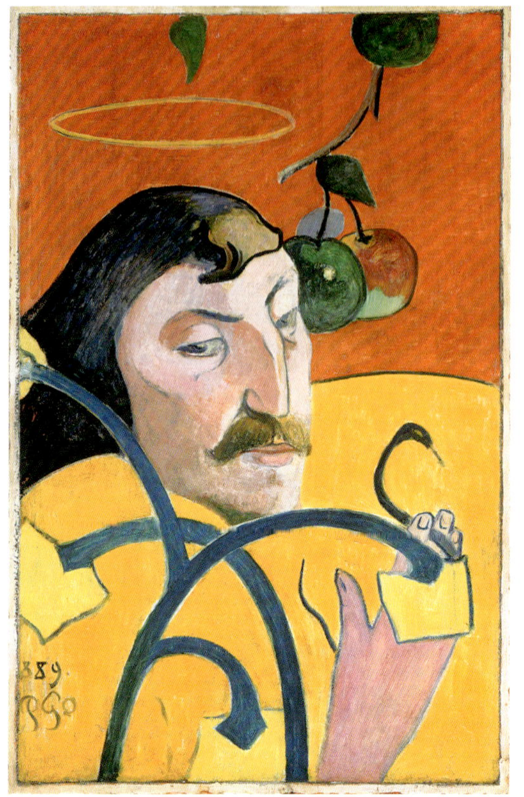

Paul Gauguin, *Self-Portrait with Halo,* 1889, oil on wood, 31⅜ x 20⅜ in. National Gallery of Art, Washington, D.C., Chester Dale Collection. Photo: Jose Naranjo. Image © 2005 Board of Trustees, National Gallery of Art, Washington.

Paris in which he urged his "dear sister" to view herself as "androgynous, without sex."[2] Instead, she became engaged to one of Gauguin's younger friends, the artist Charles Laval.

Gauguin was thus primed for the Buddha's teaching of the origin of suffering in desire when he went to live with van Gogh in their ascetic "studio of the South." (Their asceticism included regular "hygienic" visits to the brothel, part of their communal budget.) The two artists could hardly have been more different—van Gogh believed passionately in painting from life, while Gauguin preferred painting from memory and his imagination; van Gogh worked his paintings in thick, visually tactile brushstrokes, while Gauguin once bragged about the smooth surface he achieved by ironing a finished canvas; van Gogh viewed his artistic calling as the compassionate practice of a bodhisattva, while for Gauguin art was a way to express subconscious feelings and exorcise his demons. If van Gogh found it hard to attain the serenity of nirvana because of his unreliable mind, Gauguin had a major ego to contend with.

When he fled Arles and van Gogh on December 23, 1888, after the traumatic ear-cutting incident, Gauguin went to stay with his fellow artist and loyal friend Emile Schuffenecker in Paris. The previous October, while still living with van Gogh, Gauguin had written Schuffenecker, "What do you mean when you talk about my terrifying mysticism?"[3] The statement suggests the direction of their future discussions. Schuffenecker became involved with the Theosophist and Rosicrucian movements—he created, for example, the cover illustration for the French Theosophist magazine *Le lotus bleu* in 1892. But he became interested in Buddhism as well. When, in September 1895, Schuffenecker sent the writer Jules Bois (see p. 23) a copy of the *Dhammapada,* the sayings of the Buddha, he commented:

> May this lofty wisdom soothe the aching heart of my friend. This doctrine of Buddha can be easily summarized. Surrender egoism, the cause of all misery. Practice compassion, meaning all our vital effort should go toward the benefit and happiness of our species, not the satisfaction of our passions. This is simple and difficult. That which kills our fellow artists is ambition, the exaggerated development of self-love. All my efforts strain to kill these passions in myself. To the extent I have succeeded, I am happier.[4]

Schuffenecker's words call to mind the following passage from the *Dhammapada:*

> Whoever overcomes this clinging vulgar craving in the world, so hard to get over, has sorrows fall away, like the drops of water from a lotus. . . . Just as a tree will regrow even if cut, as long as its root has not been destroyed and is firm, so will this misery regrow again and again as long as the tendency to craving is not rooted out.[5]

These words from the *Dhammapada* seem also to have inspired a passage in Gauguin's 1893 manuscript, *Noa Noa:*

> In time with the sound of the ax I sang:
> Cut down the entire forest (of desires) at the base
> Cut in yourself the love of yourself, as with the hand, in autumn,
> one would cut the Lotus.[6]

In fall 1889 Gauguin was living at Marie Henry's oceanside inn at Le Pouldu in Brittany with the Dutch painter Meyer de Haan, who was also a scholar of religion and Eastern philosophy. Their decoration of the inn's dining room incorporated Buddhist as well as Christian symbolism, local proverbs, and even some Egyptian motifs—another influence of the previous summer's Exposition Universelle. Two of the most prominent features of the room were Gauguin's *Self-Portrait with Halo* and his *Portrait of Meyer de Haan,* painted on the top halves of two flanking doors.

Self-Portrait with Halo is an enigmatic work. It is helpful to know that at the time it was painted Gauguin had once again been spurned in love—by Marie Henry, who took de Haan as a lover in preference to Gauguin. Depicting himself as a saint, Gauguin places the apples of desire behind his head, where they remain unpicked as he averts his eyes. In the pendant portrait, the apples are plucked and piled in a bowl in front of de Haan, who muses darkly over copies of Milton's *Paradise Lost* and Thomas Carlyle's *Sartor Resartus.*

But perhaps as important was Gauguin's lingering memory of his time with van Gogh, exactly one year earlier. Here he was again, living and working side by side with a red-headed Dutch artist interested in alternative spirituality. Van Gogh, meanwhile, was isolated at an asylum in Saint-Rémy and continuing to paint feverishly. Gauguin sought to reassure him that he was continuing their dream of artistic brotherhood. He wrote van Gogh in the first half of November 1889: "We are, de Haan and I, set up *for work and for serenity*."[7] One way to understand Gauguin's *Self-Portrait with Halo* is as a delayed response to van Gogh's self-portrait as a Japanese Buddhist monk, painted as a gift for Gauguin the previous September.

The horizontally bifurcated background of *Self-Portrait with Halo* resembles that of van Gogh's *Self-Portrait with Bandaged Ear* from the previous January, which Gauguin would have seen at the gallery of their mutual dealer, Vincent's brother Théo van Gogh. Both paintings share red as one of the background colors, but for Vincent's orange Gauguin substituted an intense saffron yellow—indeed, he appears wrapped in it.

Yellow was not only one of van Gogh's favorite colors, it was also the color of the robes worn by some Buddhist monks, a fact of which Gauguin was well aware. The October 1889 issue of the *Livre d'or de l'Exposition Universelle (Golden Book of the World's Fair)* showed a procession of bonzes—Buddhist monks—in the Annamite pagoda, "dressed in magnificent robes, in red and yellow satin . . . the third, carrying in his hand the lotus branch."[8] Gauguin may well have seen such a procession, for it was probably repeated regularly during the Exposition Universelle, which opened on May 6, three weeks before Gauguin left Paris for Brittany. The lotus—Buddhist symbol of purity and compassion—is a likely identification for the strange plant in the foreground of the *Self-Portrait,* toward which Gauguin directs his eyes. Above his head Gauguin painted a yellow halo, echoing van Gogh's painted aureole in his self-portrait for Gauguin.

The snake winding through Gauguin's fingers links the *Self-Portrait with Halo* to the even more complex *Nirvana*. Although *Nirvana* may have been painted at Le Pouldu, it seems more likely, in view of its delicacy and use of gold paint, that Gauguin painted it after he returned to Paris in February 1890. The word "nirvana" inscribed in the bottom right corner may refer to the esoteric interests of de Haan, but it also invites the viewer to interpret this painting in Buddhist terms. The snake in de Haan's hand forms a stylized letter "G" that serves as the first letter of Gauguin's signature. The snake thus refers to Gauguin, who here presents de Haan as an acolyte or alter ego.

A multivalent symbol, the snake can stand for fertility (its resemblance to the penis links it with male generative power), temptation (its biblical meaning), and—like the lotus—regeneration (it sheds its skin). If symbols are signs of things imbued with energy, the snake is symbolic "of energy itself—of force pure and simple; hence its ambivalence and multivalencies."[9] This particular snake has a diamond-shaped head, similar to the odd diamond shapes of the yellow lotus blossoms in *Self-Portrait with Halo.* His twining body resembles the lotus stems depicted in Tibetan and other Buddhist art.

This attribute of a diamond-headed lotus/snake, along with de Haan's pointed ears, demonic eyes, and the blue and white colors of his robe, is strong evidence for identifying him with Vajrapani ("Vajra-handed")—the *yaksha,* or demonic being, who bears in his hand the diamond thunderbolt *(vajra),* which, in Tibetan Buddhism, represents the male generative organ and male power. Vajrapani is a protector of the Buddha and the manifestation of the Buddha's power to persuade others. His colors are blue and white. His *vajra* is sometimes paired with a lotus, representing in this context the female generative organ and female cosmic energy, much as de Haan is paired with female energy in *Nirvana.*

Nirvana is freedom from desire. In *Nirvana,* Gauguin presents his friend as a bodhisattva whose masculine power to cut through illusion is not a weapon of desire, but a weapon able to overcome desire. Like the earlier *Self-Portrait with Halo, Nirvana* answers the challenge Vincent van Gogh set for both himself and Gauguin with his self-portrait as "a simple bonze worshipping the Eternal Buddha."[10] But in presenting de Haan/Vajrapani as a manifestation of himself, Gauguin outdid van Gogh by identifying with the Buddha. While this may at first seem a typically egocentric Gauguin stance, it is in keeping with the Buddha's teaching that every person has the potential to be a buddha—to be "awake."

On his second and final journey to Tahiti in 1895 (he would die in the Marquesas in 1903), Gauguin took with him a copy of the manuscript for *Noa Noa,* which he had been working on in Paris. Between 1896 and January 1898, he made some additions to it, which he titled "Diverse Things." They include the following passage:

> Buddha, a simple mortal who neither conceived nor comprehended God, but who conceived and comprehended fully the intelligence of the human heart, reached that eternal bliss, Nirvana—the last stage of the soul in its progressive movement through the ages—all people, by virtue of the attainment of this wisdom, are able to become buddhas.[11]

Before his first trip to Tahiti in 1891 Gauguin had written Emile Bernard, "All of the Far East, the great philosophy written in letters of gold in all their art, all that is worth studying, and I think I will be reinvigorated out there."[12] The passage is reminiscent of van Gogh's comment in his letter to Gauguin about his self-portrait: "It will even be necessary for me to recover somewhat more from the stultifying influence of our so-called state of civilization in order to have a better model for a better picture."[13] Perhaps in part, Gauguin went to the South Seas in the hope of finding the Buddha in himself. If so, he was seemingly not much more successful than van Gogh had been. Still, he gave the last self-portrait he did to a Vietnamese Buddhist friend, author of a satirical play, *Loves of an Old Painter,* about the perils of desire.[14]

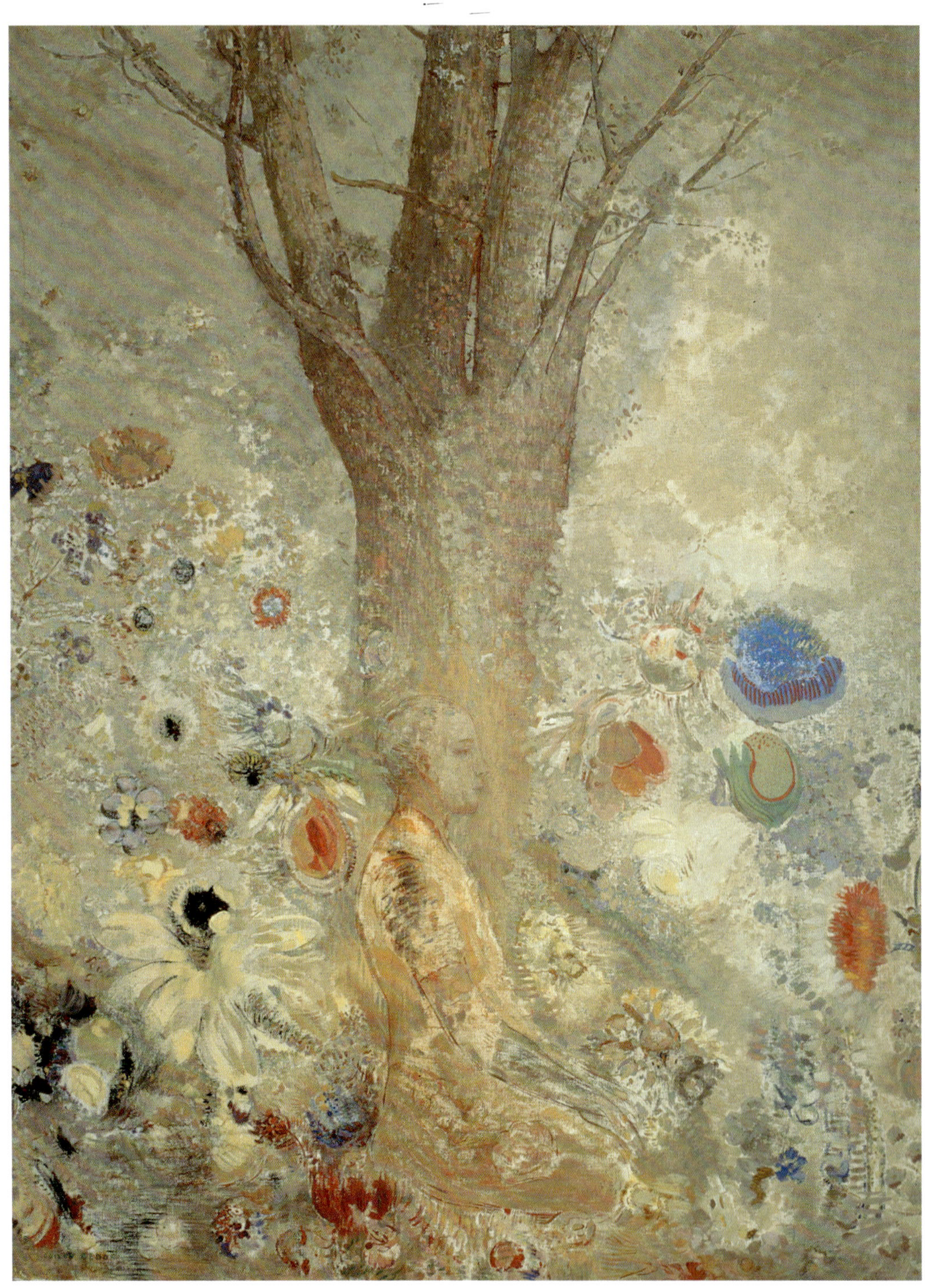

Odilon Redon, *Buddha in His Youth,* about 1904, distemper on canvas, 63 3/16 x 47 1/2 in. Van Gogh Museum, Amsterdam.

ODILON REDON 1840–1916

MORE, EVEN, THAN HIS FRIEND PAUL GAUGUIN, Odilon Redon was an artist of the unconscious. The terrors and fantasies that found visual expression in the oppressively dark works Redon called his *noirs,* or "blacks," were inspired by Romantic literature and by his own misery. In his charcoal drawing *A Drowning* (1884), for example, an immense sun, blackened in eclipse, sheds its dark rays over the face of a drowned man floating in a murky sea under an even murkier sky. In this simple drawing, made when he was forty-four years old, Redon conveyed his profound sense of abandonment leading to suicidal depression.

In contrast, the joys of serenity have rarely been as purely expressed as in Redon's later luminous works in color. At the age of sixty-four, Redon painted *Buddha in His Youth.* The subject is presumably the legendary First Trance, when the young Siddhartha spontaneously entered a meditative state as he was sitting under a tree watching his father plowing. In the Redon painting we see a meditating figure virtually overrun by vibrant flowers, much like the description of the Buddha's enlightenment at the beginning of the Flower Garland Sutra:

> Nets and garlands of precious stones and flowers are draped everywhere, emitting shining light and harmonious sounds. Above him spreads a tree—the tree of enlightenment—that has a trunk of diamonds; its boughs are lapis lazuli. The tree speaks various truths without end; its leaves supply delightful shade to every corner of the universe.[1]

The young Buddha seems as rooted in the earth as the tree behind him. Clearly, for Redon, a considerable inner transformation had occurred.

Odilon Redon and his younger friend Paul Gauguin shared family stories of dramatic ocean voyages. The one-year-old Gauguin lost his father during his family's voyage to Peru. Redon's father had gone to America to escape the draft in 1814 and made his fortune there. In 1840, three weeks before Odilon's birth, his father brought his much younger Creole wife and Odilon's four-year-old brother to France from New Orleans. Much later, in his memoir, *A soi-même (To Myself)*, Odilon wrote:

> Ocean travel then was both long and hazardous. It seems that during this return bad weather, or contrary winds, threatened to send off course the ship carrying my parents. I would have loved, thanks to this delay, by chance or by fate, to have been born among the waves, which I have since so often contemplated from the high cliffs of Brittany, with suffering, with sadness: a place with no homeland, above an unfathomable depth.[2]

His statement conveys a bottomless grief. While Gauguin remembered his early childhood with his mother in Peru as a paradise lost, Redon was cast out of paradise almost the moment he was born.

Named officially after his father, Bertrand, Odilon was called after his flighty mother, Odile, who had formed a lifelong bond with her first son during the four years Bertrand was in France preparing for the family's relocation. Odilon may have been renamed by his father in an attempt to inspire in Odile his share of motherly love. If so, the ploy was not effective: when he was three days old, Odilon was sent to live under the care of a wet nurse and then an elderly uncle at Peyrelebade, the family's wine-producing estate in the bleak Médoc region of France. He tells us in his memoir that his frail health prevented him from starting school until he was eleven years old; it was only then that he rejoined his parents and siblings (there were now four) at the family home in Bordeaux.

Odilon's exile may have been for health reasons—he suffered, it seems, from seizures—but this early rejection left a malevolent imprint on his mental health. The dominant mood of his childhood was loneliness; that of his adulthood, depression. He did not marry his own Creole wife, Camille, until he was forty years old. (He was the only one of Odile's five children who married at all.) Four years before his death in 1916, Redon wrote in response to a question about artist biographies:

> What's the use? The artist comes to life to accomplish the mysterious. He is an accident. He has no place in society. He is born completely naked on straw without a mother to prepare his swaddling clothes. As soon as he, young or old, exhibits the rare flower of originality . . . this flower's unfamiliar perfume disturbs people and causes them to turn away. Therefore the artist [experiences] unavoidable, even tragic isolation; therefore the

> sad and incurable anxiety that envelops his youth, even his infancy, and that makes him unsociable until the day he finds . . . others who understand him. It is best not to speak of these painful origins; to know them changes nothing.[3]

The art historians Douglas Druick and Peter Zegers have identified in this statement a "fantasy of autogenesis, central to the myth of creative genius, now the organizing principle of Redon's identity." But, they go on, "disclaimers notwithstanding, the past continued to hurt him."[4] Redon's art, his famous *noirs,* which eventually came to glow with brilliant color, were the means to mitigate this hurt.

An important influence on the young artist was the botanist Armand Clavaud, whom Redon first came to know in Bordeaux around 1858–59, and with whom he remained friends until Clavaud's suicide in 1890. Redon had substituted nature for his human mother, and Clavaud provided him with an intimate understanding of this emotionally nourishing source of inspiration. He also introduced the young Redon to the Romantic view of life through the paintings of Eugène Delacroix and the writings of both Delacroix's champion, the poet Charles Baudelaire, and the American master of mystery, Edgar Allan Poe.

In 1859 Charles Darwin's *On the Origin of Species* was published. Always interested in the latest scientific ideas, Clavaud no doubt discussed the theory of evolution with his young friend. An admirer of the philosophers Spinoza and Schopenhauer, he also read Hindu texts. In 1883, perhaps as a tribute to Clavaud, Redon created a charcoal drawing of a Spinoza-like figure musing before an open book inscribed "Ramayama"—the title of the classic Sanskrit epic of India. Clavaud's belief in an animating spirit of the universe and in the imaginary powers of the unconscious mind would be important to Redon's conception of his own artistic mission. At the age of thirty, Redon wrote an autobiographical essay entitled "Le Fakir," in which he expressed regret that human spiritual evolution was lagging behind physical evolution.

One of the authors whose work Armand Clavaud introduced him to was Gustave Flaubert, whose *Temptation of Saint Anthony* Redon read in 1882. It inspired him to publish three series of lithographs between 1888 and 1896. The book itself had gone through a number of stages before it was published in 1874. In the late 1840s Flaubert's manuscript reflected Spinoza's monist view that mind and body, idea and the universe, are one, an entity Spinoza called "God or Nature." Later versions show the influence of the English philosopher Herbert Spencer, who attempted to apply evolutionary theory to every aspect of reality, including the "Unknown." As finally published, the book reflects Flaubert's conclusion that science and religion are not in conflict, but rather represent two poles of a continuum of human thought. *The Temptation of Saint Anthony* ended up a virtual catalog of metaphysical belief systems, each personified by a vividly described entity encountered by the saint in

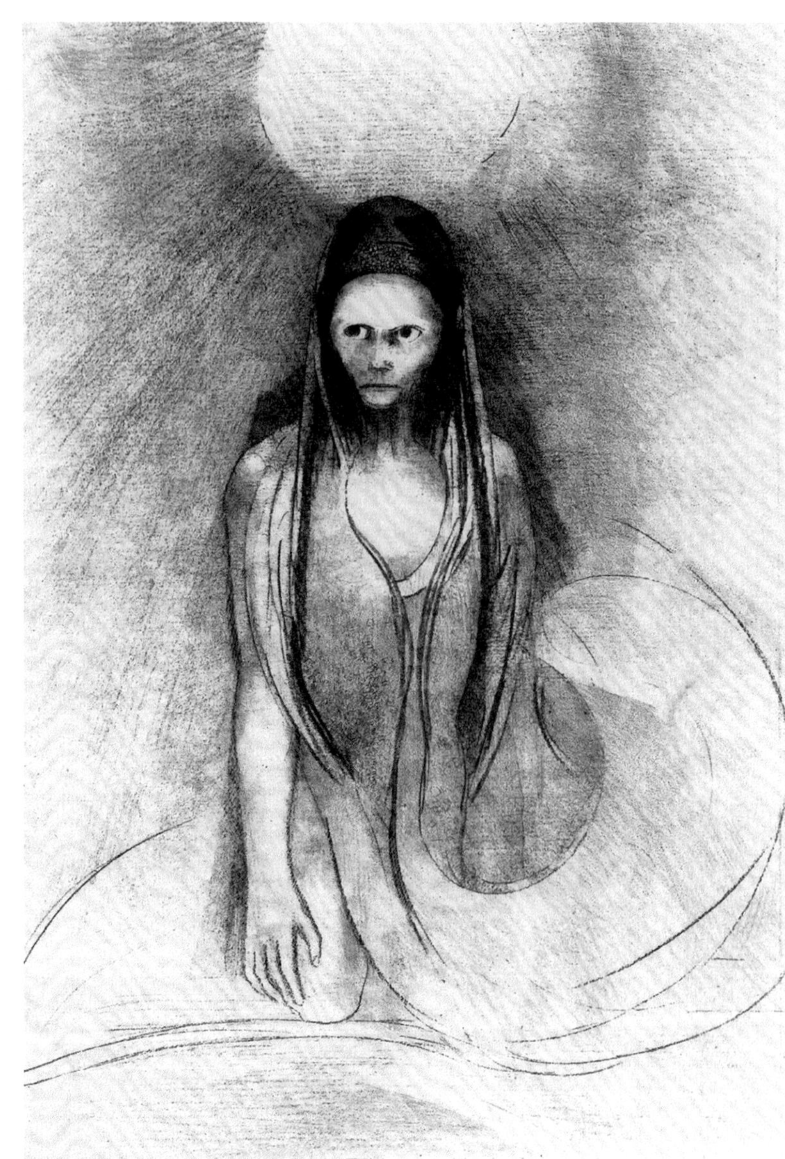

Odilon Redon, *Intelligence Was Mine! I Became the Buddha,* 1896, lithograph. Image: $12\frac{3}{8} \times 8\frac{1}{2}$ in. The Art Institute of Chicago, The Stickney Collection, 1920.1768. Photograph by Greg Williams. Image © The Art Institute of Chicago.

his search for spiritual nourishment. None of them satisfy, and Anthony finishes his journey in a state of pantheistic bliss inspired by the generation of life.

The Temptation of Saint Anthony is at once episodic and hallucinatory. Its appeal for Redon lay in the exotic variety of characters and scenarios that seem to emerge, dreamlike, from the saint's unconscious mind. Flaubert devoted a long passage to the Buddha, presenting him as the last god in the "Brahman" (Hindu) pantheon. Although Redon created his first two lithographic series based on Flaubert's book in 1888–89, he did not depict the

Buddha until 1895, when he published in the periodical *L'estampe originale* a lithograph entitled *Le Buddha* with a caption quoting Flaubert's passage, "They brought me to the schools. I knew more than the doctors."[5] The next year he published as part of his last portfolio of Saint Anthony lithographs *Intelligence Was Mine! I Became the Buddha*. Its caption is a line toward the end of Flaubert's passage on the Buddha, but it seems closer to his description of the Buddha's first appearance:

> Suddenly a naked man appears, seated in the middle of the sand with his legs crossed. A large circle vibrates, suspended behind him. The little curls of his black hair, deepening into an azure tint, twist symmetrically around a protuberance at the top of his head. His arms, of great length, fall straight down his sides. His two hands, with open palms, rest evenly on his thighs.[6]

The final words of Flaubert's Buddha are more apocalyptic than Buddha-like: "I have nothing more to do . . . everything must perish; and, until the new births, a flame will dance on the ruins of a world's overthrow."[7] Nor do Redon's two lithographs reflect either Buddhist art or Buddhist philosophy. Without their titles, his images are not particularly recognizable as depictions of the Buddha.

In July 1895, at the time he was creating these images, Redon confessed to a friend, "I have books on Buddhism that I have not yet read."[8] Redon's use of the word "yet" would seem to indicate his intention to become better educated about a religion that, for Flaubert, as well as for many of Redon's Theosophist and occultist colleagues, was still mired in the mists of orientalism. In 1885, for example, when Edouard Schuré published his essay "The Buddha and His Legend," he seemed more interested in the legend than the Buddha: "We are not entering here into an analysis of the metaphysics of the Buddha; we limit ourselves to the essential reflections: What was the secret attitude of Buddha before the sphinx of destiny? What was his response to the great enigma?"[9] Instead of directly examining the Buddha's teachings, which have nothing to do with secrets, Schuré chose to analyze two expressions of Buddhism he saw as coexisting in contemporary society: the exoteric Buddha of Schopenhauer and the positivists and the esoteric and much more appealing—to Schuré—Buddha of the "Neo-Buddhists," or Theosophists: the "Çâkya-Mouni of a transcendent spiritualism."[10]

Redon was a believer in mystery—indeed, his artistic vision depended upon it—but he was no mystic. His knowledge of Indian philosophy, which went back to the 1860s, came from his biologist friend Clavaud, who, according to Redon, "searched . . . at the edges of the imperceptible world for that intermediate life between animal and plant, flower and being, that mysterious element which is animal during a few hours of the day and only in the presence of light."[11] In his own creative search, Redon ended up advocating liberating the mind by focusing, like Clavaud, on some object of attention. In 1909 he wrote a friend who had asked his advice on behalf of another artist:

> It would be desirable, if he wants to find peace, happiness, that he close his intelligence, his too conscious clarity (that miner's light) in order to concern himself only with the simple substances that he uses. . . . When one has settled in detail all the windings of one's life, stubbornly, patiently, a kind of infused, imaginative power arises, ready to burst forth; this power is the source of suggestive art. . . . It is necessary that the painter have before him, under his hand, some *object of attention.* I don't believe that one can avoid this. No visual memory can take its place. I know that the earth turns, that everything passes, and that it is even necessary for the gods to change, as Renan has said; but I wouldn't know, in the instant when I breathe and write you, how to think of my art differently. To take a *bite* by means of the most attentive, minute analysis, pencil in hand: that's my system. . . . I beg you to believe that sweet and light is the serenity that flows from this understanding of oneself![12]

Writers on Redon and his art have tended to treat his insistence on close attention to nature as an attempt to distance himself from younger Symbolist artists and writers. This passage, however, suggests that sometime before 1909 Redon was practicing a meditation technique that emphasized stilling and releasing the mind by focusing on physical sensation.

The visual evidence shows Redon beginning to achieve the serenity of which he writes after 1895, when brilliant color infused the work of this artist previously known for his *noirs.* Redon's reference to Renan suggests that he had read Ernest Renan's *New Studies in Religious History* (1884; see p. 31), with its excellent essay on Buddhism. Thanks to the work of Roseline Bacou, we know that Redon's library also contained an 1895 edition of *The Gospel of Buddha* by Paul Carus, the German-born American proselytizer of the religion of science, and Sadakichi Hartmann's *Buddha: A Drama in Twelve Scenes,* published in 1897.[13]

"Buddhism," Carus wrote in *The Gospel of Buddha,* "is a religion which knows of no supernatural revelation, and proclaims doctrines that require no other argument than the 'come and see.' The Buddha bases his religion solely upon man's knowledge of the nature of things, upon provable truth."[14] Carus's scientific approach would have appealed to Redon's Clavaud-influenced sensibility. In contrast, Hartmann's *Buddha: A Drama in Twelve Scenes* is more fantastic even than the Buddha of Flaubert. Sadakichi Hartmann was a German-Japanese American anarchist and writer. His book's appeal for Redon probably lay primarily in its last chapter: "Darkness in Space," dedicated "To Students of Color Psychology." Here, in a kind of positivist version of the Flower Garland Sutra, "poetical license imagines that, at Buddha's entering Nirvana, a color revery *[sic]* takes place in the universe."[15] Hartmann goes on to describe "a kaleidoscopical symphony of color effects continually changing in elation

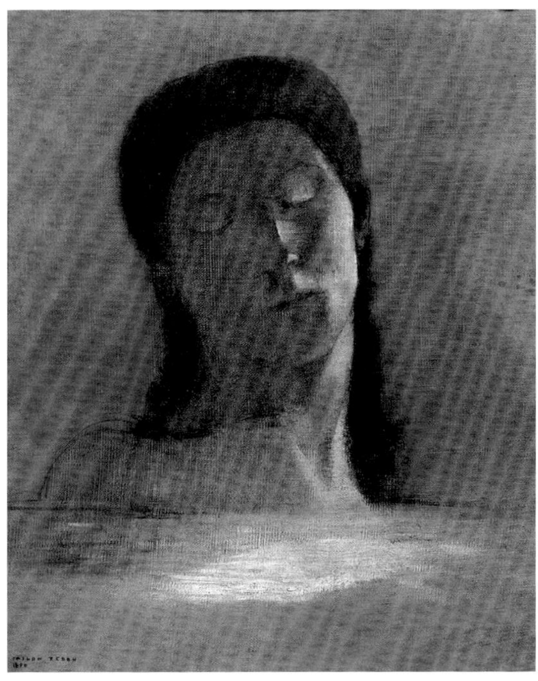

Odilon Redon, *Eyes Closed,* 1890, oil on canvas, 17⅛ x 14 in. Musée d'Orsay, Paris. Photo © Réunion des Musées Nationaux/ Art Resource, NY.

and depression, velocity, intensity, variety and sentiment, continually developing and composing new forms and designs . . . as suggested from the endless constructions, textures, phenomena revealed in astronomy, microscopy, mineralogy, geology, paleontology, etc."[16]

In 1901 Redon for the first time showed only works in color in his exhibition at the Galeries Durand-Ruel. Their subjects ranged from landscapes to portraits to flowers. One work, listed in the catalog but now apparently lost, depicted "The Death of Buddha." Around 1904 Redon painted *Buddha in His Youth,* a large canvas in which a seated Siddhartha meditating under a tree is surrounded by vibrant flowers that seem projected onto the screen of his closed eyes. A pastel by Redon from around 1905 shows the Japanese bodhisattva Jizo, protector of children, standing under the same tree in a flower-filled landscape.[17] His right hand holds a walking stick and his left hand is raised in blessing; his eyes are closed.

"Eyes closed" was a favorite theme of Redon's, a theme that began appearing in his art around 1890. The basic image is an androgynous head with naked shoulders rising above the ocean. The figure, its eyes closed in meditation, sometimes emanates a Christlike quality, but its identity is never specific. Redon did, however, change the title of one such image from *Sacred Heart* to *Buddha.* The image of a meditating head emerging from the sea is reminiscent of Redon's wish to have been born at sea: "a place with no homeland, above an unfathomable depth." The "unfathomable depth" in *Eyes Closed* is that of the mind.

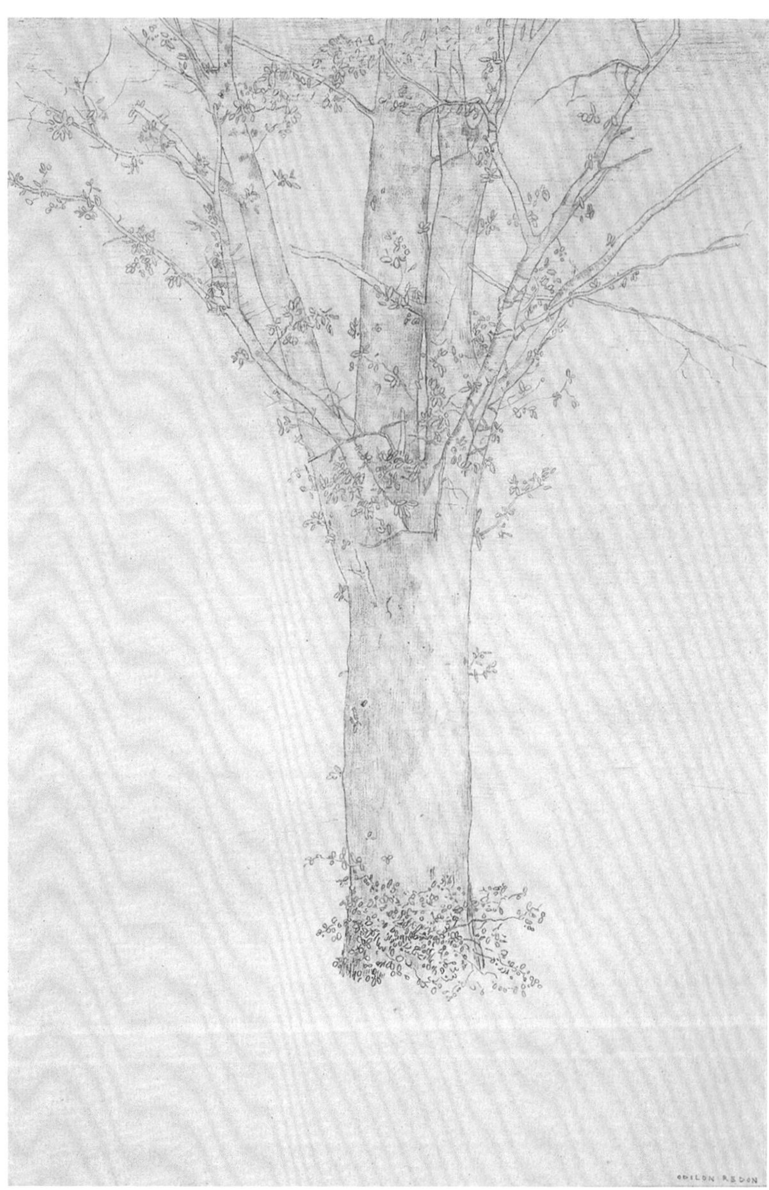

Odilon Redon, *Tree,* 1892, lithograph, $15\frac{5}{8}$ x $12\frac{7}{16}$ in. The Art Institute of Chicago, The Stickney Collection, 1920.1704. Image © The Art Institute of Chicago

The setting of *Buddha in His Youth* is similarly autobiographical: the tree under which Siddhartha meditates was adapted from a drawing of a tree at Peyrelebade, Redon's childhood home, which for him represented his connection with nature. (He had lost Peyrelebade in a dispute with his mother and siblings in 1897.) In *Buddha in His Youth,* Redon seems to be identifying his own youthful self with the young Buddha. Indeed, his descriptions of his younger self stress his reclusive, contemplative nature: "I spent hours, or later the whole day, stretched out on the grass, in the deserted places of countryside, watching the clouds pass . . . I lived only *in* myself, with a revulsion for any physical effort."[18]

The Temptation of Saint Anthony continued to exert its influence as well. In Flaubert's novel, the Buddha says of his early years: "I went continually to meditate in the gardens. The shadows of the trees used to move; but the shadow of the one that sheltered me did not move."[19] Why would a shadow not move? Either because the earth has stopped turning or because the Buddha has become his own sun. *Buddha in His Youth* is visual evidence that Buddhism enabled Redon, at the end of his life, to come to terms with the emotional suffering of his childhood, to recast his past in the light of the "infused, imaginative power" arising from his hard-won understanding of the mind.

II OTHER DIMENSIONS

Yeno, the sixth patriarch, once saw two monks watching the flag of a pagoda fluttering in the wind. One said "It is the wind that moves," the other said "It is the flag that moves"; but Yeno explained to them that the real movement was neither of the wind nor the flag, but of something within their own minds.

KAKUZO OKAKURA

BY THE END OF THE NINETEENTH CENTURY the empirical, "scientific" understanding of the material world was driving a significant number of artists toward an exploration of noumenal reality, accessible to intuition rather than the senses or the intellect. The pithiest formulation of this development is by Wassily Kandinsky's biographer Will Grohmann: "Art became the creation of reality."[1] Kandinsky was one of the most important progenitors of this concept, and his book *On the Spiritual in Art* was its gospel, gaining enormous popularity among artists and art lovers alike from the time it was published, in early 1912. For Kandinsky, art had the potential to serve as a positive spiritual force in the world:

> In a mysterious, puzzling, and mystical way, the true work of art arises "from out of the artist." Once released from him, it assumes its own independent life, takes on a personality, and becomes a self-sufficient, spiritually breathing subject that also leads a real material life: it is a being . . . [and] possesses—like every living being—further creative, active forces. It lives and acts and plays a part in the creation of the spiritual atmosphere.[2]

For Kandinsky, a "true" work of art leads a full inner life—good art has soul. Kandinsky's word for this life-force was *Klang,* spiritual reverberation.

As with the Symbolists, Theosophy continued to influence such early modern abstractionists as Kandinsky, František Kupka, and Piet Mondrian. Theosophy was an early expression of what we now think of as global culture. The Theosophical Society was founded in New York in 1875 by a Russian expatriate, Helena Blavatsky, and her spiritualist friend, Colonel Henry Olcott. By the turn of the century it was headquartered in Adyar, India, and claimed tens of thousands of members all over the world. Madame Blavatsky's goal was to create a "scientific" religion based on absolute knowledge of things spiritual rather than on faith. Her method involved not so much comparative religion as comparative occultism; the "science" part mostly concerned investigating psychic powers that she saw as latent in all but the most spiritually advanced human beings. Her many books attempted to bridge the gap between reason and faith by combining elements of Neoplatonism, Brahminism, Buddhism, Kabbalism, Gnosticism, Rosicrucianism, and Hermeticism. Blavatsky tended to use a Buddhist vocabulary, but hers was a neo-Buddhism that disguised what has been described as a "Judaeo-Christian moral ethic tempered by spiritual Darwinism—a survival not of . . . the fittest organism, but of those with the 'fittest' spirit."[3] Theosophy recast positivism in religious terms, offering a solution to the nineteenth-century problem of how to reanimate the material world with spiritual qualities.

Wassily Kandinsky might be thought of as the art world's Blavatsky. His interest in Theosophy has been well documented. Although auras and other Theosophical elements showed up in his work as late as 1912, Kandinsky's Theosophical interest seems to have peaked by 1909, the year he actually wrote *On the Spiritual in Art:*

> Even if some observers are skeptical of the theosophists' tendency to theorize and their somewhat premature delight in putting an answer in place of the great, eternal question mark, nonetheless the great, yea spiritual, movement remains. It is a powerful agent in the spiritual climate, striking, even in this form, a note of salvation that reaches the desperate hearts of many who are enveloped in darkness and night—a hand that points the way offers help.[4]

Kandinsky's phrase "even in this form" would seem to place him in the skeptics' camp. His last image—a hand pointing the way toward the light—calls up the Buddhist metaphor about not confusing the hand that points at the moon with the moon itself.

It also brings to mind Marcel Duchamp's 1918 painting *Tu m',* which might be translated "you [missing verb] me," a verbal version of the concept of interdependence. *Tu m'* includes a pointing hand signed "A. Klang." Duchamp's "Klang" is surely a reference to Kandinsky's concept *Klang* ("sound"), by which Kandinsky meant resounding, or reverberation. Kandinsky's writings help explain the jarring contrast between the abstraction of Duchamp's *Large Glass,* conceived in Munich in 1912, and the hyper-realism of his last major work, *Etant donnés* (1946–66). In May 1912, in Munich, Kandinsky published his essay "On the Question of Form" in the *Blaue Reiter Almanach.* It was certainly read by Duchamp, who arrived in Munich the following month. "The forms employed," Kandinsky wrote, "which the spirit has wrested from the reserves of matter, may easily be divided between two poles. These two poles are: 1. The Great Abstraction 2. The Great Realism. These two poles open up two paths, which lead ultimately to a single goal."[5] Kandinsky's formulation evokes the full title of Duchamp's *Etant donnés,* which translates as *Given: 1. The Waterfall, 2. The Illuminating Gas.*

"Kandinsky," wrote Duchamp, "opened to the spectator a new way of looking at painting."[6] Like Kandinsky, Marcel Duchamp set out to liberate both art and its audience. But while for Kandinsky art was form—a creation with a life of its own that connects artist and viewer—for Duchamp art was emptiness, a space wherein the viewer "brings the work in contact with the external world by deciphering and interpreting its inner qualifications and thus adds his contribution to the creative act."[7] The degree to which the artist fails to fully convey his intention creates a "gap" that is energized by the potential of this encounter: "What art is in reality is this missing link, not the links which exist. It's not what you see that is art, art is the gap."[8] In other words, art, like everything else, is empty of inherent self-existence.

Despite his emphasis on the viewer, Duchamp's was not a populist view of art. He critiqued contemporary art practice in terms that parallel the two manifestations of Buddhist practice: "Whereas the true artist, true art, is always esoteric, the modern approach to art is based on competition, on making art exoteric."[9] "The word 'art,'" Duchamp told Pierre Cabanne, "interests me very much. If it comes from Sanskrit, as I've heard, it signifies 'making.'"[10] He was probably referring to the ancient Indo-European root *ar,* which means "to join or fit" and is the root of the Sanskrit word *ara,* which signifies, among other things, the spoke or radius of a wheel. There is a Sanskrit word as well for Duchamp's viewer-response theory of art: *rasa. Rasa* resides not in the artist or the object, but in the mind of the viewer—just as the taste of wine exists not in the vintner or in its bottle, but in the mouth of the one who drinks it.

That Duchamp knew this analogy is suggested by his cover for the March 1945 issue of *View* magazine, where an illuminating gas emerges from the neck of a wine bottle.[11] *Rasa* may have been what Duchamp had in mind when he tried to explain his concept of the "aesthetic echo" at the 1949 Western Round Table on Modern Art in San Francisco: "Art cannot be understood through the intellect, but is felt through an emotion presenting some analogy with a religious faith or a sexual attraction—an aesthetic echo."[12]

Duchamp's pairing of religious faith with sexual attraction may have startled his fellow participants in the Western Round Table, but it would not have surprised his friend Constantin Brancusi. There is evidence that together Brancusi and Duchamp explored the phenomenon within Mahayana Buddhism known as Tantrayana or Vajrayana—a set of psychologically sophisticated practices that utilize yogic techniques of internal concentration or visualization to achieve release from suffering.

Mahayana Buddhism recognized two main paths to awakening: the Sutra Way, in which the practitioner patiently explores and works on the afflictions of his or her mindstream by engaging in prescribed practices such as meditation, and the Tantra Way, in which practitioners cultivate a vision of the world as a mandala and themselves as buddhas or bodhisattvas—"enlightenment beings," who vow to retain human form until everyone achieves enlightenment. As with Kandinsky's "two paths," the goal of both "ways" is the same: a state of compassionate, blissful imperturbability. This experience of *shunyata,* of emptiness, results from the energetic conjunction of wisdom, or receptivity (envisioned as female), and compassion, or skillful means (envisioned as male). The union of male and female elements within the body produces a realization of nondual reality, generating *mahasukha,* "the great bliss."

Both *sutra* and *tantra* come from Sanskrit verbs having to do with sewing. *Sutra* means "thread" or "string," in the sense of continuum. *Tantra* refers to threads that are woven into a fabric.[13] The goal of Tantric contemplative exercises is to experience *samsara* ("journeying," the cycle of existence) and *nirvana* (release) as one and the same. Tantric practices seem to have developed originally in India as a way to utilize sexual energy as a means to enlightenment. The method proved so efficacious that it was absorbed into the monastic tradition, as systems of mental practices. Tantric methods are designed not to subdue the body and mind and their passions, but to confront, transform, and transmute them into vehicles for enlightenment. Tantra's assumption of nonduality implies the collapse of all concepts, including those of purity and impurity.

The Tantras are texts that describe the mandala of a specific deity along with associated practices, such as chants and visualizations. Several Tantric systems have a female buddha or bodhisattva as their principal deity; a male practitioner will meditate upon himself in this female form, just as a female practitioner might visualize herself as a male deity. This personal deity, or *yidam,* is not a protector or intercessor, but an alter ego whose nature corresponds to the practitioner's own character and whose visualization is intended to generate psychological transformation. The union of wisdom and compassion is personified by the sexual union of buddhas or bodhisattvas and their respective consorts. These images are referred to as *yab-yum* ("father [and] mother"). Visualizations associated with *yab-yum* deities help the practitioner to merge his or her own masculine and feminine energies, thus achieving the bliss of fusion and the mental radiance that arises from the experienced continuous nature of subject and object.

The Tantric text *Mahayana-sutralamkara* appeared in a two-volume French translation with an exposition on yogic practices by Sylvain Levi, in 1907 and 1911.[14] Tantric Buddhist practices are esoteric practices requiring direct transmission from a teacher in order to be effective. However, by the end of 1907, there was at least one Tibetan in Paris: Adjourp Gumbo was brought by Jacques Bacot,[15] the explorer, collector, and future translator of Brancusi's favorite book, *The Tibetan Poet Milarepa.* Bacot's descriptions of Tibet reminded Brancusi of his own mountainous homeland of Romania, and the Tibetan sorcerer-singer-saint became his alter ego. Brancusi was fond of recounting stories in which, like Milarepa, he possessed magical powers or the ability to defy conventions of time and space.

Brancusi appears to have become attracted to non-Western art in 1907, the year his style began departing radically from that of Auguste Rodin, with whom he apprenticed in April of that year. Marcel Duchamp, who may have known Brancusi as early as 1910, when they both had work at the Salon des Indépendants,[16] would seem to have begun exploring Tantrayana in 1911–12, while trying to resolve personal issues around suffering and desire. Their mutual interest in the subject was suggested by Duchamp in a conversation about his concept of the Androgyne as "a kind of thinking that leads to a way of understanding" that is "above philosophy." He stated, "If one has become the Androgyne one no longer has a need for philosophy," and he used Tantrayana as an example, citing Brancusi: "We may also call this perspective Tantric, as Brancusi would say."[17]

The American artist Georgia O'Keeffe absorbed Buddhist perspectives first through the Japanophile attitudes of her teacher Arthur Wesley Dow and then through her own readings, which included Kandinsky's *On the Spiritual in Art,* Kakuzo Okakura's *Book of Tea,* and, later, *The Secret of the Golden Flower,* a Chinese manual of techniques for clarifying the mind. Dow was in fact ahead of Kandinsky, asserting in his 1899 book, *Composition,* that works of art, including well-designed objects of everyday use, have the power to awaken spiritual potential within the general populace. For Dow, however, abstraction was relative—unlike Kandinsky, he never abandoned reference to the material world. It would be up to his student O'Keeffe to push Dow's theory into the raw realm of psychological expression.

Buddhism found fertile ground in the United States, thanks in part to the early and active trade in cultural goods between northern New England and Asia. As early as 1844 an essay entitled "The Preaching of the Buddha" appeared in Ralph Waldo Emerson's journal, *The Dial;* the Transcendentalist educator Elizabeth Palmer Peabody translated these passages from the Lotus Sutra from Eugène Burnouf's *Introduction to the History of Indian Buddhism,* which had just appeared in Paris. The American Transcendentalists' interest in Asian thought evolved over succeeding decades into the phenomenon of the "Boston Buddhists." The most notable example was Ernest Fenollosa, author of the widely read *Epochs of Chinese and Japanese Art.* Fenollosa, who was in East Asia from 1878 to 1889 and from 1896 to 1900, developed the collection of Asian art now at the Boston Museum of Fine Arts, a collection that Dow drew upon to develop his theories. Fenollosa was succeeded as advisor there by Kakuzo Okakura, an intimate friend of Isabella Stewart Gardener and the author of several influential books in English on Japanese culture.

Meanwhile, in Chicago, the German-born Paul Carus founded the prolific Open Court Publishing Company in 1887 and began publishing his journal, *The Monist.* The goal of

Carus's "Religion of Science" was to foster comparative thinking about religion with an emphasis on Buddhism, which he presented as a philosophical and ethical system based on fact. In 1893 Carus was among the speakers at the World Parliament of Religions, held in Chicago. The conference featured a significant number of talks on Asia, including five lectures by Anagarika Dharmapala from Ceylon and no fewer than six different speakers on Japanese Buddhism. Zen Abbot Soyen Shaku's talk was translated by D. T. Suzuki, who later came to work as a translator for Carus and became one of the most important interpreters of Buddhism, especially Zen Buddhism, to the West.

Soyen's lecture, entitled "The Law of Cause and Effect, as Taught by Buddha," seems to foreshadow William James's 1898 principle of pragmatism: "The ultimate test for us of what a truth means is indeed the conduct it dictates or inspires."[18] James's thinking impressed Suzuki, who in his writings for Western audiences tended to emphasize the pragmatic aspects of Zen Buddhism, perhaps making Zen seem more familiar to Westerners.

The quintessential American pragmatist was John Dewey. Influenced by Darwinian concepts of evolution (he was born in the year *On the Origin of Species* was published), Dewey resolved Descartes's mind/body dualism by understanding the mind as a product of natural processes and the web of interactive relationships between human beings and world. According to Dewey, as far as we humans are concerned, the world is not comprised of things, or objects, but of happenings, or experience. Although he never mentioned Buddhism in his writings, Dewey was in contact with D. T. Suzuki early in his career, when he was at the University of Chicago and Suzuki was in nearby La Salle working for Carus, who was Dewey's publisher. When Dewey traveled in Japan in 1919, it was Suzuki who served as his translator. The roots of American Zen are thus tangled with those of American pragmatism in ways that are not easy to unravel.[19]

In his book *Art as Experience,* developed from his 1931 William James Lectures at Harvard, Dewey wrote: "In common conception, the work of art is often identified with the building, book, painting, or statue in its existence apart from human experience. Since the actual work of art is what the product does with and in experience, the result [of this misconception] is not favorable to understanding."[20] The statement is typically Deweyesque in its impenetrability; what Dewey is saying is that the "work" of art does not reside in the art object, but in what the object "does" within the mind of the viewer. This view is very close to Duchamp's concept of art as the "gap" in which experience occurs. A useful—one might even say pragmatic—way of thinking about Marcel Duchamp is as an American pragmatist. It is also an iconoclastic way of thinking about him. Most commentators stress Duchamp's keen analytic mind and his wit—characteristics posed as quintessentially French—and the French philosopher Henri Bergson has been thought of as a primary philosophical influence on him.

Yet Bergson and Dewey had a great deal in common. Born within two days of each other

(Bergson on October 18 and Dewey on October 20, 1859), they knew each other, and both were influenced early on by the German idealist philosophers. Duchamp may well have gotten ideas from Bergson, including his belief in the importance of humor. (Bergson described humor as the relief we feel when we free ourselves from the mechanistic.) But Dewey was closer to both Buddhism and, as we shall see, Duchamp when he described his life goal as obtaining a "moderately clear and distinct idea of what the problems are that underlie the difficulties and evils which we experience."[21]

Duchamp lived in the United States for a large part of his adult life and died an American citizen. Something about his use of everyday material objects as pointers to intuitive objects of the mind seems at once a Buddhist and a pragmatist tactic. It is also a democratic gesture, very different from the elitist "It's art because I say it is" attitude often ascribed to him. To understand Marcel Duchamp, the father of conceptual art, is to understand that conceptual art exists not in the mind of the artist, but in the mind of the observer. And to understand the origin of this perspective in Asian thought is to understand Duchamp's achievement not as a break with the past, but as part of a continuum.

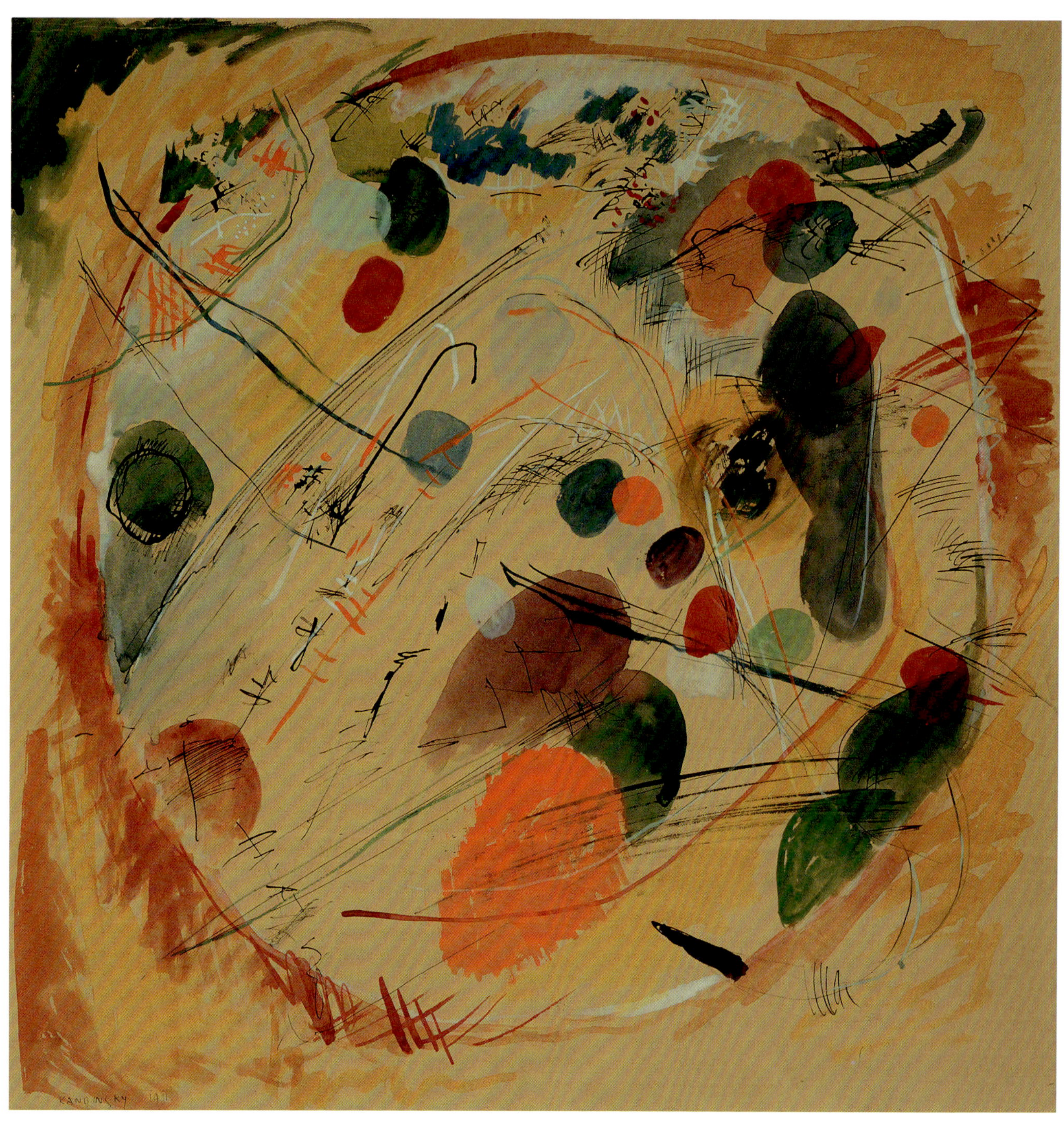

Wassily Kandinsky, *In the Circle,* about 1911–13, watercolor, gouache and ink on sepia paper mounted on cardboard, 19$\frac{1}{16}$ x 19 in. Musée National d'Art Moderne, Centre Georges Pompidou, Paris (AM 81–65–92). Reproduction © CNAC/MNAM/Dist. Réunion des Musées Nationaux/Art Resource, NY. Artist © 2005 Artists Rights Society (ARS), New York/ADAGP, Paris.

In our case, resurrection consists of not understanding art.

WASSILY KANDINSKY

WASSILY KANDINSKY 1866–1944

IN THE STATEMENT ABOVE WASSILY KANDINSKY, the expatriate Russian artist whose thinking was so important to the development of abstract art, chose the word "resurrection" rather than, for example, "revolution" or even "evolution," alerting us to the spiritual stakes of his campaign. Kandinsky set out to save the world through art. The statement comes at the pivotal point of his article "On Understanding Art," published in 1912. For Kandinsky, it was the state of not understanding, the "great, eternal question mark"—Buddhism's "mind of don't know"—that opened viewers to the experience of art. And art—with its line, form, and color—was a force equal to nature in its power to awaken the human spirit to its full potential.

Kandinsky's watercolor *In the Circle* from around 1911–13 is an early example of a form that would replace his beloved horse (still evident in his woodcut on p. 68) as a symbol of power. Some fifteen years later, he told the psychologist Paul Plaut, "If . . . in recent years I have preferred to use the circle so often and passionately, the reason (or cause) for this was not the 'geometric' form of the circle, or its geometrical characteristics, but rather my strong feeling of the inner force of the circle in its countless variations."[1] The art historian Peg Weiss has argued that possible inspirations for Kandinsky's circles include Lapp and Siberian shaman drums, as well as cosmological concepts.[2] I would add another possible source: the circle of enlightenment—the wholeness of form and emptiness expressed in "countless

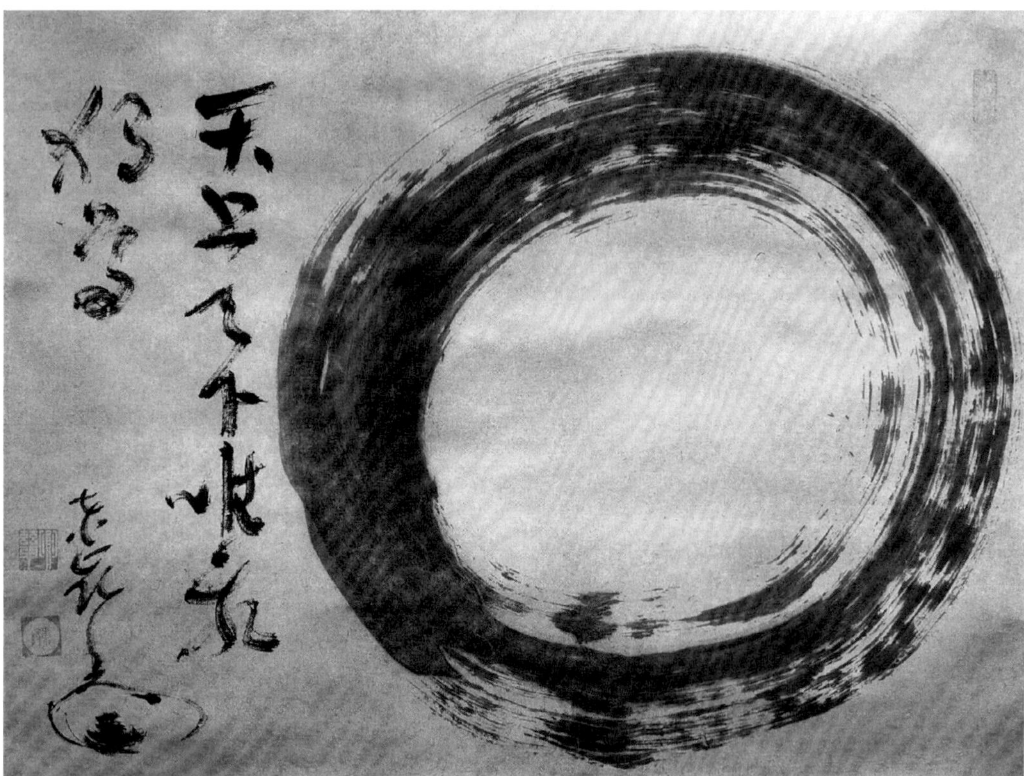

Torei (Japanese, 1721–1792), *Enso,* ink on paper, 13 x 17½ in. Private collection.

variations," from the circle of the "both vanished" stage of the Chinese Ch'an Oxherding Pictures, in which the taming of an ox is a metaphor for the taming of the mind (see Part V), to Zen brush drawings of the *enso,* Japanese for "circle." "A circle is a living wonder," Kandinsky wrote in 1937, in an essay entitled "Empty Canvas."[3]

Kandinsky's biographer Will Grohmann, who knew him personally, tells us that Kandinsky was essentially Eastern in his personality. According to Grohmann, Wassily's parents spent several decades before his birth in Kyakhta, "a Siberian city on the border of Mongolia, a center of the tea trade, the eastern section of which belonged to China. Kandinsky's father had been born in Kyakhta. There was Mongolian blood in his family: one of the painter's great-grandmothers was a Mongolian princess."[4] Buddhism came to Mongolia in the fourth century, when Chinese monks actively proselytized in this border region. Buddhism was the court religion of the Khans during the Pax Mongolica—the century of peaceful exchange and religious tolerance under the Mongols from about 1250 to 1350. Some two centuries later, Allan Khan led military expeditions into Tibet, the third Dalai Lama visited him at his palace in Khota, and Tibetan Buddhism was confirmed as the dominant form of religion in Mongolia. In Kandinsky's time Mongolia was still an important center for Buddhist philosophy.

Kandinsky's Mongolian genealogy was evident in his eyes, with their prominent upper fold, and in the olive color of his skin. An English collector, Michael Sadler, father of the first translator of Kandinsky's *On the Spiritual in Art,* provided his own description of the artist following a visit to Kandinsky's house in Murnau, near Munich, in 1912:

> He is about 35 [he was in fact 46]—dark olive skin, a thin black beard, a gentle voice & sweet smile & a Mongolian look. He told us that his father lived in Siberia, & that he had some Mongolian blood. For Chinese art & character he has a deep respect & admiration.[5]

Kandinsky's father was the manager of a tea firm and thus retained his ties with Mongolia and China after the family moved to Moscow and then Odessa. At some point in his childhood Kandinsky's parents divorced and his mother moved back to her native Moscow. Both his mother and her city were much missed by Kandinsky. As dear to him as his mother was his mother's eldest sister, Elizabeth Tikheev, who had an unforgettably "radiant inner nature"—a characteristic the artist not only aspired to in himself, but aimed to awaken in others.[6]

In his "Reminiscences," written in 1913, Kandinsky had high praise for his tolerant, supportive father. Though he extolled his mother's "severe beauty . . . inexhaustible energy, and unique accord between tradition and genuine freedom of thought," comparing her with his beloved Moscow, he did let slip in among her virtues a "pronounced nervousness."[7] It is not hard to detect his identification with this complex, nervous mother, as well as with the Moscow he had by that time abandoned:

> Moscow: the duality, the complexity, the extreme agitation, the conflict, and the confusion that mark its external appearance and in the end constitute a unified, individual countenance; the same qualities in its inner life, incomprehensible to the unfamiliar eye . . . and yet, just as unique and, in the end, wholly unified.[8]

Kandinsky also listed among his mother's virtues "heroic self-control," which in himself took the form of a self-described "tendency toward the 'hidden,' the concealed."[9] This tendency was connected with mystical experiences dating to his childhood, experiences that he could process only by making art:

> Even as a child, I had been tortured by joyous hours of inward tension that promised embodiment. Such hours filled me with inward tremor, indistinct longings that demanded something incomprehensible of me, stifling my heart by day and filling my soul with tur-

> moil by night, giving me fantastic dreams full of terror and joy. . . . I can remember that drawing alleviated this condition, i.e., it allowed me to exist outside of time and space, so that I was no longer conscious of myself.[10]

In late 1906 and early 1907, around the time he turned forty, Kandinsky underwent an emotional crisis during which he experienced a revival of these sensations. He and his mistress, the artist Gabriele Münter, had been living outside of Paris, but Kandinsky asked her to move out of their joint domicile. He wrote her on the day before his birthday: "Twice already I have felt that peculiar palpitation of my heart, which I often had in earlier times, when I was much more of a painter-poet. I . . . understand more of the theory now. But will my life and strength be enough to put this theory into practice? Tomorrow 40."[11]

Kandinsky's cognition was influenced by intense synesthesia, the tendency for sensory input of one kind to generate a sensory image of another kind, often linked with a hyperactive color sense. He drew and painted from a very early age and was encouraged in this by his father. But, despairing of ever being able to convey the effects of nature as vividly as he experienced them, he pursued a career in law and economics. He considered himself a scientist and in his "Reminiscences" tells us that his "scientific work" (in economics) was "highly thought of." Kandinsky then describes two experiences "that stamped my whole life and shook me to the depths of my being."[12]

These two events strongly influenced his decision, at the age of thirty, to finally become an artist. In 1889, he recounts, the music of Wagner's *Lohengrin* re-created in his mind the most beautiful, "pre-nocturnal hour" of the Moscow day in all its complex color, which he had often attempted to capture in paint. As Kandinsky explains, "I did not dare use the expression that Wagner had painted 'my hour' musically. It became, however, quite clear to me that art in general is far more powerful than I had thought, and, on the other hand, that painting could develop just such powers as music possesses." The leap Kandinsky describes is from perceiving music as a nonrepresentational structure of sounds with the power to evoke visual memories, to conceiving painting as a nonrepresentational structure of colored shapes with the power to create an experience in the mind. For Kandinsky, at the time, "the impossibility of seeking out these powers, let alone discovering them, made my renunciation [of art] all the more bitter."[13]

Seven years later, he had an experience with a painting by Monet that made his premonition real: "Suddenly, for the first time, I saw a painting." The catalog told him the painting was of a haystack, but he couldn't see it.

> This nonrecognition was painful to me. I considered that the painter had no right to paint indistinctly. I dully felt that the object of the picture was missing. And I noticed with astonishment and confusion that the picture not only draws you, but impresses itself in-

> delibly on your memory and, completely unexpectedly, floats before your eyes, even to the last detail. All this was unclear to me, and I could not draw the simple conclusions of this experience. . . . Unconsciously, the object was discredited as an essential element of a painting.[14]

In other words, Kandinsky's failure to recognize a haystack in Monet's painting allowed him to conceive, albeit at an unconscious level, the concept of abstract painting.

In that same year, 1896, Kandinsky moved to Munich to study art. He cited a third, "scientific" event that soon removed "one of the most important obstacles from my path. This was the further division of the atom." As he elaborated, "The collapse of the atom was equated, in my soul, with the collapse of the whole world. . . . Everything became uncertain, precarious and insubstantial. I would not have been surprised had a stone dissolved into thin air before my eyes and become invisible."[15] Kandinsky probably is referring here to the discovery of the electron by J. J. Thompson in 1897, following the discovery of X-rays by Wilhelm Roentgen in 1895 and radioactivity by Henri Becquerel in 1896. Thus, around the time that he was discovering, experientially, that a "picture" of an immaterial object can be a painting, scientists were finding out that the atom—the building block of nature in Newtonian physics—is as indistinct as Monet's haystack.

This insight occurred first in Kandinsky's unconscious mind—"in my soul." By 1913, when he wrote about it in his "Reminiscences," he had arrived, "by intuition and reflection, at the simple solution that the aims . . . of nature and of art [are] fundamentally, organically, and by the very nature of the world different—and equally great, which also means equally powerful."[16] Though simple, this experience of nondualism

> set me free and opened up new worlds for me. Everything "dead" trembled. Everything showed me its face, its innermost being, its secret soul, inclined more often to silence than to speech—not only the stars, moon, woods, flowers of which poets sing, but even a cigar butt lying in the ashtray, a patient white trouser-button looking up at you from a puddle on the street, a submissive piece of bark carried through the long grass in the ant's strong jaws to some uncertain and vital end, the page of a calendar, torn forcibly by one's consciously outstretched hand from the warm companionship of the block of remaining pages. Likewise, every still and every moving point (= line) became for me just as alive and revealed to me its soul. This was enough for me to "comprehend," with my entire being and with all my senses, the possibility and existence of that art which today is called "abstract," as opposed to "objective."[17]

When, exactly, did Kandinsky achieve the insight conveyed in this beautiful description? It would make sense to look at his art for the answer—when did Kandinsky eliminate the object from his work? But this is not as clear-cut as it might seem. Kandinsky needed years to move his realization from the unconscious to the conscious level of his mind. Like John the Baptist, Kandinsky felt the need to prepare the way for a purely abstract art: "Canceling out the object in painting makes very considerable demands of one's ability inwardly to experience purely pictorial form, so that the spectator's development in this direction is absolutely essential. This is the way to create the conditions that constitute a new atmosphere."[18] This is why Kandinsky organized, taught, and especially wrote so much: to enlighten others, as he had been enlightened, and thereby create an audience for abstract art.

So when did Kandinsky begin programmatically writing on art? After his move to Munich in 1896, aside from a piece on the state of contemporary criticism published in a Russian journal in 1901 and an exhibition review from 1902, Kandinsky's major public-education activities consisted of organizing exhibitions. (As president of the artists' association Phalanx, he showed sixteen paintings by Claude Monet in May 1903.) The typescript for Kandinsky's best-known written work—*On the Spiritual in Art,* published in 1912—is dated August 3, 1909. This was also the year Kandinsky became the Munich correspondent for the monthly Russian art journal *Apollon*. Its first issue, in October 1909, contains a "Letter from Munich" by Kandinsky, who lamented the sleepy city he had found upon his return from his Paris sojourn and other travels one year earlier. After discussing the state of the Munich art scene, he closes with remarks inspired by "a special exhibition of Far Eastern and Asiatic, predominantly Japanese art" on view "in the rooms of the so-called 'Munich Exhibition 1908.'" He describes this large exhibition of 1,276 examples of Japanese and other East Asian art, concluding:

> Again and again, so much that is part of Western art becomes clear when one sees the infinite variety of the works of the East, which are, nonetheless, subordinated to and united by the same fundamental "tone"! It is precisely this general "inner tone" that the West lacks. Indeed, it cannot be helped: we have turned, for reasons obscure to us, away from the internal toward the external. And yet, perhaps we Westerners shall not, after all, have to wait too long before the same inner sound, so strangely silenced, reawakens within us and, sounding forth from the innermost depths, involuntarily reveals its affinity with the East.[19]

The "inner tone" that Kandinsky perceived in Asian art seems to have been a synesthetic experience of its content. Here, for the first time, he uses the word *Klang,* which would become so important to his theory of the spiritual in art.

What was the source of Kandinsky's resonance with the content of Asian art? Michael Sadler's mention of the artist's "deep respect and admiration" for "Chinese art and character" implies a familiarity with Chinese aesthetics. The historian of Asian art Michael Sullivan has linked Kandinsky's concept of resonance with that "cornerstone of Chinese aesthetic

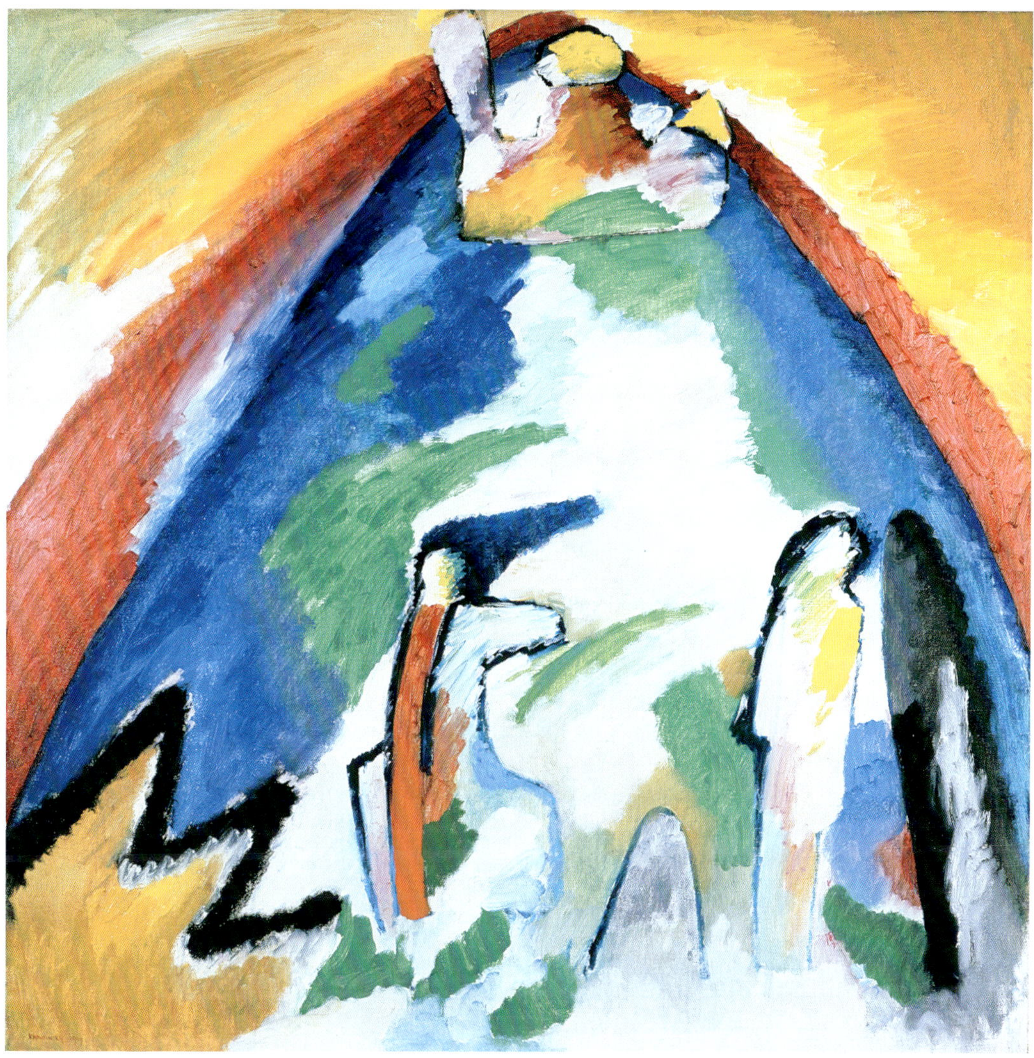

Wassily Kandinsky, *Mountain*, 1909, oil on canvas, 42⁹⁄₁₆ x 42⁵⁄₈ in. Städtische Galerie im Lenbachhaus, Munich (GMS 54). Photo © Städtische Galerie im Lenbachhaus. Artist © 2005 Artists Rights Society (ARS), New York/ADAGP, Paris.

theory"—*ch'i-yün sheng-tung* ("spirit resonance")—defined by the Chinese painter Hsieh Ho in the sixth century, when Buddhism was at its height in China: "Early Chinese painters felt that this 'spirit' was a cosmic force. . . . Later writers held that the *ch'i* was something awaiting release from within the psyche of the individual painter."[20]

Klänge was the title Kandinsky gave a book of fifty-six woodcuts and thirty-eight free-verse poems that he began writing in 1909, the same year he wrote *On the Spiritual in Art*. One of the poems, entitled "Why?"—his "great, eternal question mark"—is strikingly evocative

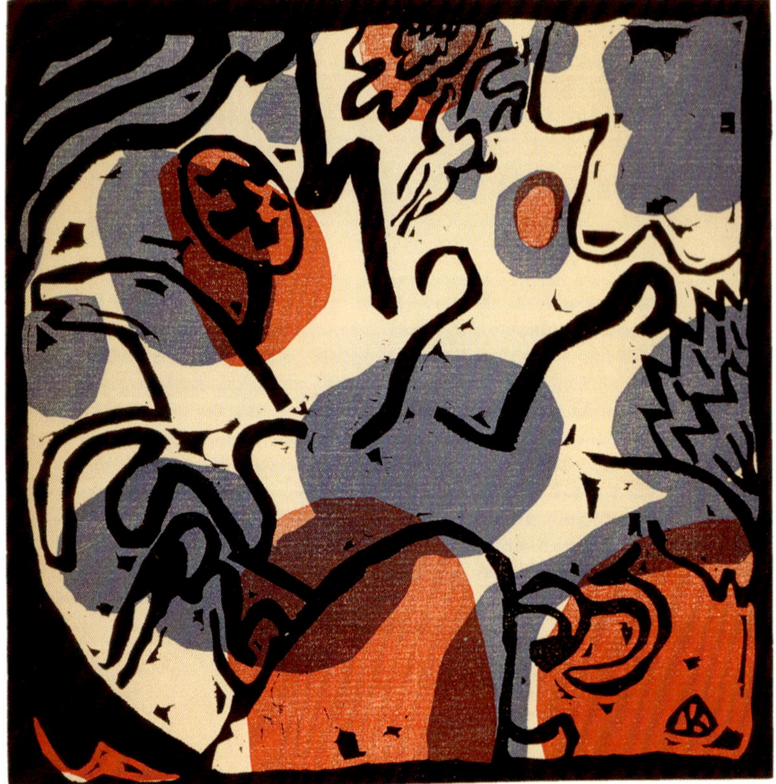

Wassily Kandinsky, woodcut with the poem "Why?" from *Klänge,* 1913, 11 x 10¾ in. The Minneapolis Institute of Arts, Gift of Bruce B. Dayton (B.83.18). Artist © 2005 Artists Rights Society (ARS), New York/ADAGP, Paris.

of the Buddhist Heart Sutra. The subject of this most popular of the Buddhist sutras is emptiness, which is described in terms of a long list of negatives: "in emptiness there is neither form, nor feeling, nor perception, nor mental formations, nor consciousness . . . no form, no sound, no smell, no taste, no touch, no object of mind . . . no understanding, no attainment."[21] Kandinsky's "Why?" goes like this:

> "No one came out of there."
> "No one?"
> "No one."
> "One?"
> "No."
> "Yes! But when I came by, there was one standing there."
> "At the door?"
> "At the door. He stretched out his arms."
> "Yes! Because he doesn't want to let anyone in."
> "No one came in there?"
> "No one."

"The one who stretched out his arms, was he there?"
"Inside?"
"Yes. Inside."
"I don't know. He just stretches out his arms so no one can get in."
"Was he sent there so No One can get in? The one who stretches out his arms?"
"No. He came and stood there himself and stretched out his arms."
"And No One, No One, No One came out?"
"No One, No One."[22]

The room is occupied by no one; in other words, it is empty.

"Why?" is also reminiscent of the chapter on "Entering the Gate of Nondualism" in the Mahayana Vimalakirti Sutra. Nondualism is the link between phenomenal and noumenal, unmanifested reality: form is emptiness, emptiness is form. In the Vimalakirti Sutra, Manjushri, the bodhisattva of wisdom, provides the final answer to Vimalakirti's question to the assembled bodhisattvas: "How does the bodhisattva go about entering the gate of nondualism?"[23]

> Manjushri replied, "Good sirs, you have all spoken well. Nevertheless, all your explanations are themselves dualistic. To know no one teaching, to express nothing, to say nothing, to explain nothing, to announce nothing, to indicate nothing, and to designate nothing—that is the entrance into nonduality."[24]

One would not want to overstate the importance of Buddhism for Kandinsky's personal philosophy. The one who stretches out his arms can also be interpreted as a Christ-figure, and Christian symbolism is what shows up most frequently in Kandinsky's art from the period 1909 to 1913. Nevertheless, the poem "Why?" is most un-Christian in its denial of a sender for the one who came, and anti-Theosophist in its espousal of the mind of don't know—buddha mind. "Why?" resonates with Kandinsky's 1912 assertion: "In our case, resurrection consists of not understanding art."

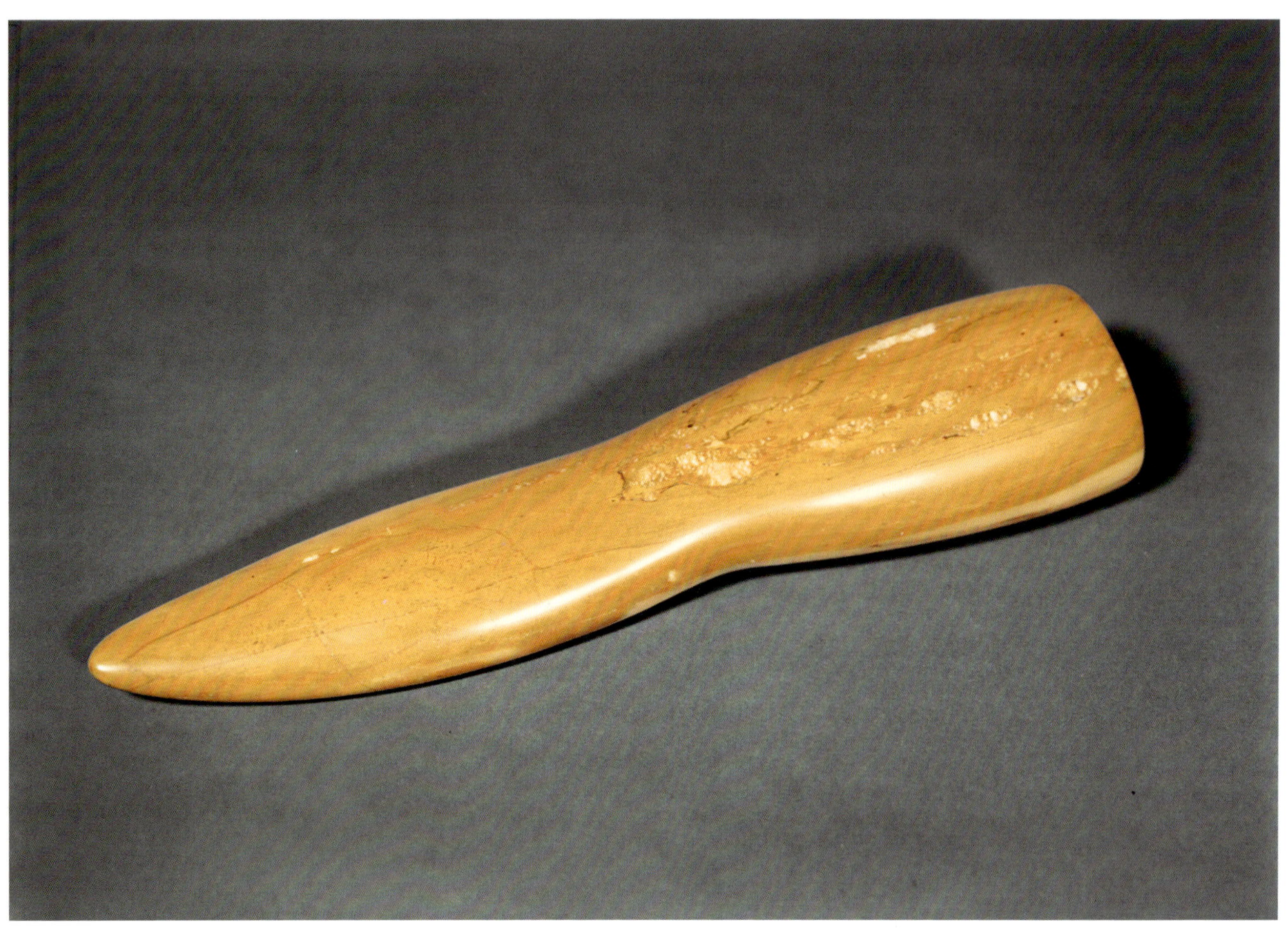

Constantin Brancusi, *Hand,* 1920, yellow marble, 11⅞ x 2½ x 2 in. Courtesy of the Fogg Art Museum, Harvard University Art Museums, Cambridge, Gift of Mr. and Mrs. Max Wasserman, 1964. Image © 2005 President and Fellows of Harvard College (photo: Michael A. Nedzweski). Artist © 2005 Artists Rights Society (ARS), New York/ADAGP, Paris.

> Buddhism isn't a religion, it is a morality and a technique through which one can come closer to the gods. Buddhism is my morality. I have neglected the technique.
>
> CONSTANTIN BRANCUSI

CONSTANTIN BRANCUSI 1876–1957

THE ABSTRACT MARBLE *HAND* THAT CONSTANTIN BRANCUSI sent as a gesture of friendship to his faithful collector John Quinn in 1920 conveys serenity, focused repose. Its honey color, smooth texture, and flat, pointed shape, as well as the fact that it was meant to be seen, not on one of Brancusi's powerful pedestals, but simply "on your desk," as Brancusi wrote to Quinn—all mark it as an object of private contemplation.[1] It is a hand like that on which Brancusi's sleeping *Muse* of 1912 rests her cheek in a pose that calls to mind the sleeping wife of the Buddha, a pose that reminded Siddhartha of death and so forcibly impressed him with the transience of life that it instigated his "Great Setting Forth." *Hand* might also remind us of the end of that story—the Buddha's *mudra,* or gesture, of "touching the earth," calling her to witness his victory over mental and emotional distortions. It is the gesture of Akshobhya—one of the five *jina,* or "victor" buddhas, whose name means "Immovable"—who appears with his earth-touching *mudra* in the crown of the Vajrasattva headdress on display in Brancusi's day at the Musée Guimet (see p. 72). *Vajrasattva,* Sanskrit for "Diamond Being," here signifies a teacher who has fully mastered Tantrayana.

One work by Constantin Brancusi has consistently been identified as Buddhist in inspiration: a large, carved oak sculpture from the early 1930s now in the Solomon R. Guggenheim Museum in New York.[2] Titled *King of Kings,* its alternate title is *Spirit of the Buddha.* Its hollowed-out, egg-shaped "head" may have to do with the concept of emptiness.

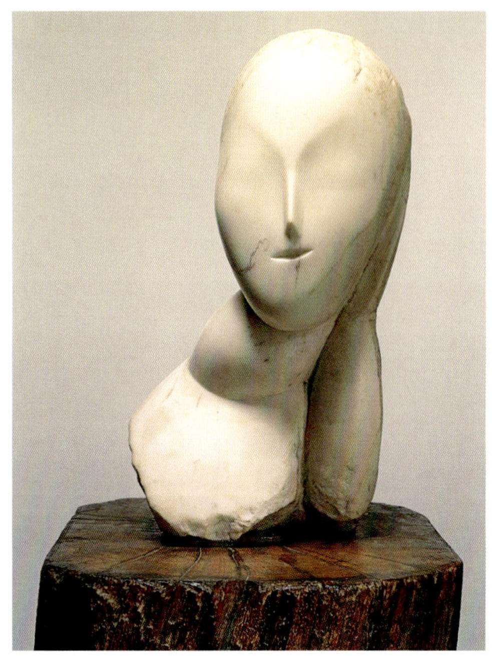

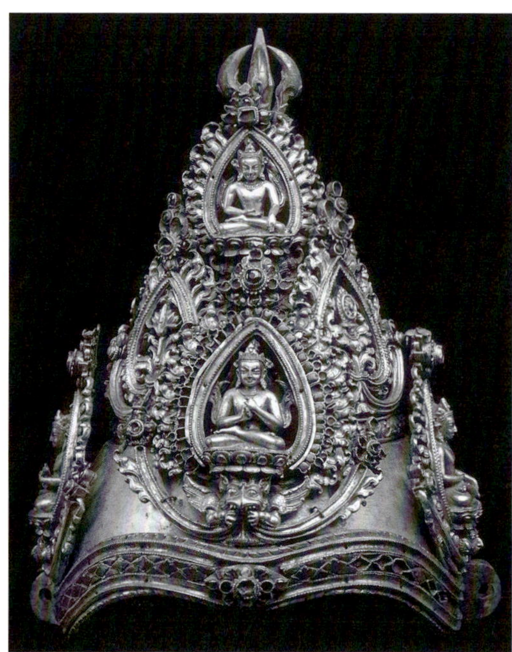

(left) Constantin Brancusi, *The Muse,* 1912, marble, 17 3/4 x 9 x 6 3/4 in. Solomon R. Guggenheim Museum, New York (85.3317). Photo: David Heald, © The Solomon R. Guggenheim Foundation, New York. Artist © 2005 Artists Rights Society (ARS), New York/ADAGP, Paris.

(right) Varjrasattva headdress, Nepal, 1145, gilt copper alloy inlaid with gemstones. Musée National des Arts Asiatiques–Guimet, Paris (MA 4929). Photo: Thierry Oliver, Réunion des Musées Nationaux/Art Resource, NY.

Commentators have linked its jagged crown to a lotus; it might also be seen as a stylized *vajra* like the one atop the Vajrasattva headdress shown here. Still, the visual connection with Buddhism is not particularly strong. In form, the piece refers more to the folk sculpture of Brancusi's native Romania than any Buddhist sculptural tradition. But an undated note by Brancusi hints at a connection between the two titles, as well as with *Hand:*

> It's finally happened:
> The muses sing of my accession;
> I am King,
> But not by the grace of men,
> I am king by my victory over myself.
> I am wholly free and God has vested me with royalty.[3]

These words bear the imprint of Buddha's "Turning of the Wheel of the Dharma" sermon, in which he presented himself as a new type of ruler who has mastery over himself. For Brancusi, the philosophy of the Buddha, the "king of kings," was a "morality" that allowed

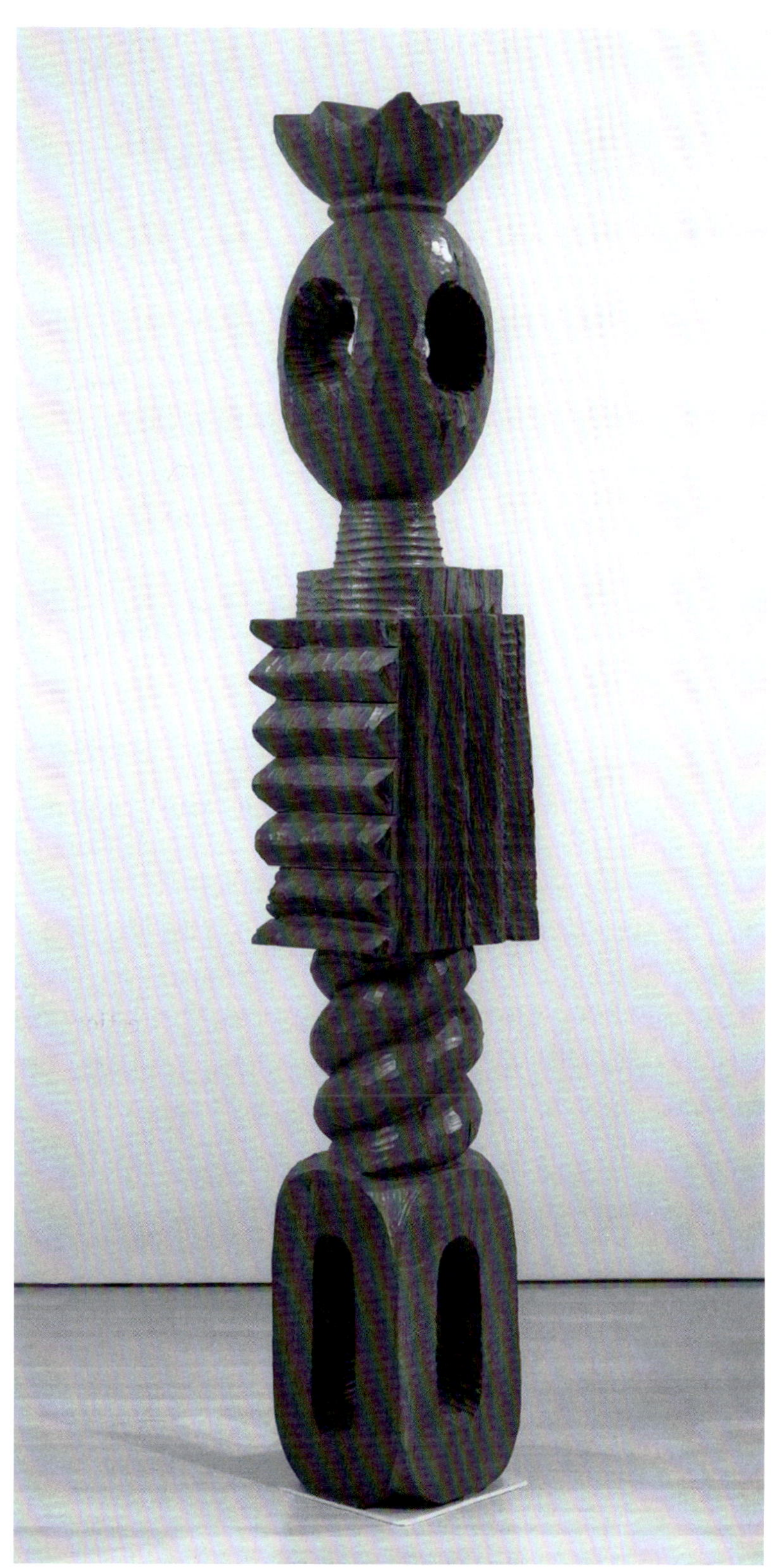

Constantin Brancusi, *King of Kings,* early 1930s, oak, overall: 118⅜ x 19 x 18⅛ in. Solomon R. Guggenheim Museum, New York (56.1449). Photo: David Heald, © The Solomon R. Guggenheim Foundation, New York. Artist © 2005 Artists Rights Society (ARS), New York/ADAGP, Paris.

(right)
Constantin Brancusi, *The Kiss,* 1907–8, stone, 34 3/4 x 11 11/16 x 7 13/16 in. Montparnasse Cemetery, Paris. Artist © 2005 Artists Rights Society (ARS), New York/ADAGP, Paris.

(far right)
Dhyani Buddha and consort, Tibetan, bronze, 5 in. high. Musée National des Arts Asiatiques–Guimet, (E.G. 1512). Photo from J. Hackin, *La sculpture indienne et tibétain au Musée Guimet* (Paris, 1931), 19, plate 49.

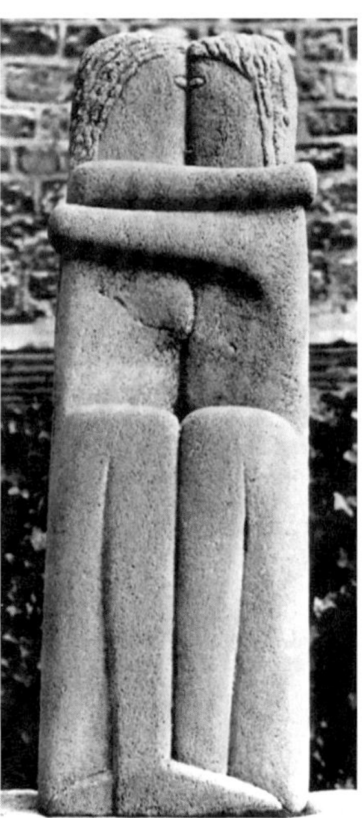

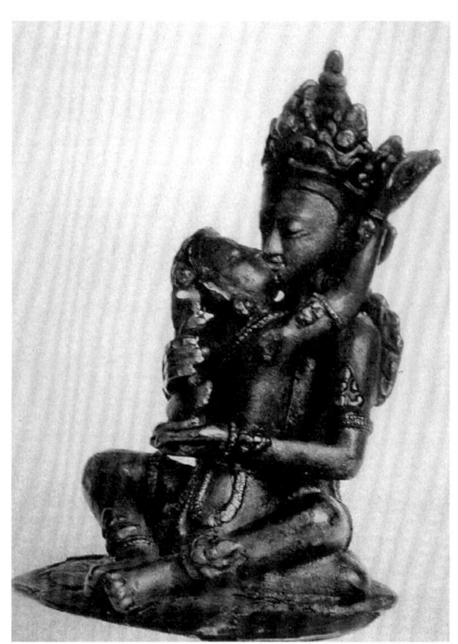

him to "come closer to the gods."[4] It gave him a way to rethink his artistic enterprise by rethinking the process of thought itself, pushing him, like Kandinsky, toward abstraction.

Perhaps the best example is Brancusi's powerfully simple *The Kiss,* whose theme he continued to refine throughout his career, ending with the cenotaph-like *Boundary Marker* (1945). Although the dating, and thus the order of early versions of *The Kiss,* is still unsettled, the Romanian art historian Sanda Miller argues convincingly that the first version, dating to late 1907–8, is the version placed on the grave in Montparnasse Cemetery of a young woman who killed herself after the end of a love affair.[5] Years later—in fact, the year before his death—Brancusi recalled:

> I received in Paris a commission for a funerary monument in memory of two lovers. Giving—as is my custom—a lot of thought to this sculpture, I realized to what extent the reflection of the exterior shape of two beings is removed from the essential truth. . . . I wanted to embody not only that unique couple but all those pairs that lived and loved on this earth.[6]

At Brancusi's funeral Henri-Pierre Roché stated that Brancusi characterized the Montparnasse *Kiss* as his "Road to Damascus."[7] The abstract form that Brancusi used to convey his concept owes more to African and Egyptian sculpture than to any Buddhist source. The specifics of that form, however—two bodies in complete embrace, including genital embrace—could have been inspired by Tibetan *yab-yum* sculptures of copulating couples. The 1900 edition of the *Petit guide illustré au Musée Guimet* describes a fierce *yab-yum* on view at the museum, calling it the "Vanquisher of Death."[8] Though this multiarmed *yab-yum* may have provided a conceptual source for the grave-marker version of *The Kiss,* a more likely visual source is an unusually sweet *yab-yum* of a Tibetan Dhyani Buddha and consort that was part of the original collection of the Musée Guimet. Seated in sexual embrace, their lips connect in a tender kiss in much the same spirit as Brancusi's lovers.

Born in rural Romania, the young Brancusi was a chronic runaway—he left home for good at the age of eleven. His conflicts seem to have been with his father, who died when he was nine, and with his three stepbrothers. A hint of his suffering is conveyed in his early sculpture *Torment* (1907), depicting the head and naked shoulders of a young boy who shuts his eyes and defensively tucks his cheek into his upraised right shoulder. *Torment* shows the influence of Auguste Rodin, in whose studio Brancusi worked in April 1907—around the time *Torment* was made. Brancusi famously commented on the shortness of his apprenticeship: "Nothing grows under big trees."[9] In a more nuanced analysis, he recalled: "When I was with Rodin, I did a sculpture a day. I adopted his way of working. I imitated him unwittingly but I saw the parody. I was unhappy. These were the hardest years of all, the years of research when I had to find my own path."[10]

Finding his own path involved visits to collections of non-Western sculpture then on view in a number of museums around Paris. In the Louvre, Cernuschi, and Guimet museums, as well as in private collections of friends such as Jacques Doucet, Brancusi found a range of alternatives to the nineteenth-century European heroic tradition of sculpture. Egyptian, African, and especially Asian art provided new models for apprehending and representing aspects of visible and invisible reality to which Brancusi was acutely sensitive. Curator Margit Rowell has pointed out the visual connections between the evolution of Brancusi's radically reductive early sculpture *Sleeping Muse* (1909–10) and specific Buddha and bodhisattva heads in the Musée Guimet.[11] Brancusi's enthusiasm for Buddhist sculpture was documented by his friend the artist Cecilia Cutescu-Storck, who in 1909 wrote to her husband of repeated visits to the Musée Guimet with Brancusi to view "the sculptures of the masters of India, Tibet, China, and Turkistan." She particularly enjoyed "Brancusi's interesting and unexpected comments on certain statuettes of the Buddha."[12]

Brancusi was fond of the Greek philosophers, but by all accounts his favorite book was *The Tibetan Poet Milarepa: His Crimes, His Trials, His Nirvana.* Brancusi strongly identified with this Tibetan sorcerer-poet turned saint, detecting in his life parallels with his own. According to two assistants who looked after Brancusi late in his life, both Brancusi and Milarepa "had lost their fathers at an early age, braved countless ordeals, performed extraordinary feats, and always lived in solitude."[13]

Milarepa was published in French in 1925—relatively late, given its evident influence on Brancusi and his work, a fact that has puzzled art historians. The answer may lie with its

French translator, Jacques Bacot. Virtually the same age as Brancusi (he was born in 1877), Bacot led two expeditions to Tibet, bringing back objects and, from his first journey in 1907, an actual Tibetan—Adjourp Gumbo, from Padong.[14] In 1908 the Musée Guimet exhibited Bacot's Tibetan objects, and he gave a public lecture (published the following year) about his "pilgrimage" to Tibet, which he described as a mountainous, religious county, a "land of prayer," much like Brancusi's beloved Romania.[15] In May 1909 Bacot departed for Tibet a second time, returning in March 1910. In 1911 he again lectured on Tibetan art at the Musée Guimet.[16] One of his illustrations was the *yab-yum* figure referred to above, reproduced in the proceedings of Bacot's lecture as "Dhyani Bouddha with his shakti."[17] The museum exhibited over three hundred of Bacot's Tibetan paintings, sculptures, and other objects in 1911, and he gave most of these to the museum in 1912.

A passage in Bacot's introduction to *Milarepa* suggests he first met Brancusi well before 1925:

> Our best sculpture expresses the effort of thought—one might be tempted to say its impotence—by a tensing of the entire body, from the forehead to the toes. But the thought that the Oriental figure conveys through the serenity of the Buddhist smile is thought released, freed from the flesh. It doesn't search; it neither strives nor tires. It contemplates.[18]

Clearly, Bacot's description of "the effort of thought" expressed by "our best sculpture" refers to *The Thinker* by Rodin, with whom Brancusi had briefly apprenticed. Bacot went on at some length about Buddhism and its differences from Western thinking, contrasting the concepts of intellect and intuition:

> As for the basis of the meditation in which Milarepa absorbed himself during the greater part of his long life, it cannot be related to any of our methods or our philosophies. From our side . . . lack of discipline of thought, which affects only very little the way we live. Contradictory systems born from intellectual effort, from introspection with its multiple contingencies, with the suspect duality of subject/object. From [Tantrayana] a single direction of thought despite a great variety of aspects, and the submission of life to metaphysical conviction.[19]

Brancusi managed to condense Bacot's somewhat incoherent formulation into a pithy statement that he was fond of repeating: "I make pee-pee on intelligence."[20]

On the subject of the ego, Bacot continues:

> It is thus that Milarepa, for whom the sensate world had about as much reality as an image in a mirror, lived. . . . Finally, the very individuality of the hermit became part of the unreal world and disappeared as an object of knowledge. The self object disappeared into the subject and became one with it. . . . It is necessary to forget—effacing totally the accidental self, the individual self—to know the self in its objective reality.[21]

When, late in his life, Brancusi remarked, "I am no longer in this world, no longer attached to my person, I am far removed from myself, among essential things,"[22] it was as if Milarepa were speaking. Perhaps more than the visual influence of Buddhist sculpture, the Buddhist concept of dissolving the boundaries of the self pushed the shape of Brancusi's heads back to the egg—symbol of the potentiality of existence.

Bacot's statement that, for Milarepa, "the sensate world had about as much reality as an image in a mirror" is paralleled by Brancusi's own comment about the exterior shapes of lovers being mere reflection and not the essential truth. It finds even more concise form in a 1919 statement by Brancusi: "We do not see real life except by reflections."[23] This view of reality showed up in his work both as heads contemplating their own reflections—for example, *Narcissus* (1909) and the startlingly phallic *Princess X* (1915–16)—and in the highly polished, mirrorlike surface of many of his pieces. Beginning in about 1910, Brancusi experimented with gilding his sculptures to look like Asian Buddhist gilt bronzes. He came to prefer a higher polish—to the point of reflectivity. His own photographs of his work tend to emphasize this reflectivity, both through the visual confusion of surface and setting, and through form-dissolving bursts of reflected light. "Works of art are mirrors in which each person sees his own likeness," he concluded.[24]

As he elaborated—or, more accurately, simplified—his theme of *The Kiss,* Brancusi increasingly emphasized the eyes of his lovers. Their conjoined eyes form single, round, bifurcated, vulvalike shapes in the *Boundary Marker* and other late permutations of *The Kiss,* such as his plan for a Temple of Deliverance. The eyes of Brancusi's sculptures look inward, not outward. Their later abstract-vulva form signifies the sight of emptiness, the site of enlightenment. This theme of inner vision was central to Brancusi's work. He urged his viewers to use his sculptures as objects of meditation: "Look at them until you see them. Those who are closest to God have seen them."[25] That Brancusi meant something other than analytic seeing is suggested by the title of one of his egg-shaped marble sculptures: *Sculpture for the Blind* (1916).

Brancusi spent the last ten years of his life living among his sculptures, making virtually nothing. This seemed odd to some, but it suggests another parallel with Milarepa, who for the last part of his long life made a point of doing precisely nothing. Perhaps Brancusi was following his example. Perhaps he finally managed to efface the boundary between subject and object, himself and his work. It would be up to his friend Marcel Duchamp to take this conundrum to the next stage. "Art," Brancusi wrote in one of his notes, "has been made to dominate, to mourn, to pray. We want to make it so it lives."[26]

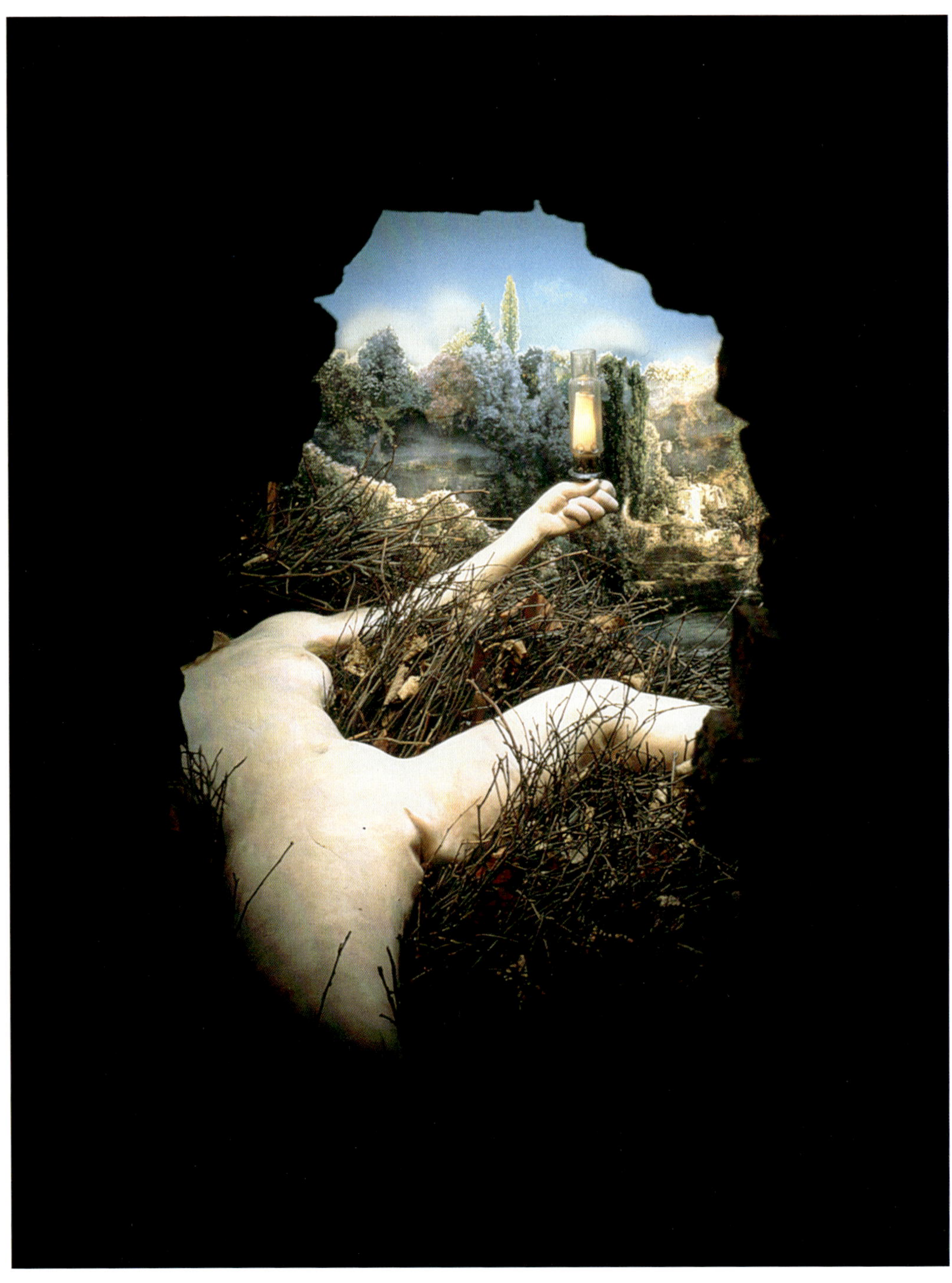

Marcel Duchamp *Etant donnés: 1° La chute d'eau, 2° Le gas d'éclariage (Given: 1. The Waterfall, 2. The Illuminating Gas),* 1946–66, about 95½ x 70 x 49 in. Philadelphia Museum of Art, Gift of the Cassandra Foundation, 1969. Artist © 2005 Artists Rights Society (ARS), New York/ADAGP, Paris/Succession Marcel Duchamp.

If you wish, my art would be that of living: each second, each breath is a work which is inscribed nowhere, which is neither visual nor cerebral. It's a sort of constant euphoria.

MARCEL DUCHAMP TO PIERRE CABANNE

I spend my time very easily, but wouldn't know how to tell you what I do.... I'm a respirateur—a breather. I enjoy it tremendously.

MARCEL DUCHAMP TO CALVIN TOMKINS

MARCEL DUCHAMP 1887–1968

WHEN MARCEL DUCHAMP DIED IN 1968 the artist Jasper Johns wrote, "The art community feels Duchamp's presence and his absence. He has changed the condition of being here."[1] With his "readymades," Duchamp shifted attention from artistic product to process, and shifted responsibility for that process to the perceiver. This profound change in the relationship of artist to artwork and audience definitively altered the cultural landscape of the twentieth century. Although Duchamp's innovations date from early in the century, they took root during the increasingly democratic social climate of the postwar period and flourished during the anti-authoritarian sixties. Only in the last decade of Duchamp's life did admiration from younger artists such as John Cage, Robert Rauschenberg, and Jasper Johns, along with a shifting cultural climate, bring Duchamp and his work into the limelight he had previously avoided. Even then he never let on that, contrary to the impression he had stopped producing art in 1923, he had in fact been working since 1946 on a complex installation: *Etant donnés: 1° La chute d'eau, 2° Le gaz d'éclairage* (*Given: 1. The Waterfall, 2. The Illuminating Gas*).

Etant donnés was finished in 1966, but its existence was not revealed until after Duchamp's death. Its title was taken from a 1912 note for his major early work, *The Large Glass,* begun in 1915 and abandoned in 1923. Duchamp published this note in 1934 in a collection of facsimile notes entitled *La mariée mise à nu par ses célibataires, même*—the formal title of *The Large Glass*. Twenty years earlier, Duchamp had published a related note in his *Box of 1914:* "Given that . . . ; if I suppose I am suffering a lot. . . . "[2] These notes suggest that with *The Large Glass* the twenty-five-year-old Duchamp was investigating the nature of suffering, the same problem the twenty-nine-year-old Siddhartha set for himself as he embarked on the period of research and meditation that resulted in his awakening.

Etant donnés offers a solution to the problem of suffering that Duchamp seems to have arrived at quite early in his career, and to which he devoted the rest of his life as an artist. Duchamp's friend the author Henri-Pierre Roché remembers him making a statement that is like a distillation of a Zen koan: "There is no solution because there is no problem."[3] From this perspective, the solution to the problem of suffering is that suffering happens, not in the world, but in our minds. Along similar lines, the solution to interpersonal problems is to understand "you" as not separate from "me." Duchamp translated the French title of his *Large Glass* as "The Bride Stripped Bare by Her Bachelors, Even." But another meaning of *même,* according to *Cassell's French Dictionary,* is "same, self, self-same . . . herself." An alternative translation would be "The Bride Stripped Bare by Her Bachelors, *Herself*." Read this way, the title resembles that of Duchamp's 1918 painting *Tu m',* which voiced out loud sounds like *Tu m'es:* "You are me." Both titles emphasize nonduality. The bride is Duchamp; she is (even) her bachelors; she is also you.

Marcel Duchamp seemed destined to be an artist. His maternal grandfather was a successful printmaker; his two older brothers, Jacques Villon and Raymond Duchamp-Villon, were well-known avant-garde artists in Paris; and the eldest of his three younger sisters, Suzanne, painted as well. Their notary-father supported his children in their artistic vocations. The only shadow on this apparently happy family life was Duchamp's deaf mother. His first biographer, Robert Lebel, wrote that Duchamp remembered "above all her placidity, even her indifference, which seems rather to have hurt him until it became a goal for him in his turn to attain."[4]

Henri-Pierre Roché tells us:

> . . . in 1916, at age twenty-nine, he appeared to me with a halo—which he always kept for me. Of what was he made? Perfect clarity, ease, swiftness, lack of ego; complete openness to those able to be naïve, spontaneous, and audacious. His presence was a grace and a gift, and he was unaware of it, despite the fact that he was surrounded by a growing crowd of disciples.[5]

By all accounts a warm and generous friend, Duchamp was elusive regarding his own activities, his sources, artistic and otherwise, and his beliefs. There has been considerable

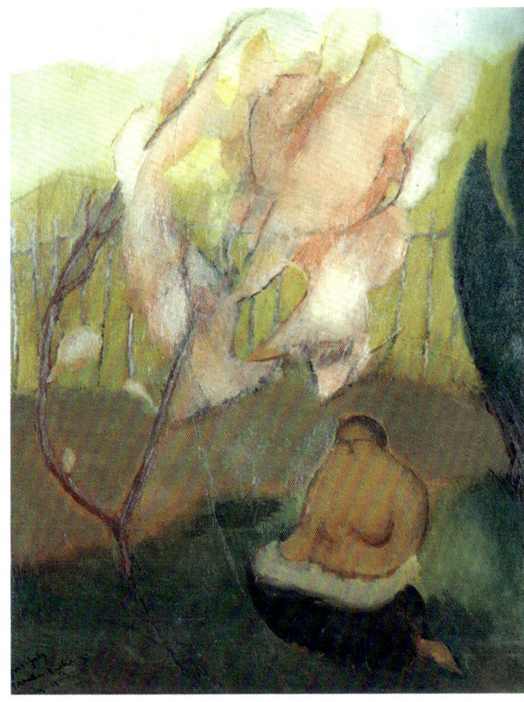

Marcel Duchamp, *Draft on the Japanese Apple Tree,* 1911, oil on canvas, 23¾ x 19½ in. Private collection, Paris. Photo from Arturo Schwarz, *The Complete Works of Marcel Duchamp,* rev. ed. (New York: Delano Greenidge, 2000), 300. Artist © 2005 Artists Rights Society (ARS), New York/ADAGP, Paris/Succession Marcel Duchamp.

speculation about the meanings of his enigmatic artworks and his equally enigmatic statements about them. Close attention to works of art can reveal multiple layers of meaning—an enterprise intensified by Duchamp's love of puns, in both French and English. Still, despite all the theories about Duchamp's philosophy of life and art, almost no one has systematically explored potential Buddhist influences within his work.[6] While looking at Duchamp through the lens of Buddhism by no means brings complete focus—his mind was too wide-ranging for that—it does help clarify his intentions in useful ways.

Two works by Duchamp cited as showing Buddhist influence are the painting *Draft on the Japanese Apple Tree* and *Fountain,* the upended urinal rejected by the New York Society of Independent Artists in 1917. The seated figure in *Draft on the Japanese Apple Tree,* described as suggesting "a Buddha-like state of enlightened meditation,"[7] is reminiscent of Odilon Redon's *Buddha in His Youth* (p. 42). Duchamp mentioned Redon as an influence more than once,[8] and Redon's large pastel had been a highlight of his retrospective at the Salon d'Automne in 1904, the year Duchamp arrived in Paris to study art.

Translated as "draft," the French *courant d'air* in Duchamp's title is literally a "current of air," which might be interpreted as breath. The model for this work was a Japanese woman who may have been Buddhist and may, in fact, have been meditating. "La Japonaise" modeled for the group of artists living in Puteaux, outside of Paris, which included Duchamp's brothers and the Czech artist František Kupka. Like Kandinsky, and at about the same time, Kupka developed a theory of abstract art as a medium for spiritual communication. Sixteen years older than Duchamp and something of a mentor to him, Kupka was a practicing medium and a Theosophist. Around the turn of the twentieth century he created several works with Buddhist themes, including *Soul of the Lotus* (1898). Acutely aware of his sense impressions, Kupka experienced coenesthesia: the feeling of existence that arises from the sum of bodily sensations, emotions, and sense impressions. Like many other believers in the occult at the time, he was passionately interested in science and technology, including explorations of the relationship between time and space via high-speed and chrono-photography and concepts of the fourth dimension, which, pre-Einstein, was thought of as a parallel invisible realm of existence.[9]

That Duchamp shared many of Kupka's interests is evident in paintings such as *Yvonne and Madeleine, Torn Up in Tatters* (1911), which shows his two youngest sisters in multiple profiles anticipating the effects of time, and *Sad Young Man on a Train* (1911), which combines motion and emotion. Duchamp later said of this period, "Perspective was very important. *The Large Glass* constitutes a rehabilitation of perspective, which had then been completely ignored and disparaged. For me, perspective became absolutely scientific."[10] He added:

> What we were interested in at the time was the fourth dimension. . . . Simply, I thought of the idea of a projection, of an invisible fourth dimension, something you couldn't see with your eyes. Since I found that one could make a cast shadow from a three-dimensional thing . . . I thought that, by simple intellectual analogy, the fourth dimension could project an object of three dimensions, or, to put it another way, any three-dimensional object, which we see dispassionately, is a projection of something four-dimensional, something we're not familiar with.[11]

A key phrase here is "which we see dispassionately." Dispassion was the "perspective" that allowed Duchamp to develop his concept of the readymade. As he explained, "Instead of choosing something which you like, or something which you dislike, you choose something that has no visual interest for the artist. In other words, to arrive at a state of indifference towards this object; at that moment it becomes a readymade."[12] But visual, or "retinal" (to use a Duchamp term), indifference is not necessarily mental indifference. Readymades may "look trivial," he said, "but they're not. On the contrary, they represent a much higher degree of intellectuality."[13] A good deal of practice is required to cultivate a relationship with things-in-the-world that obviates judgment, aesthetic or otherwise. Duchamp's goal was to replace sensual apprehension with absolute apprehension. In his "Specifications for 'Readymades'" he described the process of selection as "a kind of rendezvous"—a meeting that is the result of intention.[14]

In 1917, when *Fountain* was submitted anonymously to and immediately rejected from the supposedly open exhibition of the Society of Independent Artists, two commentators, both close to Duchamp, noted how inverting the urinal had turned it into a buddha. In the May 1917 issue of Duchamp's little magazine *The Blind Man,* Louise Norton published her essay "Buddha of the Bathroom"; a year later Apollinaire wrote in the *Mercure de France:* "The Society of Independent Artists' attitude is obviously absurd because it is based on an indefensible position that art cannot ennoble an object, and in the case in point it ennobled it singularly by transforming into Buddha an object of hygiene and male convenience."[15] Apollinaire's words, as well as the title of Duchamp's magazine, resonate with a verse from a famous Buddhist text, the *Bodhicaryavatara,* or *Way of the Bodhisattva,* by the eighth-century *Mahasiddha,* Shantideva: "Like a blind man who finds a pearl within a mound of filth, I know not by what miracle the enlightened mind is born in me."[16]

Another passage from the *Bodhicaryavatara* supports my theory that *Tu m',* created the following year, should be translated, "You [are] me." According to Shantideva, "Whoever wants quickly to attain salvation of himself and others should practice the supreme mystery: to interchange the terms of 'I' and 'other.'"[17] It is also interesting to note, in light of Duchamp's frequent assertions of his own laziness, that Shantideva was known as the "Lazy One." Until he preached the *Bodhicaryavatara,* his fellow monks had no idea that this monk who seemed only to eat, sleep, and defecate had attained great insight.

When Duchamp painted *Draft on the Japanese Apple Tree,* his personal life seems to have been in some turmoil. Two months earlier, in February 1911, his liaison with a married woman named Jeanne Serre had produced a daughter. At the time he showed an increasing interest in both metaphysics and machine technology. For Duchamp, the machine seems to have been an investigative device, a way to dissect and analyze the workings of the heart through manageable metaphors. In this he was influenced by the radical Symbolist playwright and avid bicyclist Alfred Jarry, creator of "Pataphysics," intended, among other things, to "explain the universe supplementary to this one."[18] Another influence was the writer Raymond Roussel, who impressed Duchamp with his creative use of homophones and his fantastic mock-scientific machines, one of which, in Roussel's play *Impressions of Africa,* made art.

In late 1911, for his brother's kitchen, Duchamp painted a coffee grinder, which, he declared, "I made to explode." As he explained, "The knob is seen simultaneously at several points in its circuit, with an arrow to indicate movement. Without knowing it, I had opened a window onto something else."[19] The turning of the handle is signaled not only by the arrow but by what look like multiple arms, leading Duchamp's biographer Robert Lebel to compare *Coffee Grinder* with "an astonishingly similar figure, taken from Dr. Jean Vinchon's study of the Mandala."[20]

The *Coffee Grinder* proved prophetic, for Duchamp's life took another turn in March 1912.

On the day of the press preview for the annual Salon des Indépendants, his brothers asked him, on behalf of the hanging committee, to withdraw his mechanistic *Nude Descending a Staircase, No. 2*. "That cooled me off so much," Duchamp later reported, "that, as a reaction against such behavior coming from artists whom I had believed to be free, I got a job. I became a librarian at the Sainte-Geneviève Library in Paris."[21] He neglected to mention that this unhappy young artist first took a train to Munich, where he arrived on June 21. "My stay in Munich," he wrote some fifty years later, was the scene of my complete liberation."[22] He would soon abandon painting, commenting later: "I was really defrocked, in the religious sense of the word."[23] The image calls to mind the young Siddhartha divesting himself of his princely garments before setting out to seek the solution to the problem of suffering. Whatever Duchamp's experience in Munich, it was solitary: "I never spoke to a soul, but I had a great time."[24]

It is not clear why Duchamp chose Munich. He later said he knew a cow painter there—Max Bergmann, with whom he had courted Jeanne Serre in Paris two years earlier. Through his correspondence with Bergmann Duchamp may have learned about Kandinsky's *On the Spiritual in Art,* which appeared at the end of 1911, and the *Blaue Reiter Almanach,* which appeared in early May 1912, featuring a radical mix of illustrations from the collection of the Munich Ethnographic Museum. That museum's flamboyant director, Lucian Scherman, actively cultivated friendships with artists in his efforts to increase attendance. In 1910–11 Scherman had traveled to India, Ceylon, and Burma collecting Buddhist sculptures and other devotional objects, a set of monastery doors, and items of daily use, including clothing, handicrafts, and tools. In Darjeeling he rounded out the collection with purchases from Tibet and Nepal. After his return, Scherman mounted a huge exhibition of this material, complete with photographs showing the use of these objects in daily life. Other items from the Munich Ethnographic Museum's major collection of East Asian art may also have been on view or gone up later that summer.

Scherman's exhibition was up from May through June of 1912. Duchamp arrived in Munich on June 21 and stayed through September.[25] Scherman's exhibition may even have been one of Duchamp's incentives for going to Munich, for a large exhibition of Jacques Bacot's collection of similar material had been on view at the Musée Guimet the previous year. We know from a wash drawing inscribed "Aéroplane—Münich 1912" that Duchamp visited Munich's renowned Deutsches Museum, where Germany's advanced technology was on display.[26] At that time the Ethnographic Museum was in the same building complex on Prinzregentstrasse. (The two museums have since moved to separate buildings.) Imagine seeing displays of water motors, steam engines, turbines, and diesel engines with their large, beautiful flywheels; then, in another part of the complex, coming across depictions of the Wheel of the Dharma or powerful Buddhist guardian figures from Japan with wheel-shaped, flame-bedecked halos. For someone with Duchamp's interests, such an experience might have generated powerful visual and intellectual connections between physics and metaphysics.

Although already dissatisfied with painting, the twenty-five-year-old Duchamp produced two important paintings and several large drawings during his three-month stay in Munich, including a first study for *The Large Glass*. After he returned to Paris, Duchamp studied to become a librarian, working at the Bibliothèque Sainte-Geneviève from spring 1913 until he left for New York in 1915. Although he never detailed the precise focus of his reading during these two years, he mentioned studying perspective and reading Pyrrho of Elis, a painter-turned-philosopher who had traveled with Alexander the Great to Buddhist India and advocated the cultivation of indifference toward life and alertness to the passing moment.[27] That Duchamp also read Asian philosophy is suggested by his remark to Pierre Cabanne on how in Sanskrit, the language of Mahayana Buddhism, the word "art" connects to the idea of "making" (see p. 55). From the thousands of hours spent on his *Large Glass*, to his various elaborate "boxes," to the twenty years he spent developing *Etant donnés*, Duchamp was nothing if not a maker.

The suggestion in *The Coffee Grinder* of a mandala—a "window" that opens from material to immaterial reality—hints at a Tantric influence. This work was done at the end of 1911, the same year that Jacques Bacot's Tibetan collection, which included mandalas, was shown at the Musée Guimet. Duchamp may even have attended or discussed this exhibition with Constantin Brancusi, whose *Muse* and *Kiss* had been influenced by the museum's Buddhist sculpture. How important Brancusi was to Duchamp is revealed by a comment in a letter to the American critic Walter Pach indicating that Brancusi was the only artist Duchamp felt he had to see before leaving Paris for New York in spring 1915. Confessing he hadn't "met a single artist I know," Duchamp wrote: "I absolutely must go and see Brancusi."[28]

"Rotational movement is one of the most obvious characteristics of Tibetan rites," wrote Jacques Bacot in his first published Musée Guimet lecture.[29] *Coffee Grinder* depicts a machine that through rotational movement transforms individual coffee beans, whose form resembles the female exterior genitals, into a substance that can be made into a stimulating—an awakening—liquid. Perhaps the best-known Tibetan examples of rotational movement are prayer wheels—rotating wheels or cylinders bearing or containing inscribed texts. Small ones are twirled on sticks; very large ones are turned using a mill powered by flowing water. Tibetan prayer wheels are modeled on the Wheel of the Dharma, the wheel the Buddha drew on the ground when he preached his first sermon, "Setting in Motion the Wheel of the Dharma." Sometime in 1913—the year after his return from Munich—Duchamp attached a bicycle wheel to a stool. He kept it by his chair in his studio so he could easily set it spinning.

Tosi Lee has made a convincing case for the connection between Duchamp's choice of a

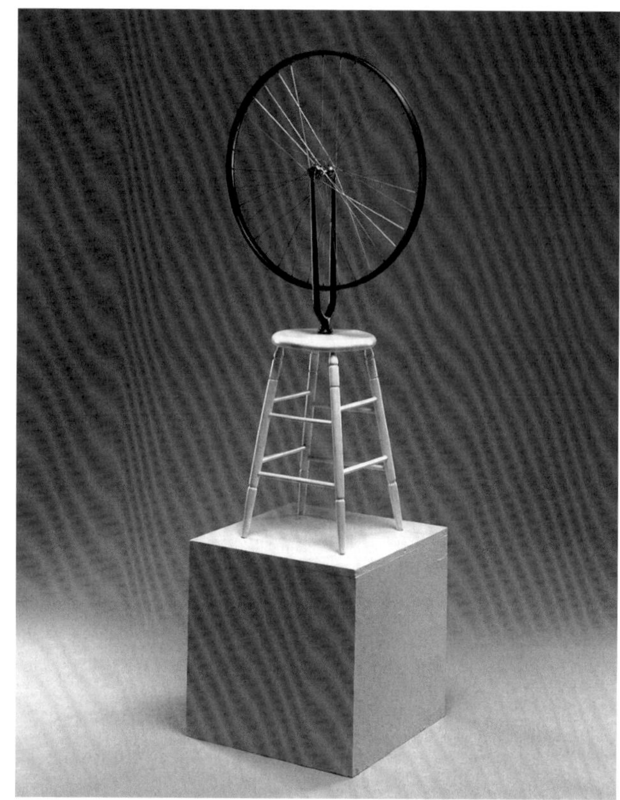

Marcel Duchamp, *Bicycle Wheel,* 1964 replica of 1913 original, 49 3/16 in. Philadelphia Museum of Art, Gift of the Schwarz Galleria d'Arte (1964-175-1). Photo: Graydon Wood, 1992. Artist © 2005 Artists Rights Society (ARS), New York/ADAGP, Paris/Succession Marcel Duchamp.

wheel for his first "readymade" and the Buddhist Wheel of the Dharma. In the Buddha's first sermon the wheel stands, among other things, for the newly enlightened Buddha's determination to turn the wheel of truth in this world. In early Buddhist art, the Wheel of the Dharma is represented by a wheel placed on top of a throne or pillar. Duchamp enthroned his wheel on a pillarlike studio stool, signifying, according to Lee, "the commencement of Duchamp's new path in art as well as his 'teachings.'"[30]

In Indian and Southeast Asian art the Wheel of the Dharma is often shown flanked or supported by lions, as on the East Gate of the Great Stupa at Sanchi. Full-scale replicas of this large gate dominated the courtyards of both the Ethnographic Museum in Berlin, where Duchamp stopped on his return from Munich, and the Musée Guimet in Paris.[31] On its left pillar, the wheel is flanked at top and bottom by lions; on the central pilasters, it is supported by lions on stool-like columns. An undated note by Duchamp, containing his typical wordplay, suggests how the Wheel of the Dharma connects to the *Bicycle Wheel:*

between the lions
______________ lines

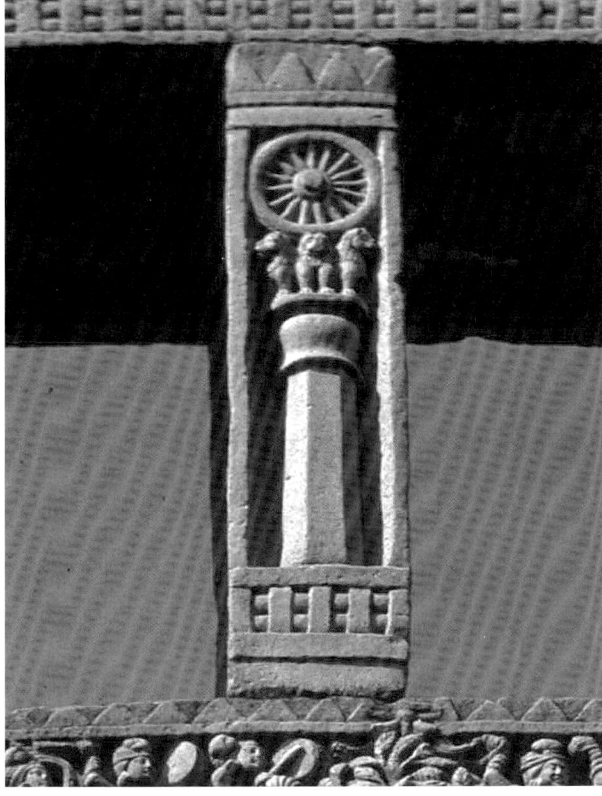

Detail, East Gate of the Great Stupa at Sanchi, India, first century, sandstone. Courtesy of the Department of the History of Art, University of Michigan, Ann Arbor. Photo © Wendy Holden.

> Riding between the lines/lions
> Reading between the lines
> Riding between the lions—[32]

Duchamp turns the pairing of reading/writing into reading/riding. In the language of Buddhist symbolism, reading between the lines of the turning wheel generates an experience of riding between the lions of Enlightenment.

According to Duchamp, the *Bicycle Wheel* was originally created, not as an art object, but as an object of contemplation:

> The *Bicycle Wheel* is my first Ready-made, so much so that at first it wasn't even called a Ready-made . . . it had more to do with the idea of chance. In a way, it was simply letting things go by themselves and having a sort of created atmosphere in a studio, an apartment where you live. Probably, to help your ideas come out of your head. To see that wheel turning was very soothing, very comforting, a sort of opening of avenues on other things than material life of every day.[33]

Marcel Duchamp, *To Be Looked At (from the Other Side of the Glass) with One Eye, Close To, for Almost an Hour,* or *The Small Glass,* 1918, oil paint, silver leaf, lead wire, and magnifying lens on cracked glass, 20⅛ x 16 x 1⅜ in. The Museum of Modern Art, New York. Katherine S. Dreier Bequest. Digital Image © The Museum of Modern Art/Licensed by SCALA/Art Resource, NY. Artist © 2005 Artists Rights Society (ARS), New York/ADAGP, Paris/Succession Marcel Duchamp.

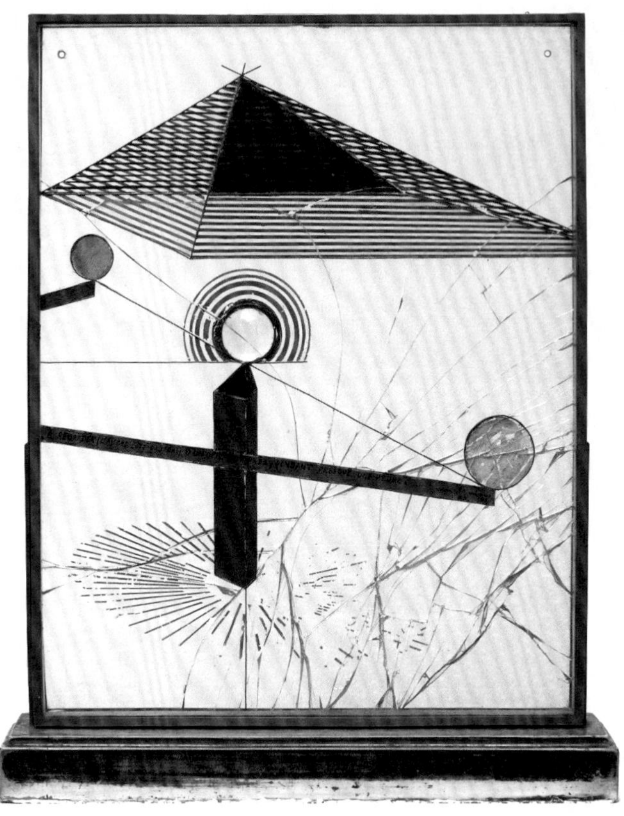

Duchamp's description of the *Bicycle Wheel* has prompted interpretations of it as a white noise machine for the eyes, but it is more than that. It is a device not so much for shutting out "material life," as for the "opening of avenues on other things," a meditation machine. Chance—the outcome of relinquishing desire and the wish to control; a state of equanimity that allows "simply letting things go by themselves"—would become a key concept for the art of the twentieth century.

Duchamp began constructing *The Large Glass* in 1915, after three years of research. Its title may have been inspired by the French term for Mahayana: *Grand Véhicule.* One translation of *véhicule* is "medium." The vehicle of glass may have been suggested to him by the experiments of Kandinsky and his colleagues with the Bavarian folk tradition of reverse painting on glass. Some of Kandinsky's works in this medium incorporated metallic foil. Duchamp would use silver, but in a way that combined transparency and reflectivity. *The Large Glass* shows you the world, the work, and yourself through, on, and reflected in its surface.

Four elements on the right side of the lower, "bachelor" half of the glass allude to a Buddhist "perspective." At the top is a small circular form described by Duchamp in his 1965 etching

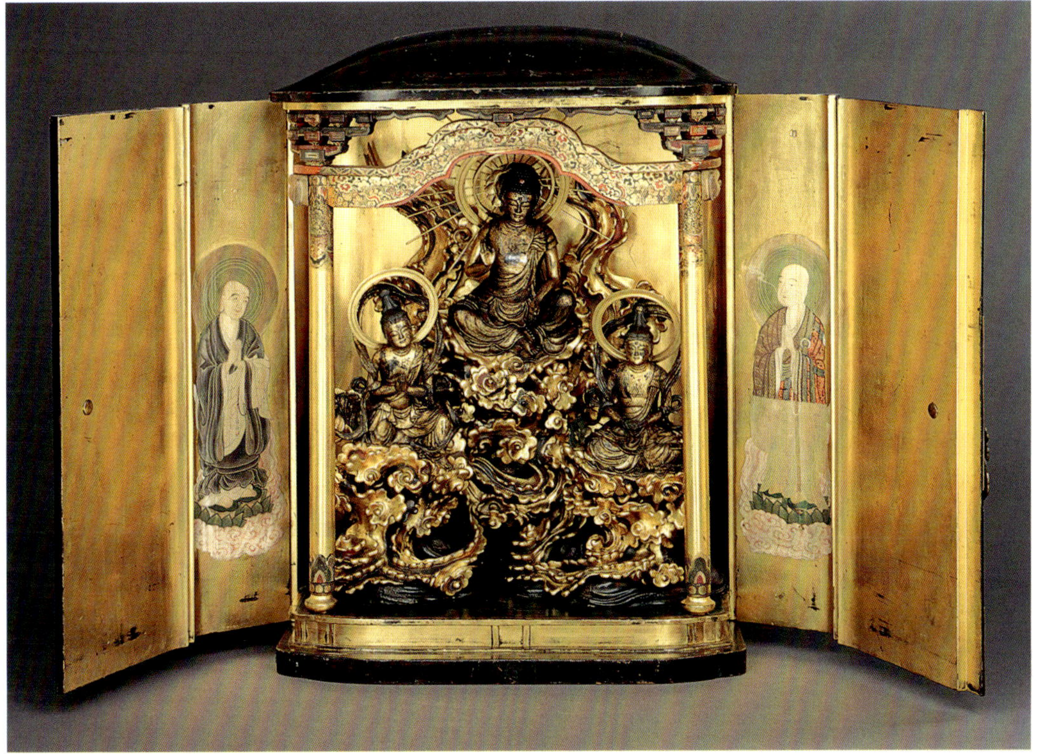

Altar with Amida triad, Japan, about 1800, wood, lacquer, gilt, paint, copper and brass fittings, 28 in. high. Staatliches Museum für Völkerkunde, Munich. Photo: Marianne Franke.

The Large Glass Completed as a "Mandala (a magnifying glass to focus the splashes)."[34] It hovers above three "Oculist Witnesses," whose wheel-like shapes were supposedly based on French oculist charts. Duchamp first developed these circular forms in 1918 in a piece he referred to as "the small 'Glass,'"[35] evoking the name of Buddhism's other main branch, Theravada or Hinayana—in French, *Petit Véhicule* ("small vehicle"), because it focuses on individual enlightenment, as opposed to *Grand Véhicule,* which focuses on the enlightenment of all beings.[36]

The "Mandala" of *The Small Glass* is an actual magnifying lens, and Duchamp inscribed the piece: "To Be Looked At (from the Other Side of the Glass) with One Eye, Close To, for Almost an Hour." When followed, this instruction transforms the viewer into a witness of the world. Indeed, Duchamp hung and photographed it on a balcony in Buenos Aires, where he had gone after the United States entered World War I. The lights of the city are visible through *The Small Glass,* which Duchamp called a "voyage sculpture."[37] His term calls to mind both "vehicle" and the Sanskrit word *samsara,* which defines life as "journeying."

The circular, radiant forms of the Oculist Witnesses closely resemble the halos of portable Japanese Amida altars, such as the striking example in Munich's Ethnographic Museum (shown here) and those in the Musée Guimet.[38] (These portable altars may have inspired Duchamp's multiple *Box in a Valise,* which he once referred to as "ready-made help."[39]) From its founding in 1879, the Musée Guimet featured a large display of Japanese Buddhist art, analyzed in regularly updated "little guides" to the collection. Amida is the Japanese name for the Buddha of consciousness, whose original Sanskrit name, Amitabha, means "Infinite Light." Some depictions show a beam of light emerging from the place at the center of his brow called the *urna.* On his right his wisdom is manifested as the bodhisattva Mahasthamaprapta, who brings to humanity the knowledge of the need for liberation. On Amitabha's left his compassion takes the form of the bodhisattva Avalokiteshvara, whose Sanskrit name means the one who observes, or witnesses, the cries of the world.[40]

Evidence suggests that, for Marcel Duchamp, the bodhisattva Avalokiteshvara was an alter ego.[41] An embodiment of compassion, Avalokiteshvara vowed not to ascend to buddhahood until he had liberated every being in all realms of existence. Called Kannon in Japan and Kuan-yin in China, Avalokiteshvara is "The One Who Confers the Gift of Fearlessness." One of his characteristic hand gestures *(mudras)* is the *abhaya,* or "fear not" gesture, in which the palm faces the viewer in the universal sign to "stop"—in this case, a reassuring order to stop being afraid. His attributes include a watering vessel and a lotus (another name for him is Padmapani, the "Lotus Holder").

When asked why he decided to stop painting, Duchamp responded, "I decided nothing at all; I am simply waiting for ideas. I've had thirty-three ideas; I've made thirty-three paintings."[42] In the Lotus Sutra the Buddha is asked how the bodhisattva Regarder of the Cries of the World preaches the dharma—"what is the character of his tactfulness?"[43] The Buddha responds with a list of thirty-three manifestations, including female ones, assumed by Avalokiteshvara to most effectively help individual sufferers. A male bodhisattva in India and Tibet, Avalokiteshvara was gradually transformed into a female, Kuan-yin, in male-oriented Chinese society. The patron bodhisattva of Tibet, he is complemented there by the female bodhisattva Tara ("star"), who is said to have been born from the tears of compassion shed by Avalokiteshvara as he contemplated the task of saving all suffering beings.

In 1921 Duchamp had his friend Man Ray photograph him as a woman he named Rrose Sélavy. Duchamp's love of homophones has generated a number of interpretations of this name. The most common is "Eros c'est la vie" (Eros, that's life)—a meaning in keeping with Duchamp's interests, as we shall see. But Duchamp himself said about the double "r" of Rrose: "The verb *arroser* takes 2 r's . . . I thought it very clever to begin a word, a name, with 2 r's, like the 2 l's in Lloyd."[44] An alternate reading of Rrose Sélavy thus becomes "Arrose c'est la vie" (Watering, that's life), alluding to Avalokiteshvara's attribute of the watering

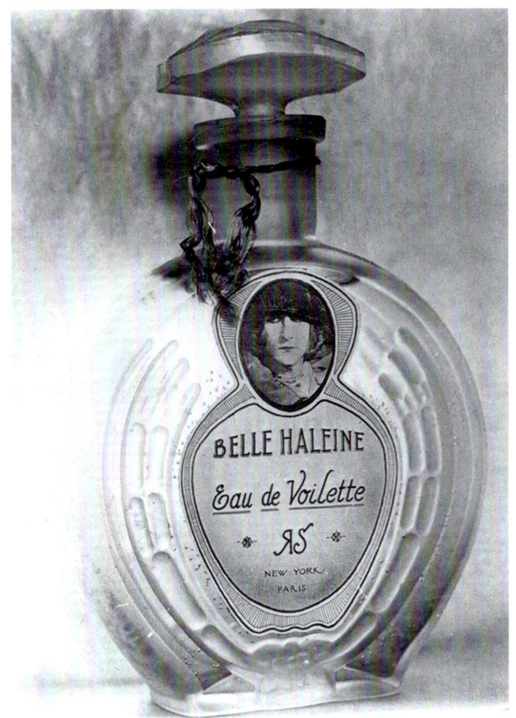

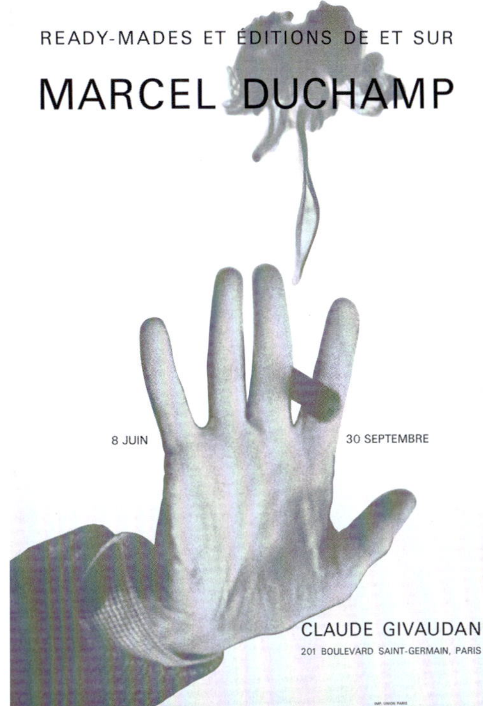

(left) Marcel Duchamp (photographed by Man Ray), perfume bottle for *Belle Haleine/Eau de Voilette (Beautiful Breath/Veil Water)*, 1921 (negative), gelatin silver print, 8⅞ x 6⅞ in. Philadelphia Museum of Art., Purchased with the Alice Newton Osborn Fund and funds contributed by Ann and Donald McPhail upon the occasion of the 100th birthday of Marcel Duchamp, 1987 (1987-36-2). Artist © 2005 Artists Rights Society (ARS), New York/ADAGP, Paris/Succession Marcel Duchamp.

(right) Marcel Duchamp, poster for the exhibition *Ready-Mades et Editions de et sur Marcel Duchamp*, 1967, 27⅜ x 18⅞ in. Courtesy 871 Fine Arts, San Francisco. Photo: John Wilson White. Artist © 2005 Artists Rights Society (ARS), New York/ADAGP, Paris/Succession Marcel Duchamp.

vessel and his tears over the suffering of humankind. According to the curator of the Musée Guimet at the time Rrose was "born," the color of the Tara corresponding to the Buddha Amitabha is "rose."[45]

Rrose created a number of artworks, including a perfume bottle whose label bears her image and her name. Titled *Belle Haleine / Eau de Voilette (Beautiful Breath / Veil Water)*, it alludes both to breath—the focus of Buddhist meditation practice, including Tantric practice, with its concept of *prana* (vital breath)—and to the nourishing fall of water through which the compassion of Avalokiteshvara is manifested. Tosi Lee notes, "Traditionally, Kuan-Yin's water vase is called 'the vase of heavenly dew' or 'nectar' or 'sweet dew' *(amrita)* . . . making Duchamp's choice of a perfume bottle especially appropriate."[46]

Perhaps the strongest visual evidence for Duchamp's identification with Avalokiteshvara is a poster he designed for his 1967 exhibition at the Galerie Givaudan in Paris. In it we see Duchamp's hand in Avalokiteshvara's signature *abhaya*, "fear not," *mudra*. The smoke from the cigar held between Duchamp's first two fingers resembles the lotus that is the attribute of both Avalokiteshvara and Tara. According to Arturo Schwarz, "Duchamp mentioned that he was amused by this photo because of the formal analogy between the shape of the lower part of the smoke cloud and the female genitalia."[47] In Tantric iconography, the lotus is a symbol for the female genitals.

In 1956 Duchamp told a graduate student, "I want to grasp things with the mind the way the penis is grasped by the vagina."[48] The presumably alarmed scholar buried this vivid statement in a footnote about the fourth dimension. But its conflation of mental and sexual energy is typical of Tantrayana, whose adherents believe that male and female bodies possess complementary energies, identified in the male as *upaya* (skillful means or compassion) and in the female as *prajna* (wisdom or insight). The goal of sexual Tantra is transcendence of dualism through sexual union.

When Duchamp's installation *Etant donnés* was revealed after his death in 1968, the art world was stunned. First, Duchamp's identity had been organized around the supposed fact that he had stopped making new works of art in 1923. Now, it was obvious that he had been working for the last twenty years of his life, diligently and secretly, on a work whose importance rivaled that of *The Large Glass*. Second, *Etant donnés* was a shocking work, even by Duchampian standards. A peephole in an old wooden door (reminiscent of the monastery door in Scherman's Munich exhibition) reveals a startling vision of a naked woman lying on her back amid twigs and leaves. Her face, right arm, and right leg are hidden, but her left leg is bent to so as to open her vulva to our view. She holds a glowing lamp in her left hand. In the background is a mountain landscape featuring a misty lake and a lit-up, moving waterfall.

We have seen that the language of Buddhism can provide clues to the significance of Duchamp's enigmatic titles. Duchamp once told Arturo Schwarz that he wanted "to transfer the significance of language from words into signs, into visual expressions of words, similar to the ideograms of the Chinese language." The statement suggests some familiarity with written Chinese. *Etant donnés* translates as "given." What is given in Buddhism is the Dharma. To know that the Chinese ideogram for "Dharma" is composed of the signs for "water" and "disappear" helps explain the subtitle of *Etant donnés:* "1. The Waterfall 2. The Illuminating Gas." It is a recipe for Enlightenment.[49]

As Duchamp indicated to Schwarz, however, the words are not the point; what is important are the visual components. The Tibetan "Chenresig empowerment" (Chenresig is the Tibetan name for Avalokiteshvara) begins with the pouring of water into the hands of disciples, who rinse their mouths with it to purify and prepare themselves to meet the deity.[50] And in the stage-one visualization called "vase empowerment,"[51] *yoginis* holding vases pour water through the crown of the head, cleansing the mind and the body of defilements and enabling the dismantling of mental obstacles.

The lamp in *Etant donnés* was based on a model from Duchamp's youth, the old Bec Auer gas lamp that burned with a green flame. Duchamp referred to its distinctive light in a conversation with Pierre Cabanne the year after he finished *Etant donnés:*

> DUCHAMP: *Portrait of Chess Players* [1911] . . . was painted by gaslight. It was a tempting experiment. You know, that gaslight from the old Auer jet is green; I wanted to see what the changing of colors would do . . .
>
> CABANNE: It's one of the rare times when you were preoccupied with problems of light.
>
> DUCHAMP: Yes, but it isn't even really the light. It's the light that enlightened me.[52]

Gas generates light and heat and vanishes. In Tantrayana, the transformative agency of wisdom is represented by female Tantric deities—*dakinis* and *yoginis*—who are personified in the Yogini Tantras as Vajrayogini, the female buddha. Vajrayogini represents *prajna anala* (wisdom fire)—the energy of inner heat by which the practitioner experiences the "spontaneous great bliss," the realization of emptiness.[53] In the second phase of Tibetan Tantric visualization, the energy centers, or *chakras* (wheels), of the inner body are opened up. "Winds," or vital energies, flow from the 72,000 subtle "channels" of the body through three main channels that run parallel to each other. The goal is to direct the winds into the central channel, which runs from the forehead up over the crown of the head, down the spine and under the body, to the tip of the sexual organ. From there, the central channel ascends through the center of the body and the chakras, emerging through the top of the head.[54] In 1919 Duchamp had his head shaved in a "tonsure" of a star shooting from his forehead up over the crown of his head. In a 1936 letter to Duchamp, Katherine Dreier reminisced: "Dee, do you recall that you told me that you had such a marvelous sensation at the base of your spine which you enjoyed?"[55] Twenty-two years later, in 1958, Duchamp produced a multiple bearing the words *Eau & gaz à tous les étages* (Water and gas on every floor). It was said to be a replica of plaques found on turn-of-the-century French apartment houses, but in the context of other evidence, its wording suggests a lifelong practice of moving energy up through the chakras.

The pose of the nude in *Etant donnés* can be compared to that typical of Himalayan sculptures of *yoginis* and *dakinis,* such as the large *dakini* in the collection of the Musée Guimet.

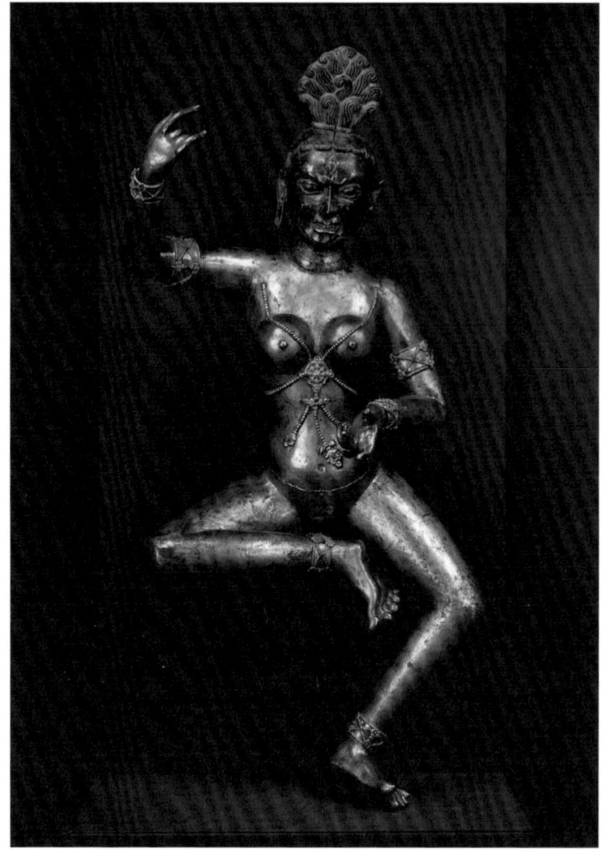

Dancing Dakini *(ardha-paryankasana)*, 19th century, from Tibet or Nepal (?), gilded copper with traces of polychrome, 49 1/16 x 24 1/8 x 15 5/8 in. Musée National des Arts Asiatiques–Guimet, Paris (MA 1631). Photo: Amaudet, Réunion des Musées Nationaux/Art Resource, NY.

Like Duchamp's nude, her arm is raised and her leg bent, although her genitals are not open, as is the vulva of the figure in *Etant donnés*. This feature, however, does resemble other Tantric depictions, showing the open *yoni* of the female buddha Vajrayogini in her aspect symbolizing emptiness.

In the highest tantras, according to Elizabeth English, a scholar of Tibetan Buddhism, "emptiness is described experientially as the ecstatic, all-consuming great bliss, the tantric metaphor for which is orgasm. Thus the experience of emptiness or bliss is said to 'arise in' or to be 'produced from' the *dharmodaya*, or the woman's sex."[56] Duchamp's phrase, "I want to grasp things with the mind the way the penis is grasped by the vagina," images his own mind as a female vagina and suggests the Tantric concept of the transcendence of dualism through sexual union. In Pierre Cabanne's interview with Duchamp the year before the artist's death, they talked about the importance of eroticism in Duchamp's work:

> DUCHAMP: Eroticism was a theme, even an "ism," which was the basis of everything I was doing at the time of the "Large Glass." . . .

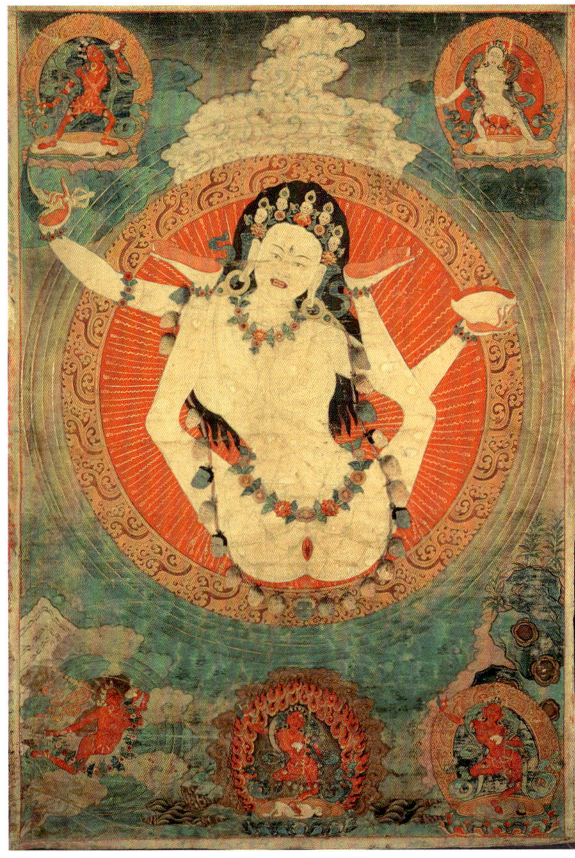

Vajrayogini, Tibet, Shangpa Kagyu lineage, ground mineral pigment on cotton. Private collection. Photo courtesy of Arnold Lieberman.

> CABANNE: Still, in your work, this eroticism has remained disguised for a rather long time.
>
> DUCHAMP: Always disguised, more or less, but not disguised out of shame.
>
> CABANNE: No, hidden.
>
> DUCHAMP: That's it.[57]

Cabanne didn't know—yet—about *Etant donnés.*

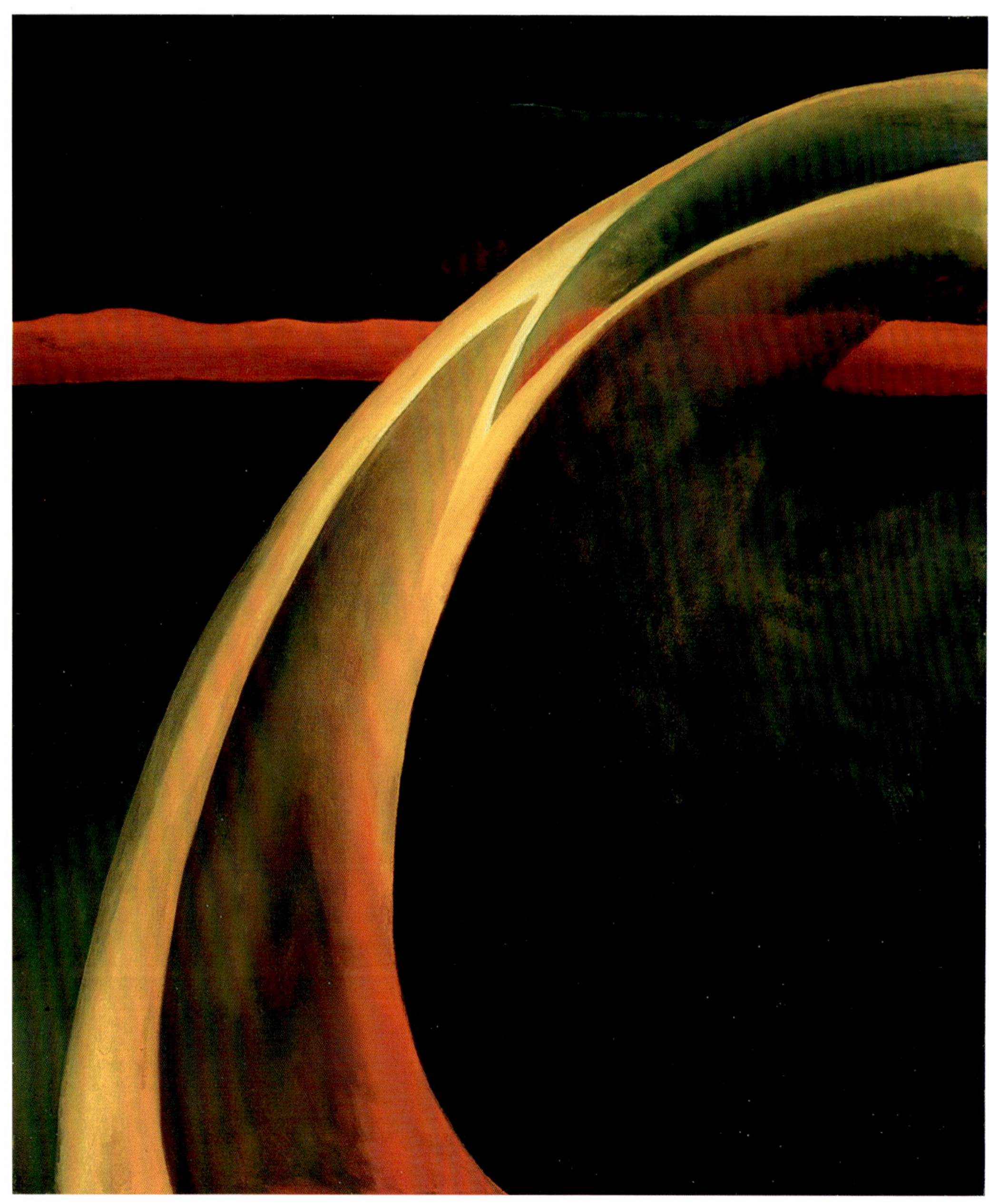

Georgia O'Keeffe, *Orange and Red Streak,* 1919, oil on canvas, 27 x 23 in. Philadelphia Museum of Art, Bequest of Georgia O'Keeffe for the Alfred Stieglitz Collection. Artist © 2005 The Georgia O'Keeffe Foundation/Artists Rights Society (ARS), New York.

By unknown—I mean the thing that means so much to the person that he wants to put it down—clarify something he feels but does not clearly understand... sometimes it is all working in the dark—but a working that must be done—Making the unknown—known—in terms of one's medium is all absorbing.

GEORGIA O'KEEFFE

GEORGIA O'KEEFFE 1887–1986

IN THE EARLY 1960S THE ART CRITIC Katharine Kuh asked the seventy-five-year-old Georgia O'Keeffe about the strongest influence on her work. "Some people say nature," O'Keeffe responded, "but the way you see nature depends on whatever has influenced your way of seeing. I think it was Arthur Dow who affected my start, who helped me to find something of my own."[1] Dow brought a Japanese Buddhist perspective to the teaching of art in America during the first decade of the twentieth century. When queried by Kuh about the influence of Asian art on her work, O'Keeffe gave a revealing answer:

> I enjoy Oriental art very much and prefer traveling in the East than in Europe. But tell me, can you find anything in my work that shows an Oriental influence? I had an important experience once. I put up everything I had done over a long period and as I looked around at my work I realized that each painting had been affected by someone else. I wondered why I hadn't put down things of my own from my own head. And then I realized that I hadn't done this because I'd never seen anything like the things in my own head.[2]

Only after studying with Dow did it become possible for O'Keeffe to give visual form to the things in her head and her heart, to what she called her "unknowns."[3]

Finding something of her own was Georgia O'Keeffe's passion; art was how she went about it. Although she tended to dismiss her childhood as either conventionally happy (a big family in a big house on a big farm in Sun Prairie, Wisconsin) or unimportant compared with her subsequent doings, her emotional complexity began at birth, with her naming. One of seven children, Georgia had one older brother, Francis, named after their father. But, as the second child, she was named not after her mother, Ida (that honor would go to a sister), but after her mother's father, George Victor Totto. Georgia Totto O'Keeffe thus began life with the name of the Hungarian count who had abandoned her mother along with the rest of his Wisconsin family, never to be heard from again. Unable to fill that hole in her mother's heart, Georgia tended to blame herself: "As a little girl, I think I craved a certain kind of affection that Mama did not give." She was, however, her father's favorite and identified with him: "I think that deep down I am like my Father. When he wanted to see the country, he just got up and went. That is how it has to be at times with me."[4]

Georgia's father, an alcoholic, eventually reduced his family to poverty and then abandoned them, much as Georgia's namesake had. Her mother died from tuberculosis after a long, sad decline in May 1916, the month of Georgia's first show in New York at Alfred Stieglitz's 291 gallery. Two years later, shortly before Georgia's thirty-first birthday, her father died unexpectedly in a fall from a roof. Not long afterward, she painted *Orange and Red Streak,* a dark and dramatic, yet lyrical painting, conveying the experience of a lightning storm just after sunset in the midst of a flat Texas landscape. Like the sixth Zen patriarch's assertion that the real movement of the fluttering flag is within the mind, *Streak* depicts inner weather. Years later, in reference to this painting, O'Keeffe recalled:

> The cattle in the pens lowing for their calves day and night was a sound that has always haunted me. It had a regular rhythmic beat like the old Penitente songs, repeating the same rhythms over and over all through the day and night. It was loud and raw under the stars in that wide empty country.[5]

It was a sad sound, an archetypal sound of loss. This passage detailing a memory from Texas—where O'Keeffe went to teach art four months after her mother's death, and from which Stieglitz extracted her the February before her father died—seems a strange thing to write, more than half a decade later, about an essentially abstract painting that balances the power of darkness with the power of light. Clearly, *Orange and Red Streak* still had the power to re-create a specific state of mind for O'Keeffe. But the painting itself speaks to a certain quality in its maker, a quality of intense identity with the primal forces of nature. In September 1916, soon after she arrived, she had written from Texas to a friend:

> Tonight I walked into the sunset . . . the whole sky—and there is so much of it out here—was just blazing. . . . But some way or other I didn't seem to like the redness much so . . .

> I walked home—and kept on walking—The eastern sky was all grey-blue . . . lit up—first in one place—then in another with flashes of lightning—sometimes just sheet lightning—and sometimes sheet lightning with a sharp bright zigzag flashing across it—. I . . . sat on the fence for a long time—looking—just looking at the lightning—you see there was nothing but sky and flat prairie land . . . Well I just sat there and had a great time all by myself—not even many night noises—just the wind.[6]

How did O'Keeffe come by her power to transform intense emotion into visual form? She credited Arthur Wesley Dow: "This man had one dominating idea: to fill a space in a beautiful way—and that interested me. After all, everyone has to do just this—make choices—in his daily life, even when only buying a cup and saucer."[7] O'Keeffe's seeming non sequitur here makes sense if you know Dow's teachings. An early proponent of relational thinking, Dow was a New England artist whose own landscape paintings, woodcut prints, and photographs were done in a soft, tonalist style. He had worked in Pont Aven when Paul Gauguin was there, in the later 1880s. Although Dow did not seem to understand what Gauguin was up to at the time, when he published the first edition of his revolutionary book for the teaching of art—*Composition*—a decade later, he decorated its cover with an emblem that combined an abstract landscape with the word "synthesis" spelled out in eight Greek letters. Gauguin had written in his own "Notes synthétiques" of 1888: "In [a painting] all sensations are condensed; contemplating it, everyone can create a story at the will of his imagination and—with a single glance—have his soul invaded by the most profound recollections; no effort of memory, everything is summed up in one instant."[8] Georgia O'Keeffe might have agreed, but Dow's goals were not so metaphysical. For Dow, "synthesis" meant the revitalization of American art and culture through the programmatic infusion of Eastern, primarily Japanese, design principles. His model was the dialectic proposed by Hegel—the first Western philosopher to integrate elements of Buddhism into his thinking—where synthesis was the product of interaction between a cultural thesis and its antithesis.

In Hegel's example, "being" (the thesis) encounters its opposite, "non-being," resolving into the synthesis "becoming." In a pragmatic American vein, Dow emphasized the "appreciation" he believed would result from reorienting Western values from representation toward implication—the Japanese aesthetic that, as Monet allegedly asserted, "evokes a presence by means of a shadow and the whole by means of a fragment."[9] For Dow, abstract form turns viewers into creators by stimulating them to develop the meaning of what they are seeing. Through his universal system of art education, Dow aimed to nurture the creative power that is "the natural endowment of every human soul, showing itself at first in the form that we call *appreciation*."

> This appreciation leads a certain number to produce actual works of art, greater or lesser,—perhaps a temple, perhaps only a cup,—it leads the majority to desire finer form and more

> harmony of tone and color in surroundings and in things for daily use. It is the individual's right to have full control of these powers.[10]

This passage is what lay behind O'Keeffe's connection between filling a space in a beautiful way and the everyday choice involved in buying a cup and saucer. Making choices means having power. "The intention," Dow wrote in his conclusion to *Composition,* "has been to reveal the sources of power; to show the student how to look within for the greatest help; to teach him not to depend on externals, not to lean too much on anything or anybody."[11] This was an intention that Georgia O'Keeffe would make her own.

Dow's partner in his subversive effort was the Boston philosopher, artist, and art historian Ernest Fenollosa. (Fenollosa's two-volume *Epochs of Chinese and Japanese Art* would be required reading for Dow students.) Also a Hegelian, Fenollosa's missionary zeal regarding Japanese aesthetics came from his having lived and taught in Japan, where (among other things) he was named an imperial commissioner of fine arts, received the precepts of esoteric Tendai Buddhism, and amassed a collection of art that ended up in the Boston Museum of Fine Arts, where he served as curator of Far Eastern art from 1890 to 1895. That is where Dow met him, in search of information about Japanese art, which, Dow intuited, might help improve the deplorable state of American visual culture. The two men joined forces, with Fenollosa providing the expertise, Dow the means. In 1903 Dow himself traveled to Japan, as well as Southeast Asia, India, and Greece.

Dow's *Composition* included examples of both Asian and Western art: Japanese woodblock prints and French Gothic sculpture were used to illustrate "Notan"—the most Japanese of the three "elements" of Dow's "art language." (The other two elements are line ["the boundaries of shapes"] and color ["the quality of light"].) Realizing perhaps that the term "Notan" might be a barrier to his readers, Dow replaced it with "Dark-and-Light" in his condensed manual *Theory and Practice of Teaching Art,* which O'Keeffe assigned to her own students. In contrast to Western concepts of chiaroscuro or shading, which Dow linked with representation, Notan "has a fuller meaning as a name for a great universal manifestation of beauty. Darks and lights in harmonic relations—this is Notan."[12] Dow cited the ink paintings of Zen Buddhist priest-painters as examples of this mastery of tonal relations.

"Notan" combines two concepts originally from the Chinese: *no,* which means darkness, depth, concentration, strength, or density; and *tan,* meaning light, pale, fleeting, or transitory. Dow's Notan was a holistic concept very like the Chinese Taoist principle of yin and yang, which had migrated from China to Japan, showing up in the Kano school of painting as *in-yo,* meaning shadow *(in)* and light *(yo)* but also negative and positive, passive and active, female and male. *No-tan,* dark and light, was the physical manifestation of *in-yo* in art.[13]

O'Keeffe's example of choosing a cup and saucer may contain another reference. In *Com-*

position, as well as his teaching, Dow recommended Kakuzo Okakura's *The Book of Tea* as a source of information about the origin and practice of the "fine appreciation" that characterized Japanese culture.[14] Okakura, who had been one of Fenollosa's students in Japan, became a controversial but knowledgeable and charismatic advocate for Asian culture. In 1902 he emigrated to Boston, where four years later he became advisor and then curator for Chinese and Japanese art at the Museum of Fine Arts. In 1906 he also published *The Book of Tea,* in which tea becomes a symbol for the essence of Asia. Chapter 3, entitled "Taoism and Zennism," contains a passage that is helpful in understanding the appeal of emptiness for O'Keeffe, in terms of both her way of life and her particular form of abstraction:

> Laotse . . . claimed that only in vacuum lay the truly essential. The reality of a room, for instance, was to be found in the vacant space enclosed by the roof and walls, not in the roof and walls themselves. The usefulness of a water pitcher dwelt in the emptiness where water might be put, not in the form of the pitcher or the material of which it was made. . . . In art the importance of the same principle is illustrated by the value of suggestion. In leaving something unsaid the beholder is given a chance to complete the idea and thus a great masterpiece irresistibly rivets your attention until you seem to become actually a part of it.[15]

Okakura's passages on "Zennism" are equally evocative of O'Keeffe's work:

> Zennism, like Taoism, is the worship of Relativity. One master defines Zen as the art of feeling the polar star in the southern sky. Truth can be reached only through the comprehension of opposites. Again, Zennism, like Taoism, is a strong advocate of individualism. Nothing is real except that which concerns the working of our own minds.[16]
>
> A special contribution of Zen to Eastern thought was its recognition of the mundane as of equal importance with the spiritual. . . . The whole ideal of Teaism is a result of this Zen conception of greatness in the smallest incidents of life.[17]

And, like Dow, Okakura stressed the black-and-white emphasis of Zen:

> The followers of Zen aimed at direct communion with the inner nature of things, regarding their outward accessories only as impediments to a clear perception of Truth. It was this love of the Abstract that led the Zen to prefer black and white sketches to the elaborately colored paintings of the classic Buddhist School.[18]

Georgia O'Keeffe began studying with Arthur Dow in the fall of 1914. A year later she moved to South Carolina for a one-year position teaching art at Columbia College. There, in October 1915, she began creating her first truly distinctive works of art. In the summer of 1915 O'Keeffe read Kandinsky's *On the Spiritual in Art,* in a translation entitled *The Art of Spiritual Harmony,* by Michael Sadler. Kandinsky's concept of the function of art was of great interest to O'Keeffe. His theories about the psychology of color struck a chord as well, but it was more likely something in her own psychology that caused her to write her friend Anita Pollitzer in October 1915: "The colors I seem to want to use absolutely nauseate me."[19] The Zen intensity of black and white, on the other hand, inspired O'Keeffe to create the smoldering charcoal drawings she called her "Specials." When she did begin bringing in color, it tended to be blue. Her *Blue Lines* of 1916 are resonant with the advice of a Chinese Sung Dynasty painter quoted in Fenollosa's *Epochs of Chinese and Japanese Art:* "With regard to inking, sometimes light ink is to be used, sometimes deep and dark . . . sometimes receding ink . . . sometimes ink mixed with *sei-tai* (blue). . . . After making sharp outlines, they are to be retraced with blue and ink. Then the forms will seem to come out of mist and dew."[20]

The penultimate chapter of *The Book of Tea* is entitled "Flowers." It is the darkest of Okakura's chapters, inspiring him to muse on death:

> Tell me, gentle flowers, teardrops of the stars, standing in the garden, nodding your heads to the bees as they sing of the dews and the sunbeams, are you aware of the fearful doom that awaits you? . . . Tomorrow a ruthless hand will close around your throats.[21]

In another letter to Pollitzer from October 1915 O'Keeffe wrote, "Anita—do you feel like flowers sometimes?"[22] Flowers became the forms through which O'Keeffe began attempting to make "the unknown known." The art historian Anne Middleton Wagner has argued that O'Keeffe's apparently sexualized flower paintings were an evasive action on her part and can tell us much about the aims of her art. Irritated by the tendency of critics to interpret her "Specials" and other abstractions as fecund expressions of a feminine sensibility, O'Keeffe shifted toward the supposedly more objective mode of still life. To the novelist Sherwood Anderson she wrote about her upcoming exhibition of 1924:

> My work this year is very much on the ground—There will be only two abstract things—or three at most—all the rest is objective—as objective as I can make it. . . . I suppose the reason I got down to an effort to be objective is that I didn't like the interpretation of my other things—so here I am with an array of alligator pears—about ten of them—calla lilies—four or six—leaves . . . horrid yellow sunflowers—two new red cannas—some white birches with yellow leaves—only two that I have no name for and I don't know where they came from.[23]

O'Keeffe's strategy backfired, of course. Critics simply lit on those subjects associated with notions of the feminine—her flowers—and made precisely the same point.

O'Keeffe's phrase "that I have no name for" is telling. She was working at a preverbal level of experience for which there is no language beyond metaphor. Metaphors depend on

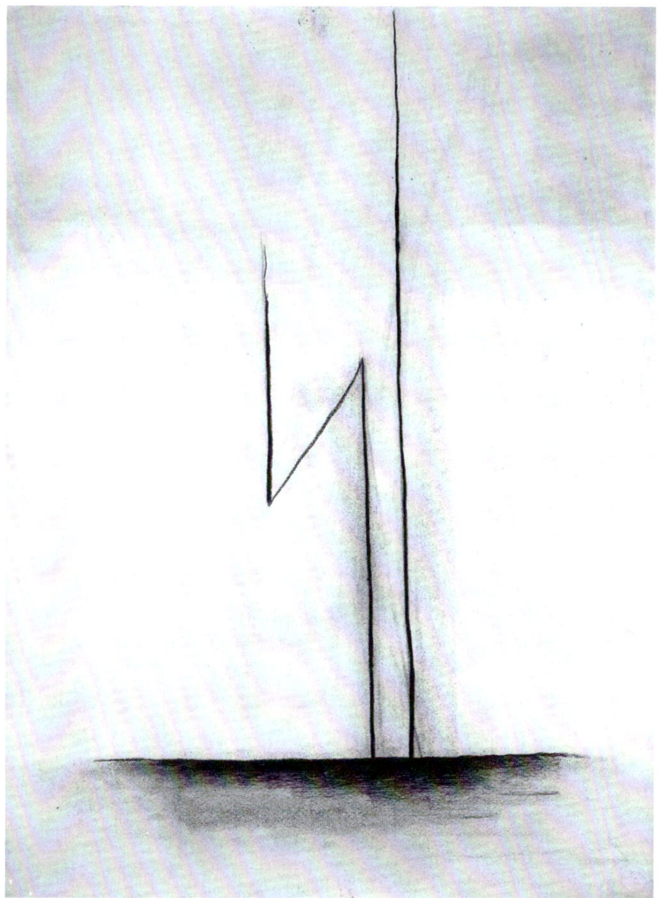

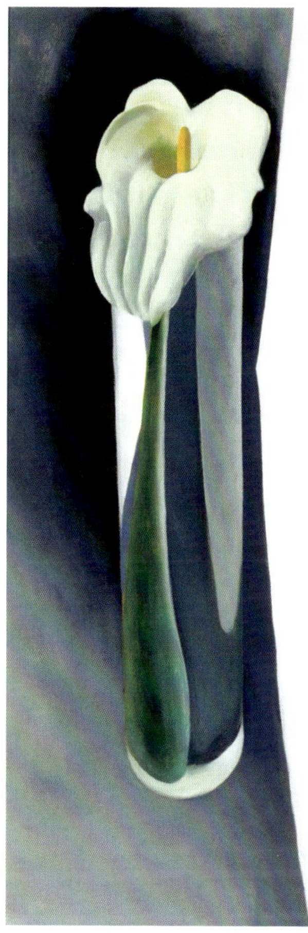

(left) Georgia O'Keeffe, *First Drawing of Blue Lines,* 1916, charcoal on laid paper, 24¾ x 18⅞ in. National Gallery of Art, Washington, DC. Alfred Stieglitz Collection (1992.89.11), Gift of The Georgia O'Keeffe Foundation. Image © 2005 Board of Trustees, National Gallery of Art, Washington. Artist © 2005 The Georgia O'Keeffe Foundation/Artists Rights Society (ARS), New York.

(right) Georgia O'Keeffe, *Calla Lily in Tall Glass—No. 2,* 1923, oil on board, 32⅛ x 12 in. Georgia O'Keeffe Museum, Santa Fe, NM, Gift of the Burnett Foundation (1997.06.10). Image © Georgia O'Keeffe Museum, Santa Fe/Art Resource, NY. Artist © 2005 The Georgia O'Keeffe Foundation/Artists Rights Society (ARS), New York.

mutual understanding, and it was on this level that O'Keeffe ran into trouble. In 1939 she addressed her critics directly in a catalog statement:

> Everyone has many associations with a flower—the idea of flowers. You put out your hand to touch the flower—lean forward to smell it—maybe touch it with your lips almost without thinking—or give it to somebody to please them. Still—in a way—nobody sees a flower really—it is so small—and we haven't time—and to see takes time like to have a friend takes time. . . . So I said to myself—I'll paint what I see—what the flower is to me but

III THE SPACE OF ART

America now presents this curious spectacle of success. The artist has to all intents and purposes won his battle for freedom of expression. It approaches the Nirvana we all dreamed of. The only question now remaining is, what now our role?... It is understandable... that having lost contact with the old revolutionary attitude which stemmed from Europe, Americans now turn more and more to the Orient and seek there some direction and criterion for the further development of their art. To many, Japanese Zen seems to offer a solution to their dilemma.... However, in this Zen may be misunderstood in that it is no means to ends other than its own.

ISAMU NOGUCHI, AROUND 1960

The painted space
The space of painting
seems mutable...
What seems literal can twist or be twisted
into something else—as rigidly
literal works tend to become transcendental.
The space of works of Zen
seems mutable.

JASPER JOHNS, AROUND 1992–93

SINCE THE 1960S A NUMBER OF WESTERN ARTISTS have directly addressed the affinities between Zen Buddhism and art-making, whether skeptically, as in the statement by the sculptor Isamu Noguchi, who associated Zen with his childhood in Japan and had conflicting feelings about it, or more analytically, as in the notes by the American painter Jasper Johns, implicitly recognizing the parallel between painting practice and Zen practice. Although Zen is by no means the only form of Buddhism, it is the best known in the West. (Indeed, for many Westerners, Zen is Buddhism and Buddhism is Zen.) Zen is the Japanese name for Ch'an, which is, in turn, Chinese for the Sanskrit word *dhyana,* meaning meditative absorption. Dhyana Buddhism spread in the sixth century from India to China, where it merged with Taoism, becoming a form of Buddhism that emphasizes the enlightenment experience and downplays intellectual analysis. Controversies arose over the nature of this experience, epitomized by the difference between the "gradual enlightenment" advocated by Shen-hsiu (606–706) and the "sudden enlightenment" expounded by Hui-neng (638–713). Hui-neng became the sixth Chinese patriarch, and his view won out. Subsequent Ch'an rhetoric emphasizes sudden enlightenment, but its practitioners continued training the mind through meditation and observing the precepts. Zen arrived in Japan via Korea (where it is called Sŏn) in the twelfth century. There, it developed two main branches: the Soto school, which emphasizes the realization of our innate enlightened nature through sitting meditation, and the Rinzai school, a more active and goal-oriented practice that uses tools such as intuiting the "solution" to logical paradoxes called *koans.*

The prolific writer and teacher Daisetsu Teitaro Suzuki (1870–1966) spent a lifetime interpreting Buddhism, specifically Zen Buddhism, to the West. Suzuki is usually given credit for the second "great wave" of Japanese culture in Europe and the United States, after World War II (the first "great wave" was in the second half of the nineteenth century[1]). There was, however, more continuity than the wave metaphor might imply. Suzuki began publishing in English in 1898. Kakuzo Okakura's and Ernest Fenollosa's writings appeared in the early twentieth century, and Laurence Binyon first published *The Flight of the Dragon: An Essay on the Theory and Practice of Art in China and Japan* in 1911. The Englishman Arthur Waley began producing books on Chinese and Japanese poetry and Asian art, publishing *Zen Buddhism and Its Relation to Art* in 1922.

Suzuki first came to the United States in 1897 to work for Paul Carus, and his English writings and translations began appearing the following year. He returned to Japan in 1909, but his translations of Buddhist texts and writings on Zen Buddhism continued to appear in Europe and the United States. The most influential of his many books in America was probably the 1949 English edition of *An Introduction to Zen Buddhism,* with its foreword by C. G. Jung. *The Zen Doctrine of No-Mind,* which appeared in the same year, was also widely read, and his 1960 *Manual of Zen Buddhism* was particularly popular with artists. In 1949 the seventy-nine-year-old Suzuki returned to the United States, where he taught in Hawaii and in Claremont, California, before going on a lecture tour of American universities and finally settling in New York in 1951. His famous classes at Columbia University, where he was professor of religion until 1957, were attended by writers, artists, and musicians such as Thomas Merton, Philip Guston, and John Cage.[2]

Following Japan's defeat by the Allies in 1945, Zen can truly be said to have invaded the West. As Noguchi suggested, the Holocaust and Hiroshima produced a dramatic loss of faith in the utopian ideals of previous generations, sending artists on a quest for a way of conceiving existence that was nontheistic, but less bleak than existentialism. For many, Suzuki's Zen, with its reification of the aesthetic, validation of the idiosyncratic, and offer of *satori,* or enlightenment, as an achievable human goal, was the answer—or at least one of the answers—to this quest. Zen Buddhism became a path to recovery of artistic purpose. Noguchi may have been correct in asserting that the postwar climate did not produce all that many authentic Zen Buddhists in the West, but there is no question that Zen offered a way to reimagine the authentic creative act.

Zen in the Art of Archery, by the German Eugen Herrigel, appeared in an English edition in 1953. It was a key reading for artists in the fifties. "Fundamentally," Herrigel wrote, "the marksman aims at himself and may even succeed in hitting himself."[3] For "marksman," read "artist." Art as a spiritual practice, a way to make contact with, as Noguchi said, "depths of inner experience from which to draw substance for further development,"[4] appealed to a number of artists trying to make their way in a fragmented postwar world. With both U.S. and U.N. forces stationed in Japan during the Korean conflict and a number of European and American artists traveling to Japan independently, firsthand experience with Japanese Buddhism increased along with secondhand reading and listening.

Zen was more than an influence on the Beat poets of the 1950s such as Jack Kerouac, Allen Ginsberg, and Gary Snyder—it was their inspiration. Again, the beginnings of this trend went back to an earlier generation. William Butler Yeats and Ezra Pound were both strongly influenced by Japanese Noh plays and haiku poetry. These two seminal modernist poets were influenced by Ernest Fenollosa, who, with Pound, translated *Certain Noble Plays of Japan* (1916). Another important influence was Isamu Noguchi's father, the bilingual Japanese poet and critic Yone Noguchi, whose *Spirit of Japanese Poetry* (1914) circulated widely among the literati of England and America. Also the author of the ten-volume *Spirit of Japanese Art* (1915), the elder Noguchi was probably the best-known interpreter of Japanese art to the West between the wars.

In addition to Suzuki and Herrigel, the postwar generation of American artists and writers were inspired by the writings and radio broadcasts of Alan W. Watts, whose perennially popular publications include *The Spirit of Zen: A Way of Life, Work and Art in the Far East* (1936), and *The Way of Zen* (1957). Also popular with artists was Paul Reps's *Zen Flesh, Zen Bones* (1957), an anthology of Zen stories, koans, and Oxherding Pictures that Reps had originally published in the 1930s.

The American Abstract Expressionist painters Jackson Pollock, Franz Kline, and Philip Guston were all influenced by Zen to a greater or lesser degree. Franz Kline, for example, told Katharine Kuh, "I don't decide in advance that I'm going to paint a definite experience, but in the act of painting, it becomes a genuine experience for me."[5] Kline's formula owes a good deal to Herrigel, who in *Zen in the Art of Archery* quoted his Zen master as insisting, "The right art is purposeless, aimless!"[6] This view of creation as an experiential act is usually cited as the link between postwar expressionist painting and Zen, but the connections between the two are more subtle and complex.

Early in 1964 the thirty-four-year-old Jasper Johns was given a retrospective at the Jewish Museum. In the catalog for the show, the museum's director, Alan R. Solomon, wrote:

> For the past seventy-five years a crisis of sensibility has been brewing in modern art, a crisis which, for a number of reasons, has been submerged beneath the level of general awareness until quite recently. . . . Yet the plain fact remains that the issues of sensibility raised by Dada, and subsequently raised again by the new generation of American

> artists, together with the broad reexamination of the meaning of objective reality stimulated by exploration of these issues, challenge all of our basic premises defining the esthetic experience.[7]

Solomon dated the start of this "crisis" to Paul Gauguin, who challenged the "preoccupation with 'observed' phenomena."[8] Solomon credited "a new contemporary attitude" with finally allowing for the recognition of Duchamp's revolutionary role and the emergence of artists such as Robert Rauschenberg and Jasper Johns, who were originally dubbed "Neo-Dadaists" by critics who also understood Duchamp only within an "anti-art" context. It is true that, along with his friend John Cage, Johns was one of those artists who "got" Duchamp. Far from being "anti-art," his own work furthered Duchamp's task of bringing the viewer into the art project as an active participant—Duchamp by demanding that viewers create meanings for the objects he "gave" them, Johns by stimulating their emotions along with their minds through sensuous, evocative combinations of shared and personal symbolism.

But other artists had also been exploring "issues of sensibility." The Japanese American sculptor Isamu Noguchi served as a bridge, linking spatial concepts developed in the American Midwest, where spent his teens; the abstract spirituality of Brancusi, with whom he studied in Paris; and Asian aesthetics and philosophy from China, India, Indonesia, and especially Japan, where he spent his early childhood. The aesthetic richness and emotional poverty of Noguchi's childhood endowed him with a strong sense of the "seen and unseen" (to quote the title of one of his sculptures) and an equally strong social conscience. In a different way from Duchamp, Noguchi brought art into the realm of the everyday with his seamless aesthetic that encompassed children's playgrounds, furniture, and light itself as sculpture.

Working in the medium of painting, Ad Reinhardt adapted Zen practice and Zen language to art practice and art language, eventually producing dramatically reductionist but somehow eventful paintings. Reinhardt's forceful, koanlike writings would prove influential on two generations of artists, from his friend and contemporary Agnes Martin to Vija Celmins. From the mid-1950s until his death in 1967, Reinhardt painted single-color paintings: red, blue, and, finally, black.

The roughly contemporary single-color paintings of the younger French artist Yves Klein, who called himself "Yves le Monochrome," would eventually devolve into literally nothing. If Reinhardt aimed to reduce painting to its absolute fundamentals, to its "end," Klein's goal was nothing short of the destruction of all categories in order to make art a vehicle to the absolute. In this Klein's program was more like that of Duchamp, who spoke of wanting to access a "fourth dimension" and of the artist's role as that of a "mediumistic being."[9] Klein has been labeled a conceptualist, in addition to a number of other things, including "the George M. Koan of French Neo-Dada."[10] What Reinhardt and Klein may have had most in common, in the end, was that they both were influenced by Zen Buddhism in the development of their artistic philosophies, although—like Duchamp—Klein seems to have absorbed a dose of Tibetan Buddhism as well.

Like Reinhardt and Klein, Jasper Johns produced several monochrome paintings in the mid-1950s. Johns's work, which includes sculpture as well as paintings, prints, and drawings, has commonly been understood as linking the "hot" emotional painting of the Abstract Expressionists with the "cool" cerebral work of Pop artists, such as Andy Warhol, who brought recognizable, popular imagery back into American art. As Johns's career has progressed, however, personal content has assumed an ever greater role in his work. At the same time, Tantric Buddhist subject matter has become explicit, suggesting that a Zen Buddhist reading of his earlier work may be helpful to its interpretation. For the artists in this section—Noguchi, Reinhardt, Klein, and Johns—the nondualistic realm in which space and time are one is accessed through sensual engagement with the tangible. In the words of Jasper Johns, "literal works tend to become transcendental. The space of works of Zen seems mutable."

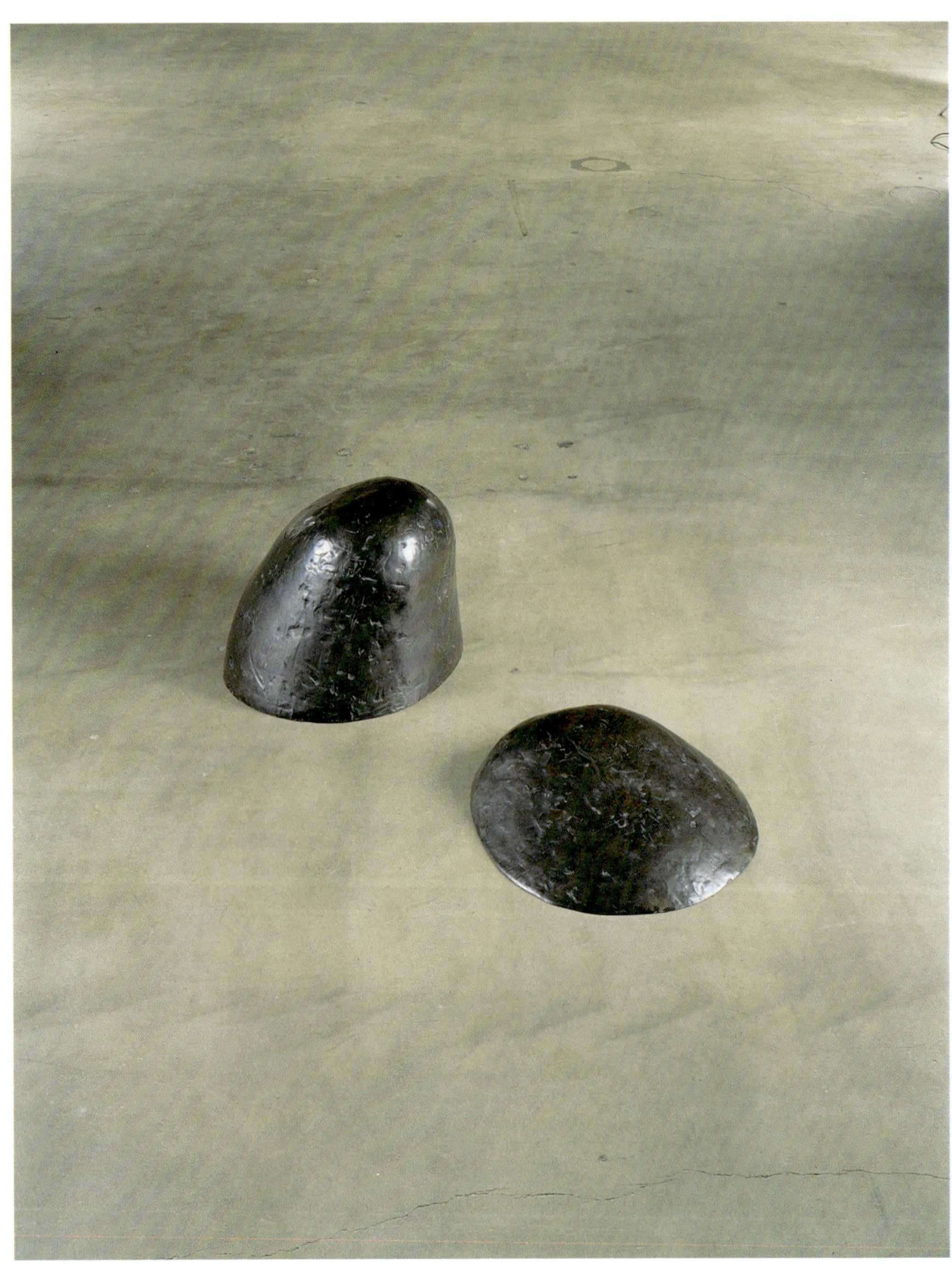

Isamu Noguchi, *Seen and Unseen,* 1962, bronze, 19½ x 27 x 24 and 6½ x 27 x 26 in. (528 A 3/3). Photo: Kevin Noble. Reproduced with the permission of The Noguchi Museum, New York.

I don't think that art comes from art. A lot of artists apparently think so. I think it comes from the awakening person.... Everything tends toward awakening, and I would rather use the word awakening than a word derived from some system—because there are many systems.

ISAMU NOGUCHI, 1987

ISAMU NOGUCHI 1904–1988

THE MODEST CAST-BRONZE TWIN SCULPTURE *Seen and Unseen,* by Isamu Noguchi, seems to emerge from the floor on which it rests. It bears the marks of its making: cast from clay molded by hand (other sculptures from this time show traces of footprints), its surfaces are rough and pitted, like those of stones. Stones are what *Seen and Unseen* calls to mind—the artfully arranged stones of Japanese Zen gardens, which are largely submerged in the earth. Noguchi wrote: "In Japan the rocks in a garden are so planted as to suggest a protuberance from the primordial mass below. . . . We are made aware of this 'floating world' through consciousness of sheer invisible mass."[1] From what is seen, we sense what is unseen.

Noguchi's title for this work contains another, hidden reference. His father was the Japanese art and literary writer Yone (Yonejiro) Noguchi, who began his career as a poet in the California Bay Area at the end of the nineteenth century. The title of his first book of poems, published in San Francisco in 1897, was *Seen and Unseen or, Monologues of a Homeless Snail.* As it happened, the subtitle would fit the lonely, peripatetic son better than the father, who transformed himself from a pathetic exile into a dogmatic nationalist after returning to Japan in the year of Isamu's birth. The irony would not have been lost on his son, who wrote in his autobiography, published in 1968: "I notice how themes stated long ago recur in various guises. Discontinuity I see in all its aspects. In gardens it is with rocks, the continuity is implied underground, an effect sought also in bronze with *Seen and Unseen.*"[2]

Indeed, the two elements of *Seen and Unseen* are perhaps better described, not as twins, but as father and son. (One is, in fact, notably larger than the other.) Throughout his life, Isamu Noguchi sought to mine the buried veins of continuity and connection with his father and with Japan, where he spent his childhood. From his mentor Brancusi, Noguchi may have heard the aphorism "When we are no longer children, we are already dead," although Noguchi put it slightly differently: "Who is no longer a child is no longer an artist."[3]

Born in Los Angeles after his father had left for Europe and then Japan, Isamu Noguchi and his American mother, Léonie Gilmour, did not join his father until Isamu was two. Yone proved to be a self-involved soul. His own autobiography, published when Isamu was ten, contains a chapter entitled "Isamu's Arrival in Japan." It paints a painful picture:

> Isamu noticed that I clapped my hands to call my servant girls, and they would answer my clapping with "Hai!"—that is the way of a Japanese house. And he thought to himself, of course to my delight, that it was proper for him to answer "Hai" to my handclapping, and he began to run toward me before the girls, and kneel before me as they did, and wait for my words.[4]

Yone had taken a Japanese "wife," with whom he eventually had nine children. (He married her formally in 1913.) Yone dedicated his autobiography not to his eldest son, but to the eldest of his Japanese children: "to Hifumi, my daughter six years old." Isamu's few memories of this time were "not happy":

> In the garden were two large cherry trees, and surrounding it was a high bamboo fence over which I could peer when riding the maid's back. The cherry blossoms came and then the wind that scattered them over the ground, so sadly. Not far from the house I came to know a playground, or open space, that filled me with foreboding.[5]

Isamu did not see much of his father. Yone did make an ineffectual attempt to prevent Isamu's mother from sending her son off alone, at age thirteen, to an experimental school in Rolling Prairie, Indiana. As Isamu described it:

> At this crucial moment I was again made aware of my father, whom I had not seen in many years. He came to the boat to try to stop my going. For my part, there wasn't much choice. I was to be an American, banished as my mother had decided.[6]

The experimental school fell victim to the First World War before Sam Gilmour—Isamu's new, midwestern identity—could receive its benefits. A children's camp in the summer, by fall 1918 it became a military training camp.

> While all the other children went home, I was left alone to watch soldiers, trucks, mess halls and barracks take over the grounds. I became a sort of mascot. Then there was the

> Armistice. Winter came, and I had no place to go, since my mother could not afford to send me elsewhere. Nobody seemed to be in charge of me.[7]

Fifty years later, the grown-up castoff would rhetorically ask, "Is fortune or misfortune the better teacher?"[8]

Thereafter, Isamu was more fortunate in his teachers. The following summer the school's founder, Dr. Edward A. Rumley, learned of his plight and placed him with the family of a homeopath turned Swedenborgian minister in La Porte, Indiana. Isamu finished high school while earning his keep by mowing lawns in the summer, tending furnaces in the winter, and delivering papers year-round. During this time, "I constantly worried about my mother in Japan and developed a moral loathing for my father."[9] By the time his mother finally returned to the United States in 1923, Isamu was attending Columbia as a premedical student, thanks to Dr. Rumley. "If she had thought to break my dependence in sending me away, my own reaction had been to feel deserted. My extreme attachment never returned, and now the more motherly she became, the more I resented her."[10] Isamu linked his taking the name Noguchi around this time to his resentment, as well as to the support of Hideyo Noguchi, another kindly doctor, who urged him to fulfill his dream of becoming an artist, "as my father was."

> There was no hint of Japan about me. Yet when I finally became conscious that I was to be a sculptor, I decided almost involuntarily to change my name, adopting one that perhaps I had no right to. I could see my mother's consternation, but she did not object, helping me rather in my travail, away from her, toward Japan, and the way that I had chosen.[11]

Three years later, he applied for a Guggenheim fellowship to support three years of study and travel in Paris, India, China, and Japan. This itinerary may have been inspired by reading Kakuzo Okakura, whose *Ideals of the East* emphasized the development of Asian culture from India through China to Japan. In his Guggenheim application Noguchi stated what would be his lifelong goal: "My father, Yone Noguchi, is Japanese and has long been known as an interpreter of the East to the West, through poetry. I wish to do the same with sculpture."[12]

In Paris, Noguchi worked for a time as an assistant to Brancusi, who taught him the art of carving stone (he had learned woodworking in Japan as a child), gave him the courage to create abstract sculpture, and reinforced his attitude regarding the continuum of man and nature. (Noguchi had begun his Guggenheim application: "It is my desire to view nature through nature's eyes, and to ignore man as an object for special veneration."[13]) Brancusi taught him something else—focus: "The one thing Brancusi could not stand was lack of absolute concentration. . . . I could understand his saying that if I were not at one with the work, do something else, but don't try to be a sculptor."[14]

Quickly settling into a studio of his own, Noguchi thrived in the rich artistic climate of Paris in the twenties. In preparation for his promised travels to India and East Asia, he spent a month in London, reading up on "Oriental matters" at the library of the British Museum.[15] But he found himself unable to leave Paris, and his fellowship was not renewed. Returning to New York in 1928, he reluctantly abandoned abstraction in order to raise funds by selling his work, primarily portrait heads: "The pursuit of art based on reflective leisure had now to be superseded by application to a job. . . . By Spring [1929] I had finally managed to acquire the means to pursue my repeatedly interrupted trip to the Orient, and self discovery."[16] He again started out in Paris, where, in another heartbreaking rejection, he received a letter from his father asking him not to come to Japan bearing the name of Noguchi. None of Isamu's efforts to gain recognition as an international artist his father could be proud of counted in the face of this stubborn insularism. (Yone would blame the potential upset of his Japanese wife, about to give birth to another child.) Isamu changed his plans and spent eight months in China, where he developed his skill in brush painting.

His money almost gone, Isamu finally traveled to Tokyo in 1931. There, he was given a house to live in by his kindly uncle Totaro Takagi, of whom he made a sensitive, realist portrait head in the Zen tradition. Although his father did visit him ("we would hold long silent conversations"), Isamu's painfully mixed emotions caused him to flee (his word) from Tokyo to Kyoto, where he learned to work in clay.[17]

> I was all alone. I had a potter I went to, I did things in ceramics. But I was also exposed to all these [Zen] gardens and a way of life which was then very somnolent. Nobody ever went there. Everything was full of dust. But there I perceived an art which was beyond art objects. It's the way of life, you might say.[18]

Isamu Noguchi would not return to Japan for twenty years, until after the end of World War II and the death of his father. In the 1930s he became close friends with the utopian engineer Buckminster Fuller, collaborated with the dancer Martha Graham, and, in the spirit of the time, committed himself to the social uses of art. He even traveled to Mexico, where he created a three-dimensional, antifascist mural in a public market entitled *History as Seen from Mexico in 1936*.[19] Strongly influenced by the Zen gardens he had experienced in Kyoto, Noguchi became a pioneer in the concept of sculpture as space that connects. "By sculpture," he wrote, "we mean those plastic and spatial relationships which define a moment of personal existence and illuminate the environment of our existence."[20]

Noguchi meant "illuminate" literally as well as figuratively. By 1933 he was beginning to incorporate light into his sculpture *(Musical Weathervane)*, and ten years later he made his first "Lunar" illuminated sculpture. After his 1950–52 stay in Japan, Noguchi would invest considerable aesthetic energy in developing and marketing his *akari*—sculptural paper

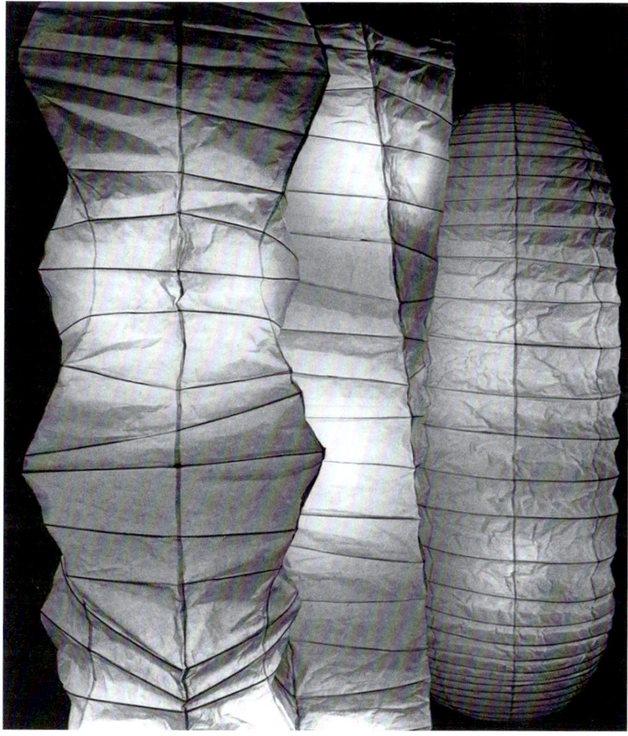

Group of *akari* light sculptures designed by Isamu Noguchi. From left to right: models 33N, J1, and 32N. Photo © Michio Noguchi. Reproduced with the permission of The Noguchi Museum, New York.

lanterns intended for sale to a broad public. "The ideal of *akari,*" he wrote, "is exemplified with lightness (as essence) and light (for awareness)." He stressed their impermanence: "the quality is poetic, ephemeral, and tentative."[21] The *akari* also represented a connection with Noguchi's father. Though he doesn't give the title, the one poem by Yone that Isamu quotes in his autobiography is "Like a Paper Lantern." Its last four lines read:

> To the Eastward, to the Westward? Alas,
> Where is Truthfulness?—Goodness?—Light?
> The world enveils me; my body itself this night enveils my soul.
> Alas, my soul is like a paper lantern in the rainy world.[22]

Again, the father's lines describe the son's experience. At the end of the 1930s, Noguchi's idealism was seriously challenged. He was denied participation in the Works Progress Administration projects on the grounds that, as a successful portrait artist, he didn't need the money. He believed, however, that it was because he was not considered American enough. The Japanese attack on Pearl Harbor brought this painful issue into the foreground. Noguchi worked to counter negative stereotypes of his fellow Japanese Americans in the press and committed himself voluntarily to the relocation camp at Poston, Arizona. (Although he was in California at the time, he was officially a New Yorker and thus not subject to the evacuation order.) He hoped, with the support of a friend in the government, to be able to design and develop recreation areas at Poston.

> It soon became apparent, however, that the purpose of the War Relocation Authority was hopelessly at odds with that ideal. . . . They wanted nothing permanent or even pleasant. My presence became pointless . . . it took me seven months to get out and then on a temporary basis. So far as I know, I am still only temporarily at large.[23]

By the end of the war, Noguchi was doing work about the "enclosure of space" and impermanence: "Like cherry blossoms, perfection could only be transient—a fragile beauty is more poignant."[24] The American bombing of Hiroshima in August 1945 emphasized just how fragile we are. His father wrote him from Tokyo, "Takagi, my elder brother whom you lived with while in Japan, passed away under the noise of fire. . . . If you come to Japan again, you will see her in an entirely different aspect. I am getting old and feel so sad and awful with what happened in Japan."[25] Isamu later wrote of this time: "The winds of the imagination by now blew on me with force from the East."[26] His father died in 1947, and his close friend Arshile Gorky killed himself the following year. "My depression was increased by the ever-present menace of atomic annihilation."[27]

In 1949 Noguchi applied for and received a grant from the Bollingen Foundation for a traveling fellowship "to prepare material for a book on leisure (which allows for meditation on the meaning of form in relation to man and space)."[28] Critics have been confused by Noguchi's use of the seemingly frivolous word "leisure" in this context, tending to ignore it in favor of his parenthetical statement regarding the meaning of form. But Noguchi's concept of an "art based on reflective leisure"[29] was probably suggested to him by *Tsurezuregusa,* a popular collection of essays written during the second quarter of the 1300s by Yoshida Kenko, a court official turned Buddhist monk. This work was first translated into English by Ryukichi Kurata in 1931 under the title *The Harvest of Leisure.* Kenko's opening statement reads:

> My life is not one of occupation; it is a life of leisure. Everyday is like the day that went before. My ink-dish lies before me. My heart is like a mirror—all the world is reflected in it. I write as I see, and it may seem strange and mad enough, for I think of strangely mingled things.[30]

Although Noguchi's formal proposal to the Bollingen Foundation stressed the social aspects of his research, he did say that "special attention will be given to the contemplative uses of leisure (for the re-creation of the mind)."[31]

In his introduction to *The Harvest of Leisure,* L. Adams Beck wrote that Kenko's meditations were "the natural effusion of a heart sufficiently at leisure from itself to contemplate mankind with serene impartiality" and that "in retiring from the world he . . . chose a little lonely house in the wilds of Arashiyama far enough away from the imperial bustle of Kyoto."[32] Noguchi, after traveling in Europe, Egypt, India, Cambodia, Bali, Java, and finally Japan, settled down in 1951–52 in a little two-hundred-year-old farmhouse in Kamakura, from which he wrote:

> Here in the hillside at the edge of ricefields have been spent the days of this year—a segment of Japan. The changing seasons have now made one round—each day a wonder of discovery to me, so intimate is nature here. . . . Whatever quality my work now has is I hope that of nature—that is to say the result of our communion. . . . There has I trust been a minimum of the imposition of will and thought. The medium which is the earth itself has its own way—and the fires of the kilns burn away my petty prides.[33]

When he had first arrived in postwar Japan, Noguchi had been deluged with distracting attention from fellow artists. Because he was not fluent in Japanese (despite having lived in Japan between the ages of two and thirteen), he asked the abstract painter Saburo Hasegawa to travel with him and help him "re-experience the beauty of ancient temples and gardens, and to imbibe the tranquillity of Zen."[34] Hasegawa was the perfect choice—around 1940 he himself had retreated to a remote farm to practice Zen Buddhism and study Taoist and Zen classics. Hasegawa described how hard Noguchi studied Zen at this time, including rereading D. T. Suzuki's *Introduction to Zen Buddhism*. Later, around 1960, on a train from Kyoto to Tokyo, Noguchi had the opportunity to discuss contemporary Zen forms of expression with Suzuki himself. The conversation seems to have stimulated Noguchi's insecurity regarding his identity:

> I had said that in the West the ideal was to triumph over gravity, and that in doing a rock garden in America it would be logical to have the rocks themselves levitate (as I was then doing in the Chase Manhattan Garden). He replied, "Ah, that is why they will eventually have to come back to us." Did he include me in "us"?[35]

When Noguchi returned to Tokyo in 1950, he was asked to help design a memorial room and garden in honor of his father for the university where his father had taught for forty years. *Mu*—Japanese for "nothingness"—was the sculpture Noguchi created for the garden in memory of his father. This piece is essentially a three-dimensional *enso* ("circle," see p. 61). Its title refers to the solution to a famous Zen koan that is often the first koan given to Zen students. Asked whether a dog has Buddha-nature, the master Chao-chou answered, "*Mu*" ("It does not"), which might mean "no," or it might mean "nothingness"—in other words, "yes."

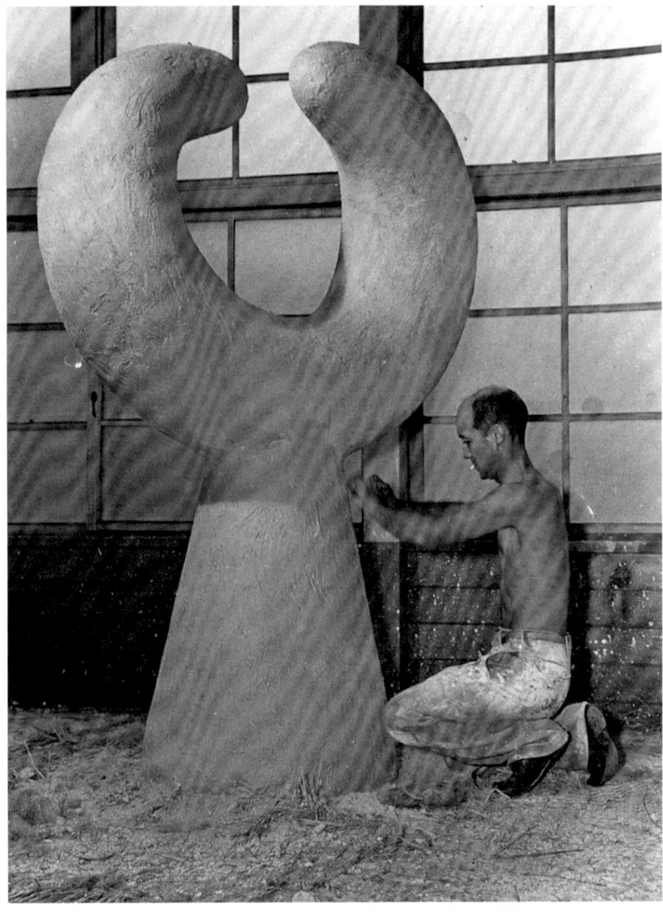

Isamu Noguchi at work on *Mu* for the garden Shin Banraisha, Keio University, Tokyo, 1952, cast stone, about 8 ft. high. Photo: Michio Noguchi. Reproduced with the permission of The Noguchi Museum, New York.

Publicly, Noguchi dismissed the significance of his title, describing the work as a "sculpture like the circle made by thumb and index finger, which I inadvertently called *Mu,* meaning nothingness, a Zen term well-known in Japan, but provoking innumerable wisecracks and cartoons."[36] His description evokes the Buddhist *vitarka* ("teaching") *mudra* in which the thumb and first finger form a circle, symbolizing emptiness—an apt reference for a memorial to a father who was a teacher. On the one hand, Noguchi was a proselytizer only for art, and had no ambition to educate the public about Zen Buddhism. On the other hand, his response was very Zen. As D. T. Suzuki wrote in the book Noguchi read:

> To reach the goal of Zen, even the idea of "having nothing" ought to be done away with. Buddha reveals himself when he is not more asserted; that is, for Buddha's sake Buddha is to be given up. This is the only way to come to the realization of the truth of Zen. So long as one is talking of nothingness or of the absolute one is far away from Zen, and ever receding from Zen.[37]

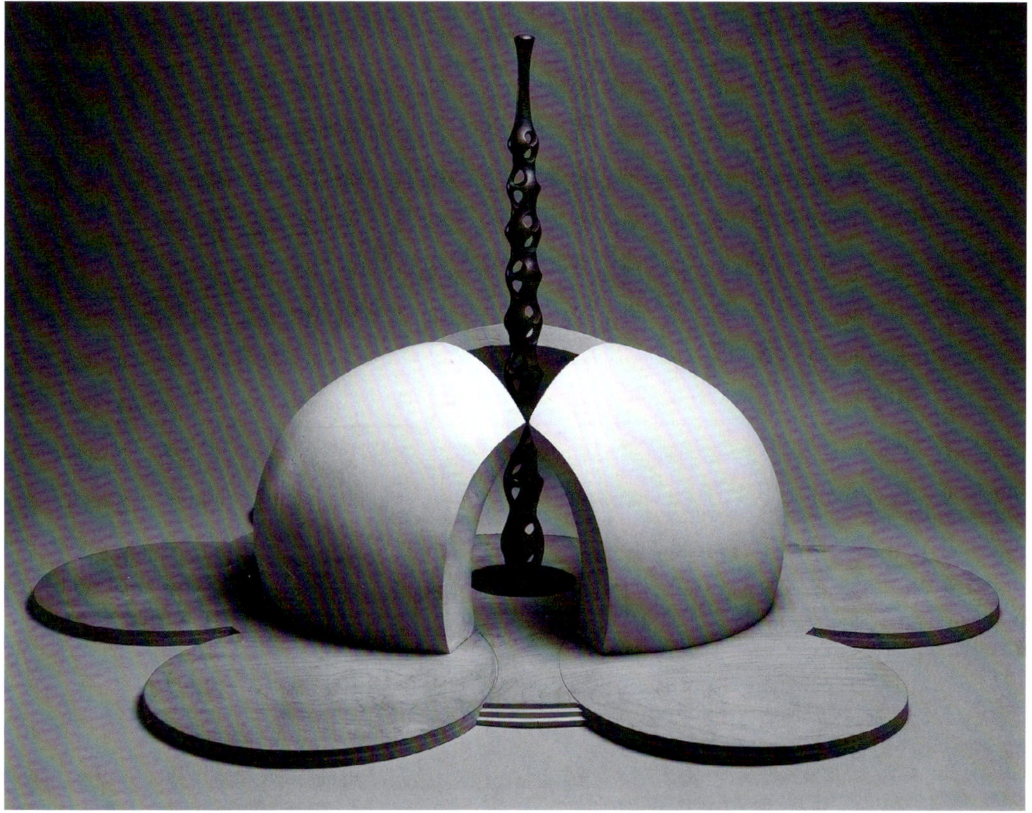

Isamu Noguchi, *Study for a Memorial to Buddha,* 1957, plaster model. Photo: Kevin Noble. Reproduced with the permission of The Noguchi Museum, New York.

An explicit link to Buddhism in Noguchi's work came in 1957, when he was asked to join a group of young Japanese architects in submitting a proposal for a memorial in New Delhi, commemorating the twenty-five-hundredth anniversary of the death, or *parinirvana,* of the Buddha. Noguchi had already given some thought to this subject, as several years earlier UNESCO had inquired if he would be interested in helping to design a park in Lumbini, Nepal, the birthplace of the Buddha. Noguchi had even stopped there on his way to Japan, so he "entered this competition with the wonderful memory of Nepal in my mind."[38]

The team chose the lotus flower as their motif. In their entry application Noguchi wrote, "In the blossom so closely related in significance to the teachings of the Buddha, we found the theme of recurrent change and rebirth. We came to realize it was not only the birth of Buddhism that we wished to celebrate, but the significance of universal birth and awakening."[39] The proposal was rejected. Their design, with its proposed seventy-foot-high cast-bronze "nine-bulbed spire, somewhat like the lotus root," would have been expensive and,

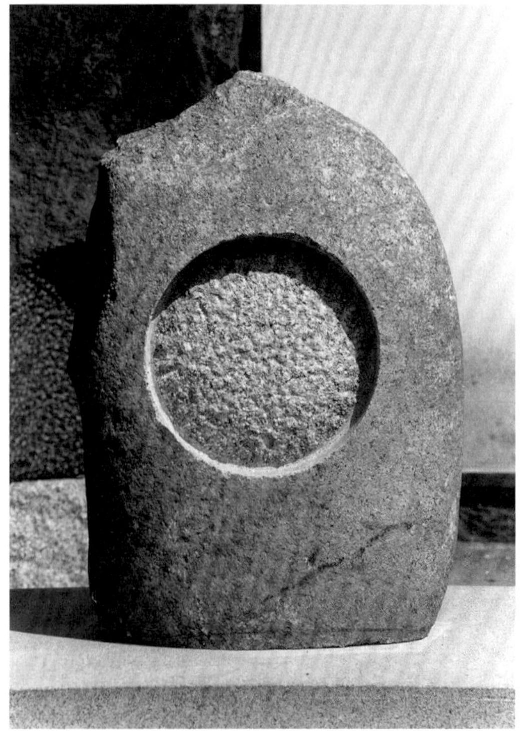

Isamu Noguchi, *Ojizousama (Circle Stone)*, 1980, andesite, 19 x 13 x 5 in. Reproduced with the permission of The Noguchi Museum, New York.

in truth, a bit ungainly: Brancusi's *Endless Column* meets Buckminster Fuller's geodesic dome. Noguchi's response reveals his antireligious, humanist bias: "Failure to have our design chosen only leaves me more convinced that such a monument should be built to mark the Buddha's holy birth rather than the birth of his religion."[40] Buddhism as a religion was born when the Buddha died. Noguchi seems to be saying we should honor the spirit of the person, not the "ism." (He may also have been hinting that UNESCO should build that park in Lumbini.)

In the last decade of his life Noguchi made *Ojizousama,* a nineteen-inch, slightly vertical stone with a circle carved in its middle. When the former relocation camp internee represented the United States at the 1986 Venice Biennale, he showed *Ojizousama* in an exhibition entitled "What Is Sculpture?" Noguchi had the piece photographed in two versions—one with, one without a little red bib like the ones that in Japan commonly adorn figures of Ojizousama—Jizo, for short.

The bodhisattva Jizo is the compassionate protector of the dead, especially children, and of travelers. His Sanskrit name, Kshitigarbha, means "womb of the earth"—Noguchi would have liked that. Jizo's stone form, which can be as simple as a barely carved rock, appears along Japanese roads, at intersections, in mountain passes, and at the entrance to graveyards. The circle carved into Noguchi's Jizo could be a reference to the womb or to the wish-granting jewel that is his attribute. It is also another *enso,* resonant with *Mu,* nothingness. *Ojizousama* may have been Noguchi's gesture of gratitude for "the luck that attends little boys,"[41] as he characterized his lonely journey from Japan to northern Indiana some sixty years before. It may also have been an offering to help him on the journey he would shortly undertake.

In his life and work Isamu Noguchi incorporated contrasting realms—Japan and the United States, the traditional and the new, the changeless and the transient, the Zen garden and Buckminster Fuller. The teachings of the Buddha provided a way, not to integrate these oppositions, but to allow the extremes of life as he experienced it to coexist in his mind and in his art:

> Sculpture in the traditional sense is, by definition, something with built-in values of permanence. . . . But then there is the other reality of the evanescent new—that truth born of the moment. Cherry blossoms in old Japan, or one jump ahead of obsolescence in the modern. I have thought of this, too, as sculpture. . . . We all look to the past and to the future to find ourselves. Here we find a hint that awakens us, there a path that someone like us once walked.[42]

Ad Reinhardt, *Abstract Painting No. 5,* 1962, oil on canvas, 60 x 60 in. Tate Gallery, London. Photo: Tate Gallery, London/Art Resource, NY. Artist © 2005 Estate of Ad Reinhardt/Artists Rights Society (ARS), New York.

The one standard in art is oneness and fineness, rightness and purity, abstractness and evanescence. The one thing to say about art is its breathlesssness, lifelessness, deathlessness, contentlessness, formlessness, spacelessness, and timelessness. This is always the end of art.

AD REINHARDT, 1962

AD REINHARDT 1913–1967

PACKED INTO THE ABOVE CONCLUSION TO HIS frequently quoted essay "Art-as-Art" is Ad Reinhardt's radical Zen perspective. The "one" thing to say about art, which in the opening sentence of this essay is simply "that it is one thing," turns out to be quite a bit more than that. By the end of the essay, it has become a litany: "breathlessness, lifelessness, deathlessness, contentlessness, formlessness, spacelessness, and timelessness"—all words for emptiness. To understand Reinhardt's esoteric brand of Zen is to understand that there is no contradiction between one thing and many things or, more accurately, many not-things.

The critic Lawrence Alloway said he once wrote Ad Reinhardt how much he liked an "exuberant list of denials" Reinhardt had published about some works he had done in the Virgin Islands. Reinhardt had claimed that these abstract paintings "contain no sea shells or undersea caves, no blinding sand or wild winds or superstitions, no terror of the deep, no west-Indian magic, nor zombies, no sea-urchins. There is in them no trace or taste of lobster or turtle, mango or mongoose, no rum or coca-cola, no bamboo or barracuda or outboard motor [and so on]." Reinhardt wrote back to Alloway, "Yes, but the funny thing was they were in the paintings."[1] It is helpful to know that Ad Reinhardt once defined nirvana as: "one-ness, nothingness, all-in-one, nothing."[2]

Reinhardt was often described as monklike; indeed, the critic Harold Rosenberg dubbed him the "black monk" of Abstract Expressionism.[3] But he was no mystic. He was austere and moralistic intellectually as well as artistically, which is perhaps why the humor in his mordant writings tends to be missed now that Reinhardt the person is gone. He published numerous, increasingly impassioned diatribes on behalf of abstraction and artistic integrity, and his scathing cartoons satirized the art world so incisively that they were sometimes interpreted as straightforward analyses. One, entitled "A Portend of the Artist as a Yhung Mandala," manages to poke fun simultaneously at the art world, at religious/cosmic symbolism, at Jung ("Yhung"), and at the hyper-classification of Tantric Buddhism. Reinhardt even developed his own, tongue-in-cheek "Chronology" of his life for the catalog to his 1966 Jewish Museum retrospective.[4]

In his chronology Reinhardt begins in 1913 with: "Born, New York, Christmas Eve, nine months after Armory Show." Conceived during the Armory Show—which is generally agreed to mark the advent of modern art in the United States—and born on Christmas Eve (in Buffalo, but this detail didn't fit the program), Ad Reinhardt was the self-appointed savior of "pure" art during a century in which the United States achieved imperial ambitions in the realms of both global politics and art. He was active as an artist in antiwar and civil rights protests. As an undergraduate at Columbia College in the early thirties, Reinhardt studied with the great historian of modern art Meyer Schapiro. John Dewey and Ananda Coomeraswamy, the influential historian of Asian art and religion, were also on the faculty at the time. Reinhardt studied painting at the American Artists School in 1936–37 and was a member of the American Abstract Artists group from 1937 to 1947. He returned to school for a master's degree in Asian art history at New York University's Institute of Fine Arts from 1946 to 1951, and taught both design and art history at Brooklyn College from 1947 until his death twenty years later. The only mention of anything like a personal life in his chronology is for the year 1949, where he notes, cryptically: "Paints water colors in Virgin Islands waiting for divorce."[5]

For 1960 he notes only: "Writes about Buddha images";[6] the entry, however, is printed in boldface type. The article to which he refers, "Timeless in Asia," published in *Art News*, was a disguised diatribe against the "unconscious" spontaneity of Abstract Expressionism: "Nowhere in world art has it been clearer than in Asia that anything irrational, momentary, spontaneous, unconscious, primitive, expressionistic, accidental or informal, cannot be called serious art. Only blankness, complete awareness, disinterestedness."[7] Reinhardt emphasized that Buddha images are made according to preordained rules: "In Asia, all sculptures are diagrams, conventionalized schemes. . . . Standard forms and identical patterns are repeated and refined for centuries. The intensity, consciousness and perfection of Asiatic art comes only from repetitiousness and sameness."[8] It was no coincidence that in this way these ancient sculptures of the Buddha were exactly like contemporary paintings by Ad Reinhardt. Reinhardt was a passionate believer in the end of art, in both senses of that word: art as

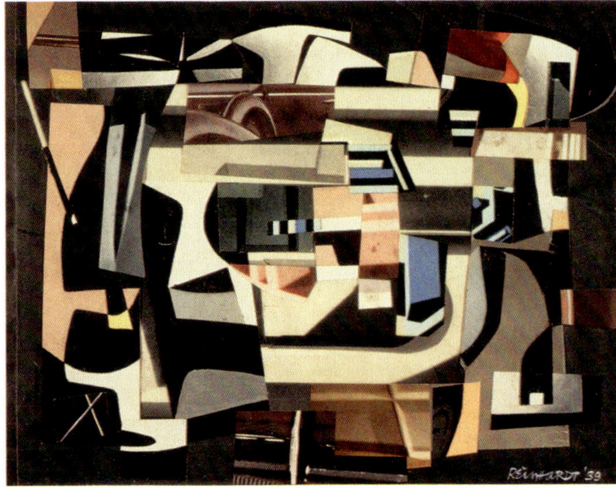

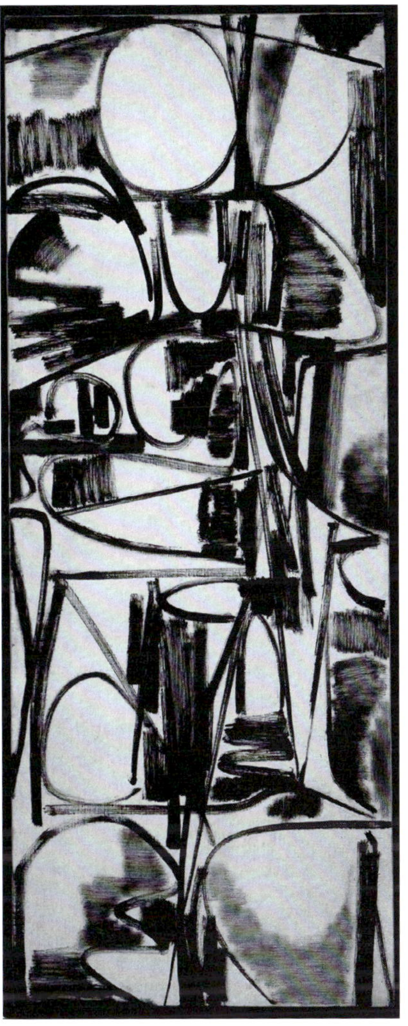

(above) Ad Reinhardt, *Collage,* 1939, paper collage on board, 7⅛ x 9¼ in. Collection of David and Vicki Cox, San Francisco. Artist © 2005 Estate of Ad Reinhardt/Artists Rights Society (ARS), New York.

(right) Ad Reinhardt, *Calligraphic Painting,* 1949–50, oil on canvas, 50 x 20 in. Private collection, Switzerland. Photo © 2005 Malcom Varon, New York. Artist © 2005 Estate of Ad Reinhardt/Artists Rights Society (ARS), New York

meditative practice and as outside of time. "In such a framework," he noted, "where all artists work within the same traditions, the possibility of achieving true originality exists."[9]

Ad Reinhardt eschewed the ego expression of Jackson Pollock and Franz Kline in favor of a patient pursuit of the experience of emptiness in art. Over the course of the 1940s and 1950s he gradually eliminated imagery of any kind, eventually reducing his surfaces to broad swaths of subtly varied tones of a single color that, by 1960, darkened to no color at all. Around 1940 he had abandoned Cubist-influenced abstraction in favor of the overall pattern of collage, and by the late 1940s he was creating black-and-white "calligraphic" paintings and luminous "brick" paintings. His shapes gradually became larger and more contingent until he achieved the brilliant variations on a single color exemplified by *Red Painting* of 1952. For the next four years, Reinhardt focused on two colors: red and blue. In 1955–56 he began

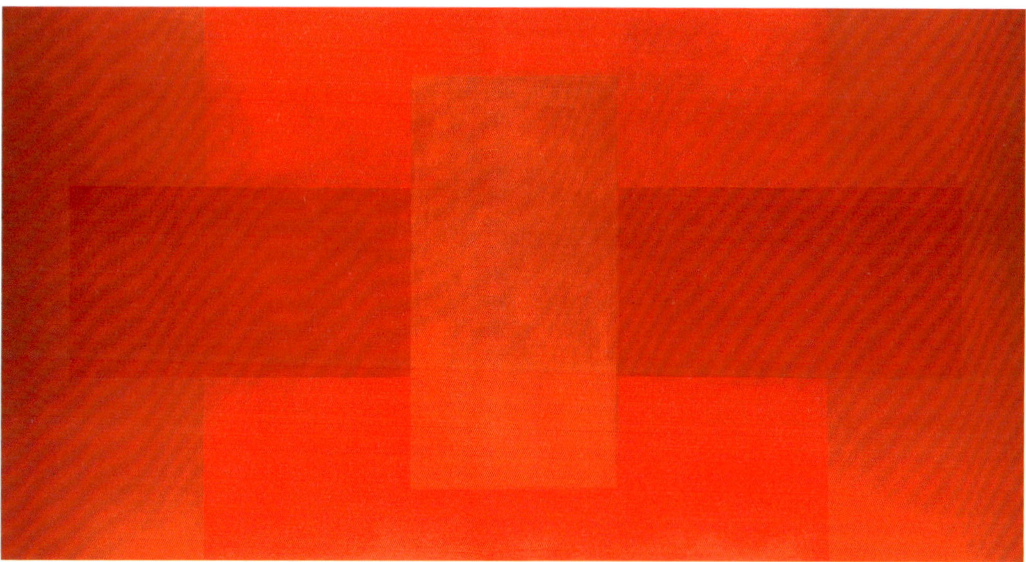

Ad Reinhardt, *Red Painting*, 1952, oil on canvas, 78 x 144 in. The Metropolitan Museum of Art, Arthur Hoppock Hearn Fund, 1968 (68.85). Photo © 1979 The Metropolitan Museum of Art. Artist © 2005 Estate of Ad Reinhardt / Artists Rights Society (ARS), New York.

to darken his colors dramatically, first in vertical canvases and then in five-foot-square paintings bearing nine black squares arranged in a symmetrical cross or mandala shape. "Five feet wide," he was quoted as saying, "just the width of a man's reach."[10]

His statement pointedly relates these apparently austere paintings to the human body. In Buddhism, all things are relative. This is even—perhaps especially—true of black, which is composed of colors that almost cancel each other out. About Reinhardt's Black Paintings, the art historian and critic Yve-Alain Bois wrote: "Only Reinhardt could almost suppress almostness."[11] The subtle images of these five-by-five-foot canvases are revealed only by the angle of light across his strokes of black paint. Reinhardt had finally achieved the goal described in a passage he copied to his notes from the Chinese self-help manual *The Secret of the Golden Flower*: "When purpose has been used to achieve purposelessness, then the thing has been grasped."[12]

For Ad Reinhardt, who was not only a painter but a historian of Asian art, the end of art was also its beginning. His mind took naturally to the kind of intellectual oxymorons favored both in Taoism and in Zen Buddhism, which he knew not only through his own study but also from his lifelong friendship with the spiritual writer Thomas Merton. An "Autointerview" from *Art News* is a straight-out parody, for those in the Zen "no," of the story of the Ch'an master Jui-yen Shih-yen, who every morning called out to himself, "Master!" and answered, "Yes?" He would ask himself, "Are you awake?" and answer, "Yes!"—telling himself, "Don't let yourself be deceived by others," and replying, "No! No!" Reinhardt's 1965 art-world version goes like this:

> "You were a vanguard pre-abstract-expressionist in the late thirties, a vanguard abstract-impressionist in the middle forties and a vanguard post-abstract-expressionist in the early fifties, weren't you?" I asked.
>
> "Yes," he said.
>
> "You were the first painter to get rid of vanguardism, weren't you?" I asked.
>
> "Yes," he said.
>
> "Is this the bench you paint on, these the bottles you mix paints in, these the brushes you paint with?" I asked.
>
> "Yes," he said. . . .
>
> "There's nothing else to say?" I asked.
>
> "No," he said.[13]

Reinhardt was temperamentally drawn to Zen's spirit of iconoclasm, conveyed by the admonition: "If you encounter the Buddha, kill him."[14] His own take on the "worth" of art is apparent in the first of "Seven Quotes" he offered to readers of the short-lived art journal *It Is:*

> HIT SEMES THAT THIS OFFRYNE YMAGES IS A SOTILE CAST OF ANTICHRISTE AND HIS CLERK—is for to draw almes fro pore men . . . certis, these ymages of hemselfe may do nouther gode nor yvel to mennis soules, but thai myghtten warme a man's body in colde, if thai were sette upon a fire.[15]

A bit of translation seems called for. The quote, allegedly from "England, 1389," refers to the worth of devotional images. They may not have much effect on the state of the soul of someone purchasing them, but they would surely warm the body if burned. Reinhardt is using the quote to comment on the usefulness of imagery in art. His message is identical to that of a Zen parable, related by Alan Watts in his book *The Spirit of Zen*. The Ch'an master Tan-hsia was reprimanded by the keeper of a temple in which he had spent a cold night for burning a wooden sculpture of the Buddha to warm himself.

> Tan-hsia merely scratched about among the ashes, remarking, "I am gathering the holy relics from the burnt ashes." "How," asked the keeper, "can you get holy relics from a wooden Buddha?" "If there are no holy relics," replied Tan-hsia, "this is certainly not a Buddha and I am committing no sacrilege. May I have the two remaining Buddhas for my fire?"[16]

Typically, Reinhardt's insistence on the location of artistic value outside of the physical object stresses the negative—ill-gotten profit from the sale of images. On the subject of the commercial success of his colleagues, Reinhardt could be scathing:

> It is not right for artists to act as if "abstraction" and "representation" do not make a difference. Artists who do not remember Clive Bell's sentence . . . that "every sacrifice made to representation is something stolen from art," and who paint "abstract-expressionist" flames, girders, grasses, and sunsets, should be apprehended for fencing hot merchandise.[17]

Reinhardt's affinities with Zen, however, extend beyond overt iconoclasm to touch on the nature of consciousness. Many commentators have written about the apparent incongruity of light becoming an active presence within the dark surfaces of Reinhardt's Black Paintings. All agree that this phenomenon has something to do with the element of time—time spent absorbing and being absorbed by the surface of a Reinhardt painting. The subtle geometry of these paintings, almost invisible within the bottomless darkness of their surfaces, cannot be conveyed in a reproduction. Their reticence belies the heartfelt responses they elicit from patient viewers. The art editor Thomas Hess, for example, wrote, "The Black squares have a flicker to them, not an after-image—because the flicker is there, in front of you, in the paint—but a kind of tangible resonance."[18] Yve-Alain Bois claimed that Reinhardt "reduces the spectator to the sole organ of his or her vision. . . . What one then perceives, in the blackest of the 'black' paintings, is no longer the infinitesimal variation of color, but the always fleeting, always dubitable, beginning, the promise of a speck of light, the 'last vestige of brightness.'"[19] The painter John Zurier once described to me the seemingly opposite effect—a sense of corporeality, of bodily being—as the sensation engendered by encounters with Reinhardt's Black Paintings.

In 1966, one year before his death, the Jewish Museum in New York presented a retrospective of Reinhardt's work that focused on these last paintings. In his preface to the exhibition catalog the museum's director, Sam Hunter, commented:

> Reinhardt's implacable icons involve the artist and observer in an "action," no matter how distilled or recessive its visible evidence. . . . By means of the element of duration—the enforced acclimatization of the observer to refined contrasts which operate slowly in time on mind and eye—by the introduction of perceptual problems and choices among shifting formal configurations within an open-end symmetrical system, Reinhardt creates an ambiguous rather than an absolute order. . . . The subliminal dynamism of Reinhardt's severe ascetic orders links them to sensation, and through sensation to the idea of the work of art not as a contained and perfect classical system, but as a moment in a process of consciousness.[20]

Although some critics have described these paintings as Minimalist, as primarily intellectual and conceptual, they are the product of an artist who was of the generation of the Abstract Expressionists, and they more properly belong with this earlier movement. Hunter identifies why: as with Zen, their emphasis is on experience, "a moment in a process of consciousness."

In 1957, in *Art News,* Ad Reinhardt published his influential "Twelve Rules for a New Academy." It is hard to know whether Reinhardt's attraction to Buddhism was the cause or the effect of his fondness for lists, but his "Six Traditions to Be Studied," "Six General Canons or the Six Noes to Be Memorized," and "The Twelve Technical Rules (or How to Achieve the Twelve Things to Avoid)" poke fun at Buddhism's Three Refuges, Four Noble Truths, Five Precepts, and Eightfold Path as unsubtly as his "Portend of the Artist as a Yhung Mandala" poked fun at Tantric Buddhism. His "Twelve Rules" are surely modeled on Buddhism's Twelve Links of Dependent Origination, a list of interrelated phenomena in the cycle of life, each of which gives rise to the next, and the lack of understanding of which leads to suffering. The connection with the Heart Sutra and its repeated "nos" is equally clear. Reinhardt's recipe boils down to:

1. No texture
2. No brushwork or calligraphy
3. No sketching or drawing
4. No forms
5. No design
6. No colors
7. No light
8. No space
9. No time
10. No size or scale
11. No movement
12. No object, no subject, no matter. No symbols, images, or signs. Neither pleasure nor paint.[21]

Neither pleasure nor pain. "The fine artist," Reinhardt wrote in his penultimate sentence, "should have a fine mind, 'free of all passion, ill-will and delusion.'" This could have been written by a Zen literati brush painter. But Reinhardt would not have disagreed with Noguchi's assertion that Zen "is no means to ends other than its own." Reinhardt's Zen was the esoteric form, which renounces all goals and all identity, even as Buddhism. For Ad Reinhardt, art was not a practice leading to enlightenment; art *is* enlightenment.

Yves Klein, *Blue Monochrome (IKB 42),* 1960, pigment, resin on fabric on board, 78⅜ x 60¼ in. The Menil Collection, Houston (80–13 DJ). Photo: Hickey-Robertson, Houston. Artist © 2005 Artists Rights Society (ARS), New York/ADAGP, Paris.

I am the painter of space. I am not an abstract painter, but on the contrary a representational one, a Realist.

YVES KLEIN

YVES KLEIN 1928–1962

THE EXPERIENCE OF A WORK OF ART BY YVES KLEIN is like nothing else—except, perhaps, an encounter with an exceedingly strange natural object or event, like a fungus or a sudden change in atmospheric pressure. Klein's signature color was blue—"IKB" (International Klein Blue), which he patented. It was an intense blue with a violet undertone, also known as ultramarine. "Ultramarine," which comes from the Latin for "beyond the sea," became the name for a ground mineral pigment, lapis lazuli, that came from the East: Persia, Afghanistan, China. Giotto used it for his fresco panels of pure, unmodulated blue. Once he spotted these at Assisi in 1958, Klein characteristically declared Giotto his forerunner.

Lapis lazuli is a precious mineral and thus expensive. Klein used an artificial ultramarine pigment produced since 1828 by heating clay, soda, sulfur, and coal. It can be differentiated from true lapis only under the microscope and by the fact that, unlike lapis, it cannot be used in fresco painting because the mineral acids in plaster tend to bleach it. What Klein patented was not the color so much as a formula for its application—the ratio of pigment to the binder he developed: a polyvinyl acetate dissolved in ethyl alcohol and ethyl acetate. This binder allowed the blue pigment to remain totally present—stable and visually available—on the surface of Klein's paintings. Its fumes are dangerous. Some people think they contributed to his early death of a heart attack at the age of thirty-four.

The use of volatile binders was not the only dangerous practice Klein engaged in. He also flung himself from buildings, painted with fire, and exposed his art and himself to the elements, including lightning. The intensity of his investment registers in the work. Many have noted the uncanny presence of these objects. The critic and historian of philosophy Thomas McEvilley notes that "an IKB monochrome viewed out of context on the other side of the world still breathes the fierceness of Yves's ego and his fiery drive toward transcendence." According to McEvilley,

> An immaterial substance, which Yves called "pure pictorial sensibility," is injected into the art work by the alchemist/artist who has isolated and purified this sensibility in himself; it can be experienced in the painting, after any number of years, by a viewer whose own sensibility is sufficiently developed. Art, then, is not a sensory but an extrasensory experience.[1]

Klein's work is the expression of his way of being in the world, a way of being that was tremendously influential in the world of art. A number of artistic trends were affected if not inspired by him, from *Nouveau Réalisme* to Minimalism, Process Art, Earthworks, and Performance Art. Part of the reason for this range of influence is the both/and quality of his work. Although he challenged the idea of what art is, Klein's work—unlike Duchamp's—is antiphilosophical; although it is about transcendence, it is, unlike Reinhardt's, aggressively physical. In both ways, the work of Yves Klein is very much like Zen Buddhism.

Klein spent the greater part of his childhood and youth in Nice, on the Côte d'Azur, where the intense blue of the sea and the sky stimulated conceptions of space "beyond" what he could see—an "ultra" marine. Most of us think of the sky as the surface of our ocean of air, but the young Yves conceived the sky as art: he visualized himself signing its other side. He thought about other colors as well, not just blue. Toward the end of his short, eight-year career he was working with gold, the color of light. An autobiographical account from his "journal of one day," *Dimanche* (Sunday), hints at why his friends later said of him that his was a Zen spirit:

> The child is in bed. The room is dark. He closes his eyes and presses his fingers against his eyelids, and he sees great flames; he sees them, and they are there, where his eyes are, in fact deeper inside his head. And yet there is nothing there, no inside, no outside, no objects, no eyes. The child sees intense color in complete simplicity. . . . But this astonishing light is not of the day or of the night. It is unchanging, yet trembles sweetly. It is always there inside the head. And will it stay there always? . . . The child calls its mother and asks, "What is it that you see when your eyes are closed?" At first the mother doesn't understand; he explains; then she says: "Don't do that! You'll go blind." The interior light is all color.[2]

It was also pure sensation.

Yves's mother, like his father, was a painter. More even than most mothers, she might have feared his damaging his eyesight through his fascination with inner light. Klein consistently described himself as a painter while engaging in a wide range of art activities. His mission may have been as simple, or as complicated, as making his painter-mother see the light; taking his viewers to a space where, in a description based on the Heart Sutra, "there is no inside, no outside, no objects, no eyes"—where there is "nothing there."[3]

Klein claimed that he began painting monochromes in order to see the absolute. The word "absolute" is related to the verb "absolve"—to release. Klein covered many metaphysical bases and subjected himself to a number of disciplines in his attempts to achieve release into total freedom. His yearning had its origins in the wartime privations he and his family endured, but also in his childhood emotional environment. During his first year of life his Aunt Rose became a surrogate for his wayward artist-mother, Marie Raymond. Yves was both regularly abandoned by his mother and indulged by his adoring aunt and grandmother—a situation pretty much guaranteed to produce a narcissist, intensely craving attention and grandiose in his ambitions.

Thanks to the devotion of Aunt Rose and his grandmother, Yves became a lifelong supplicant of Saint Rita of Cascia, patron saint of lost causes and a popular saint in Nice. They had dedicated him to her as a baby, and as an adult he made at least five pilgrimages to her shrine. His interest in spirituality took him in a number of directions. From the age of nineteen Klein was a faithful student and then an equally faithful follower of the writings of Max Heindel, the German-born founder of the Rosicrucian Society of Oceanside, California. Although Heindel characterized his "cosmo-conception" as "mystic Christianity," it was really a takeoff on the Theosophy of Madame Blavatsky and the Anthroposophy of Rudolf Steiner—in other words, an attempt to theorize "scientifically" an evolution of the spirit. Finally, in his late twenties, Klein began reading the phenomenological writings of French philosopher Gaston Bachelard, who provided him with an acceptably intellectual language in which to couch his mystical beliefs.

These beliefs would seem to place him at a far distance from the earthy rigor of Zen Buddhism. Klein's connection with Zen appears to have come primarily through the Japanese martial art of judo, which makes sense, given the edginess of his stance in life and in art. Through Kodokan judo, Klein found for himself a way to experience and express the relationship between the realm of the spirit and the physical realm of the body.

The metaphysically inclined Klein probably first read about Buddhism in the context of his two earliest jobs, both of which were with bookstores. At the age of eighteen he went to work at the Librairie des Champs-Elysées in Paris and then, after moving back to Nice in August 1947, he managed a bookstore that Aunt Rose set up for him in her appliance store. Despite the quotidian context, Klein focused his bookstore on philosophy and art, including poetry and books on judo. According to his lifelong friend the poet Claude Pascal, "Yves . . . ordered [books] more for himself than for business."[4] Klein had met Pascal and another lifelong friend, the artist Arman, at the police athletic league, where, at the age of nineteen, he was engaged with his usual passion in learning judo.

Judo, which translates as "gentle *[ju]* way *[do]*," is a refinement of jujitsu, a weaponless system of self-defense that was one of twenty-some martial arts based on the principles of Zen practiced by the samurai warrior caste of medieval Japan. These martial arts included archery and horsemanship. We know from the testimony of his friend Arman that Klein, who identified strongly with the knightly code of conduct, read *Zen in the Art of Archery* by Eugen Herrigel, a book that was winning a cult following among artists in Europe and America. His attraction to knightly romance may also have lain behind Klein's strange obsession with learning horsemanship so that he could ride to Japan on horseback.

The jujitsu fighter aimed to develop flexibility and skill in carrying out prescribed maneuvers. He conquered, not through force, but through economy of energy, balance, and willingness to yield in order to win. Over the centuries, as the importance of the warrior caste declined in Japan, the martial arts developed into forms of body-based spiritual discipline. Kokodan judo was developed around 1880 by the reformer and pacifist Jigoro Kano, who had studied jujitsu under a number of different masters. Kano took from jujitsu a number of throws and grappling techniques, while eliminating the more violent foot and hand strikes. He put forward two "unifying principles": first, maximize mental and physical efficiency by using the energy of the opponent to defeat aggression; and, second, realize that prosperity can only come through mutual benefit. Kano and his successors traveled the world proselytizing on behalf of judo. Shortly before his death in 1938, the Japanese tourist industry board published a book of Kano's writings on judo. There, we read that "Kodokan literally means 'a school for studying the way,' 'the way' being the concept of life itself."[5]

According to Klein, "Judo is, in effect, the discovery by the human body of a spiritual space."[6] It was during the time he first studied judo, 1947–48, that Klein began a lifelong practice of meditation. According to Arman, Klein developed the ability to sit in the full-lotus position for up to three hours—a feat normally possible only for seasoned practitioners. He also cast himself as a poet: "I am a poet. I am sure of this and yet I have nothing to say."[7] This self-characterization points to another potential source of inspiration: Jacques Bacot's life of the Tibetan poet-adept Milarepa, who was a fierce meditator. In terms with which Klein would have identified, Milarepa compared the Buddhist experience of emptiness with the sky:

> [The awareness of voidness]
> is like the feeling of staring

into a vast and empty sky . . .
Thinking of the magnitude of the sky
Meditate on the vastness with no center and
No edge.[8]

This is the feeling that Klein would aim to stimulate in the viewers of his blue monochromes.

As a highly developed *Mahasiddha*, one of Milarepa's skills was projecting himself physically through space, a capability that the young *judoka*, Yves Klein, was attempting to emulate, and which he would later present as an art action in his *Leap into the Void* (1960). Milarepa was also famous for his fasting and for his celibacy, both of which the young Klein also attempted to emulate. His enthusiasm registers in a 1949 photograph, in which he strides confidently through the streets of Nice wearing a shirt painted with question marks and hand- and footprints like those on Tibetan paintings of great spiritual adepts he could have seen in the Musée Guimet in Paris.[9]

Much as Kano had aimed to make judo accessible to everyone, Max Heindel, Yves Klein's other role model, tried to bring Rosicrucian ideas to a broad public. Born in Copenhagen in 1865, Heindel eventually moved to California and became, in 1904–5, vice-president of the Theosophical Society of Los Angeles. In 1907 Heindel went to Germany, where, the story goes, an Elder Brother of the Rosicrucian Order offered to impart the sect's teachings, but only if Heindel would promise to keep them secret. This Heindel refused to do. It turned out this was a test: having passed it, Heindel was told how to reach the Temple of the Rose Cross, where he was given information that eventually made its way into his tome, *The Rosicrucian Cosmo-Conception*. This book became Klein's bible.

Thomas McEvilley has written extensively about how crucial Heindel's writings were to Klein's way of conceiving his role as an artist. Klein would not have seen Heindel's Rosicrucianism and Buddhism as contradictory. On the contrary, there is a heavy dose of Buddhist philosophy in Theosophy, and Heindel himself wrote, "There is an invisible and spiritual sun whose rays promote soul-growth upon one part of the earth after another as the physical sun promotes the growth of form, and this spiritual impulse also travels in the same direction as the physical sun; from east to west."[10] Like Kano and Heindel, Yves Klein set himself a missionary task. He would become Yves le Monochrome and share with the world his insights regarding "the way" into infinite space, into freedom:

> It was in 1947 that the "idea," the conscious vision of the "monochrome," came to me. I must say that it came to me rather intellectually; it was the result of all my passionate research at that time. Judo (1946), the Rosicrucian cosmogony (1947) (interpreted by Max Heindel, Oceanside, California), jazz, I played piano and dreamed of having a big orchestra, of composing music with a single tone, "a great monotone symphony."[11]

To develop himself further for this task, which was probably still rather vague in his mind, Klein decided to travel, not to California and the Rosicrucians, but to Japan—on horseback, no less. To learn to ride, he and Claude Pascal went to Ireland, where they worked in a stable. First, however, the two friends went in November 1949 to London, to learn English. Klein got himself a job in the shop of a framer, where he learned skills that would prove more valuable than horseback riding. The son of two painters, Klein surely knew how to handle paint materials. But the simple rituals of a frame shop—gilding and laying down pigment to tone canvas-covered wooden frames—revealed to him how his "intellectual" theory might be transformed into sensuous presence.

> It was there, during the year at "Savage's," that I received enlightenment into matter in its profound physical quality. Returning in the evening back to my room, I executed gouache monochromes on pieces of white cardboard and increasingly I used lots of pastel. I really liked the pastel tone! It seemed to me that in the material of pastel, each grain of pigment remained free and individual without being killed by the fixative medium. . . . Obviously the possibility of leaving the grains of pigment in total freedom, as they are found in the powder, mingled perhaps but independent, was quite intriguing to me. "Art is total freedom, it is life."[12]

He showed his first monochromes to Pascal, then hung them on the walls of his room and invited friends in to see them. This was, in his mind, his first exhibition.

Klein did not make it to Japan until 1952. He went alone, by boat—Pascal was recovering from tuberculosis, and Arman had better things to do. He stayed for fifteen months, studying Japanese and traveling to sites that included Mount Fuji, Hiroshima, and Buddhist temples and gardens. He also continued making monochromes, which, as in London, he "showed" in the rooms where he was living. For the most part, however, Klein dedicated himself to judo. He enrolled at the Kodokan Institute, determined to achieve the fourth-level black belt that would, he believed, allow him to return in triumph to France, where he intended to revolutionize the teaching of judo based on Japanese Kodokan methods.

His first goal turned out not to be so easy, and the second, impossible. He was awarded the fourth level in the short time he wanted to spend only by enlisting his aunt and others in a campaign to persuade the head of the Kodokan Institute that the institute would benefit if it awarded Klein a black belt, allowing him to open a Paris club devoted "exclusively to Kodokan Judo."[13] This was a judo tactic: Kano himself had recommended that, "although giving way to the opponent's strength is often very important, the principle of leverage is sometimes more important for the purpose of throwing."[14] Klein did eventually open a judo club in Paris, in addition to publishing a book and producing a film on Kodokan judo. But he was never accepted by the French judo establishment, which refused to recognize his Japanese credentials. Although deeply disappointing, this turn of events eventually (after a stint teaching judo in Spain) forced Klein to make peace with his parents' legacy and accept his calling: he would be a painter.

Klein continued his unconventional methods of getting his work into the world by publishing, in 1954, a booklet entitled *Yves Peintures.* The "preface" by "Pascal Claude" consists of three pages of horizontal lines. The ten tipped-in color plates are monochromes printed in different colors labeled with the names of cities where Klein had spent time over the previous four years—London, Madrid, Tokyo, Nice, Paris. His dates of residence are attached to the city names, implying that the reader is looking at reproductions of paintings done, for example, in Tokyo in 1953.

This impression is bolstered by measurements given in parentheses, with no unit specified. One would normally interpret the numbers as centimeters. However, as millimeters they correspond precisely to the sizes of the colored papers. Further confounding the issue of what the book represents is a simultaneous publication by Klein entitled *Haguenault Peintures,* which has an identical format, except for the addition of fictitious collection credit lines in the captions. Klein later claimed that Haguenault was a brand of gingerbread. The influence of Duchamp is not hard to detect in the evasiveness of this presentation, and Duchampian as well is the sheer industry of the books' production. But as a device for launching Klein's reputation as a monochrome painter, *Yves Peintures/Haguenault Peintures* is quite Kleinian in its brilliance and audacity.

Klein's inclusion of a preface consisting only of horizontal lines is revealing of his attitude to his audience. Unlike Reinhardt, who wrote a great deal about exactly what he intended with his monochromes, Klein never specified meanings for his work. The art historian Sidra Stich has written, "More than merely appealing to the eye or mind, the paintings aim to affect all the senses and to go beyond thinking into the realm of feeling, to combine corporeal with spiritual invigoration."[15] Klein wanted his viewers to react to what they saw, free of conditioning either from statements by the artist or from habit. He later credited his audience with determining two of his most important directions as an artist: his shift from using a range of colors to a focus on blue and his incorporation of natural sponges into the surfaces of his painted works. About a 1956 show of his monochromes in various colors, he wrote:

> I immediately noticed an important thing: in the presence of a wall on which canvases of different colors were hung, the public reconstituted the elements into a decorative polychromy. Prisoners of their habitual way of looking, the members of the public, although a select group, didn't place themselves in the presence of the "COLOR" of a single picture. This is what provoked my Blue Period.[16]

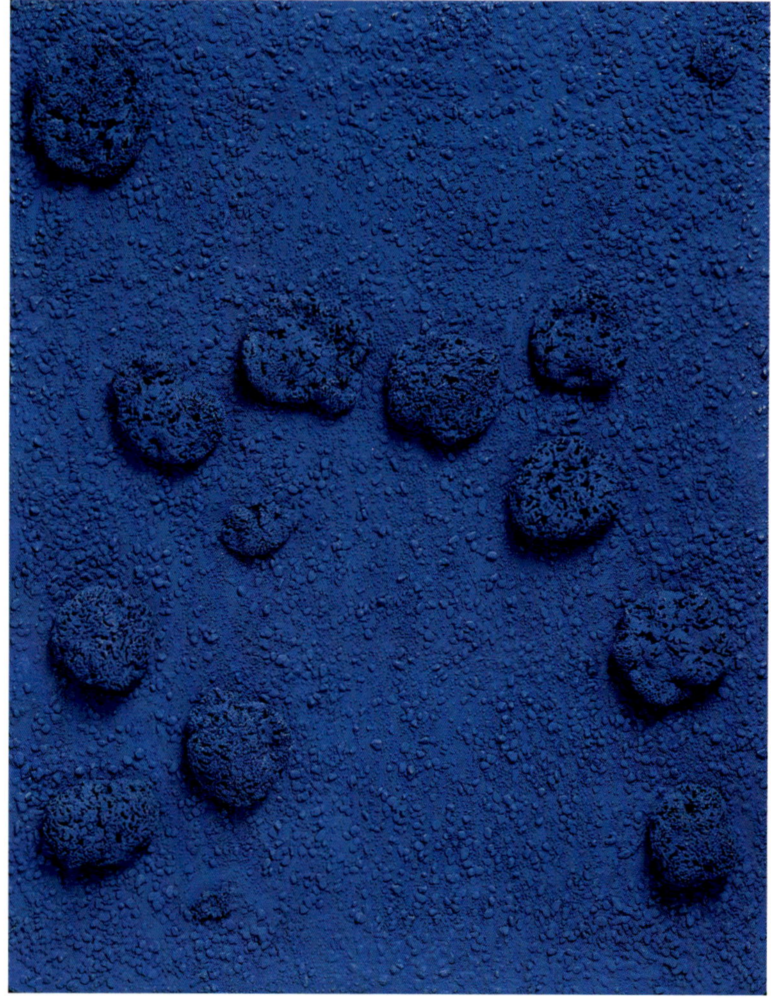

Yves Klein, *Blue Monochrome Sponge Relief (RE 24),* 1960, sponges, pebbles, dry pigment in synthetic resin on wood board, 57⅛ x 44⅞ x 5⅛ in. Hood Museum of Art, Dartmouth College, Hanover, New Hampshire; Gift of Mr. and Mrs. Joseph H. Hazen (P.961.288). Artist © 2005 Artists Rights Society (ARS), New York/ADAGP, Paris.

Our minds have been conditioned to compare and judge, to choose favorites rather than to experience something directly. Klein recognized that even art aficianados have habits of looking. His goal was to gently guide them, like a Buddhist teacher, to *seeing,* to opening themselves to the presence of a particular pigment-saturated object by giving them objects that were apparently all alike. Marcel Duchamp, as quoted by Jasper Johns, put this goal another way: "to reach the impossibility of sufficient visual memory to transfer from one like object to another the memory imprint."[17] Klein aimed to give his viewers paintings with such infinitesimal visual differences that any memory of them would be lost from one painting to the next. To focus his viewers' minds further, he gave these apparently identical paintings different prices.

In 1957 Klein had two simultaneous shows in Paris. One, at the Iris Clert Gallery, consisted of monochrome blue paintings with one large, blue-infused sponge sculpture. The other, at Colette Allendy, consisted of a variety of blue works. The sponge sculpture at Clert's led Klein to another discovery:

> It was . . . on this occasion that I discovered the sponge. While working on my paintings in the studio, I sometimes used sponges. Very quickly they obviously became blue! . . . Thanks to the wild living material of sponges, I was going to be able to do the portraits of the beholders of my monochromes, who, after having seen them, after having traveled through the blue of my paintings, come back totally impregnated in sensibility, like sponges.[18]

This concept of the beholders beholding themselves in the work via sponges, which suggest wiping or cleaning as well as absorbing, calls to mind the career of the Sixth Zen Patriarch, who was elevated from kitchen worker to Patriarch on the basis of his instinctive absorption of the essence of Zen. Hui-neng modified a more obvious successor's summary of Zen teachings—"The body is like the Bodhi-tree, the mind to a mirror bright; carefully we cleanse them hour by hour, lest dust should fall upon them"—with: "Neither is there Bodhi-tree, nor yet a mirror bright; since in reality all is void, whereon can the dust fall?"[19] Klein wrote his own variation in 1952, just before his trip to Japan:

> If you become like a mirror
> Those who look at you
> See themselves in you.
> You are then invisible![20]

The works Klein showed at the Colette Allendy Gallery revealed a strong Japanese influence. Two blue folding screens were included, along with *Blue Rain,* a group of thin blue dowels hung from the ceiling (the title evokes images of Hokusai woodcuts). *Pure Pigment* was a large rectangle of blue powder spread on the floor and patterned with a small rake, like the gravel in a Zen garden. Klein's sponge reliefs also show the influence of Japanese Zen gardens, with their apparently randomly placed rocks amid gravel. The most famous example—which Klein surely visited—is the garden of the Rinzai Zen Buddhist temple, Ryoanji, in Kyoto.

The most radical work at the Allendy Gallery in 1957 was not particularly accessible to the public. *Surfaces and Blocks of Invisible Pictorial Sensibility* was a small room with empty white walls on the second floor that Klein showed to a few friends, as he had done with his early monochromes in London and in Japan. Its title indicates that Klein did not think of the room as empty. It was full of the same pictorial sensibility as his monochromes, perhaps more so. Two years later, reflecting on this show, Klein wrote: "I realized that the paintings are but the 'ashes' of my art. The authentic quality of the painting, its very 'being,' once created, is found beyond the visible, in pictorial sensibility in the raw material state."[21]

Klein took this concept of pictorial sensibility public on his thirtieth birthday—April 28, 1958—when he opened his exhibition of emptiness at the Iris Clert Gallery. It was entitled "The Specialization of Sensibility in the Raw Material State into Stabilized Pictorial Sensibility: The Void." Over the previous two days he had painted the gallery white, consciously filling it in the process with his artistic sensibility through a kind of meditative action. In a lecture at the Sorbonne the following year, he described both his intention and his process:

> With this endeavor I desire to create, establish, and present to the public a sensible pictorial state within the limits of an exhibition gallery . . . one is to be literally impregnated by the pictorial atmosphere, specialized and stabilized beforehand by the painter in the given space. . . . How to realize that? I enclose myself alone forty-eight hours before the opening in the gallery, to repaint it entirely in white. . . . My presence in action in the given space will create the climate and the radiating pictorial ambiance that habitually reigns in the studio of an artist endowed with real power.
>
> A sensible but real abstract density will exist and live by itself and for itself in places which are empty in appearance only. In short . . . I must simply say that the experience was decisive and made me deeply understand that painting is not a function of the eye.[22]

The opening was a typically theatrical event—the drinks served caused visitors to urinate blue for several days, impressing upon them the fact that their bodies had absorbed Klein's "pictorial atmosphere." And the crowds kept coming—hundreds each day for the duration of the show. At least some of them must have been repeat visitors. Clearly, the pictorial ambiance was radiant for those willing to be "impregnated" by an artist who had worked hard to develop spiritual power.

Klein's productions continued to multiply. He showed the void elsewhere. He worked with "living paintbrushes"—naked women whose bodies became matrices for transferring blue paint to canvas. He worked with nature directly, exposing his canvases to the elements. He sold "Zones of Immaterial Pictorial Sensibility," taking in return only pure gold, half of which he returned to the earth by throwing it into the Seine. Reflecting his early experiences at the London frame shop and with gold-leaf screens in Japan, he began to produce gold-surfaced paintings that he called "monogolds." He painted with fire. He appropriated a day—Sunday, November 27, 1960—calling it the "Theater of the Void" and creating a one-day newspaper, *Dimanche*. Page one featured an alarming photograph of Yves Klein leaping off the ledge of a building, about to either take flight or crash to the street below. The headline read, "Man in Space!" and the photo was captioned, "The painter of space throws himself into

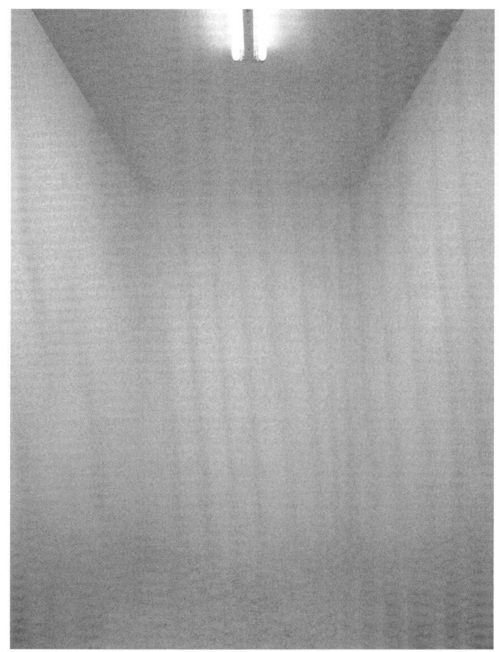

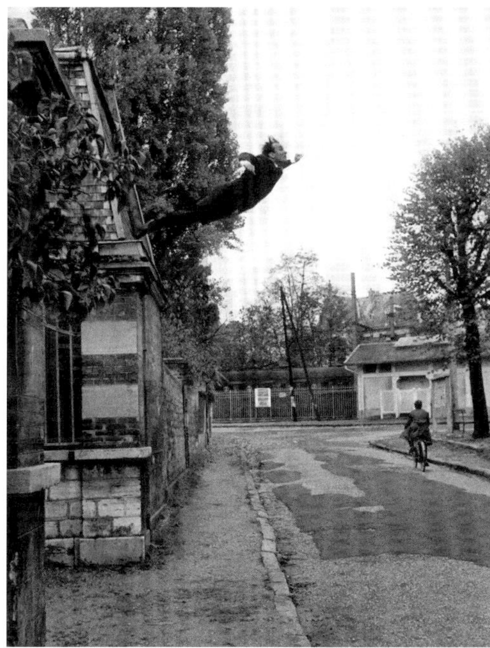

(left) Yves Klein, *Void,* 1961, white painted room (paint with fine white gravel), $14\frac{1}{2}$ ft. long x $5\frac{1}{2}$ ft. wide x $9\frac{3}{8}$ ft. high. Museum Haus Lange, Kaiser Wilhelm Museum, Krefeld, Germany. Photo: Krefelder Kunstmuseen. Artist © 2005 Artists Rights Society (ARS), New York/ADAGP, Paris.

(right) Yves Klein, *Yves Klein Leaping into the Void,* 1960, Paris, photograph, 14 x 11 in. Albright-Knox Art Gallery, Buffalo, New York, Gift of Seymour H. Knox, Jr., 1976. Photo: Harry Shunk. Artist © 2005 Artists Rights Society (ARS), New York/ADAGP, Paris.

the void." Although the photograph was a composite, it commemorated an actual leap witnessed by at least one of Klein's friends.

Unfortunately, Klein was throwing himself into his work in all too many ways. One of the unhappy side-effects of his stint studying judo in Japan was an amphetamine habit, and he continued to rely on stimulants even after he stopped teaching judo to devote himself fully to producing art in 1959. Dropping judo seemed to cause him to lose his emotional balance: he became increasingly temperamental and frantic. About two years later, Yves Klein died of a heart attack. He had been prophesying his death for years: "Now I want to go beyond art, beyond sensibility, beyond life; I want to go into the void."[23]

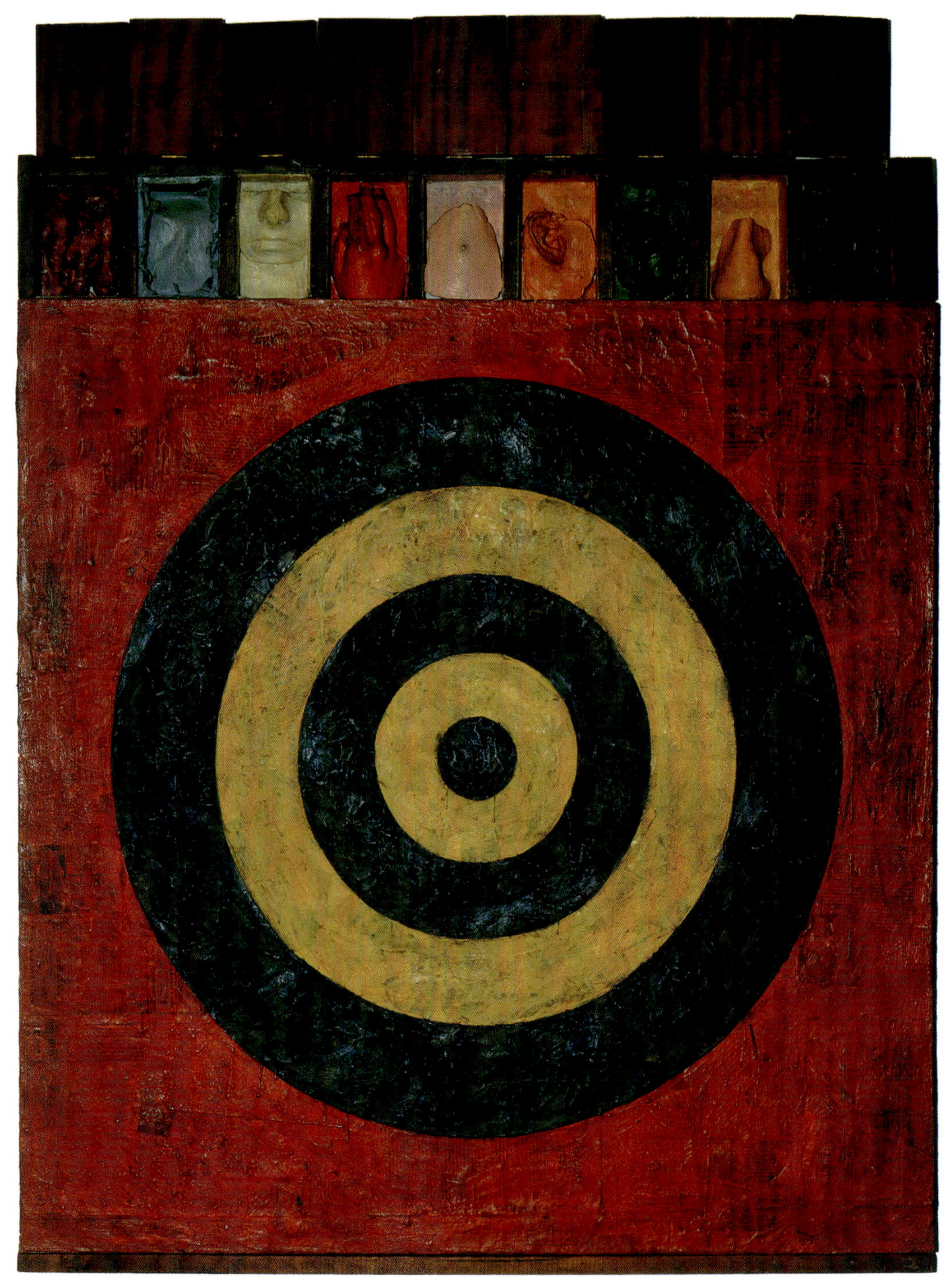

Jasper Johns, *Target with Plaster Casts,* 1955, encaustic and collage on canvas with plaster casts in hinged wooden boxes, 51 x 44 x 3½ in. Private collection/Bridgeman Art Library (BBC196585). Artist © Jasper Johns/Licensed by VAGA, New York, NY.

In the earlier paintings . . . I looked for subject matter that was recognizable. . . . These were things people knew, and did not know, in the sense that everyone had an everyday relationship to numbers and letters, but never before had they seen them in the context of a painting. I wanted to make people see something new. . . . When something is new to us, we treat it as an experience. We feel that all our senses are awake and clear. We are alive.

JASPER JOHNS, 1969

JASPER JOHNS 1930–

JASPER JOHNS BECAME AN ART-WORLD SENSATION at the age of twenty-seven when *Target with Plaster Casts* was shown at Leo Castelli's new gallery in January 1958 alongside other unconventional works, such as *Flag*. *Flag* was the exact shape and color of an American flag; yet it was a painting. Not just any painting: it was painted in encaustic—pigmented wax laid on with lots of texture but thinly enough so that the newsprint layer underneath showed through. *Flag* exudes intense physical presence as a painting. At the same time, it conveys an immediately recognizable, emotion-laden "design," to use a Johns word. *Flag* has long since become an icon of postwar American art and thus lost the shock of the new that Johns was aiming for: is it a painting or is it a flag? The answer—it seems obvious, now—is not either/or but both/and. Johns is philosophical about the shifting aesthetic fortunes of *Flag*. Asked by an interviewer twenty years after its making whether *Flag* could have retained its shock value as a work of art, Johns replied, "Well, I don't think it can. Things change. . . . The use that people have for things changes. There's no way to avoid that."[1]

Johns has repeatedly said that the idea for *Flag* came to him in a dream in 1954, when he would have been twenty-four years old. This doesn't tell us much, beyond the fact that the American flag was an energetic presence within the young artist's unconscious mind at this age. Speculation has been rife. But knowing, for example, that Johns was named for his feckless father, who was in turn named for a Revolutionary War hero—William Jasper—

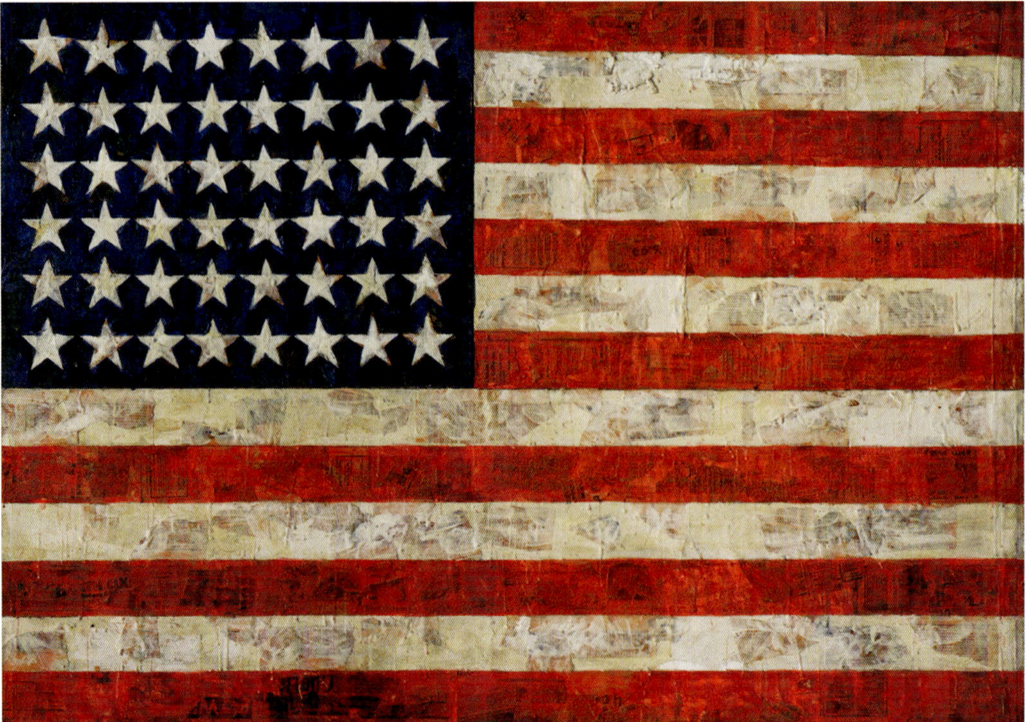

Jasper Johns, *Flag,* 1954–55, encaustic, oil, and collage on fabric mounted on plywood (three panels), 42¼ x 60⅝ in. The Museum of Modern Art, New York, Gift of Philip Johnson in honor of Alfred H. Barr, Jr. (106.1973). Digital image © The Museum of Modern Art/Licensed by SCALA/Art Resource, NY. Artist © Jasper Johns/Licensed by VAGA, New York, NY.

who bravely rescued the flag under fire, tells us less about *Flag* than does Johns's statement about its "both/and" identity as flag and as art. The image of the flag must have held complex meaning for him, as it does for us, but what came to him in the dream was an insight having to do with the relationship between seeing and identity.

The origin of the subject of Johns's target paintings—not to mention their object—is less obvious. *Target with Plaster Casts* was the most complex work in Johns's first show. It must have been even more shocking than *Flag* at the time, for its content—concentric circles topped by a row of sensual body fragments that include a mouth, a nipple, an ear, and a penis—is frankly sexual. Disturbingly so, for not only have the casts obviously been made from a real body (whose?), but they are strongly evocative of love and loss. They include the back of a hand (obeisance?), the front and back of a foot (coming and going?), a bone fragment (death?), and an empty box with ragged edges from which something appears to have been torn. The target and its background are rendered in primary colors—red, yellow, and blue—implying primal emotions. The body parts are painted in secondary colors and each resides in its own hinged box with a lid, implying hiddenness. The question presented by *Flag*—is it a flag or is it a painting?—multiplies into mind-boggling complexity: Is *Target with Plaster Casts* a painting or a sculpture or both? Who is the target and who is doing the aiming? We feel somehow implicated by this work in a mysterious, troubling process that we don't quite understand.

Neither, perhaps, did Johns. But it seems likely that Johns had read Eugen Herrigel's *Zen in the Art of Archery,* which states, "It is necessary for the archer to become, in spite of himself, an unmoved center. Then comes the supreme and ultimate miracle: art becomes 'artless,' shooting becomes not-shooting."[2] The target, in other words, is both the self and the place of transformation. For something to be transformed, it must, on some hidden level, be destroyed, taken apart, dismantled. Just as Johns's flag was both object and symbol, the fragmented body parts are both objects and symbols for fragmented feelings, the fragmented self.

The lids or doors of the boxes may also be connected with the archer-artist's quest:

> The demand that the door of the senses be closed is not met by turning energetically away from the sensible world, but rather by a readiness to yield without resistance. In order that this actionless activity may be accomplished instinctively, the soul needs an inner hold, and it wins it by concentrating on breathing.[3]

The prescription of breathing meditation for developing an "inner hold" would seem to relate even more directly to *Target with Four Faces* (1955), a work made around the same time as *Target with Plaster Casts.* Here, the target is surmounted by four boxes with one long door. Each box contains a separate cast of the same object: a nose and closed mouth. The mouth is, of course, another kind of potential target—the target of an intended kiss. It could also stand for taste and touch, the nose for smell. But this line of sensual association leaves out sight and sound, and thus feels less than satisfying. The erotic feels like the focus of *Target with Four Faces,* but the repetition of the nose and closed mouth has a soothing, rhythmic quality, like breathing. Johns presents us here with a problem containing its own solution: the Zen antidote to sensual and emotional confusion is centering the mind, coming back to the present by "concentrating on breathing."

If *Flag* was ambiguous as an object, Johns multiplied the ambiguity geometrically in *Target with Four Faces* and again in *Target with Plaster Casts.* These early works by Johns resemble Zen koans—paradoxes that stimulate the mind to go beyond rational thinking. D. T. Suzuki wrote about koans in his *Essentials of Zen Buddhism:* "The worst enemy of Zen experience, at least in the beginning, is the intellect, which consists and insists in discriminating subject from object."[4] In 1978 an interviewer raised the object issue with Johns by commenting, "I remember a discussion in which somebody confessed to not understanding why you use objects to paint." Johns replied: "Well, that person could just as well have asked the opposite question, why I use painting for these objects."[5] His comment is very like a line from Herrigel, about the childlike mind: "We could say that it was playing with things, were it not equally true that the things are playing with the child."[6] "For me," Johns concludes, "the decisive factor is my interest in ambivalence."[7]

"Ambivalence" might be seen as another word for relationship or, perhaps better, interrelationship. A connection between this liberating relational ambivalence and focused attention is provided by D. T. Suzuki in his 1949 book, *The Zen Doctrine of No-Mind.* Regarding the Zen term *chien-hsing,* Suzuki wrote:

> *Chien* . . . signifies the pure act of seeing. When it is coupled with *hsing,* Nature, or Essence, or Mind, it is seeing into the ultimate nature of things, and not watching. . . . The seeing is not reflecting on an object as if the seer had nothing to do with it. The seeing, on the contrary, brings the seer and the object seen together, not in mere identification but the mind becoming conscious of itself, or rather of its working. The seeing is an active deed, involving the dynamic conception of self-being; that is, of the Mind.[8]

The passage helps illuminate the content of a much-analyzed inscription in Jasper Johns's notebook from 1964:

> The Watchman falls "into" the "trap" of looking.
> The "spy" is a different person
> "Looking" is & is not "eating" & also "being eaten"
> That is, there is continuity of some sort among
> the watchman, the space, the objects.
> . . .
> The watchman leaves
> his job & takes away
> no information.
> The spy must remember
> & must remember himself
> & his remembering.
> The spy designs himself
> to be overlooked. . . .
> Somewhere here, there is the question of "seeing clearly."
> Seeing what?
> According to what?[9]

The "spy" has been identified by commentators with the artist, Johns himself. The "watchman" has been associated with the viewer, but he might better be interpreted as another,

As Bucky Fuller is fond of pointing out: the movement with the wind of the Orient and the movement against the wind of the Occident meet in America and produce a movement upwards into the air—the space, the silence, the nothing that supports us.

JOHN CAGE

This is John Cage's definition of America: When you go to Asia from America, you go with the wind, and when you go to Europe from America, you go against the wind. Both winds meet in America and rise to heaven.

NAM JUNE PAIK

There is a wind that never dies.

YOKO ONO

WITH THE WORK OF THE COMPOSER AND ARTIST John Cage, the relation of Buddhism to Western art came out of the closet. Cage freely acknowledged the significant impact of Buddhist philosophy on his life and his work. This is no coincidence, as Cage's fundamental artistic contribution was to definitively eliminate the boundary between art and life. Critical to this radical accomplishment was his realization that not only was communication of personal emotion through art not possible, it was not the point. For Cage, the purpose of art, for both maker and perceiver, was "to sober and quiet the mind so that it is in accord with what happens."[1] Thanks to Cage, the integration of art and life reached its culmination in the discipline of music. We can close our eyes and direct our gaze, but we can't close our ears. Cage's breakthrough was to teach us that our listening is as directed by habits of the mind as our seeing; that our likes and dislikes—attractions and aversions, to use Buddhist terminology—warp our experience of the flow of reality in all of its richness. The purpose of art is to open our hearts and minds to the experience of that richness.

Fortified by the teachings of Zen Buddhism, Cage broke ground in three areas. First, more effectively than the hermetic Duchamp, who greatly influenced him, the gregarious Cage incorporated chance happenings from "real" life—specifically ambient sound—into his work. Second, Cage eliminated the hierarchies between composer and performer and performer and audience by "letting go" of creative responsibility and by incorporating his audience into his performances. But perhaps his greatest legacy as far as visual artists were concerned was the experiential, performative nature of his work, which emphasized the process of creation over its product:

> It reminds me of what Thoreau said, and I feel so too. "It's not important what form the sculptor gives the stone. It's important what sculpting does to the sculptor." People can be plumbers or street cleaners or be like artists if they do their work as their lives; what and how they do makes how they live, and gives them the love and pleasure of living.[2]

Recollecting the Sixth Zen Patriarch's comment about movement belonging neither to the wind nor to the flag, but to the mind, we might liken John Cage's mind to a wind that swept up both Asian and Euro-American culture and disseminated the results around the globe. Through his work, his teaching, and his friendships, Cage had an impact on many of the new music artists who emerged in the 1960s and 1970s. Even earlier, he inspired Robert Rauschenberg, Jasper Johns, and various artists involved with Happenings, Fluxus, and Performance Art. Fluxus artist Nam June Paik, for example, took the "wind" initiated by Cage and in his use of broadcast media literally made it rise toward heaven. The international artists involved in Happenings and Fluxus were decidedly rowdier and more socially committed than the American Abstract Expressionists who preceded them or the Pop artists who were their contemporaries. Like Noguchi, they wanted to give art back to the social realm, to make it continuous with everyday living.

The first art event formally described as a "Happening" was Allan Kaprow's *Eighteen Happenings in Six Parts,* presented in New York at the Reuben Gallery in 1959. Happenings were events of indeterminate length with no narrative, usually involving members of the audience and incorporating everyday as well as artist-made objects. The generally acknowledged forerunner of Happenings was John Cage's 1952 "concerted action" at Black Mountain College. This multimedia affair included paintings, slide and film projections, prepared piano and phonograph music, poetry, improvised dance, and a "lecture" by Cage. There was no script, nothing had been rehearsed; there was only general agreement about order. John Cage helped spark the evolution of Happenings through his course on experimental composition at the New School for Social Research from 1956 to 1960. Kaprow was among his students there, as were others involved in Happenings, including Fluxus musicians and artists George Brecht, Al Hansen, Dick Higgins, Jackson Mac Low, and La Monte Young.

Cage was an equally important influence on artists involved with the international Fluxus movement, a consciously "Neo-Dada" revival of the post–World War I, "anti-art" Dada movement. Fluxus artists took up the earlier Dada artists' targets: nationalist and hierarchical cultural traditions that had led to the social catastrophe of the First World War. "Purge the world of . . . 'intellectual,' professional & commercialized culture, purge the world of dead art, imitation, artificial art, abstract art, illusionistic art, mathematical art,—PURGE THE WORLD OF 'EUROPEANISM'!"[3] exclaimed George Maciunas, a Lithuanian who immigrated to the United States in 1948 at the age of seventeen. Trained as an architect and a graphic artist, but also intensely interested in avant-garde music, Maciunas was a maniacal organizer who invited a remarkably interdisciplinary group of people to join Fluxus. His Marxist goal was the "gradual elimination of fine arts . . . motivated by desire to stop the waste of material and human resources . . . and divert it to socially constructive ends." In this process, Fluxus art "could temporarily have the pedagogical function of teaching people the needlessness of art including the eventual needlessness of itself."[4]

Not surprisingly, Fluxus performances tended toward the anarchic, and Maciunas's productions were heavily weighted toward the didactic in both content and presentation. Despite the overtly political nature of the enterprise, Fluxus products were leavened with considerable humor. The Fluxus artist and writer Ken Friedman dubbed this aspect "Zen Vaudeville," while Maciunas characterized Fluxus's humorous one-liners as "Neo Haiku Events."[5] The humor suggests a Zen perspective, as does Maciunas's definition of the term "Fluxus," in which he refers (among other things) to the "act of flowing: a continuous moving on or passing by . . . a continuous succession of changes."[6] A number of the artists associated with Fluxus have acknowledged the importance of Zen. Ben Patterson, for example, stated: "I, and my generation of Fluxus artists, were all more or less twelve to fourteen years old when the first atomic bomb exploded. . . . Perhaps only Zen or existentialism could begin to deal with such finality."[7]

A significant Zen influence on Maciunas was the Japanese musician and artist Yoko Ono. They became intimate friends in early 1961, and Maciunas gave Ono her first show in June of that year. Another influence was Nam June Paik, like Ono a musician who early on became an artist. Paik had mixed feelings about the value of his Asian cultural heritage, including Zen, which he saw as "responsible of *[sic]* Asian poverty."[8] But Paik clearly signaled Zen's relevance to changing world culture in the titles of his works, often pairing the words "Zen" or "Buddha" with a Western technological term, such as "TV."

In the June 1964 edition of the Fluxus newspaper *cc fiVe ThReE,* Paik wrote:

> Zen consists of two negations.
> The first negation:
> The absolute IS the relative.
> The second negation:
> The relative IS the absolute.
> The first negation is a simple fact, which every mortal
> Meets every day: everything passes away . . . mother,
> lover, hero, youth, fame . . . etc.

The second negation is the KEY-point of Zen.
That means . . .
The NOW is utopia, what it may be.
The NOW in 10 minutes is also utopia, what it may be.
The NOW in 20 hours is also utopia, what it may be.
The NOW in 30 months is also utopia, what it may be.
The NOW in 40 million years is also utopia, what it may be.
Therefore
We should learn,
how to be satisfied with 75%
how to be satisfied with 50%
how to be satisfied with 38%
how to be satisfied with 9%
how to be satisfied with 0%
how to be satisfied with –1000%
Zen is anti-avant-garde, anti-frontier spirit, anti-Kennedy.[9]

The "frustration" of Zen for Paik was this acceptance of "what is," which Paik wittily characterized in Zen terms as "NO catharsis."[10] This was precisely what Cage liked about Zen. "You can feel an emotion," Cage once said, "just don't think that it's so important. . . . Take it in a way that you can then let it drop! Don't belabor it!"[11] In an interesting postwar flip of dualities, the "Eastern" artist Paik valued catharsis, while the "Western" artist Cage valued integration. Clearly, by the late 1950s "Eastern" and "Western" had lost their value as descriptive generalizations.

Despite his acknowledged importance for her work, Yoko Ono, like Nam June Paik, rebelled against John Cage's rejection of emotion. She seems to have regarded him as overly intellectual: "Mental richness should be worried just as physical richness. Didn't Christ say that it was like a camel trying to pass through a needle hole, for John Cage to go to heaven?"[12] Her use of a Christian metaphor is telling. The daughter of a Japanese Protestant father and a Buddhist mother, Ono grew up in both the United States and Japan, where she experienced the tragic denouement of World War II. The most transcendental of the Fluxus artists, Ono attempts to lure her audiences into realms of imagination and transformation.

Ono's models for this project to save the world were the meaning-packed insights contained in Zen koans and poems. She ended a 1966 lecture with contrasting versions of Zen mind contained in two poems by rivals for the role of Sixth Zen Patriarch:

The body is the Bodhi Tree
The mind like a bright mirror standing

Take care to wipe it all the time
And allow no dust to cling.

SHEN-HSIU

There never was a Bodhi Tree
Nor bright mirror standing
Fundamentally, not one thing exists
So where is the dust to cling?

HUI-NENG[13]

The paradox, which the paradoxical Yoko Ono appreciated, is that both versions are "true." But, like the Fifth Patriarch, who chose Hui-neng as his successor, Ono instinctively gravitated to the freedom represented by the floating dust. Her most famous instruction-piece consists of one word: "Fly."

Happenings, Fluxus, and Performance Art were international art movements, not just because they surfaced in more than one place at a time, but because the people involved tended to travel a lot—thanks in part to the development of commercial air travel in the period following the Korean War. It is no coincidence that George Maciunas claimed to have conducted postgraduate studies at New York University in the "European and Siberian Art of Migrations," or that Nam June Paik described himself as a "Mongolian-Manchurian-Korean nomad."[14] Things were happening simultaneously in the United States, Western Europe, Eastern Europe, and Japan. The cultural dichotomy between East and West had all but disappeared, and Buddhism was as likely to inform the art of a Western artist like Laurie Anderson as artists with Asian backgrounds, like Paik and Ono.

Although she has performed all over the world, Laurie Anderson has always been based in New York and her work is nominally about the United States—the title of her major four-part performance piece of 1980–83. Anderson is closer to Paik than to Ono in her drive to affect people beyond the relatively circumscribed art audience. Over a decade younger than either of them, she got her start in the avant-garde Performance Art world of the 1970s. By the early 1980s, the success of her song "O Superman" had launched her into a recording and performing career. Like Yoko Ono, Laurie Anderson studied music seriously as a child, and she aims to engage the emotions by way of the senses. But while Ono is a visual poet, creating sensuous, highly focused images and actions for the mind, Anderson is a self-described storyteller whose medium is multilayered, multidisciplinary narrative.

All four of the musician/artists in this section—Cage, Paik, Ono, and Anderson—have applied and extended Thoreau's observation that music is always present in our environment; it is only our hearing that is intermittent. As Cage put it, "Art is everywhere; it's only seeing which stops now and then."[15]

John Cage, *HV2 (#6)*, 1992, from series of fifteen color etchings in three impressions each, 11½ x 14½ in., ed. 45. Published by Crown Point Press. Artist permission courtesy of the John Cage Trust.

There's an idea I had in the forties, and now that I'm a little bit older I still have the same idea more or less: that one of the ways of saying why we make art is that it helps us in the enjoyment of life. The way of enjoying life keeps changing, because of changes in our scientific awareness. The way you enjoyed life in, say, 1200 is different from the way you enjoy it now. And that accounts for the changes in Art.

JOHN CAGE

JOHN CAGE 1912–1992

JOHN CAGE'S BUDDHIST-INFLUENCED IMPACT on the arts, worldwide, has arguably been greater than that of any other artist in the second half of the twentieth century. Cage was a genius, both in the sense of possessing extraordinary qualities of mind, and in the sense of personifying the spirit of his time. If any one word can describe the twentieth century, that word is "change"—"increasingly rapid change." Cage not only accepted, he embraced change, attempting to live his life and create his art "in accord with what happens." Thanks to his eloquence, charm, and refusal to observe disciplinary conventions—he was friends with as many artists as musicians—a large chunk of the cultural world ended up changing with him.

Around 1949–50 John Cage gave a "Lecture on Nothing" at the New York Artists' Club founded by the painter Robert Motherwell and frequented by the Abstract Expressionists. It opened with the statement, "I am here and there is nothing to say."[1] His own account of that lecture gives some idea of what it was like to experience a John Cage performance:

> This Lecture on Nothing was written in the same rhythmic structure I employed in my musical compositions. One of the structural divisions was the repetition, some fourteen times, of a single page in which occurred the refrain, "If anyone is sleepy let him go to sleep." Jeanne Reynal, I remember, stood up part way through, screamed, and then said,

> while I continued speaking, "John, I dearly love you, but I can't bear another minute." She then walked out. Later, during the question period, I gave one of six previously prepared answers regardless of the question asked. This was a reflection of my engagement in Zen.[2]

Cage's concerts were even more disorienting than his lectures. They might consist of silence, as in *4′33″* (four minutes and thirty-three seconds was the length of time pianist David Tudor did *not* play the piano), or contain painfully loud feedback sounds. (Cage once made the remarkable suggestion that loud sounds in a concert hall might help people deal with the loud sounds they encounter in their daily lives.) To run screaming from the room was not a unique response to a Cage performance. Nevertheless, when someone suggested to Cage that the most surprising thing he could do would be to give a conventional lecture, he replied: "I don't give these lectures to surprise people, but out of a need for poetry."[3]

For John Cage, poetry, music, and art all had the same purpose: "to sober and quiet the mind so that it is in accord with what happens."[4] He was fond of telling the story about where he got the phrase "to sober and quiet the mind." It was the answer to a question he had asked an Indian musician about what her Indian teacher thought the purpose of music was. Not long afterward a friend, the composer Lou Harrison, came across a statement by the seventeenth-century English composer Thomas Mace "expressing the same idea in almost exactly the same words. I decided then and there that this was the proper purpose of music." The modern Western "idea of self-expressive art was therefore heretical."[5]

In a 1992 interview with Laurie Anderson for *Tricycle: The Buddhist Review,* Cage explained how he came to Buddhism:

> I had read *The Gospel of Sri Ramakrishna*. I became interested, in other words, in Oriental thought. And I read also a short book by Aldous Huxley called *The Perennial Philosophy,* and from that I got the idea that all the various religions were saying the same thing but had different flavors. . . . So I browsed, as it were, and found a flavor I liked and it was that of Zen Buddhism. It was then that Suzuki came to New York, and I was able to go to Columbia once a week for two years to attend his classes.[6]

Cage seems to have begun reading about Zen Buddhism in the late 1940s, before he began attending the lectures of D. T. Suzuki around 1950.[7] In a 1966 interview Cage described his first exposure to Zen as a lecture he heard while teaching at the Cornish School of Applied Arts in Seattle between 1938 and 1940: "I had heard one lecture given [there] by Nancy Wilson Ross . . . late in the thirties on Zen and Dada, which had impressed me very much, but which had not impressed me sufficiently to get me to reading Zen texts."[8]

So what did get Cage reading Zen texts? In 1945 Cage faced an emotional crisis. His marriage ended, and he felt an urgent need to come to terms, personally and professionally, with his homosexuality. In his 1944 piano composition *The Perilous Night,* he had attempted to convey "the loneliness and terror that comes to one when love becomes unhappy." The suite received negative critical reviews, and Cage was devastated: "I had poured a great deal of emotion into the piece, and obviously I wasn't communicating this at all."[9] Friends advised him to see an analyst, but he did not find the psychological approach effective:

> I always had a chip on my shoulder about psychoanalysis. I knew the remark of Rilke . . . [who] said, "I'm sure they would remove my devils, but I fear they would offend my angels." When I went to the analyst for a kind of preliminary meeting, he said, "I'll be able to fix you so that you'll write much more music than you do now." I said, "Good heavens! I already write too much, it seems to me." That promise of his put me off.[10]

One of Cage's angels was his colleague and lover, the dancer Merce Cunningham. The American Psychiatric Association still included homosexuality on its list of pathologies (where it would remain until 1973). "Well," Cage asked himself, "if you had a disturbance both about your work and about your daily life, what are you going to do?" And he answered:

> None of the doctors can help you, our society can't help you, and education doesn't help us. . . . Furthermore, our religion doesn't help us. . . . There isn't much help for someone who is in trouble in our society. I had eliminated psychiatry as a possibility. You have Oriental thought, you have mythology.[11]

Cage's reference to "mythology" comes from his connection to Joseph Campbell, with whom Cage and his wife lived briefly when they moved to New York in 1942. Campbell may have steered Cage toward his first serious exploration of "Oriental thought": the writings of the Indian aesthetician Ananda Coomaraswamy—most likely Coomaraswamy's influential 1934 book, *Transformation of Nature in Art,* which looks at Indian and Chinese aesthetics along with writings by the fourteenth-century German mystic Meister Eckhart. After reading Coomaraswamy, Cage began working on another, longer composition*, Sonatas and Interludes* (1946–48), in which he attempted to convey the "nine permanent emotions" of Indian aesthetics. And he would become quite fond of quoting Coomaraswamy's "Art is the imitation of nature in her manner of operation."[12]

Cage continued reading Asian philosophy in search of solutions to both his emotional and professional quandaries. Finally, in Zen Buddhism he found a perspective that accorded with his own understanding and experience of life. Cage seems to have grasped early on the benefits of escaping the ego. At fifteen, he had won an oratorical prize with a speech entitled "Other People Think," in which he urged "silence on the part of the United States, in order that we could hear what other people think, and that they don't think the way we do, particularly about us."[13] He also paid attention to the effect of states of mind on perception.

In 1937 he gave a talk to a Seattle arts society entitled "The Future of Music: Credo," which began: "Wherever we are, what we hear is mostly noise. When we ignore it, it disturbs us. When we listen to it, we find it fascinating. . . . We want to capture and control these sounds, to use them not as sound effects but as musical instruments."[14]

So Zen Buddhism found fertile ground in the mind of John Cage. But it would bring something new to his outlook as well—it enabled him to give up his need to "capture and control" in art, as well as in life, to accept rather than resist change. His next major composition, finished in 1951, would be entitled *Music of Changes*. Cage's absorption of Zen principles allowed him to revolutionize the conventions of Western music by using chance and indeterminacy as organizing principles in both the composition and the performance of his works. For Cage, chance was a basic law of nature; by using chance as a creative device he was working in accord with nature. Cage used chance to determine what would be fixed, both in composing his music and making his art. Indeterminacy, on the other hand, has to do with the social reality of making, as opposed to composing: "I was intent on making something that didn't tell people what to do. . . . What I would like to arrive at, though I may never, . . . would be a situation in which no one told anyone what to do and it all turned out perfectly well anyway."[15]

Using chance both helped Cage escape his own preferences and opened him up to change. To generate answers to his aesthetic questions, Cage turned to the ancient Chinese book of wisdom—the *I Ching*, or *Book of Changes*. He told Laurie Anderson in 1992:

> I use chance operations instead of operating according to my likes and dislikes. I use my work to change myself and I accept what the chance operations say. The *I Ching* says that if you don't accept the chance operations you have no right to use them. Which is very clear, so that's what I do.[16]

The *I Ching*, which became a common source of wisdom for both Confucian and Taoist philosophy, was first developed in ancient China as a set of linear signs used as oracles. The lines themselves are produced mathematically by a variety of means—by casting yarrow sticks or tossing coins, or even by computer, the method Cage eventually adopted. What makes the *Book of Changes* a book of wisdom rather than a fortune-telling manual is that each of the sixty-four signs or situations is linked with an appropriate course of action based on natural law. The fundamental question is: what is the right course of action in a given situation? The *I Ching* foretells not fate, but what should be done to meet the requirements of the moment.

Although Cage occasionally used the *I Ching* for personal guidance, in his work he used it "simply as a kind of computer, as a facility":

> The mechanism by means of which the *I Ching* works is, I think, the same as that by means of which the DNA—or one of those things in the chemistry of our body—works. It's a dealing with the number sixty-four, with a binary situation with all of its variations in six lines. I think it's a rather basic life mechanism. I prefer it to other chance operations. . . . Some people think that I'm enslaved by it, but I feel that I am liberated by it.[17]

The *I Ching*'s foregrounding of questions, its grounding in the natural world, and its mathematical complexity all appealed to the questing, transcendental, rigorous mind of John Cage. As for the principle of chance as a compositional device, Cage told printmaker Kathan Brown: "Most people who believe that I'm interested in chance don't realize that I use chance as a discipline. They think I use it—I don't know—as a way of giving up making choices. But my choices consist in choosing what questions to ask."[18] He further elaborated this thought in another interview:

> If you work with chance operations, you're basically shifting—from the responsibility to choose to the responsibility to ask. People frequently ask me if I'm faithful to the answers, or if I change them because I want to. I don't change them because I want to. When I find myself at that point, in the position of someone who would change something—at that point I don't change it. I change myself. It's for that reason I have said that instead of self-expression, I'm involved in self-alteration.[19]

Another aspect of Cage's self-alteration emerged from indeterminate situations—his relationship with his performers and his audiences. He wanted to empower the performer, and for this reason, despite an early interest in writing and in visual art, he was most interested in "making" music. Cage believed that the performance of music offered a model for the kind of freedom with which the individual might ideally exist within society. Most performers—particularly traditional musicians—are not used to being empowered, and Cage sometimes found them to be downright hostile. His preferred performer was the pianist David Tudor, whose own unique musical skills enabled him to manifest the potential contained within Cage's indeterminate instructions. Tudor typically performed on the "prepared piano," which Cage developed in the late 1930s—a piano transformed into a percussion instrument by inserting various objects under the strings.

The people in his audiences were as important to Cage as the performers. His efforts to engage them generated a "concerted action" that served as a precursor of Happenings. This historic event—called both *Theater Piece No. 1* and *Black Mountain Piece*—took place at Black Mountain College near Asheville, North Carolina, in 1952. It included Cage's music for piano performed by David Tudor, improvised dance by Merce Cunningham, four all-white paintings by Robert Rauschenberg that were hung from the rafters, poetry read from a ladder by M. C. Richards and Charles Olson, the projection of slides and films, Rauschenberg playing an old-fashioned phonograph, and a "lecture" by Cage. Each performer in this unscripted, unrehearsed event had a randomly assigned time slot. The performance took place in and around the audience. As Cage described it, the seating arrangement was "a square composed of four triangles merging toward the center, but not meeting. . . . The audience could see itself. . . . In each one of the seats was a cup, and it wasn't explained to the audience what to do with this cup—some used it as an ashtray—but the performance was concluded by a kind of ritual, pouring coffee into each cup."[20] Cage later said the only parts he could recall were the coffee cup ritual and telling a woman who had come early and asked him which was the best seat that the seats were all equally good.[21]

Another seminal composition from 1952 by Cage is *4'33"*, which he considered his most important piece. As he explained:

> It has three movements and in all of the movements there are no sounds. I wanted my work to be free of my own likes and dislikes, because I think music should be free of the feelings and ideas of the composer. I have felt and hoped to have led other people to feel that the sounds of their environment constitute a music which is more interesting than the music which they would hear if they went into a concert hall.[22]

The three movements were signaled by David Tudor's opening and closing the piano. What *4'33"* engendered in its first audience was anger: "People began whispering to one another, and some people began to walk out. They didn't laugh—they were irritated when they realized nothing was going to happen, and they haven't forgotten it thirty years later: they're still angry."[23]

Cage said he first came up with the concept for *4'33"* in 1948, at a conference at Vassar College "involving artists and thinkers in all fields."

> I was just then in the flush of my early contact with Oriental philosophy. It was out of that that my interest in silence naturally developed: I mean it's almost transparent. . . . It stands to reason, the absence of activity which is also characteristically Buddhist. . . . Life is Activity, sometimes translated as Life is Pain. . . . The marvelous thing about it is when activity comes to a stop, what is immediately seen is that the world has not stopped. There is no place without activity.[24]

Cage was attempting to nudge his audience toward an enlightenment experience by asking them simply to listen, in an unfiltered way, to reality. He did this by providing the "frame" of a musical piece that would consist of a specified period of silence. In fact, as Cage often observed, there is no such thing as complete silence. He did worry that his intention would be lost on most audience members—that a musical composition consisting of silence would be taken as a "joke." He mulled the idea over for four years, and was finally incited to materialize it by the example of Robert Rauschenberg's 1951 white paintings, in which Rauschenberg applied house paint with a roller to achieve smooth, uninflected surfaces. Cage described these pieces as "airports for particles and shadows. A way of making emptiness visible."[25] "When I saw those, I said, 'Oh yes, I must; otherwise . . . music is lagging.'"[26]

If the realization of *4'33"* was instigated by the work of a painter, its conception was preceded by a musical composition incorporating silence dreamed up by a painter. Would-be painter is more accurate, for it was in 1947–48, when he was nineteen years old, that Yves Klein said he conceived his *Monotone-Silence Symphony,* a musical composition consisting of a single chord held for a specific length of time—twenty minutes when it was performed in 1960—followed by an equal period of silence. Klein later wrote that the "theme" of the piece was "what I wished my life to be."[27] Still later, he defined a more audience-directed agenda: to create "a sensation of vertigo, whirling the sensibility outside time."[28] This is not so different from Cage's description of "flowing full circle [between the ego and the relative world] so that you would come out, in the end . . . like Rilke looking at a tree and wondering whether you were yourself or were the tree."[29] About the kind of coincidence that had John Cage and Yves Klein simultaneously dreaming up similar concepts, Cage said, "The mind in Buddhist terms is part of the air, so to speak . . . there *can* be a flow. In fact there must be one, otherwise we can't explain the fact that several people invent the same thing at the same time independently."[30]

According to Calvin Tomkins, Cage liked the thought that his title *4'33"* could be interpreted either as four minutes, thirty-three seconds (the length of the piece), or as four feet, thirty-three inches—"a sort of personal space-time continuum."[31] Though Cage was trained as a musician and thus involved with time, at the beginning of his career he had also been interested in the spatial arts—architecture and, as he called it, "graphic" art. During the early years of the Depression, spent in his hometown of Los Angeles, he used his energy and charm to make connections with important collectors and musicians. He showed his paintings to the former and his musical compositions to the latter and noticed a trend: "the people who heard my music had better things to say about it than the people who looked at my paintings had to say about my paintings. And so I decided to devote myself to music."[32] Perhaps not surprisingly, Cage gave his music a strong visual dimension. *Water Music* of 1952, for example, had both a visually engaging score, consisting mostly of sets of instructions, and a visual as well as an aural realization that included shuffling a deck of cards and pouring water back and forth from one container to another at different rates of speed. The

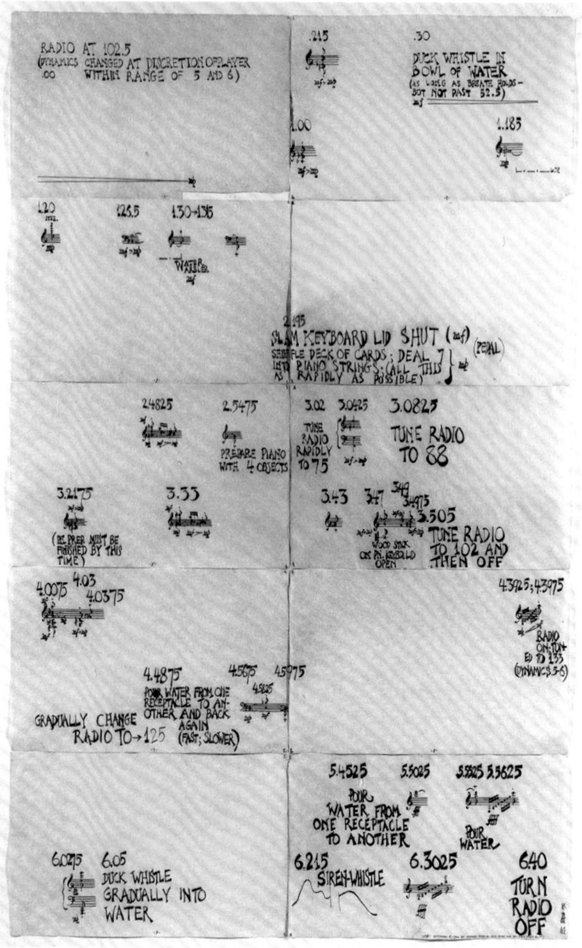

John Cage, *Water Music,* 1952, India ink on paper, ten sheets, each 11 x 17 in. Whitney Museum of American Art, New York; Purchase, with funds from an anonymous donor (82.38a-j). Photo © 1997 Whitney Museum of American Art, New York. Artist permission courtesy of the John Cage Trust.

score was large enough so that the audience could read it and thus know as much as the composer and the performer about what was happening.

Cage did more than break down the barriers between disciplines; he breached the barrier of individual creativity—of art as the unique expression of the mind and hand of the artist. In 1953 he collaborated with Robert Rauschenberg in the creation of *Automobile Tire Print*. They glued together twenty sheets of paper edge to edge and laid them in the street outside of Rauschenberg's New York studio. Cage drove the inked back wheel of his Model A Ford down the entire twenty-two-foot length of the paper, which they then mounted as a handscroll. The result—literally a tire print—exudes the aura of Zen brush painting. It is also, as curator Paul Schimmel has noted, "the visual equivalent of a sustained single note."[33]

In its wit and its subtle evocation of Buddhism, *Automobile Tire Print* shows the influence of Marcel Duchamp. Like Jasper Johns, some five years later, John Cage was strongly influenced by the example of the older artist. Cage first met Duchamp in 1942, when he and Duchamp were fellow houseguests of Peggy Guggenheim, who had agreed to pay Cage's expenses in connection with a concert he was going to give at the opening of her Art of This Century Gallery. When she learned that Cage had also promised to give a concert at the Museum of Modern Art, Guggenheim canceled the concert and refused to pay the shipping expenses to get his instruments from Chicago, where he had been living, to New York. Some thirty-five years later, Cage recalled the moment:

> I burst into tears. In the room next to mine at the back of the house Marcel Duchamp was sitting in a rocking chair smoking a cigar. He asked why I was crying and I told him. He said virtually nothing, but his presence was such that I felt calmer. . . . He had calmness in the face of disaster.[34]

Since his youth, Cage had been seeking the kind of emotional centering Duchamp had achieved. He attached significance to the belief that Duchamp had begun experimenting with chance operations the year in which he, Cage, had been born. It is hard to know exactly what Cage had in mind. It may have been Duchamp's notes for *The Large Glass,* or it may have been *Erratum Musical,* the piece of music Duchamp composed in 1913—the year *after* Cage's birth—by drawing notes randomly out of a hat. Cage so revered Marcel, as he called him, that he "didn't want to disturb him in any way."[35] So he kept his distance, but in the late 1940s, after writing the music for Duchamp's section of Hans Richter's film *Dreams That Money Can Buy,* Cage caught sight of Duchamp across the street. Duchamp greeted him with an "A-OK hand sign":[36] the hand extended palm out with the thumb and forefinger joined at the tips and forming a circle. The gesture is the Buddhist *vitarka* or teaching *mudra,* a variation of the "fear not" *mudra* that symbolizes the dispensation of the dharma. (The circle represents emptiness resulting from the union of wisdom and compassion.) Cage took it as a signal of approval for his contribution to Marcel's film bit, which no doubt it was.

At a New Year's party in 1966 Cage noticed that Duchamp looked as though his health were failing. He began spending as much time with the older artist as he could, using chess lessons as a pretext to be with him. "When he would instruct me in chess, rather than thinking about it in terms of chess, I thought about it in terms of Oriental thought."[37] This is not quite the non sequitur it seems, as chess originated in India. But when Cage asked Duchamp "if he had any relation to Eastern philosophy, because so much that he said and did was more like, say, Zen or Eastern philosophy in some form than it is like Western thought . . . he denied any connection with it."

> I think that even if he were involved consciously with Eastern philosophy, his answer would have been that he had no connection. . . . One of his goals was to go underground—which is an Eastern goal—to be a white animal, in the winter, when it's snowing, and so to climb

> up in the tree, knowing your footsteps are covered by new snow—so nobody knows where you are![38]

The shorthand version of this Zen attitude is "to leave no tracks."

Among other things, Duchamp helped Cage understand visual art as a social act. Cage told an interviewer in 1983, "Marcel Duchamp said it was the function of the observer, or the listener, to complete the work of art; so that he brought this social aspect of music over into the art of painting."[39] Yet Cage felt his version of art dharma was different from that of Duchamp, more socially engaged:

> What I like very much to think about in this connection is the final image from the Ox-Herding Pictures, the Zen text that teaches by means of illustrations instead of words. There are two versions of the Ox-Herding Pictures, you know. One version ends with an empty circle—nothingness—the example of Duchamp. In the other version the final picture is of a big fat man, with a smile on his face, returning to the village bearing gifts [see p. 208]. . . . The idea being that after the attainment of nothingness one returns again into activity.[40]

This generous attitude was one of the reasons Cage had gravitated originally toward the more social discipline of music. His absorption of Duchamp's perspective may have allowed him to return to making art. As a matter of fact, his first visual art project, in 1969, was in honor of Duchamp: *Not Wanting to Say Anything About Marcel,* two lithographs on black paper and eight screen prints on Plexiglas panels in a wooden base that can be arranged in any way. Cage called them "Plexigrams."

The title of this piece came from an incident in 1968, after the death of Marcel Duchamp. An art magazine sent Cage a letter asking him for a statement. When Cage received the letter he was with Jasper Johns, who had also received a letter. Johns said he didn't want to say anything about Marcel, and Cage took Johns's words as the title for his piece.

> It wasn't my original statement, it was Jasper's original statement. And then, instead of saying it alone or by myself, I said it together with Calvin Sumsion . . . who had been . . . a graduate student at the University of Illinois where I was when Marcel died. The reason I chose to work with him is because he knew all the techniques of doing graphic work, and I knew all the business of composing. So I composed the graphic work and he executed it, just as I would write a piece for a pianist and she would play it, or he would play it. In other words, in moving from music to graphic work, I took with me the social habits of musicians, the division of labor, so to speak. Composer to performer.[41]

The collagelike letters, images, and symbols of *Not Wanting to Say Anything About Marcel* show the influence of Robert Rauschenberg's printed collages. Cage's compositions, how-

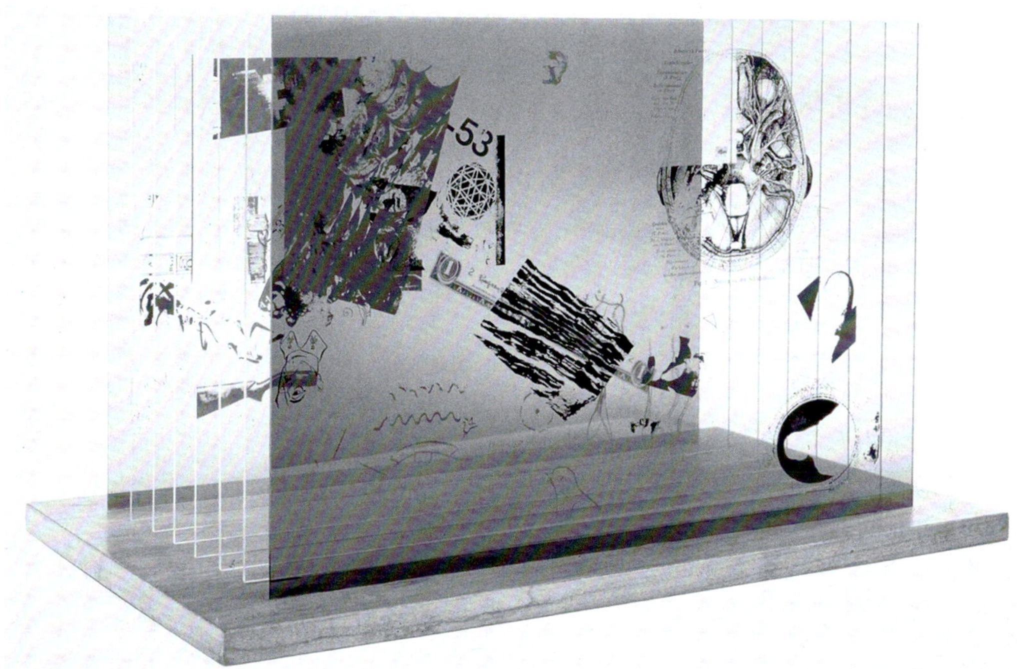

John Cage with Calvin Sumsion, *Not Wanting to Say Anything About Marcel, VIII,* 1969, screen prints on Plexiglas, from a series of eight printed in an edition of 125, eight panels 14½ x 24 in. Photo courtesy of Crown Point Press. Artist permission courtesy of the John Cage Trust.

ever, are sparer, more random. The placement, size, and even subject of the images were all determined by chance, using the *I Ching:*

> I would give him . . . chance-determined readings for horizontal and vertical. . . . I would gather, say, twenty-five images having to do with a word that came out of the dictionary—all by chance operations; and then I would go to the library and find images that corresponded with this word; and then, faced say with fifty-seven different images, I would take number thirty-seven because chance operations said I should; and then number thirty-seven should be reduced or enlarged to such and such dimensions, because those were prescribed by chance operations.[42]

Basing art processes on "Dictionaries and Atlases" was something Marcel Duchamp had thought up,[43] so the process of making *Not Wanting to Say Anything About Marcel* seems to have been a way to help Cage process his grief: "The important thing I think is that Marcel died. And that the way I chose . . . to not say anything about that was to use the dictionary, to subject it to chance operations, and then to let the words die."[44] Cage let the words die by using the *I Ching* to determine a percentage of the word or image that would be excised by

Carl Sumsion's razor blade. This is how Cage let go of his grief—by letting go of control over the viewing and even the making of *Not Wanting to Say Anything About Marcel*. While he is telling us something about himself and his relationship with Marcel, he is also telling us something about death and how to live our lives in its presence.

Aside from Marcel Duchamp, the artist who had the single greatest effect on the artwork of John Cage—certainly on how it *looked*—was Mark Tobey (1890–1976). Tobey and Morris Graves were the two most important artists of the school known as the "mystical painters of the Northwest" (Tobey became a member of the Baha'i World Faith in 1918). A generation older than Cage, Tobey moved to Seattle and began teaching at the Cornish School there in 1922, a year in which he also began to explore Chinese calligraphy. Widely traveled, Tobey spent a month in a Zen monastery near Kyoto in 1934 while visiting China and Japan. His "white writing" style of painting—white or light-colored calligraphic shapes on an abstract field—evolved following this stay.

Cage came to know Tobey soon after he moved to Seattle in 1938 to teach at the Cornish School. In addition to painting and teaching, Tobey began studying the piano and music theory around this time. Cage was struck by Tobey's willingness to look at everything in the world with equal interest. Tobey "had a great effect on my way of seeing, which is to say my involvement with painting, or my involvement with life even."[45] When Tobey's white paintings were shown in New York at the Willard Gallery in 1944, Cage saw the show:

> [It] brought about a change in my relation to art, so that when I left the Willard Gallery exhibition, I was standing at a corner on Madison Avenue waiting for a bus and I happened to look at the pavement, and I noticed that the experience of looking at the pavement was the same as the experience of looking at the Tobey. Exactly the same. The aesthetic enjoyment was just as high.[46]

Years later, in 1978, when John Cage came to make etchings at Crown Point Press at the invitation of Kathan Brown, he adopted the same all-over aesthetic as Tobey—except, he admitted space. "I don't tend to think of a foreground and a background," Cage told Brown. "I think whatever appears does so by virtue of the emptiness of the space."[47]

Cage returned annually to Crown Point Press, continuing to work with the *I Ching*, altering his aesthetic "questions" each time, and gradually learning to etch and engrave. One of his most successful series—*HV2* of 1992—contains no marks beyond accidental ones on copper plates he salvaged from the scrap pile. The plates for these fifteen color aquatint etchings were not cleaned prior to etching, so they retained traces left by the oil from hands that had touched them previously. Their color mixtures were determined by chance operations; Cage recorded the results on scores that the printers could follow and drew a map to show how the plates should be arranged on the press. These pieces of paper printed with soft,

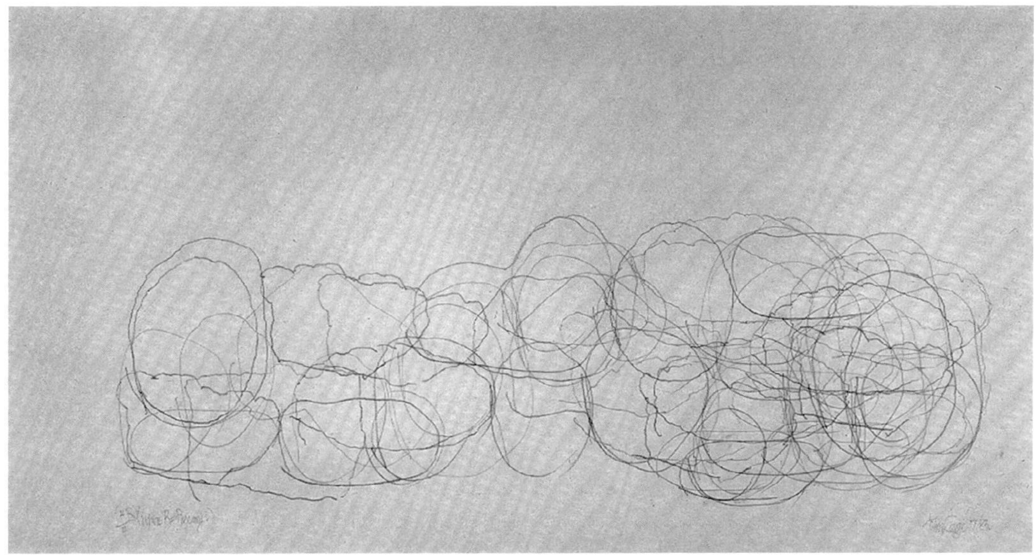

John Cage, *Where R = Ryoanji (4R)/4 7 -83,* 1983, graphite on Japanese paper, 10 x 19 in. Courtesy Margarete Roeder Gallery, New York. Artist permission courtesy of the John Cage Trust.

mottled colors contain a quiet serenity that comes as close as any of Cage's artworks to achieving his goal: "to sober and quiet the mind."

Like Yves Klein, John Cage experimented with fire and with water to create visual images. He also used rocks, which he was fond of collecting. For Cage, as for so many postwar artists, the garden of the Rinzai Zen Buddhist temple Ryoanji was an important source of inspiration. Its apparent randomness and its emptiness of anything but gravel and a few rocks appealed to him. He composed both music and art that explored its "givens," to use the title of Duchamp's last artwork. Ryoanji contains fifteen stones. Cage used fifteen stones in composing his own *Ryoanji* series of etchings, drawings, and music—the same fifteen each time. He also replicated the proportions of the garden in the paper for the *Ryoanji* prints he did at Crown Point Press beginning in 1983.

Perhaps the most lyrical pieces in the *Ryoanji* series are the graphite drawings Cage began making later that year. He would place each stone on the paper, its location determined by chance, and trace around it a certain number of times, also determined by chance, until the paper carried the tremulous images of all fifteen stones. Their shapes overlapped; Cage liked that, for at Ryoanji "the stones are arranged in such a way that there appear to be three, but in actuality there are fifteen."[48] In the end, this meditative process was all about perspective: the relationship between the Ryoanji garden and its stones, the relationship between the mind and its objects, and the mutable, elusive nature of both.

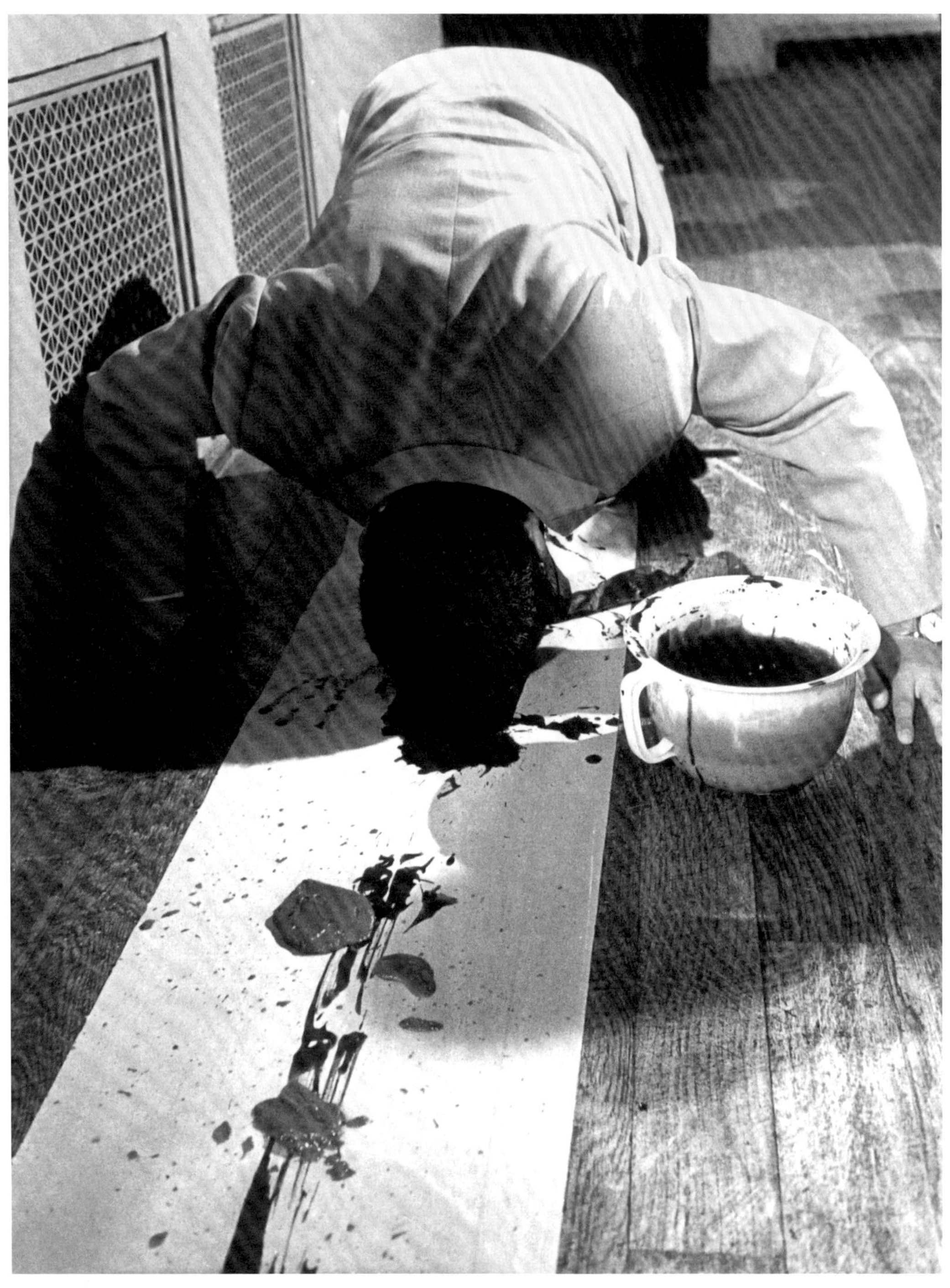

Nam June Paik, *Zen for Head,* performance, Städtisches Museum, Wiesbaden, Germany, September 1962. Photo: Gottert/DPA/Landov. Courtesy of Nam June Paik.

My TV is not always interesting,
but not always uninteresting.
As nature,
who is beautiful,
not because it changes beautifully,
but because it
simply changes.

NAM JUNE PAIK

NAM JUNE PAIK 1932–

UNLIKE JOHN CAGE, WHO HAD, ONE MIGHT SAY, a "Buddhist" temperament, Nam June Paik was a born iconoclast. Educated in Japan, a refugee both from his divided native country of Korea and from his privileged childhood, Paik once responded to a question about whether he was a Buddhist with, "No, I'm an artist."[1] Nevertheless, it was arguably Zen Buddhism that allowed Paik to begin, as an artist, in a more radical place than where Cage ended. Early on, Paik rejected the fatalism and respect for tradition of "China and Asians, who live the Confucian edict of complete obedience to one's elders, have little space for individual freedom."[2] In contrast, Zen Buddhism, with its valuing of the idiosyncratic and its incorporation of violence as a path to *satori,* held a certain appeal. If Cage sought serenity in the Buddhist perspective, Paik was drawn to the aspect of Zen that might be expressed through shock and surprise as easily as in quietude. More easily, in fact, in his early career, when youthful anger and alienation fueled his production.

A generation younger than Cage, Paik was a product of the international politics and dynamic cultural changes of the 1950s. At the age of seventeen he emigrated with his Korean family to escape the Korean War, first to Hong Kong and then to Japan. He studied music and art history at the University of Kyoto, where he wrote his thesis on John Cage's teacher, Arnold Schoenberg. The year of his graduation, 1956, Paik began studying modern music in West Germany. In 1958 he moved to Cologne to work at the Studio for Electronic Music of West German Radio. That summer he met John Cage, who was in residence at the International Vacation Course for New Music in Darmstadt. Under Cage's influence Paik began to compose and perform "action music"—startling, sometimes violent acts aimed at rousing his audience from their passive state in much the same way Renzai Zen teachers aimed to startle their students to another plane of consciousness.

Cage was not thrilled. On a panel in connection with a retrospective of Paik's work in 1982, he described his first experience of a Paik performance:

> I found myself in Cologne attending a performance by him of his *Etude for Pianoforte*. Behind Paik as he performed was an open window, floor to ceiling. His actions were such we wouldn't have been surprised had he thrown himself five floors down to the street. When at the end he left the room through the packed audience, everybody, all of us, sat paralyzed with fear, utterly silent, for what seemed an eternity. No one budged. We were stunned. Finally, the telephone rang. "It was Paik," Mary Bauermeister said, "calling to say the performance is over." I determined to think twice before attending another performance by Nam June Paik.[3]

What Cage doesn't mention is Paik's pause upon departure to douse him and David Tudor with shampoo and—in an act widely interpreted as blatantly oedipal—to cut off Cage's necktie. Cage confessed that he had trouble thinking of Paik as a composer at all. He considered the most "musical" of Paik's works to be "those for which he has given no performance directions, for which the accompaniment is simply the sounds of the environment."[4] He was thinking, perhaps, of pieces like the *TV Buddhas,* which are at the serene end of the Paik spectrum. Cage did, however, innately understand a rather difficult Paik piece, *Zen for Film* of 1964, which consists of an hour's worth of blank celluloid:

> Paik invited Merce Cunningham and me to Canal Street to see his *Zen for Film*, an hour-long film without images. "The mind is like a mirror; it collects dust, the problem is to remove the dust." "Where is the mirror? Where is the dust?" In this case the dust is on the lens of the projector and on the blank developed film itself. "There is never nothing to see."[5]

He was referring, of course, to the contrasting Zen views of Shen-hsiu and Hui-neng.

Allan Kaprow commented that in the early sixties Paik was known as a "cultural terrorist," concluding: "Paik was the all-too-live embodiment of his ironic assertion that the relative is the absolute, and vice versa."[6] Just how "ironic" Paik's assertion was intended to be is questionable. Inspired by Cage, Paik had studied up on Zen Buddhism, electronics, the socially engaged scholar of electronic media Marshall McLuhan, the socially engaged engineer Buckminster Fuller, and Heisenberg's uncertainty principle, in which electrons can appear as either particle or wave, depending on the moment and place (time and space) in which they're observed. If Paik wanted to destroy anything, it was dualistic, hierarchical thinking about culture and its relation to society; in other words, cultural tradition. The object of Nam June Paik's attack at the conclusion of *Etude for Pianoforte* may have been precisely the necktie of John Cage.

Paik has always been evasive about his attitude toward Buddhism, but the word "Zen" popped up early and often in his titles. At the very least, this tactic forced observers to consider the meaning of the term within the context of contemporary Western culture. One of Paik's Fluxus activities was a 1963 mail art project entitled *The Monthly Review of the University for Avant-Garde Hinduism*. Avant-garde Hinduism is one way of thinking about Buddhism.

The performance Cage witnessed and witlessly participated in took place in 1960. In the course of the 1960s and 1970s, Paik would be in the forefront of a radical group of young international artists who took the interdisciplinary, iconoclastic approach of John Cage in new directions. Paik's unique contribution to Performance Art was his adaptation of the technology of the moving image—film, single-channel video, and, most notably, television—to sculptural and installation formats that could be displayed in galleries and museums. Paik also worked directly with the broadcast media. Through electronic technology, he transformed Performance Art, making it broadly accessible, even engaging. His ultimate goal, however, was more ambitious: to, as he put it, "enrich the synapses between the brain cells of humanity."[7]

First, though, Paik had to break a few eggs—and a few pianos. In his *Homage to John Cage: Music for Tape Player and Piano*, first presented in Dusseldorf in November 1959, Paik played a collaged tape while performing a set of actions. According to one of the audience members that night, "In this 'music' for tape recorders and piano the most bizarre things happen in five minutes: there are howls of electronic noise, eggs splash against the wall, a motorbike clatters off, a musical box tinkles, the radio blares out political news, Paik plays Czerny-like exercises on the piano, a rosary flies past my head, an old piano has to produce its last sounds on strings that have been torn out, then it is hurled over with a thunderous noise; suddenly there is silence and complete darkness, and finally Paik's unyielding face, illuminated by a stump of candle."[8]

At the first official Fluxus festival—the "Fluxus International Festival of Very New Music" presented at the Städtisches Museum in Wiesbaden, Germany, in September 1962—Paik performed a piece by La Monte Young, which Paik renamed *Zen for Head*. (Paik had debuted his interpretation of Young's *Composition 1960 No. 10* the previous year in Cologne.) Young's score directs the performer: "Draw a straight line and follow it." Paik carried out this instruction by inking his hair with a mixture of ink and tomato juice and using his head as a brush that his body, of necessity, "followed" as he drew a line down a scroll of paper.

The crude result resembled nothing so much as a Zen literati brushstroke. Young's "score" collapses art and life in Fluxus fashion; *Zen for Head* proffers a shockingly simple Zen insight about the most direct way to perform it: use your head as a brush. The blood-red tomato juice Paik mixed with the ink evokes both human nature and human fragility. It was a brilliant performance.

The culmination of Paik's career in Germany was his "Exposition of Music—Electronic Television" of 1963. In one of the rooms at the Galerie Parnass in Wuppertal, Paik took Cage's concept of the "prepared" piano a notch further by turning three pianos into assemblages so abused that they could no longer function as pianos. The only survivor, *Integral Piano,* is gutted and encrusted with objects including toys, a clock, a lamp, a brassiere, and eggshells. Eggs—which are ubiquitous in Paik's work, especially in his early pieces—call to mind the adage that you can't make an omelet without breaking some. Paik's intention with all this mayhem was to rearrange our sensibilities by breaking down our preconceptions.

The point is reinforced by the other cultural object, besides the traditional piano, radically altered by Paik for this 1963 exposition: the television. In another room of the Galerie Parnass, he presented twelve "prepared" television sets, scattered around the floor. Their reception was altered in various ways. For example, visitors could adjust the size of the light spot at the center of the television entitled *Point of Light* by turning the volume dial of a radio hooked up to it. Paik reduced the image on the screen of *Zen for TV* to a horizontal line of light, which he made vertical by turning the set on its side. His title implies both that this television is meant to be an aid to meditation and that the set itself is in a meditative state. "I am proud to be able to say that all [the] sets actually changed their inner circuits," Paik joked at the time.[9]

In 1964 Nam June Paik moved to New York, where he renewed associations with musicians and artists he had met at Fluxus activities in Germany, including the cellist Charlotte Moorman, who would become an important collaborator. The following year Paik had his first one-person show in the United States, at Galeria Bonino in New York. At this influential exhibition, which he entitled "Electronic Art," Paik again presented his prepared television sets. "Electronic Art" generated a flurry of activity among artists and inspired the wave of video art that began in the late 1960s. But Paik wanted to reach a broader audience. A follower of McLuhan, he had a pretty good idea about how to attract media attention.

The evening of February 9, 1967, Nam June Paik and Charlotte Moorman performed Paik's *Opera Sextronique* in New York City. The poster for this event, which was open "by invitation only," proclaimed:

> After three emancipations in 20th century music (serial, indeterministic, actional), I have found that there is still one more chain to lose, that is, PRE-FREUDIAN HYPOCRISY. Why

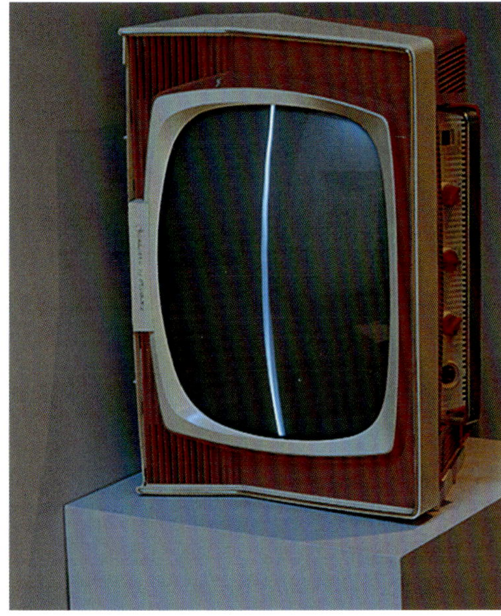

Nam June Paik, *Zen for TV,* 1963/78, altered television set, 20¾ x 15⅜ x 12⅛ in. Hood Museum of Art, Dartmouth College, Hanover, New Hampshire; gift of the artist (9GM.978.211).

> is sex a predominant theme in art and literature prohibited ONLY in music? . . . Music history needs its D. H. Lawrence, its Sigmund Freud.[10]

Act I, according to Moorman's notes (probably written by Paik), began:

> In complete darkness—two to three minutes of silence—then a Buddhist gong recording begins (Eihiji's Morning Ceremony . . . a spectacular discovery made by U.S. musicologists), symbolizing *the transience of versatile life.* In accordance with these gongs, Paik, by remote control, flashed on and off intermittently and rhythmically . . . the *Electric Bikini* I was wearing—a three-piece "light bikini" ingeniously contrived of triangles filled with 45 six-volt bulbs—representing the eternal beauty of womanhood. I walked very slowly, as in a Japanese Noh play, to my chair and began to play Paik's variations of Massenet's "Elegie" (Takehisa Kosugi then flashed the lights, while Paik played the piano accompaniment). . . . In this aria, Paik modernized Buddhism, beautified the electronic age, and criticized the commercialized so-called Sex Revolution, and sublimated it to the level of Faust/Freud/Lawrence.[11]

In the second act, Moorman appeared "seminude in a long, formal black skirt" for her role as a "live Greek female torso sitting still at a cello."[12] During this act, she and Paik were both arrested by the New York City police. Three months later, Moorman was found guilty of indecent exposure and given a suspended sentence. Paik was found not guilty because the judge found the concept of "pornographic music" impossible.

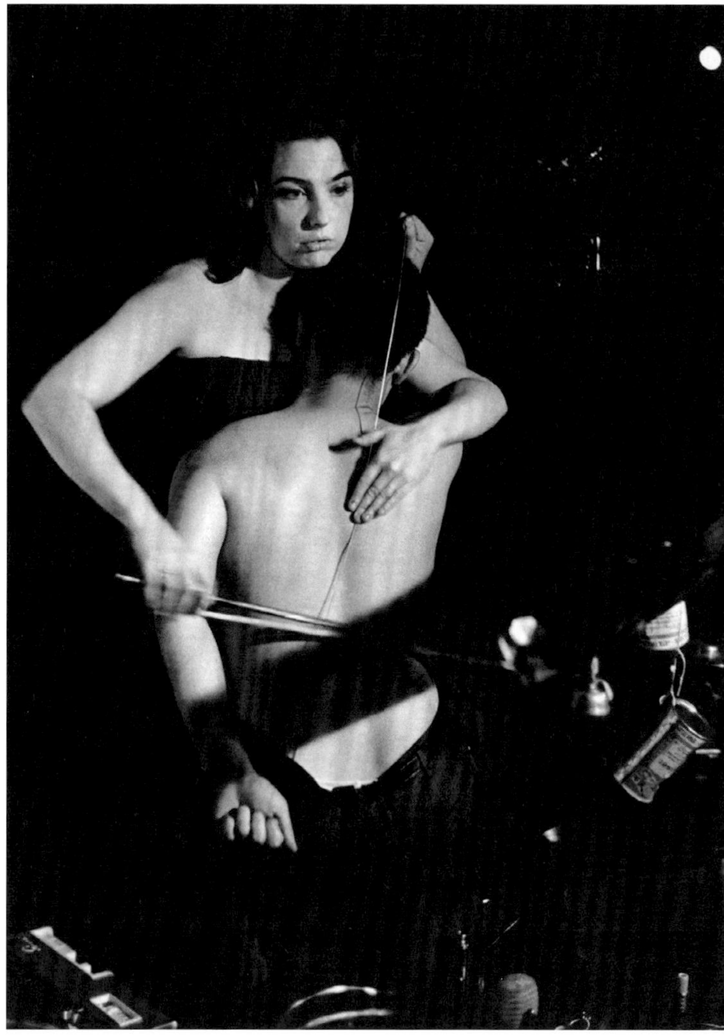

Nam June Paik and Charlotte Moorman performing John Cage's *26'1.1499" for a String Player*, 1965. Photo: Peter Moore, © Estate of Peter Moore/VAGA, NYC.

Opera Sextronique turned out to be a brilliant move. Moorman became a television talk show favorite, and the two were a popular and provocative performance team through the seventies—he, the wild man of Fluxus; she, a concert cellist gone AWOL, but always the lady. (According to Paik, she was a tough southern girl—"wild oats.")[13] Paik created many pieces for her, including a cello made of three television sets, each of them playing an image of her playing them. Perhaps the best-known is *TV Bra for Living Sculpture* of 1969. Their most poignant pairing was the 1965 performance in which his seminude body became her cello as she played a piece by John Cage. His face buried in her (clothed) bosom, Paik held the vertical single string at top and bottom behind his head and lower back. Her arms embraced him as she played. This time, it was the single string that became the vertical line,

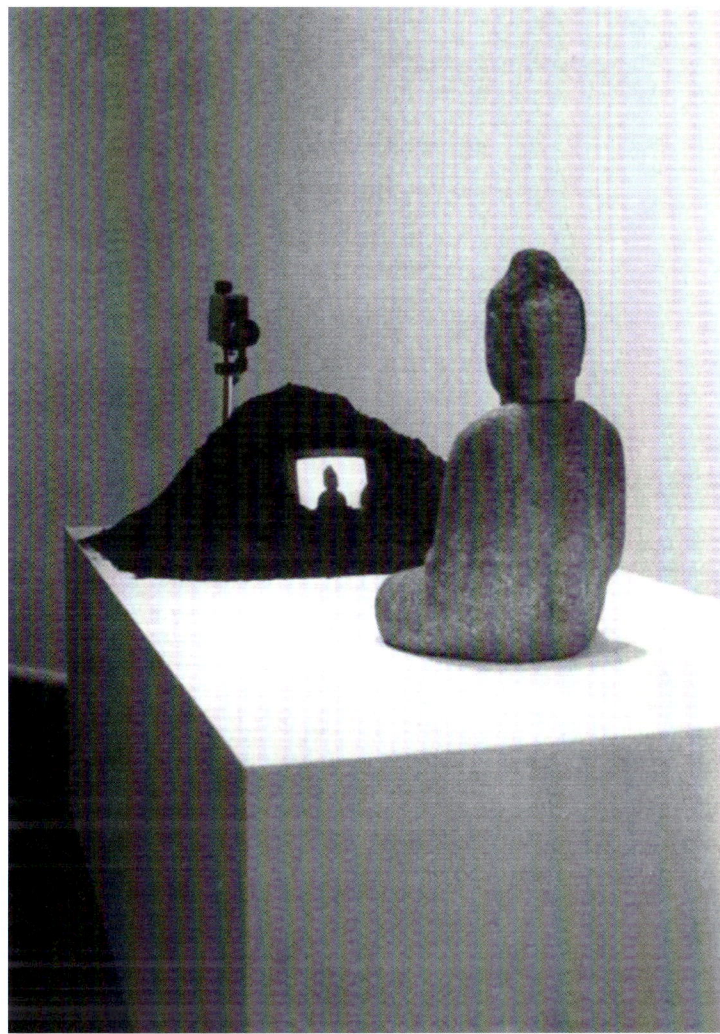

Nam June Paik, *TV Buddha No. X* (Whitney-Buddha-Complex), 1974–82, seventh-century Korean Buddha statue, monitor, camera, soil. Installation at the Whitney Museum of American Art, New York 1982. Courtesy of Nam June Paik.

connecting two bodies locked in embrace, making music. It was a particularly Paikian conception of the transcendence of dualism.

One way of thinking about transcendence is as simultaneous self-absorption and connection. Paik's most successful expression of this concept was *TV Buddha,* which he created in a number of formats, beginning in 1974. On an obvious level, *TV Buddha* refers to the fact that by 1974 television had come to occupy the place that would have been reserved, in Buddhist households, for the family altar. Paik himself told one interviewer: "I was a social thinker. TV was so prevalent, so we had to think about it. I was going to make TV high art, like Johann Sebastian Bach."[14] Earlier, in another interview, he had commented: "I react to Zen in the same way as I react to Johann Sebastian Bach."[15] Paik's intention in bringing together a television set with an image of the meditating Buddha was to raise television to the level of highest consciousness. This reading is reinforced by another piece Paik occasionally paired with *TV Buddha*—*TV Rodin* (1976–78), his first video multiple, which similarly combines a TV with a small version of Rodin's *The Thinker.*

Like any good work of art, however, *TV Buddha* carries meaning on more than one level. The historian of Asian art Walter Smith has analyzed the version of *TV Buddha* created for Paik's 1982 Whitney Museum retrospective within a traditional Buddhist context. In the Whitney version, a stone Buddha sits facing its own image on a television monitor contained in a mound of dirt. Smith compares Paik's two Buddha images facing each other to the tradition in Asian art of pairing the historical Buddha, Gautama or Shakyamuni, with Prabhutaratna, a Buddha of the distant past. This dual-Buddha image comes from the Lotus Sutra, where it illustrates Gautama's teaching that he is only one manifestation of universal buddha mind; there have been others in the past and will be others in the future. Prabhutaratna is a past Buddha who has been in the state of highest enlightenment for eons. Before his death he vowed he would reappear each time this doctrine was taught.

Smith points out that "in the Lotus Sutra, when Prabhutaratna appears to Gautama, he appears seated within a resplendent and light-filled *stupa*."[16] In its simplest form, a stupa is a grave mound. Prabhutaratna's appearance within one signals his status as a Buddha from a former age. What could be more apt than a television screen—where the image is literally made of light—within a stupa-shaped mound of dirt, referring to interment? In the Lotus Sutra, the two Buddhas carry on a dialogue. In Asian artworks that portray this scene, they commune with each other, as do Paik's two Buddhas—the one made of stone, the other of light.

Paik has said that in 1974, when he first came up with the concept for *TV Buddha,* he "had just bought four Japanese Buddhas—very good antiques—as an investment." Shigeko Kubota, a Japanese artist who would become his wife three years later, "liked the Buddha very much. She kind of prayed on this Buddha and her prayer came to me."[17] This explanation of how the concept for *TV Buddha* occurred to Paik is somewhat suspect, if only because Paik always stressed his poverty. Investing in Buddhas would seem to have been an unlikely activity. He was investing in his art.

When Zen practitioners meditate on an image of the Buddha, they are focusing on their own buddha minds—they become buddhas. This, surely, is the core meaning of *TV Buddha.* A 1989 variant of the *TV Buddha* theme paired a bronze sculpture with Paik's own facial features and a monitorless set containing a burning candle. In this contemporary altar, the flickering light of a flame replaces the electronic light of a monitor. The situation is reminiscent of the conclusion to Paik's early performance of his *Homage to John Cage:* "suddenly there is silence and complete darkness, and finally Paik's unyielding face, illuminated by a stump of candle."[18]

By the 1980s Paik no longer needed violence to contrast with Cage's silence. His message had become empowerment through enlightenment. Paik succeeded in going global with his message, creating satellite broadcasts such as "Good Morning, Mr. Orwell" (1984), "Wrap around the World" (1988), and a "final" millennial global broadcast on New Year's Eve 1999. Nam June Paik may not have had much of an effect on commercial television broadcasting, but he has done quite a lot to show that television, like music, can connect human minds and hearts. It is a proposition that deserves to be contemplated.

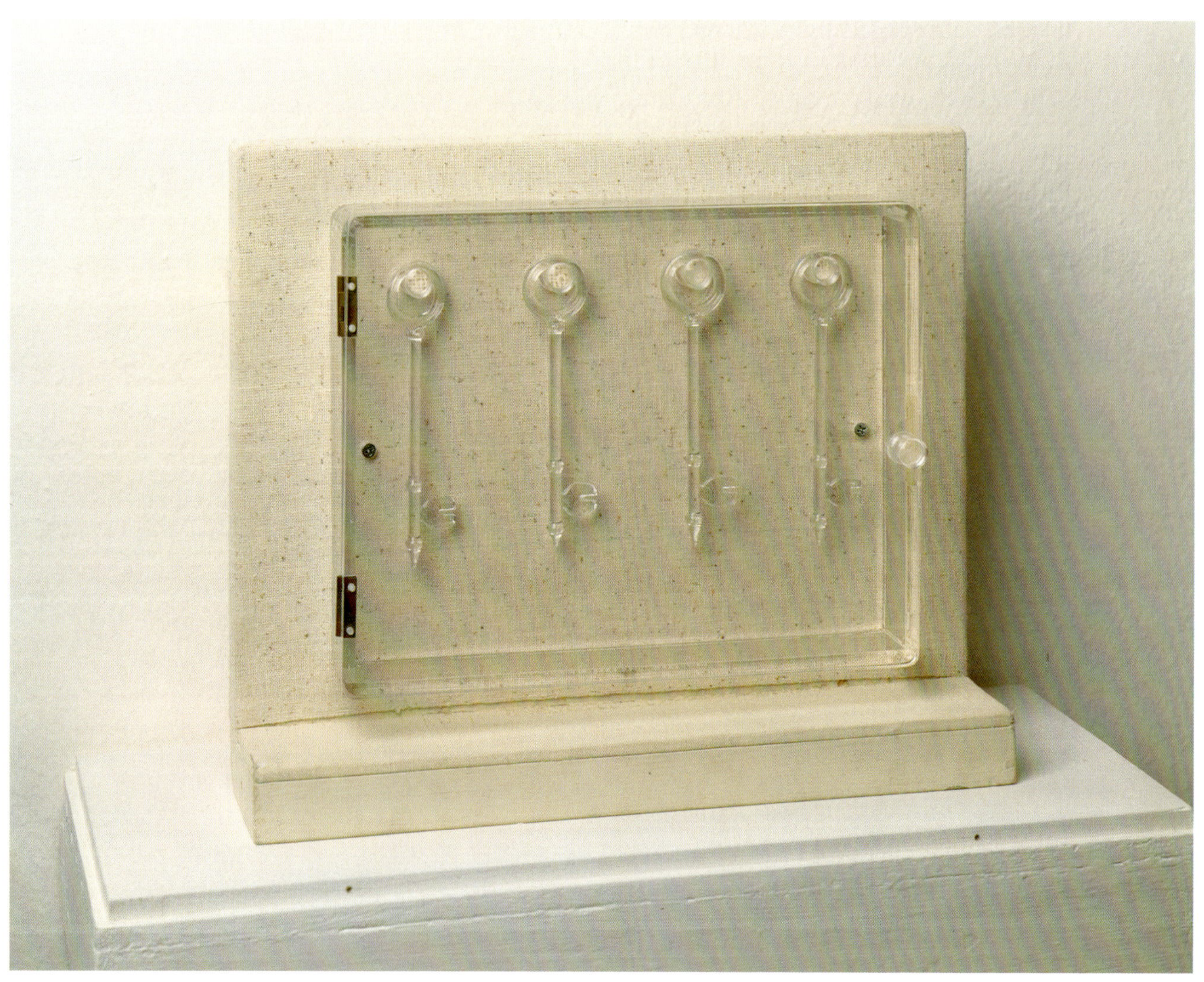

Yoko Ono, *Glass Keys to Open the Skies,* 1967, glass keys in Plexiglas box with brass hinges, 7½ x 10 x 1½ in. Collection of the artist. Courtesy of Yoko Ono.

Art is not merely a duplication of life. To assimilate art in life, is different from art duplicating life.

YOKO ONO, 1966

YOKO ONO 1933–

LIKE NAM JUNE PAIK, YOKO ONO EXPANDED into the visual arts from music within the heterogeneous artistic environment created by John Cage. Unlike Paik, she has never left music behind. Her particular contribution, in work ranging from music to poetry to visual art to performance and filmmaking, has been radical simplification. By focusing on a single action, gesture, or instruction, Ono reduces the structural complexity of Cage and the emotional complexity of Paik to a basic, relational experience. She frankly considers Cage's use of chance to be inadequate to the task at hand: the complete transcendence of consciousness. As she explained in a 1962 essay for a Japanese journal:

> We . . . are so invaded by the falsehood of consciousness we cannot even become random operational by using such a loose method as random operation. Instead, if we assign the most fictional rules, only then, may we possibly transcend our consciousness. . . . We can call these rituals a means to rationalize the irrationality in us, humans. . . . I wish not to be confused with the high-minded types who feel they have achieved Satori by becoming plantlike. I am still groping in the world of stickiness.[1]

She wants us to grope with her, and she seduces us to do so through poetic "rituals" she developed, rituals that are revealed to us through brief, tantra-like works of conceptual art.

Like Cage, Ono was influenced by the work of Marcel Duchamp: her 1961 *Painting for*

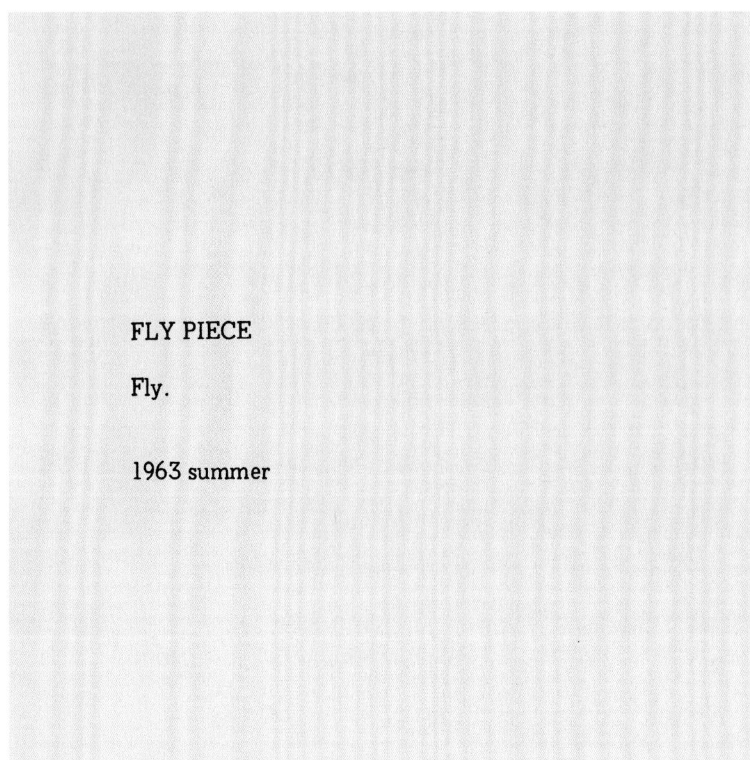

Yoko Ono, *Fly Piece,* 1963. © Yoko Ono. Courtesy of Yoko Ono.

the Wind (make a hole in a canvas; leave it in the wind) is the offspring of his 1919 *Unhappy Readymade* (hang a geometry book from a balcony; expose it to the wind and rain). And Yves Klein's *Leap into the Void* (p. 143) was clearly foundational for her *Fly Piece*. But both Yoko Ono's art and her music have a simplicity and interactive intensity that is unique to her, as well as a certain generosity. Another version of her *Painting for the Wind,* for example, reads: "Cut a hole in a bag filled with seeds of any kind and place the bag where there is wind."[2] And her *Fly Piece* offers an invitation to fly, rather than merely presenting evidence that it can be done, as Klein's *Leap* does.

For Ono, there are many ways to fly. A 1964 version of *Fly Piece* instructs: "Skin two thousand balloons. Fly them in the air."[3] In the announcement for the first formal performance of *Fly* in Tokyo, in April 1964, the instruction, "Fly," was accompanied by a hint, "come prepared to fly." For this performance, a group of Ono's artist friends, including Nam June Paik, took turns "flying" from a tall ladder. Ono was not present. Her point was that "the piece had its own life, and the participation of others, in fact, made the piece."[4] In later performances, audience members were invited to fly. In 1970 Ono made a film entitled *Fly* based on a 1968 "film score": "Let a fly walk on a woman's body from toe to head and fly out of

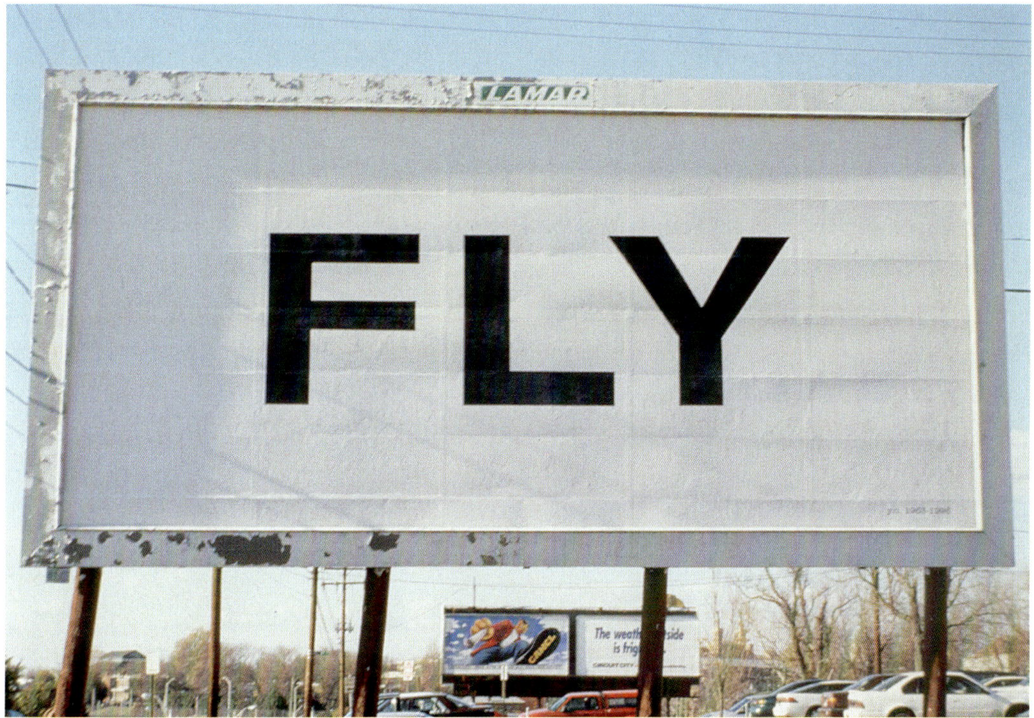

Yoko Ono, *Fly*, 1996, billboard in Richmond, Virginia. Photo: Stephen Salpukas. Courtesy of Yoko Ono.

the window."[5] The next year, *Fly* was the title of an album she did with John Lennon. *Fly*'s earliest appearance, however, was as "Instructions for Poem No. 86 / Fly," on the 1963 birth announcement for Ono's daughter, Kyoko.[6] Instead of the baby's footprint, the announcement features an ink impression of her wrist and hand in the Buddhist "fear not" *mudra*. For Ono, the instruction to "fly" is an instruction not to be afraid: "If the butterflies in your stomach die, send yellow death announcements to your friends," she wrote in 1966.[7] Ono's goal, like the Buddha's, is nothing less than the end of suffering.

Yoko Ono's background is an international mixture of Japanese and American, Buddhism and Protestantism. Born in Japan, she lived in the United States with her banker-father, mother, and brother from 1933 to 1937 and again in 1941–42. She moved to the United States yet again at the age of nineteen, when her family joined her father in Scarsdale, where he was director for the American operations of the Bank of Tokyo. Ono enrolled at nearby Sarah Lawrence College, where she majored in poetry and music composition. Yoko experienced her mother, who was from a Buddhist banking family, as beautiful but distant. Her Protestant father was a pianist who had given up a concert career to join the family business. Yoko's goal as a child was to help him vicariously achieve his early aspiration. She received classical training in both piano and voice. Her later vocal pyrotechnics were grounded in techniques of German lieder and Italian opera, and her event scores were informed by her knowledge of music composition and poetry. By the early 1950s, however, Ono was in full rebellion against the restrictions and expectations of her family, Japanese culture, and a violent world.

Like Nam June Paik, who came from an upper-class background but suffered discrimination as a Korean in Japan, Yoko Ono, with her elite schooling both in America and in Japan, became an object of derision when U.S. firebombings of Tokyo caused her family to flee to the countryside in 1945. In addition to the displacement, taunting, and wartime terror, she recalls being always hungry at this time. To escape her misery, Yoko and her younger brother would hide. She remembers lying together on their backs: "looking up at the sky through an opening in the roof, we exchanged menus in the air and used our powers of visualization to survive."[8] Twelve-year-old Yoko was no doubt the instigator in this imaginative escape from the pain of existence. It would set a pattern for her life as an artist of the imagination, and for the persistence of the sky as a presence in her work. In her 1967 sculpture *Glass Keys to Open the Skies,* for example, the four transparent keys in their clear, Plexiglas box and the plural "skies" in the title imply different imaginative possibilities. To unlock the sky, you'd have to be able to reach it, which isn't possible. But neither is it necessary, for the sky is always open to us. As Ono herself said, "Even when everything was falling apart around me, the sky was always there for me."[9]

With her childhood sky "menus" and training as a musician, it is no surprise that Ono was attracted to the work of John Cage. The art historian Alexandra Munroe has foregrounded the importance to Ono and her fellow Fluxus artists of Cage's method of creating a "score" for everything, including his artworks. According to Munroe:

> These terse instructions proposed mental and/or physical actions to be carried out by the reader/performer. . . . The early Fluxus scores were characterized by clarity and economy of language. . . . They could be performed in the mind as a thought, or as a physical performance before an invited audience. . . . Along with Brecht and the composer La Monte Young, Yoko Ono was among the first to experiment with the event score and its conceptual use of language as a form of art.[10]

An example of an event score is La Monte Young's "draw a straight line and follow it" of 1960, which Nam June Paik performed to dramatic effect in 1962 (see p. 178). A much earlier example is Yoko Ono's *Secret Piece,* which she dates to the summer of 1953:

> Decide on one note that you want to play. Play it with the following accompaniment:
> The woods from 5 A.M. to 8 A.M. in summer.[11]

These instructions are the verbal version of her original drawing of a score with the bass stave showing a sustained note, and a vacant treble stave with handwriting running along the top that reads: "with the accompaniment of the birds singing at dawn." One can imagine the willful, twenty-year-old Sarah Lawrence poetry and composition major coming up with this score, which combines the focused intensity of Yves Klein's *Monotone-Silence Symphony* with the Zen openness of John Cage's *4'33"*.

The influence of Zen koans—paradoxical statements to which a "solution" comes in a flash of insight—is evident throughout Ono's work. Her *Stone Piece (Tape Piece I)*, from 1963, instructs: "Tape the sound of the stone aging."[12] *Map Piece* from 1964 says, "Draw a map to get lost."[13] Her *Snow Piece (Tape Piece III)* begins:

> Take a tape of the sound of the snow
> falling.
> This should be done in the evening.
> Do not listen to the tape.
> Cut it and use it as strings to tie
> gifts with.[14]

Snow Piece is a good example of the connection between Ono's work and haiku poetry, which relies on nature imagery. *Water Piece* (1964) is totally Zen in its imagery of moon and water and bucket:

> Steal a moon in the water with a bucket.
> Keep stealing until no moon is seen on
> the water.[15]

But not all of Ono's work is so serene. Her work tends toward the two ends of the emotional spectrum. It can be meditative and lyrical, as in *Snow Piece* or *Fly Piece*, but it can also be anguished, as in *Voice Piece for Soprano* from fall 1961:

> Scream.
> 1. against the wind
> 2. against the wall
> 3. against the sky[16]

Another example, from the previous winter, when Ono and La Monte Young presented a series of events in her New York loft, is *Painting to Be Stepped On*. This piece of canvas, as its title implies, was on the floor. Visitors were invited to step on it—that is, to do violence to it.

Step Piece derives a good deal of its conceptual power from the fact that its creator is a woman. In this, it was a forerunner to one of Ono's most impressive performance pieces:

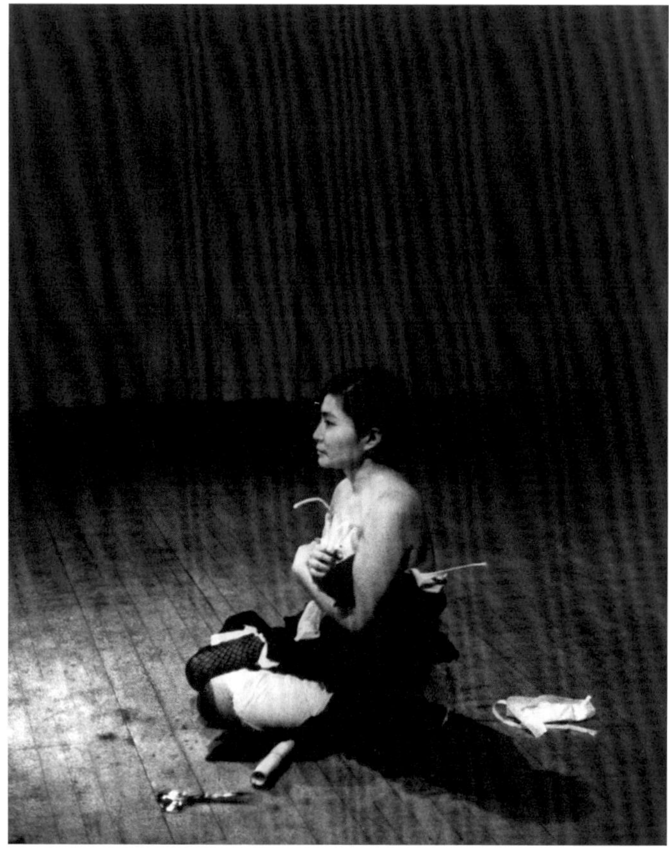

Yoko Ono, *Cut Piece,* March 21, 1965, Carnegie Recital Hall, New York. Photo: Minoru Niizuma. Courtesy of Yoko Ono.

Cut Piece, first performed in Kyoto in 1964. The instruction for the piece states simply: "Cut." In her book *Grapefruit,* she added the following gloss:

> It is usually performed by Yoko Ono coming on the stage and in a sitting position, placing a pair of scissors in front of her and asking the audience to come up on the stage, one by one, and cut a portion of her clothing (anywhere they like) and take it. The performer, however, does not have to be a woman.[17]

This apparently simple concept turns out, in performance, to be emotionally charged with violent and sexual content. Its most provocative element is contained in the last sentence of Ono's description: "The performer, however, does not have to be a woman." It is almost impossible to imagine a man performing this piece, which is the point.

It is instructive to compare the violence of *Cut Piece* with the violence of Nam June Paik's 1960 performance of *Etude for Pianoforte.* Paik ended the performance by cutting audience member John Cage's tie, as well as his shirttail, with scissors. Ono reversed the situation, giving her audience the opportunity to cut her clothes. In response to their aggression she stoically maintained a meditative state that critiqued both societal expectations regarding feminine behavior and art-world expectations that artists be self-revealing. *Cut Piece* is related to Marcel Duchamp's *Bride Stripped Bare by Her Bachelors, Even,* as both Ono and Duchamp's bride theoretically retain their emotional distance from the actions to which they are subjected. And, just as the experience of a performance of Cage's *4'33"* depends completely on its context, so Ono's experience in *Cut Piece* depended on her audience: she retained discreet remnants of her clothing in Japan and none in London, while in the United States she was left with something in between.

Ono showed *Painting to Be Stepped On* with twelve other "instruction paintings" at George Maciunas's AG Gallery in June 1961. Although there were a few written instructions, she or Maciunas mostly gave visitors oral instructions to indicate that the thirteen unstretched, ink-covered canvases they saw were simply examples of paintings they themselves might undertake. The following year, in Tokyo, she took the radical step of exhibiting only the instructions. This, she believed at the time, "would open up a whole new horizon for the visual arts. I was totally excited by the idea and its visual possibilities."[18] The negative popular and critical response sent her, temporarily, into a mental institution. In retrospect, however, she remembers this as "one of the most exciting moments of my life. It was great! It was fresh! It was a revolution! . . . It was like a love affair." But, like most passionate love affairs, "somehow, it's too sad to do again."[19] In exhibitions since then, Ono has resumed including an example along with each instruction.

Another of Ono's "instruction paintings," *Smoke Painting,* is at once a meditation aid and a comment on the value of painting, as opposed to the value of what happens in the maker/viewer's mind:

> Light a canvas or any finished painting with a
> cigarette at any time for any length of time.
>
> See the smoke movement.
> The painting ends when the whole canvas or painting is gone.[20]

The instruction pointedly conflates the maker of the "painting" and the viewer/reader. (Ono's instructions are, perhaps, best performed in the mind.) No matter who made the "canvas or any finished painting" selected, the "painter" of Ono's *Smoke Painting* is the one who "finishes" it by burning the last bit. The "end" of the painting thus refers at once to the completion of the instruction, the fate of the canvas, and its consumption as an occasion to "see the smoke movement." It is this complexity within the apparent simplicity of Ono's work that marks her as a "fine artist," as Ad Reinhardt might have put it.

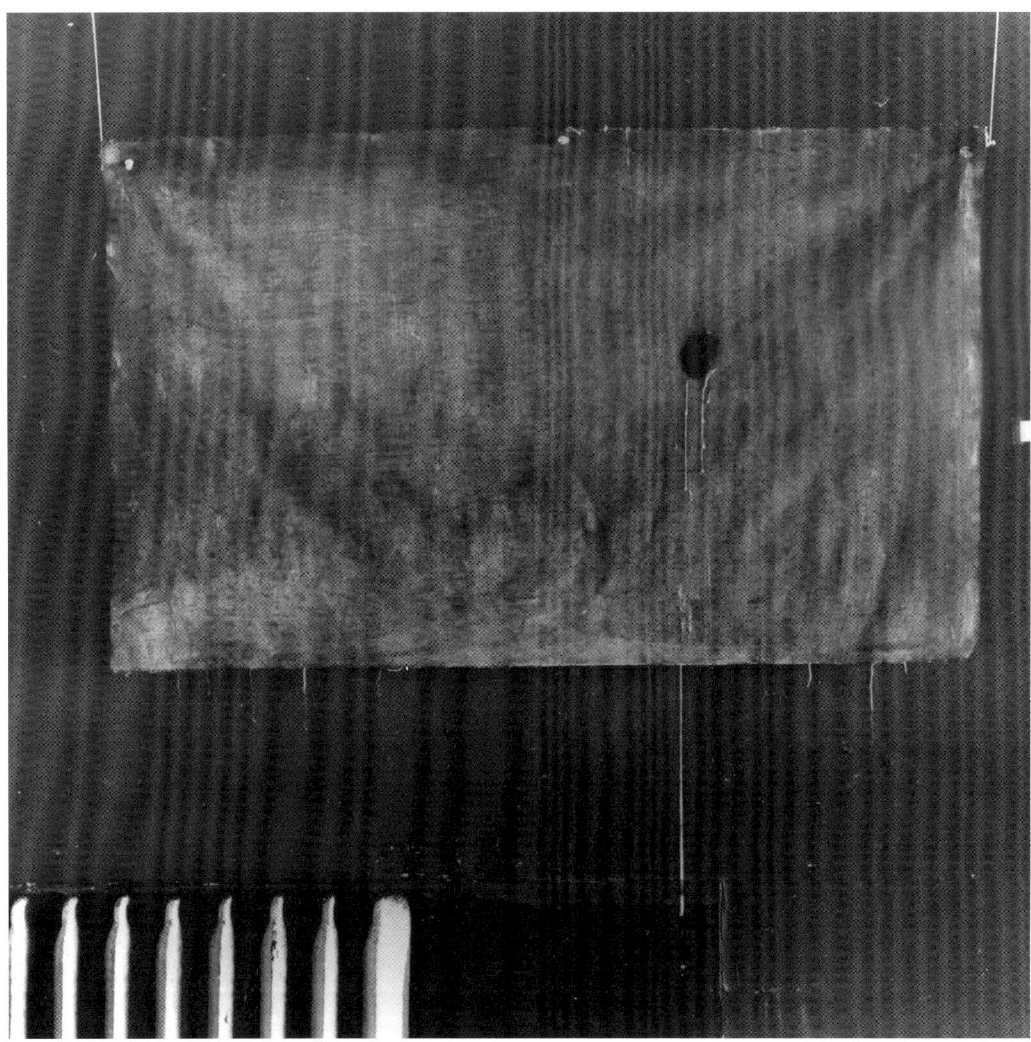

Yoko Ono, *Smoke Painting*, 1961, installation view, AG Gallery, New York. Photo: George Maciunas. Courtesy of Yoko Ono.

Whatever it may be for us, among the things *Smoke Painting* must have evoked for Yoko Ono was death by burning—something she may have learned more about from the firebombings of 1945 than she could process at the time. Her wish "to assimilate art in life" is fundamentally a wish to make life assimilatable through art. Like Siddhartha, she wanted to put an end to suffering; like George Maciunas, she wanted to eliminate the role of the person who "executes" art on behalf of others. She realized, however, that this utopian ambition might take a long time to achieve. In a 1965 letter proposing a show to Ivan Karp, then director of Leo Castelli's gallery, she wrote:

> I can just see a Bronxville housewife saying to her guests, "do add a circle to my painting before you have a drink," or a guest saying, "I was just admiring your painting by taking the previledge *[sic]* of adding another hole to it," etc. That is my dream, and something to come very much later, I suppose. . . . I hope many other instructions will come from people who take up this idea of painting. Soon there will be no need of artists, since people will start to write their own instructions or exchange them and paint.[21]

Karp's negative response at least showed a certain awareness of what she was up to:

> Thank you so much for your urgent missive. It is indeed laden with pungent metaphysics and adventurous aesthetics. It seems . . . that the kind of show you have in mind fails to suit our temperament which is essentially restless, driven, aggressive, fiercely Western and concrete—not materialistic mind you—perish the thought—but terribly concrete . . . you'll have to seek in other realms.[22]

In her lecture "To the Wesleyan People," which she delivered the following year as something of a manifesto, Yoko Ono stated: "The only sound that exists to me is the sound of the mind. My works are only to induce music of the mind in people." She added: "There is a wind that never dies."[23] That wind is the moving mind, the mind that, according to John Cage, "is part of the air,"[24] the mind that is able to transcend "the falsehood of consciousness" and fly.

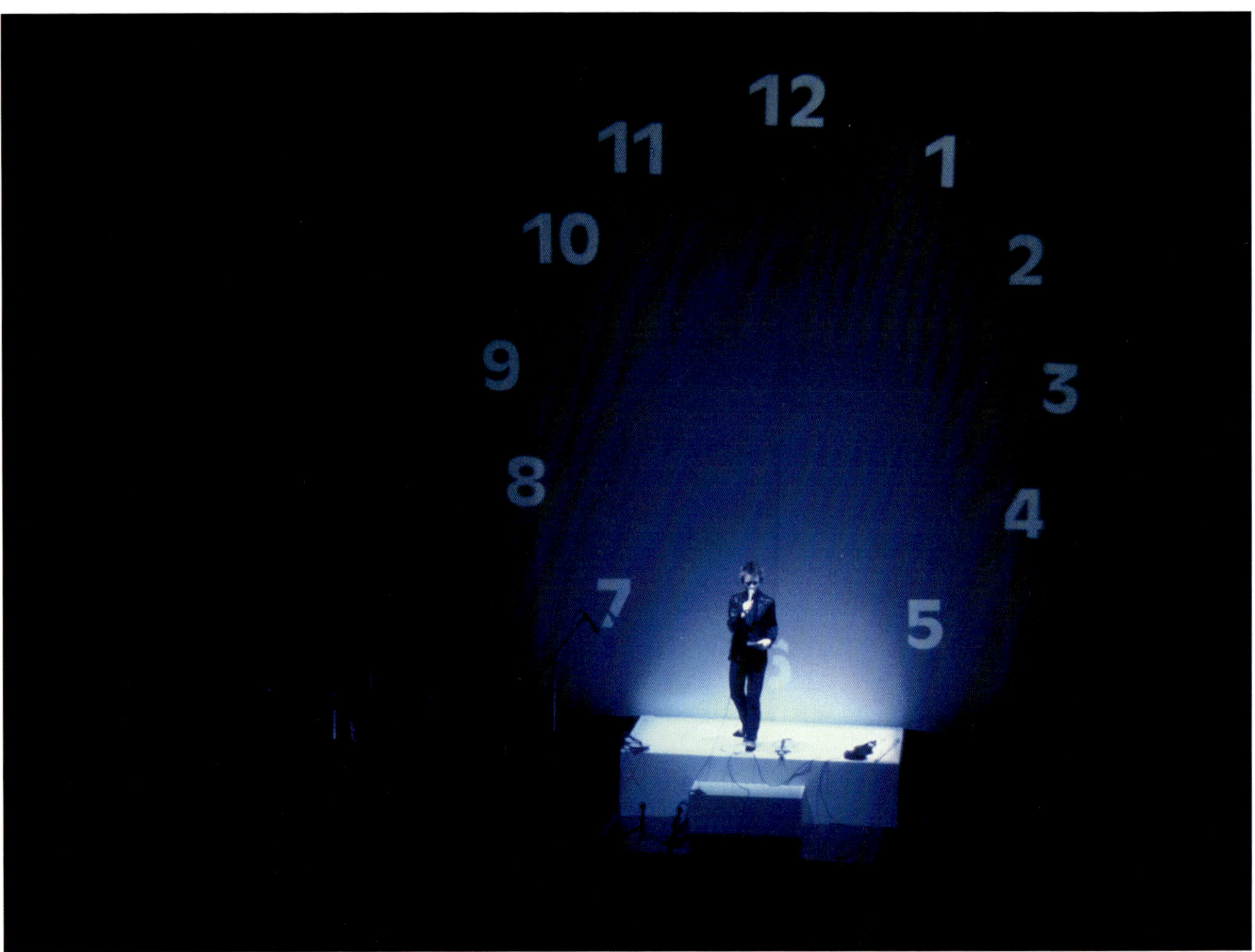

Laurie Anderson, clock set from *United States,* 1983, performance at Brooklyn Academy of Music. Courtesy of Canal Street Communications.

I am not a sitter. I am, let's say, a committed beginner of zazen. What has encouraged me as I come and go are the words of a teacher I had in 1975.... He said something like, "Now, of course you understand that when you leave some of you will continue to meditate many hours a day, some of you will meditate only a few hours and some of you won't meditate at all. You'll simply forget. But don't worry about this. Because next time you'll meditate a little longer and then you'll forget again. And then maybe a little longer and then you'll forget again." As I listened to him I realized that this was the first time I had heard effort described... in a way that described the way we move through time, remembering and forgetting and remembering again.

What time is it?... it's always the same time.

LAURIE ANDERSON

LAURIE ANDERSON 1947–

LAURIE ANDERSON IS FIFTEEN YEARS YOUNGER than Nam June Paik and Yoko Ono, and almost two generations younger than John Cage. Her career trajectory has been the opposite of their move from music into visual art. Although Anderson played violin as a child, when she launched her career in the early seventies she was a graduate student at Columbia University majoring in sculpture. By the mid-seventies she was doing Performance Art, and by the end of the decade she had expanded into songwriting and recording. But Anderson has retained her connection with the visual arts through photography, filmmaking, and her performances, for which the visuals are as important as the sound.

More than any other artist, Laurie Anderson has made Performance Art accessible to wide audiences. The content of her art replicates the complex workings of the mind—its meanderings from the past into the future, always driven by some concern of the present. Anderson's performances are grounded in both words and images through which she blends cultural, social, and political comment with personal philosophy and insight. Her words can range from insouciant and amusing to elegiac to scathingly political. Often, however, they are lyrically transcendent. Popular songs don't get much more Buddhist than "Monkey's Paw," from Anderson's 1989 album, *Strange Angels*. What's missing from the following excerpt is Anderson's wry delivery of these lines:

> I know a man he lost his head
> He said: The way I feel I'd be better off dead.

> He said: I got everything I ever wanted
> Now I can't give it up
> It's a trap, just my luck![1]

Anderson's "trap" of desire is reminiscent of the ego-traps alluded to in Jasper Johns's notes about the "watchman" and Marcel Duchamp's coatrack (see p. 150).

By the time Anderson came of age as an artist, Buddhism had become a very present element in American culture:

> Much of what I think is beautiful was shaped by the first groups of artists I worked with. This was the early and mid-seventies. And in some ways the art scene was about paying very close attention, recognizing and using shapes and forms that were already there rather than inventing brand new ones, using tools in new ways. Buddhism in many forms was in the air. Spirituality was stylish. Artists wore white. There were a lot of drugs.[2]

Anderson, whose persona at this time was that of a wholesome midwestern girl, "wore white" and went on meditation retreats. In 1972, while still in college, she made a series of sculptures from pulped newspapers, including a series of "Mudras." These early pieces already reveal Anderson's interest in the communicative conflation of hand and word. Each day she read the *New York Times,* pulped it, formed her hand into a *mudra,* and pressed the blob into it to form a shape. One of her "Mudra" pieces—*Handwriting*—took the form of the "fear not" *mudra,* with a snakelike form in the center. Made of papier-mâché, these ephemeral sculptures referred to the body both through their shapes and through their relation to time. They went very much against the grain of how art was thought about at Columbia and many other art schools at the time. "The aesthetic was that sculpture should be a) heavy and b) made of steel. I didn't fit into this aesthetic very well."[3]

Anderson was also doing performance work, such as *An Afternoon of Automotive Transmission*—a car-horn concert on the town green in Rochester, Vermont, in the summer of 1972. Anderson turned the local audience's attention on themselves and their lifestyle by reversing their custom of listening to performances on the town green in their cars and applauding by honking their horns. She auditioned cars for the pitch of their horns and then proceeded to conduct pieces such as "The Well-Tempered Beep" from the gazebo by touching previously agreed-upon colors, which the cars' occupants translated into pitch and duration.

Increasingly, Laurie Anderson would combine her interest in music with an affinity for technology. What John Cage did to the piano, and Nam June Paik to the cello, Anderson did to the violin, and then some:

> Although I was trained as a classical violinist, I abandoned the instrument when I was sixteen. . . . Years later when I began to play the violin again I redesigned the instrument

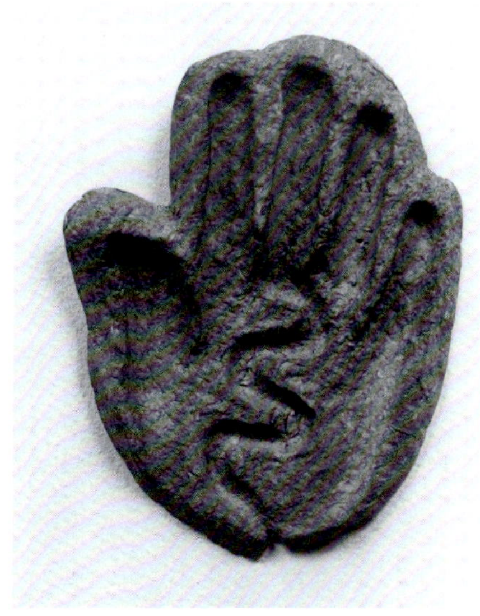

Laurie Anderson, *Handwriting (Mudra),* 1972, pulped, shaped, and dried newspaper, about 6 x 5 x 4 in. Courtesy of Canal Street Communications.

> in as many ways as I could think. Was this revenge on the classical tradition? Yes, a bit, but it was also the desire to make a violin that could play a different kind of music, speak another language.[4]

Her alterations (assisted by Bob Bielecki) include the *Self-Playing Violin* with a concealed speaker; the *Tape Bow Violin,* which instead of a bridge has a tape-head that "plays" a tape attached to its bow; and the *Viophonograph,* with its turntable and its bow fitted with a stylus. For Anderson, technology at its best is an extension of the body—and vice versa. In 1978 she created the *Handphone Table* for a Museum of Modern Art installation:

> I got the idea . . . when I was typing something on an electric typewriter. It wasn't going very well and I got so depressed I stopped and just put my head in my hands. That's when I heard it: a loud hum coming from the typewriter, amplified by the wooden table and running up my arms, totally clear and very loud. So I built a table and rigged it for sound. . . . When you put your hands over your ears, it was like putting on a pair of powerful stereo headphones. The whole head became a speaker and in a sense, an amplifier; it's more like remembering sound than hearing it really.[5]

This attention to the nuances of how our minds experience sound is related to aspects of Zen meditation. Anderson recalls similar experiences related to sight:

> When I open my eyes after a long meditation period, I suddenly seem to have about ten additional degrees of peripheral vision, like through a fisheye lens. The first time this happened, I felt like I was understanding space for the first time the way an architect might. It became pure volume. No place was more important than another. . . .

> Obviously I wasn't actually *seeing* more, but I had less desire, less of what I think of as the vision of desire: I want that, focus on it, see it as if through a gun sight.
>
> Then go get it.[6]

On one level, Laurie Anderson's ambitious multimedia performances are an attempt to share this experience of the unity of one's self with what one perceives. In Zen this is referred to as "big mind." Anderson has other ways, besides meditation, of experiencing it:

> One thing I try to do for fun once in a while is to use the wrong sense. Sometimes it's easy. You can listen with your hands by putting them on vibrating surfaces. Or you can listen with your eyes (sometimes called reading). But it's very hard to smell with your eyes. Or hear with your nose. So I try to use these impossible exercises to explain my lack of comprehension of dimensions such as time.[7]

These "impossible" koanlike exercises can be shortcuts to a direct kind of enlightenment experience. The fourteenth-century Zen master Bassui put it this way:

> When awareness of even emptiness disappears, you will realize that there is no Buddha outside Mind and no Mind outside Buddha. Now for the first time you will discover that when you do not hear with your ears you are truly hearing and when you do not see with your eyes you are really seeing Buddhas of the past, present and future. But don't cling to any of this, just experience it for yourself.[8]

Most critics date Anderson's leap from avant-garde to popular culture to 1981, the year Warner Brothers took on distribution of her song "O Superman," which became an unlikely hit. An Orwellian comment on authority, "O Superman" was inspired by a poignant performance of Jules Massenet's *O Souverain* that Anderson had heard three years earlier, in 1978. In fact, her breakthrough insight "that it was possible to work outside the world of the New York avant garde" happened that same year.[9] Anderson had been invited to do a performance at the Contemporary Art Museum in Houston,

> but the museum had no chairs, no sound system, no lights. So they decided to do the concert in a country and western bar. . . . The night of the show the regulars showed up dressed in cowboy hats and jeans and they got all the good places around the bar. Then the art crowd arrived all dressed in black. And I thought, "Oh no! This is never going to work!" But I started to do the show playing the violin and telling stories. And the stories were pretty weird but then again Texan stories are also pretty weird. And suddenly I realized that the cowboys were really getting it. And it immediately opened a whole new world for me.[10]

The shift registered in her work. Later the same year: "The Nova Convention [a festival in honor of William Burroughs in which she participated] was the first time I really used the word 'you' meaning specifically 'you in the audience.'"

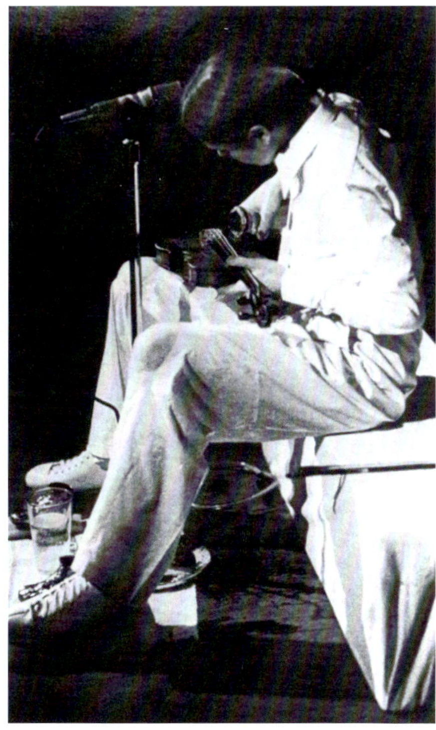

Laurie Anderson, *As:If*, 1974, performance at Artists Space, New York. Courtesy of Canal Street Communications.

> As a performer I had used "I" until I ran out of stories. Then I tried having other people read my words. But this, this was different! Finally, I wasn't just remembering things out loud! I was actually talking directly to people and it felt completely different.[11]

The "new world" that opened up for Anderson in Houston was in some ways a return to the world she had come from. A product of the Chicago suburbs, Anderson always relished the way midwestern salesmen, like her father, liked to spin tales. She had seven brothers and sisters, and learned early how to stand out in a crowd. Anderson's maternal grandmother was a Southern Baptist missionary, and that complicated storybook that is the Bible was an early influence on her storytelling style. A diary entry from 1972 reads: "In my memory, my childhood merges with the Old Testament: a series of obscure events in a distant and barbarous land."[12] Baptists tend toward the performative end of Christianity—and Anderson retains a vivid memory of her public baptism by total immersion at the age of eleven. She was dressed only in a thin white robe that became transparent as she was "washed in the blood of the lamb" and then had to testify about the experience.[13]

The vulnerability and strangeness of that moment, and others, would be exorcised through her performances. Anderson worked the baptism story into her first complex performance piece at Artists Space in New York in 1974. Titled *As:If*, the piece was organized around

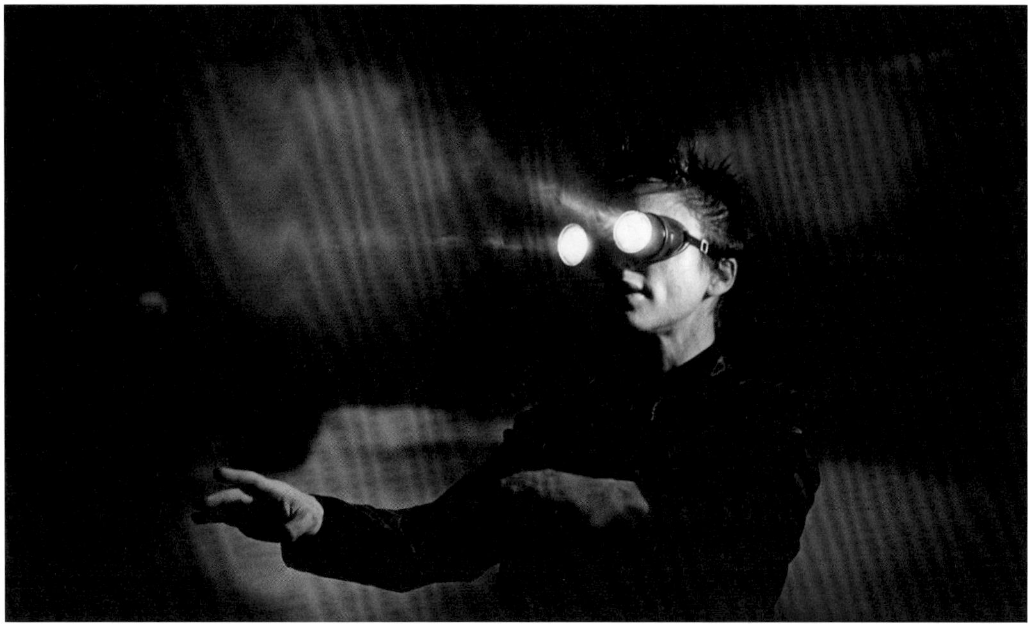

Laurie Anderson, finale of *United States,* 1983, performance at Brooklyn Academy of Music. Courtesy of Canal Street Communications.

pairs of words having to do with the relation between language and memory. An iconic pairing was "word: water"; almost every story she told had something to do with water. In addition to baptism, there was the story about the day after her grandmother died:

> We went out to skate on the pond. The temperature had dropped suddenly the night before. There were a lot of ducks out on the ice and I got close to them and they didn't move. When I got closer, I saw that their feet had been frozen into the new layer of ice.[14]

During her Artists Space performance, Anderson was wearing ice skates whose blades had been frozen into blocks of ice. She went on to recount the thought she remembered occurring to her, when she saw the ducks: "They were honking and flapping their wings. I remember thinking of the ducks' feet as little conductors that carried the honking down into the ice, turning the frozen surface into a giant sounding board."[15] Her grief-benumbed mind had transformed the ducks from suffering victims into performance artists.

Word: water. There was also the story about the diving board—how when Anderson was nine she did a flip off the high board and missed the swimming pool. She broke her back and had to wear a back brace for a year and a half. This tale, like others Anderson tells, has resurfaced in various forms. In the finale to her eight-hour 1983 performance, *United States,* Anderson, blinded by goggles containing two lights, walked tentatively toward the audience on a diving board that extended over the orchestra pit. More recently, in her 2002 performance *Happiness,* Anderson reported the recovery of a lost memory from the time just after her diving board accident. She had been in traction in a ward with burn patients. Many years later, during a back massage, a somatic memory of the intensely disturbing smell of that place suddenly was released, bringing with it other sense-memories: the sounds, the dreadful sights. They all came flooding back in a vivid re-creation of the sensual experience of that traumatic time. It was, however, a time that pushed her to engage the power of her mind. The doctors told her she would never walk again. "I decided they were wrong," she told me, "and I was right."[16]

Another theme in Anderson's work is the loss and recovery of balance. She has worn ice skates frozen in blocks of ice in other performances, partly as a "timing mechanism": "When the ice melted and I lost my balance, the concert was over."[17] Walking, she proposes, is a form of directed "falling. With each step, you fall forward slightly. And then catch yourself from falling. Over and over, you're falling. And then catching yourself from falling."[18] To move forward, you have to trust your ability to catch yourself, to keep your balance. For Anderson, making music, too, is a "constant state of imbalance followed by balance followed by imbalance."[19] So, she implies, is life. This is a point made by Shunryu Suzuki, founder of the San Francisco Zen Center, in his influential 1970 book, *Zen Mind, Beginner's Mind:*

> To live in the realm of Buddha nature means to die as a small being, moment after moment. When we lose our balance we die, but at the same time we also develop ourselves, we grow. Whatever we see is changing, losing its balance. The reason everything looks beautiful is because it is out of balance, but its background is always in perfect harmony. . . . So if you see things without realizing the background of Buddha nature, everything appears to be in the form of suffering. But if you understand the background of existence, you realize that suffering itself is how we live, and how we extend our life.[20]

Buddhism has been only one strand in Laurie Anderson's art, but it has become an increasingly important one:

> We build on top of our beliefs the way the Aztecs built on top of the pyramids they found in a huge valley; the way the Catholics built their churches on top of the Aztec temples; the way the Turks built on top of the Byzantines on top of the Christians on top of the Greeks on top of the Acropolis. And with all these history towers, I'm thinking of the teaching that speaks to me most clearly and most eloquently: that all of time is happening in this very moment. Exactly now.[21]

"Tape the sound of the stone aging," Yoko Ono instructs. Time is a wind that is always present, a wind that never dies.

V LIGHT AND INSIGHT

The dharmas are one and the ox is symbolic. When you know that what you need is not the snare or set-net but the hare or fish, it is like gold separated from the dross, it is like the moon rising out of the clouds. The one ray of light serene and penetrating shines even before days of creation.

D. T. SUZUKI'S TRANSLATION FROM KAKUAN SHIEN,
ZEN OXHERDING PICTURES

IN 1960 GROVE PRESS PUBLISHED D.T. SUZUKI'S *Manual of Zen Buddhism*. The purpose of this book, Suzuki explained in his preface, was to share with Western students of Zen what "the Zen monk reads . . . , where his thoughts move in his leisure hours, and what objects of worship he has."[1] This simple book with its numerous illustrations was popular with American artists. It was no doubt John Cage's source of information when he compared Duchamp's career and his own with the contrasting final images of Chinese and Japanese versions of the Zen Oxherding Pictures. Suzuki reproduces an early Chinese woodcut version that ends with an empty circle and a Japanese version of Kakuan Shien's twelfth-century elaboration, in which the empty circle is only stage eight. Kakuan's final image is "Entering the City with Bliss-bestowing Hands," where the young cowherd has been transformed into the wonder-working Pu-tai, an incarnation of the Buddha of the future with whose generosity Cage identified. Kakuan, Suzuki tells us, thought the shorter version "somewhat misleading because of an empty circle being made the goal of Zen discipline. Some might take mere emptiness as all important and final."[2]

The career trajectory of the painter Agnes Martin, born in the same year as John Cage, more closely resembles the sparer earlier ending, "Both Vanished." Its concluding verse, by the sixteenth-century Chinese poet Pu-ming, reads:

雙泯

"Both Vanished," number 10 of *The Ten Oxherding Pictures, II,* in D.T. Suzuki, *Manual of Zen Buddhism* (New York: Grove Press, 1960).

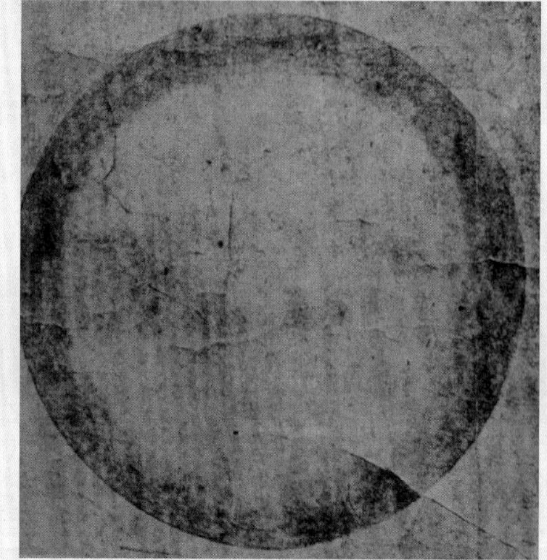

Kakuan Shien, "The Ox and the Man Both Gone out of Sight," number 8 of *The Ten Oxherding Pictures, I,* in D.T. Suzuki, *Manual of Zen Buddhism* (New York: Grove Press, 1960).

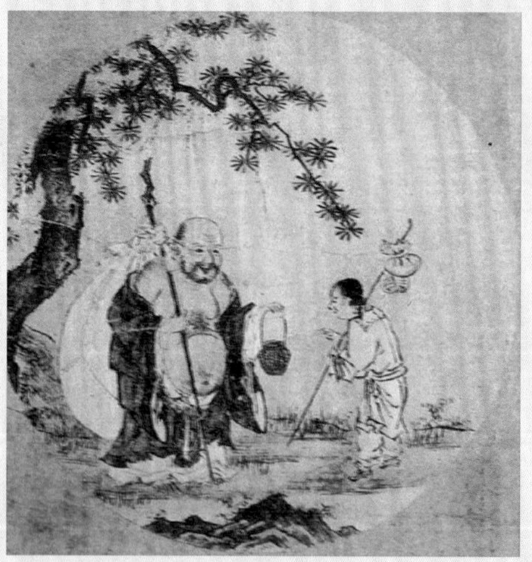

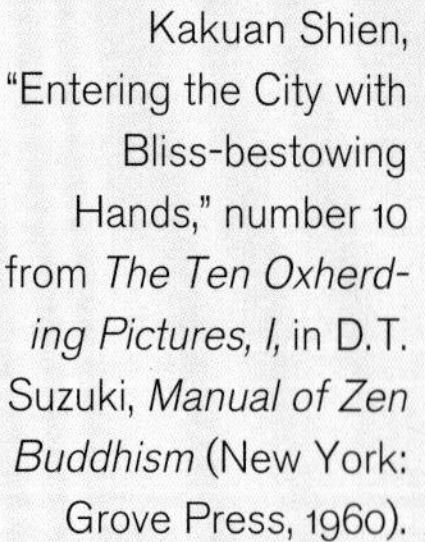

Kakuan Shien, "Entering the City with Bliss-bestowing Hands," number 10 from *The Ten Oxherding Pictures, I,* in D.T. Suzuki, *Manual of Zen Buddhism* (New York: Grove Press, 1960).

> Both the man and the animal have disappeared, no traces are left,
> The bright moon-light is empty and shadowless with all the ten-thousand objects in it;
> If anyone should ask the meaning of this,
> Behold the lilies of the field and its fresh sweet-scented verdure.[3]

In the early 1960s Martin gave her paintings and drawings, which were empty of anything but simple grids, titles like *Flower in the Wind* and *Grass* (p. 218), evoking Pu-ming's "lilies of the field and its fresh sweet-scented verdure." Agnes Martin was among the first, along with her friend Ad Reinhardt, to absorb and reflect the lessons of Zen Buddhism in her art. If in his paintings Reinhardt contains and conveys the rich darkness of the mind, Martin strives to contain and convey the elements of the natural world within the elements of two-dimensional expression. These are primarily line and color, though line and light might be a better way to describe it, for some of Martin's most powerful paintings have no color at all.

The Los Angeles artist Robert Irwin initially followed Martin's painterly pursuit of pure perception. By 1970 he reached the same "empty" gallery end-point that Yves Klein came to in 1957. Ten years later, however, Irwin bounced back in a gift-bearing mode, exemplified by his exuberant Getty garden project of 1992. According to Irwin: "At one point I thought the term 'nonobjective' was going to translate to nonobject, this idea of the phenomenon, but all of a sudden I discovered that it had nothing to do with object/nonobject at all; it had to do with relationships, and the whole idea of conditioned relations."[4]

Light is a primary medium for Robert Irwin, who is acutely conscious of his moment in time:

> There is simply no real separation line, only an intellectual one, between the object and its time environment. They are completely interlocking: nothing can exist in the world independent of all the other things in the world. To me, the whole history of contemporary art starts out as a highly informed and highly sophisticated pictorial activity. But by the time I arrive on the scene, as a post abstract expressionist, there is at least the possibility of looking at the world as a kind of continuum, rather than as a collection of broken up and isolated events.[5]

An awareness of Buddhist philosophy helped make possible this sense of the world as a "continuum" encompassing the self, the work of art, and the viewer within a boundless universe of time and space, a universe of interrelationship.

By the late 1960s radically abstract Indian Tantric art—made to be used as perceptual aids to meditation—was increasingly available to artists like Martin and Irwin. In 1969 the Los Angeles County Museum of Art presented "Fifty Tantric Mystical Diagrams," the first exhibition of Tantric diagrams in an American museum. Ajit Mookerjee's *Tantra Art,* which influenced the art of Jasper Johns, came out in 1966, with new editions in 1971 and 1977.

In addition to these visual sources, two philosophical trends during the 1960s and 1970s reinforced the impact of Buddhism on artists. The French philosopher Maurice Merleau-Ponty, whose *Phenomenology of Perception* was published in English in 1962, analyzed the "phenomenal body," opening the door for artists to understand their work not as figuration or gesture, but as experience within time and space. The experiential, constructive nature of the act of seeing was also emphasized in the philosophy of D. T. Suzuki's friend Kitaro Nishida, whose work blended Asian and Western thought. Nishida's *Zen no Kenkyu,* or *Study of Good,* appeared in English in 1960, to be followed by other books, including *Art and Morality* (1973), which had an impact on the thinking of Richard Tuttle.

Unlike Yves Klein or Yoko Ono, who want to send us transcendentally beyond ourselves, all four of the artists in this section nudge us to experience ourselves *in* the world, in all of its presence and fullness, and in all of its beauty. Both Richard Tuttle, for whom Agnes Martin was a friend and mentor, and Vija Celmins, who was once Robert Irwin's student but whose work has gone, at least superficially, in a different direction from his, offer us an experience of the world through physical form—articulated in her art, intimated in his.

Through her obsessively worked surfaces, Vija Celmins achieves visions of the universe that open our eyes to the beauty inherent in the apparently random patterns of endless ocean and the bottomless night sky. Her work evokes what Shunryu Suzuki has described as life's background of perfect harmony—buddha nature, without which "everything appears to be in the form of suffering."[6] Her recent paintings of mist-enshrouded spiderwebs, in particular, are evocative of Kakuan's lesson that "what you need is not the snare or set-net but the hare or fish." Celmins's webs are not traps, but targets intended to focus the mind, which is her prey. In this way they are connected to Jasper Johns's targets and Marcel Duchamp's coatrack.

Duchamp once pointed out what a waste of time it is to try and define art, since each moment in history has its own requirements. The interesting question is: what art, over time, do viewers continue to relate to? When first shown at the Whitney Museum in 1975, Richard Tuttle's low-key work was beneath the threshold of most critics' definition of art. The show got its prescient curator, Marcia Tucker, fired. While this event was not quite as dramatic as the death sentence meted out to Rikyu, the sixteenth-century Japanese creator of the modern tea ceremony, there is a parallel between Rikyu's revolutionary incorporation of everyday objects into the tea ritual and Tuttle's deceptively modest presentations. Tuttle's definition of quality in art is as pragmatic as the Buddha's definition of *dharma*—teachings that lead to freedom from bondage, not to bondage. Queried by an interviewer about what keeps people from opening themselves to a work of art, Tuttle responded, "Nameless fears. Fear itself . . . and finally, ego." Ego "that they see in art." According to Tuttle, "The more art frees you, the better it is. What is freedom? Is it a feeling, here one moment, gone the next? Or is it concrete, the foundation of something, if never realizable? Art is the realization of that foundation, while we are experiencing it."[7]

It is appropriate to end this study with Richard Tuttle, who was influenced by *wabi-sabi* (the Japanese aesthetic of impermanence) and by Chinese calligraphy, but who has more recently been engaged in an effort to shift his (and our) energy from an east/west to a north/south axis:

> I like thinking about the north/south, its characteristics, feeling its energy flow through me. If I were standing, it would come to my head and through my body, leaving at the back of my feet, where east/west would come from the middle of my right side passing out my left side.[8]

Such a haptic, four-dimensional conception of energy is reminiscent of the Tantric Buddhist mandala, whose visualization cultivates profoundly aesthetic as well as spiritual perceptual awareness, and which is organized in reference to the four directions. The earth turns from west to east, so east-west energy has to do with time. North-south energy, on the other hand, is related to the poles of our planet—to space.

The historical Buddha, so the story goes, achieved enlightenment just before dawn. He was sitting on the ground under a tree with its head in the heaven and its roots in the earth. Enlightenment occurred when he saw the bright morning star rising, just as the full moon was about to set. It is a mental image of extraordinary luminosity and beauty. But enlightenment, as Robert Thurman has pointed out, "is not just to slip into some disconnected euphoria, an oceanic feeling of mystic oneness apart from ordinary reality."

> Rather it is supposed to be an experience of release from all compulsions and sufferings, combined with a precise awareness of any relevant object of knowledge; both of which naturally issue in a powerful sense of unbounded connectedness with the conditions of other beings, which gives limitless energy to an infinite love that wants those beings to become happier.[9]

What is it that energizes Agnes Martin and Richard Tuttle, Robert Irwin and Vija Celmins, to devote their lives to art? It is not mysticism, that "feeling of mystic oneness apart from ordinary reality." The creative consciousness these artists are after is not the end—it is a means to the end, which is release from our habits of perception, combined with a "precise awareness" of the work of art—a "relevant object of knowledge" in which we see ourselves, as in a mirror, and smile.

Agnes Martin, *Untitled #7*, 2002, acrylic and graphite on canvas, 60 x 60 in. Private collection. Photo: Ellen Page Wilson, courtesy PaceWildenstein, New York. © Agnes Martin.

I hope I have made it clear that the work is about perfection as we are aware of it in our minds but that the paintings are very far from perfect—completely removed in fact—even as we ourselves are.

AGNES MARTIN

AGNES MARTIN 1912–2004

THE STATEMENT ABOVE BY AGNES MARTIN EVOKES the words of Shunryu Suzuki: "The reason everything looks beautiful is because it is out of balance, but its background is always in perfect harmony."[1] To draw near a painting by Agnes Martin is to experience this tension between balance and imbalance. Her compositions are exceedingly regular—grids or stripes on a perfectly square canvas. As one approaches them, however, it becomes clear that her graphite lines are applied by hand across the uneven canvas. They tremble slightly, and her pale washes of color vary in their amount of pigmentation. The result is a tender luminosity that emerges not so much from the canvas or the color as in the mind of the observer, a luminosity generated by the exhilarating dissonance between our perception of imperfection within an experience of perfection.

Agnes Martin's painting *Untitled #7* consists of a single horizontal line running across the middle of a white canvas. Because the line doesn't quite reach the edges, *Untitled #7* evokes yearning. Still, it is an oddly comforting painting. Agnes Martin has said that "suffering is necessary for freedom from suffering."[2] Shunryu Suzuki put it another way: "If you understand the background of existence, you realize that suffering itself is how we live, and how we extend our life."[3] That experiential understanding can be achieved through meditation practice. It can also be achieved by taking in the work of Agnes Martin:

> We perceive—We see. We see with our eyes and we see with our minds. We want to see the truth about life and all of beauty. Both are a great mystery to us. Perceiving is the same as receiving and it is the same as responding. Perception means all of them. It goes on all the time whether we are asleep or awake.[4]

Agnes Martin was ninety years old when she painted *Untitled #7*. Her work represents a lifetime of thinking, feeling, and meditation, which she considered essential to the life of the artist. "By looking into my mind I can see what's there," she said; "by bringing thoughts to the surface of my mind I can watch them dissolve."[5]

Martin's statement quoted at the beginning of this section was written toward the end of a self-imposed seven-year retreat from the art world. It was also a retreat from the world. In 1967 Martin agreed to an exhibition of work she had done in New York over the previous decade. That same year, she left the city, her gallery, and her artist colleagues for an eighteen-month camping trip through Canada and the western United States. She was fifty-five years old at the time; sixty-one by the time of her next exhibition, at the Institute of Contemporary Art in Philadelphia. The following year, in 1974, Martin returned to painting, but not to New York—she had come to rest on a mesa near Cuba, New Mexico, where she built herself an adobe and log house, to which she added a studio.

John Cage talked a lot about silence, but Agnes Martin lived it. For much of her life, her only companion was herself and her "voices," which spoke to her inner ear. Born on a wheat farm in northern Saskatchewan, Agnes lost her father when she was two. The family lived for a time with her mother's father, a devout Presbyterian to whom Agnes became very close. With her mother, two brothers, and sister (Agnes was the third child and second daughter), she next moved to Calgary and then Vancouver, where her mother supported the family by renovating and selling houses. (It was surely from her mother that Agnes learned her self-reliance and her building skills.) Because of its location on the Pacific Rim, Vancouver has always had a vibrant Asian cultural presence; it may have been where Martin first came into contact with Buddhist culture. At the age of nineteen she moved to Bellingham, Washington, to help her pregnant sister. Martin responded positively to what she calls the "American character,"[6] and she decided to stay in the United States.

Martin's attraction to Buddhism was grounded in the same egalitarian impulse that led her to become a citizen of the United States: the belief that everyone has within themselves the potential to recognize truth and behave accordingly. She read the writings of the visionary artist and poet William Blake, and was influenced by the pro-democracy American educator John Dewey, whose *Art as Experience* was published in 1934. Between 1934 and 1937 Martin earned her teaching credentials at Western Washington College and then taught in Washington public schools through the spring of 1941. That fall, she enrolled at Columbia Teachers

College—which Georgia O'Keeffe had also attended—receiving a bachelor's degree with a major in fine art and art education.

Over the next four years Martin alternated between teaching and—when she had saved enough money—painting. In 1946 she enrolled as an art student at the University of New Mexico, Albuquerque, where she was asked to teach. She returned to New York in 1951, earning a master's at Columbia Teachers College in 1952, and returning again for postgraduate work in 1954. In between she continued to alternate painting in New Mexico with teaching—often devoting her energy to children who were considered difficult or were otherwise disadvantaged. Finally, in 1957, the art dealer Betty Parsons made it possible for Martin to live in New York and devote herself to painting full time.

That year the interest in Japanese Zen Buddhism in the New York art world was at its peak. With her grounding in American pragmatism, Martin would have easily assimilated the Zen teachings of D. T. Suzuki, who had been associated with Dewey and delivered his famous lectures at Columbia University at same the time Martin attended Columbia Teachers College. She herself indicated that her own philosophy integrated heavy doses of both Taoism and Buddhism: "My greatest spiritual inspiration came from the Chinese spiritual teachers, especially Lao Tzu. . . . My next strongest influence is the Sixth Patriarch Hui Neng. . . . I have also read and been inspired by the sutras of the other . . . Buddhist masters."[7]

Zen influence is readily apparent in Martin's *Cow,* a painting from 1960. Its brown circle could almost represent the "Both Vanished" episode from the Zen Oxherding Pictures about the taming of the mind (p. 208). I am not suggesting that Martin's intention was so literal, however. Her own goal was to generate an experience in the mind of the observer. Martin's ultimate subject was perfection, of which the circle is symbolic:

> The Greeks made a great discovery. They discovered that in nature there are no perfect circles or straight lines or equal spaces. Yet they discovered that their interest and inclination was in the perfection of circles and lines, and that in their minds they could see them and that they were then able to make them. They realized that the mind knows what the eye has not seen but that what the mind knows is perfection.[8]

Still, Martin did entitle this painting *Cow,* and another painting from 1960, *Grass.* The meaning of these titles is surely related to the "meaning" of the Oxherding Pictures' "Both Vanished," which *Cow* so closely resembles: "Behold the lilies of the field and its fresh sweet-scented verdure."[9] Martin told her friend the artist and critic Ann Wilson:

> Saint Augustine says that milk doesn't come from the mother
> I painted a painting called *Milk River*
> Cows don't give milk if they don't have grass and water . . .
> Living is grazing

Agnes Martin, *Cow*, 1960, oil on canvas, 69 x 69 in. Private collection. Photo: Bill Jacobson. © Agnes Martin.

> Memory is chewing cud . . .
> Everyone is chosen and everyone knows it
> Including animals and plants
> There is only the all of the all
> Everything is that.[10]

So *Cow* is about the cycle of life, and about the interrelationship of all being. But Martin also told Wilson, "I don't like circles—too expanding. When I draw horizontals you see this big plane and you have certain feelings like you're expanding over the plane."[11]

Agnes Martin, *Song,* 1962, ink and watercolor on canvas, 24 x 24 in. Private collection, San Francisco. © Agnes Martin.

Agnes Martin was acutely aware of the limitations and possibilities of the two-dimensional picture plane. She was of the same generation as the Abstract Expressionists. Although she admired the paintings of Mark Rothko and Barnett Newman, it was Ad Reinhardt's rigorous, restrained geometries that seem closest to the direction her own work would take. Reinhardt's evocative "black paintings" from 1960 to 1967 (the year of his death and of Martin's departure from New York) are 60 by 60 inches, the same square dimensions that Martin's own late paintings would assume. ("Five feet wide, just the width of a man's reach," according to Reinhardt.[12])

By 1962 Martin had begun developing compositions based on the grid, a format that, because no part of the surface is more important than any other, she thought of as exemplifying the Taoist-Buddhist ideal of being without ego. As she told an interviewer: "When I first made a grid I happened to be thinking of the innocence of trees and then this grid came into my mind and I thought it represented innocence, and I still do, and so I painted it and then I was satisfied. I thought, this is my vision."[13] These words seem particularly applicable to *Song,* a painting whose title may allude to William Blake's *Songs of Innocence* and whose articulated grid contains leaflike forms.

Agnes Martin, *Grass,* 1963, ink on paper, 9 x 9 in. Collection of Richard Tuttle. © Agnes Martin.

The sensitivity of Martin's grids appealed to Richard Tuttle, who belongs to a younger generation of artists strongly influenced by her work, as well as by her philosophy. Tuttle first got to know Martin when he visited her New York studio around 1963. After buying a grid drawing from her entitled *Grass,* he reflected:

> I remember asking myself what the difference was between graph paper and Agnes's grids. Eventually I decided it had to do with the difference between the loved line and the unloved line. Agnes's line is extremely sensitive to the actual event of making the line. . . . She's saying what a human being is, is something that is free of nature.[14]

Martin explained: "The line doesn't have to describe anything. It focuses you, beyond it and beyond yourself."[15] This statement, which reminds us of the powerfully focused line of *Untitled #7,* also calls to mind the mantra at the end of the Heart Sutra: *Gate, gate, paragate, parasamgate; Bodhi—svaha!*—which translates, more or less: "Gone, gone, gone beyond; totally gone; enlightenment—hooray!"

To be free of nature is to be free of one's own nature. Martin's paintings have the poten-

Agnes Martin, *Lovely Life*, 1999, acrylic and graphite on canvas, 60 x 60 in. Private collection. Photo: Gordon R. Christmas, courtesy PaceWildenstein, New York. © Agnes Martin.

tial to generate a contained enlightenment experience through the contrast between the first impression of her work, which is that of perfect regularity, and what closer inspection reveals about their slightly trembling lines and uneven washes of color: their imperfection, their humanness. About what she referred to as this "abstract response," Agnes Martin believed "that it is infinite, dimensionless, without form and void. But it is not nothing because when we give our minds to it we are blissfully aware."[16] Not nothing. Is there a better definition of abstract art than this Zen-inflected double negative of Agnes Martin?

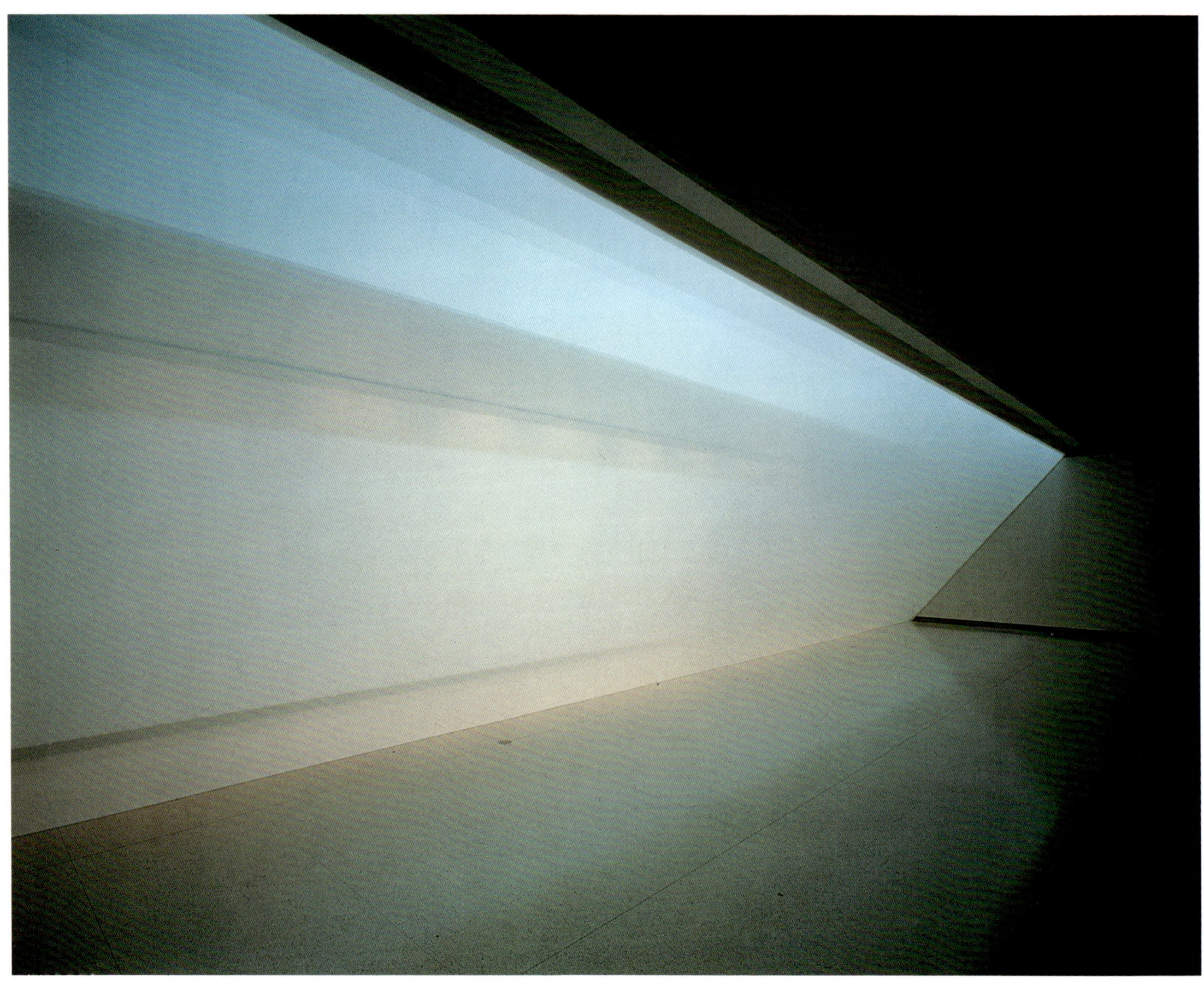

Robert Irwin, Untitled, 1971, synthetic fabric, wood, fluorescent lights, floodlights, 8 x 47 ft. overall installed. Collection Walker Art Center, Minneapolis, Gift of the artist, 1971. Artist © 2005 Robert Irwin/Artist Rights Society (ARS), New York.

If you asked me the sum total—what is your ambition?—basically it's just to make you a little more aware than you were the day before of how beautiful the world is.

ROBERT IRWIN

ROBERT IRWIN 1928–

ROBERT IRWIN MADE THE ABOVE STATEMENT AROUND ten years ago to Lawrence Weschler, who earlier had published an insightful book on the artist, *Seeing Is Forgetting the Name of the Thing One Sees*. The statement is similar to the "Epilogue" in Irwin's own 1985 book of writings, *Being and Circumstance,* in which Irwin describes his challenge as seeking "to discover and value the potential for experiencing beauty in everything."[1] Beauty, for Irwin, is an intense perceptual awareness of the "infinite richness" of reality. In 1992 he wrote, in Reinhardtian terms:

> As artists, the one true inquiry of art as a pure subject
> is an inquiry of our potential to know the world around us
> and our actively being in it, with a particular emphasis on the aesthetic.
> This world is not just somehow given to us whole.
> *We perceive, we shape the world,* and as artists we discover and give value
> to our human potential to "see" the infinite richness (beauty?) in everything,
> creating an extended aesthetic reality.[2]

It is we, his audience, who are being addressed as Irwin's co-inquirers—when Irwin speaks of "artists," he means everybody. Weschler ascribes the interchangeability of pronouns in Irwin's speech to an egolessness so profound it can sometimes seem egomaniacal:

In his conversation, "I" and "you" regularly blur—and this is no mere rhetorical evasion. The dialogue of immanence, as he calls it (the sense that "certain questions become demanding and potentially answerable at a certain point in time, and that everyone involved on a particular level of asking questions . . . is essentially involved in asking the same questions").[3]

Irwin's ambition is nothing less than the elimination of the "gap" Duchamp described between the intention of the artist and its realization in the artwork. For Duchamp, this gap is filled by the aesthetic experience of the viewer. Irwin aims to close the gap, to make the artist's quest and the viewer's quest the same. Duchamp's rhetorical title *Tu m'* could serve as the title of Irwin's life project.

Like John Cage, Robert Irwin grew up in Los Angeles, experiencing a seemingly carefree, if somewhat frenetic, youth. In his mid-twenties, like Marcel Duchamp (and, at a later age, Agnes Martin), he undertook a voluntary exile from the world. The precocious young artist had been traveling to Europe whenever he saved up enough money. On one of these trips, after graduating from the Chouinard Art Institute, he rented a little cabin on the then-remote island of Ibiza. Irwin claims not to have had a conversation with anyone for eight months:

> What was happening to me as I was on my way to Ibiza was that I was pulling all those plugs out, one at a time: books, language, social contacts. And what happens at a certain point as you get down to the last plugs, it's like the Zen thing of having no ego: it becomes scary, it's like maybe you're going to lose yourself. . . . But when you get them all pulled out, a little period goes by, and then it's absolutely serene, it's terrific. It just becomes really pleasant, because you're out, you're all the way out. . . . Time became kind of unreal.[4]

He thought about thinking: "When you peel all those layers away and you arrive at just the qualities of the ideas themselves, it becomes very clear and very simple as to why they are what they are and do what they do."[5]

Irwin's retreat had certain similarities to the Beat poet Gary Snyder's well-known stint as a fire lookout in 1952. Irwin would quote passages from Snyder's *Cold Mountain Poems: Twenty-Four Poems by Han-Shan* in the catalog to his first exhibition at the Ferus Gallery in Los Angeles in spring 1959. The paintings Irwin showed have been referred to as his "Zen paintings." Several titles from the catalog, like *Daisetz* and *Ten Bulls,* do seem to have Zen references. Ferus co-founder Walter Hopps remembered Irwin reading "everything in English he could get his hands on about Zen."[6] Irwin, on the other hand, told Weschler: "None of the people I knew really read, and I didn't either."[7] Zen, however, is experiential, not intellectual. Whatever the extent of his actual reading in Zen, Irwin's attraction to Buddhist philosophy had a strong experiential basis as a result of his own interest in the workings of the mind.

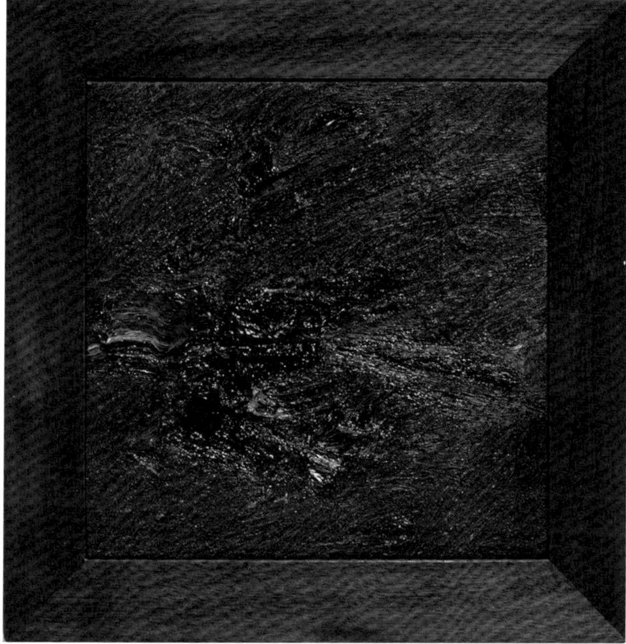

Robert Irwin, Untitled, about 1959–60, oil on canvas in wood frame, 13 x 13 in. Photograph courtesy the artist and PaceWildenstein, New York. Artist © 2005 Robert Irwin/Artist Rights Society (ARS), New York.

The "Zen paintings" are Abstract Expressionist in style, as one would expect from a thirty-year-old artist painting in the late 1950s. Following his first Ferus show, however, Irwin produced something quite new. The surfaces of his new paintings were still painterly and expressive, but their gestures are calligraphic, and their colors so dark as to be almost black. They are small in size—about one foot square—and flush-mounted in furniture-like frames that allowed them to be handled. That was, in fact, the intention: these "hand-held paintings" were to be shown on their backs, to be picked up and held.

This attempt to change the "viewing" experience into a haptic experience—connected with the body by touch as well as by sight—was suggested to Irwin by the tactile Japanese raku tea bowls collected by his colleague Allen Lynch—an influence that does not diminish the radical nature of Irwin's idea. "Those hand-held paintings got very quote-unquote 'Zen-like' in a meditative sense, as opposed to an open gestural sense," Irwin told Weschler. "And the fact that you were meant to hold them meant that they could only be experienced privately, intimately."[8] There were other Zen-like things about these paintings. Their frames were finished with the oil from Irwin's own hands and face, so they were connected in a very direct way with his body as well as that of the viewer. And their backs were as finished as their fronts. "The Zen stuff was just reinforcing something I'd learned long before while working on my cars," he said. "It's absolutely essential that everything be done all the way through."[9]

Irwin decided, however, that something was still interfering with the perceptual experience of his works, and that something was gesture, however abstract. The tendency of our busy minds is always to focus on the mark as meaning, a reference to or symbol for something other than itself. "Imagery for me constituted representation, 're-presentation,' a second order of reality, whereas I was after a first order of presence."[10] It was the Zen conundrum of focusing on the pointing finger rather than the moon.

Irwin took his paintings through a number of phases in an attempt to deal with this problem. Initially he worked with straight lines—at first painterly, then regular horizontals. Next, for two years—from 1962 to 1964—Irwin worked on ten paintings of two horizontal lines on a solid-color background. This period of relative isolation in his studio turned out to be phase two of the meditative research into the mind he had begun on Ibiza:

> I found out during that period when I was alone for eight months that my head, on a day-to-day basis, is really very superficial. I mean, it responds and bounces around like a rubber ball. . . . But if I gave it no other purposes or activities . . . except simply to sit there and weigh my own feelings, my own attitudes, my own thoughts about things, well, then I began to know something about those things. So I really applied that during those two years.[11]

By sustaining over an extended period his full attention "on a single point,"[12] Irwin turned the creative act into a meditative discipline.

One of the things he began to notice is "how incredibly discerning the human eye can be,"[13] how, for example, a smudge on the wall of the studio affected his perception of the painting he was working on. His vocabulary—straight lines—had not changed, but everything else had:

> On an experiential level, [the paintings of two lines] are in an entirely different world. . . . They're about the basic relationships of the three or four primary aspects of existence in the world: being-in-time, for example, space, presence . . . time and space seem to blend in the continuum of your presence. You lose your bearings for a moment. You finally end up in a totally meditative state.[14]

But the "you" losing all bearings, ending up in a meditative state, was, of course, the artist. Most viewers quite simply would not have invested the time needed to be able to experience a painting of two horizontal stripes in this way; in most cases, "a totally meditative state" wasn't what they were looking for anyway. Irwin had to pull us into his project. He did this in Rinzai Zen fashion by throwing us perceptually off-balance. He began painting tiny red and green dots on a white ground so that his paintings seem to glow; he bowed his canvases slightly, curving their corners, so that they seem to reach out toward us; he abandoned the

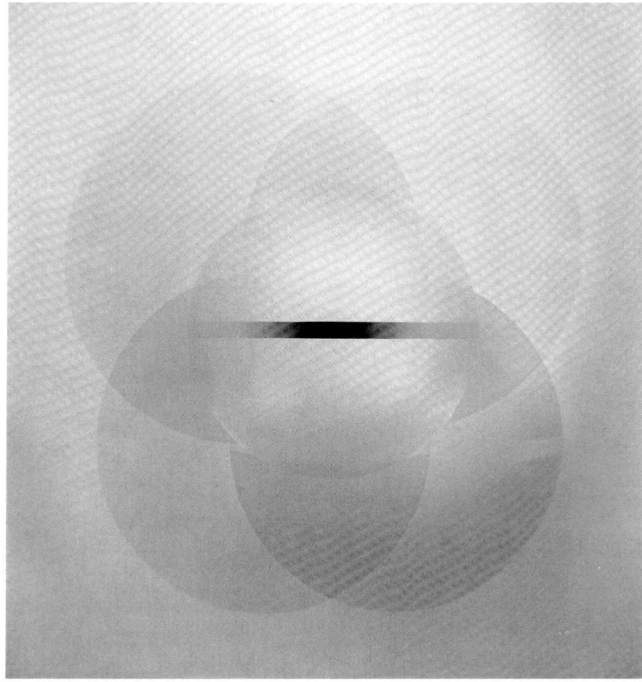

Robert Irwin, Untitled, 1969, acrylic lacquer on shaped acrylic plastic disc, 53¼ in. (diameter). University of California, Berkeley Art Museum. Photo: Benjamin Blackwell. Artist © 2005 Robert Irwin/Artist Rights Society (ARS), New York.

canvas altogether, experimenting with curved discs whose highly controlled lighting and subtle surfaces bring into visual question where the painting-as-object ends and its space—which is also our space—begins.

Even more than with most works of art, the effect of Irwin's pieces cannot be conveyed by photographs. He in fact forbade photography of his work during this period. There are thus no illustrations in the catalog for the 1966 Los Angeles County Museum of Art exhibition of Irwin's dot paintings. *Artforum* founder and editor Philip Leider wrote in a perceptive essay for the catalog:

> In Robert Irwin's most recent paintings one is confronted by what at first appears to be an immaculate white picture plane, about seven feet square, and nothing more. Some time must pass—a minute, or two, or three—before the viewer becomes fully aware of an indistinct, irregularly-shaped mass which seems to have emerged out of the white plane, roughly centered. The coloration is so subdued that there is no possibility of defining what one sees in terms of it, but rather in terms of what it suggests: a quality of energy.[15]

Leider totally got what Irwin was about: "first of all, the dedication of the work of art to the creation of an immensely human aesthetic encounter between viewer and painting, and second, a complex disassociation, in Irwin's mind, between art and the art-object."[16] The risk,

Leider points out, is that, if the viewer is not willing to slow down enough to achieve this subtle perceptual level of experience, "he will not—quite literally—see the painting at all." For Irwin, however, "The name of the game, after all, is Art, not Looking at Pictures."[17]

Irwin was obsessive in his attempts to control the environments of his works from this period. Over time, he became more and more interested in what gave these environments their particular qualities—details of the floor, the walls, the ceiling, the sources of light. Light is, of course, a form of energy. By 1969 he had moved toward using light itself as his medium, as a way to energize space and the people in it. But he still had to get their attention, to somehow make the light visible. Dust motes do this, when their slow movement is caught up in a shaft of sunlight, which, in their laconic way, they energize. Irwin's discs, with their play of light and shadow, were already moving in that direction:

> Visually it was very ambiguous which was more real, the object or its shadow. They were basically equal . . . that was the real beauty of those things, that they achieved a balance between space occupied and unoccupied in which both became intensely occupied at the level of perceptual energy.[18]

He made some tall, transparent acrylic plastic columns. What happened with them was something anyone but Irwin might have predicted: people looked at them as sculpture. It was the old pointing-finger-instead-of-the-moon problem.

His breakthrough occurred in 1970 in the form of a stealth exhibition at the Museum of Modern Art in New York, where a young curator, on her own, made an unused gallery available to him. The space was a "clumsy" one, and experiments that had been so effortlessly successful in Irwin's pristine California studio were simply unworkable here. But Irwin managed to turn the obstacles into an opportunity: "Instead of my overlaying my ideas onto that space, that space overlaid itself on me."[19] One of the three things Irwin did was to replace the standard fluorescent tubes with ones that alternated warm and cool—pinkish white and greenish white. "It was almost as if the room had a rainbow in it. It was all very strong, almost too strong, too romantic in a way; and yet, on the other hand, a lot of people didn't see it at all. So, go figure."[20] Another thing Irwin did was to string at eye level, in front of the longest wall, a wire that was painted white at both ends, "so that even walking within a foot of it, you could not see the wire going into the wall." As he explained, "I daubed a little bit of white at various other places as well, so that the wire seemed to come and go. You had this visual element that you couldn't really hold in focus, no matter how hard you tried. . . . And yet, at the same time, you couldn't ever really look at the back wall either, because your eye was always getting caught up by this line."[21] Finally, he stretched a translucent white scrim underneath one of the two banks of lights. As with the wire, this gesture was intended to make visitors to the gallery unusually aware of their own focus: "It's very hard to focus on that material; it sets up an ambiguity that makes everything do one of two things: either become ambiguous or razor sharp by comparison."[22]

Light and white scrim, which catches the light, became Irwin's most successful media for doing what he wanted: making visitors aware of their own experience of seeing (see p. 220). The scrim serves the same purpose as dust motes—or snow, which is what visitors to Irwin's room installations tend at first to think they're seeing. In 1977, the year he installed a piece called *Scrim Veil—Black Rectangle—Natural Light* at the Whitney Museum of American Art, Irwin remarked: "When people walk into a gallery where I've installed some of the kinds of things I've been doing recently, a lot of people just say, 'Oh, it's an empty room.' The question then, of course, is emptied of what?"[23] It's not nothing, as Agnes Martin might say, or, as Jasper Johns asked himself in 1964: "Seeing what? According to what?" What John Cage did for music, Robert Irwin did for art. "What I'm really trying to do," he said of the almost imperceptible additions or adjustments to art spaces he was making in the mid-seventies, "is draw their attention to, my attention to looking at and seeing all of those things that have been going on all along but which previously have been too incidental or too meaningless to really seriously enter into our visual structure, our picture of the world."[24]

After developing the Museum of Modern Art installation, Irwin closed his studio and began driving in the desert. He was doing what he had been trying to get his audience to do: experiencing the world as art.

> It's all just flat desert, no particular events, no mountains or trees or rivers. And then . . . it takes on an almost magical quality. It just suddenly stands up and hums, it becomes so beautiful, incredibly, the presence is *so* strong. Then twenty minutes later, it will simply stop. And I began wondering why, what those events were really about, because they were so close to my interests, the quality of phenomena.[25]

Unlike Agnes Martin, Irwin didn't camp; he's never been particularly interested in landscape as nature. (He likes to live at the top of a high-rise with a light-filled view.) And, unlike contemporary earth artists such as Robert Smithson or Michael Heizer, he wasn't interested in leaving his mark. What he eventually decided to do was, as Weschler puts it, "absorb the lessons of the desert and apply them,"[26] bring them back, like Pu-tai with his gifts, into the world: "I said I would go anywhere, anytime, for anybody, for anything. I made myself very available—and I made it for free."[27] He made himself, as he put it, "available in response."[28] He taught, did room installations, and gradually moved beyond art environments into the "real" world: college campuses, public buildings. He began seriously reading philosophy, particularly phenomenology, developing an academic language to try and convey through words what he was up to.

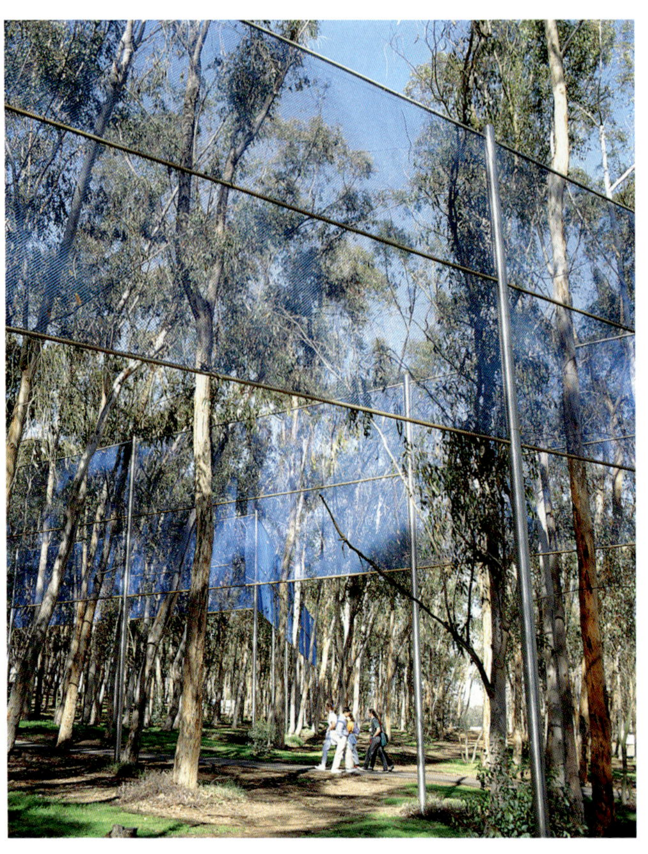

Robert Irwin, *Two Running Violet V Forms,* 1983, plastic-coated fencing, stainless steel poles, and iceplant. Two V-shaped forms each about 28 ft. high and 196 ft. long; poles 5 in. in diameter, site about 3,000 sq. ft. Stuart Collection, University of California, San Diego. Funding provided by the Stuart Foundation with additional support from the MacArthur Foundation. Artist © 2005 Robert Irwin/Artist Rights Society (ARS), New York.

And, slowly, the richness of the world began to enter his art. Irwin is perhaps best known today as the creator of the ambitious, 134,000-square-foot Central Garden at the Getty Center in Los Angeles. The process of creating the Central Garden began for Irwin in 1992, when he started working with the J. Paul Getty Trust in an attempt to humanize Richard Meier's massive architecture. The design of the Central Garden encompasses the natural ravine between the museum and the research institute with a meandering, tree-lined walkway that traverses a stream flowing over various textures of rock through a variety of grasses and gradually descends to a plaza. There, Irwin's large, vase-shaped bougainvillea arbors made of rebar provide color, scale, and a seating area. The stream continues through the plaza and ends in a cascade of water over a stone waterfall into a pool filled with an azalea maze, which appears to float. Around the pool is an array of gardens, each with a variety of plant material.

The contrast of the Getty's expansive, expensive, and expensively maintained garden with Irwin's lyrically simple installations from the 1970s is dramatic. But it is the place he has come to, like the oxherder in Kakuan's version of the Zen Oxherding Pictures. In the 1970s,

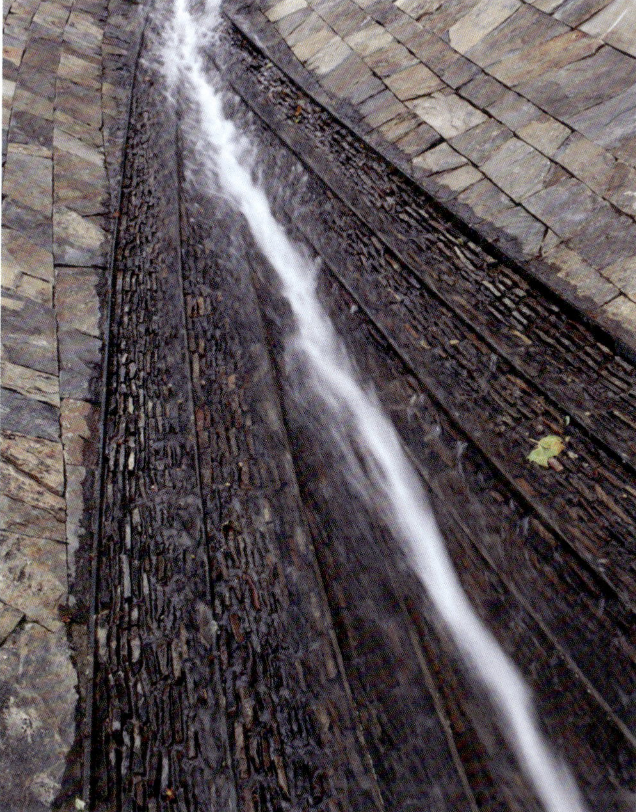

Robert Irwin, detail of Central Garden stream at the Getty Center, Los Angeles, California. Photo: Dominique Vorillon. Copyright: © 2000 J. Paul Getty Trust. Artist © 2005 Robert Irwin/Artist Rights Society (ARS), New York.

both Irwin and his art were "gone out of sight"; in the 1980s, he was "returning to the Origin, Back to the Source" in the world; in the 1990s, "entering the city with gift-bestowing hands."[29] Already in 1971 Irwin believed: "If light is the medium and space is the medium, then, in a sense, the universe is a medium. I know the impracticality of it right now but when I say that the medium is the universe, that maybe the world is an art form, then the gardening of our universe or our consciousness would be the level of our art participation."[30]

Robert Irwin has always been driven by questions. He has extended his activity as an artist out of the studio, out of the museum, into the world. The questions he is now addressing are:

> What would a non-hierarchical order look like?
> What would be its operative (extended) frame of reference?
> How might it work?
> And what kind of world would it make?[31]

A world, "not just something given to us whole," but a world in which value is given "to our human potential to 'see' the infinite richness in everything."

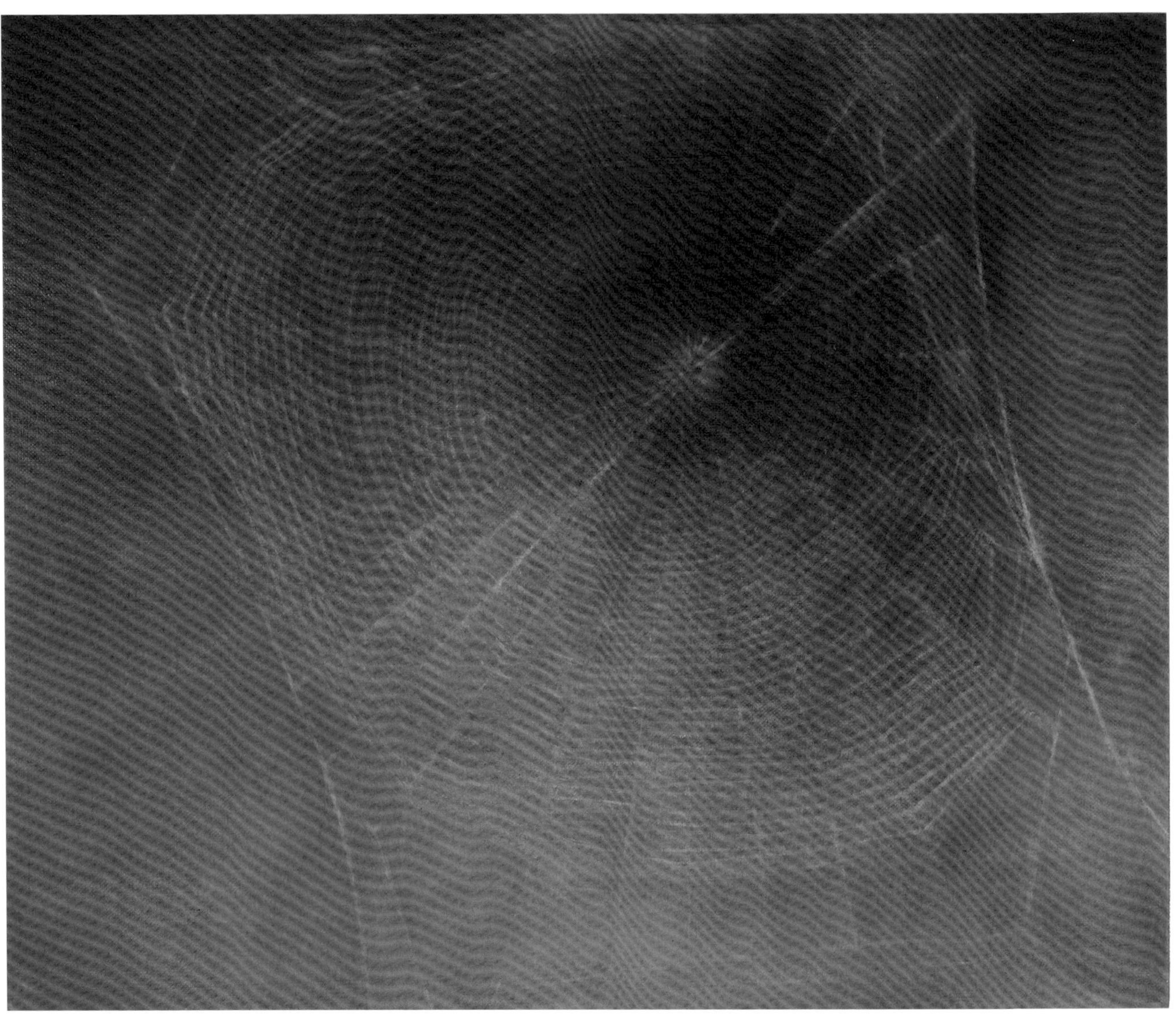

Vija Celmins, *Web #3,* 2000–2002, oil on linen, 15 x 18 in. The Edward R. Broida Collection. Photo: Michael Korol, New York. Courtesy McKee Gallery, New York.

Painting is very specific, but it is not specific to things that you can say.

VIJA CELMINS

VIJA CELMINS 1938–

THE PRECISE RENDERINGS OF VIJA CELMINS seem very different from the work of the other artists in this section—indeed, in this book. Celmins is always showing us some *thing*. Her early still lifes of electrical appliances, her paintings based on gray halftone photographs of disintegrating World War II bombers, her paintings and drawings from her own photographs of Los Angeles freeways and the surface of the Pacific Ocean, and her grainy graphite drawings of the moon's surface, rock-strewn deserts, and the depths of the night sky have brought her to a recent focus on spiderwebs. These little paintings, which capture all of the luminosity and delight of an actual spiderweb spotted on a misty morning, are the paradoxical result of Celmins's wish to "pull away" from what she had begun to regard as her "too distilled and refined" images of sea and sky.[1] Like Celmins, spiders make the same two-dimensional design over and over again; like her, they are trying to catch something.

Born in Latvia in 1938, five-year-old Vija fled with her family ahead of the advancing Russian army into West Germany, where she experienced firsthand the Allied bombing at the end of World War II. She has said she thinks of her childhood as being "full of excitement and magic, and terror too—bombs, fires, fear, escape—very eventful. It wasn't till I was ten years old and living in the United States that I realized living in fear wasn't normal."[2] Her family was relocated by the Church World Service, first to New York, then Indianapolis, "a safe place in the middle of the country."[3] An incessant drawer, Celmins entered art school at the age of sixteen. For the next five years she painted almost every day. In 1961 Celmins won a scholarship to attend Yale Summer School, where she met other young artists from New York who would become lifelong friends; they include the painters Chuck Close and Brice Marden, both of whom, like her, would develop an interest in Buddhism.

In 1962 Celmins traveled with a friend to Europe "to visit all the large museums." She was particularly attracted to the rich surfaces and subdued palette of Velázquez—"the beautiful grays, blacks, and pinks."[4] Later that year she entered on scholarship the master's program in art at the University of California, Los Angeles, where there was a thriving Zen Buddhist community. She writes of this new environment: "I know no one in Los Angeles but the landscape is exotic and exciting to me. I spend a lot of time driving around and looking, sometimes painting from my car."[5] Celmins was a student of Robert Irwin's at UCLA, where he taught for a semester in 1963. This was the period when Irwin was intensely engaged with his ten line paintings. She recalls spending "hours having heated conversations in his office about the nature of art and painting."[6] You only spend "hours" having conversations, however heated, with someone who is close to your way of thinking. Between Celmins and Irwin, the point of connection is experiential perception:

> My work . . . is for the spectator. That is, you find your relationship to it physically, not just mentally or by imagination. It asks participation to come alive. I mean spatial, visual participation. The body, the eyes complete the work.[7]

The words are those of Vija Celmins, but they could almost be those of Robert Irwin.

That same year, Celmins rented a studio that would affect her art for years to come. While driving on Venice Boulevard she saw a storefront with a "for rent" sign on it.

> I stopped and looked in these giant store windows and there was a big expanse of dust on the floor. It was all gray and went back for about ninety feet and I thought, "This is the place for me." I was going to have rooms of dust and you'd have to look through telescopes to inspect them.[8]

But Celmins is a painter, not a creator of environments like Irwin. "When I get down to making things, ideas sort of slip away and I tend to end up doing the same thing. . . . My idea of painting a single image over and over on the same canvas is not really what I would call a 'brilliant' idea. It is an act of trying to reach some physical presence beyond 'idea.'"[9] When the dust finally settled into her work in 1969 to 1972, it would be in the form of graphite drawings of moonscapes and barren desert landscapes, which do resemble dust seen "through telescopes."

What might have been the attraction of all that dust in the studio Celmins came to love, where she felt, as she put it, "free"?[10] One possibility is that it was a safe place to explore

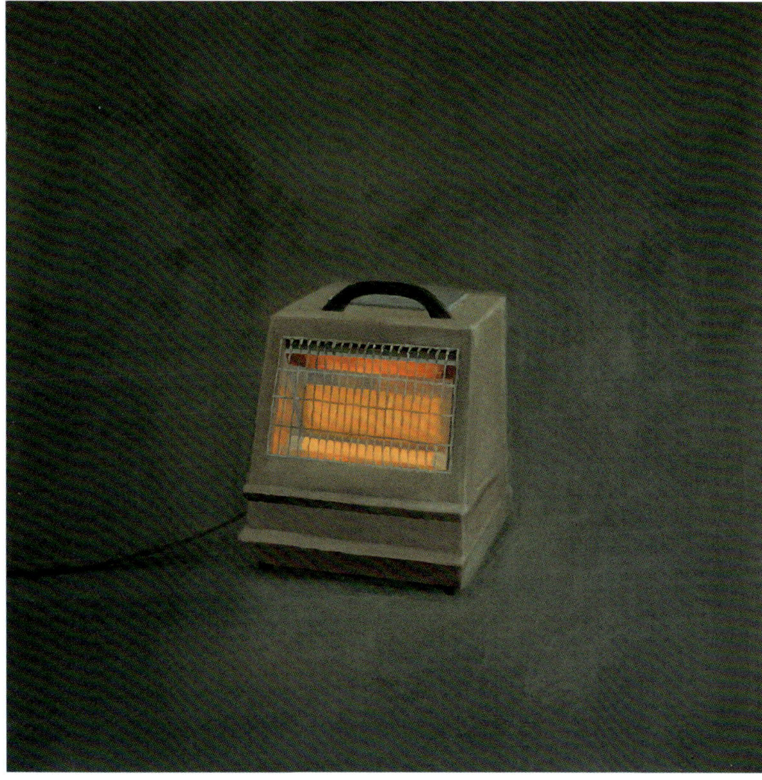

Vija Celmins, *Heater,* 1964, oil on canvas, 47⁷⁄₁₆ x 48 in. Whitney Museum of American Art, New York; Purchase, with funds from the Contemporary Painting and Sculpture Committee (95.19). Photo © Whitney Museum of American Art, New York.

memories from her war-torn childhood, when she "often cut classes . . . to explore the ruins and rubble."[11] She began tentatively, with lonely images of electrical appliances—a lamp, a hot plate, an electric frying pan, a heater, a fan. Isolated against a Velázquez-gray background, a patch of fiery orange often glows somewhere inside. Celmins has described these as "second-hand objects in my studio." Photographs of her studio from this period, however, show inert objects: tables, boxes, a chair, a cot. The objects she chose to paint are all electrified, lending them undertones of danger and anger.

The undertones became overtones in her subsequent paintings of a smoking pistol and of a television set with the image of a falling, exploding plane on its screen. Her contemporaneous sculptures *House #1* and *House #2* (1965) are painted on the outside with similar images of smoking, flaming mayhem. Celmins's *Time Magazine Cover* from 1965 shows scenes from "The Los Angeles Riot," an event that may have helped surface memories of World War II that had been buried in the safety of the American Midwest. The most haunting paintings from the mid-1960s are her war images taken from old newspaper clippings, paintings in which the single appliance has been replaced by a single war plane, often in distress. *Flying Fortress,* for example, elicits a shiver of horror as we notice the barely

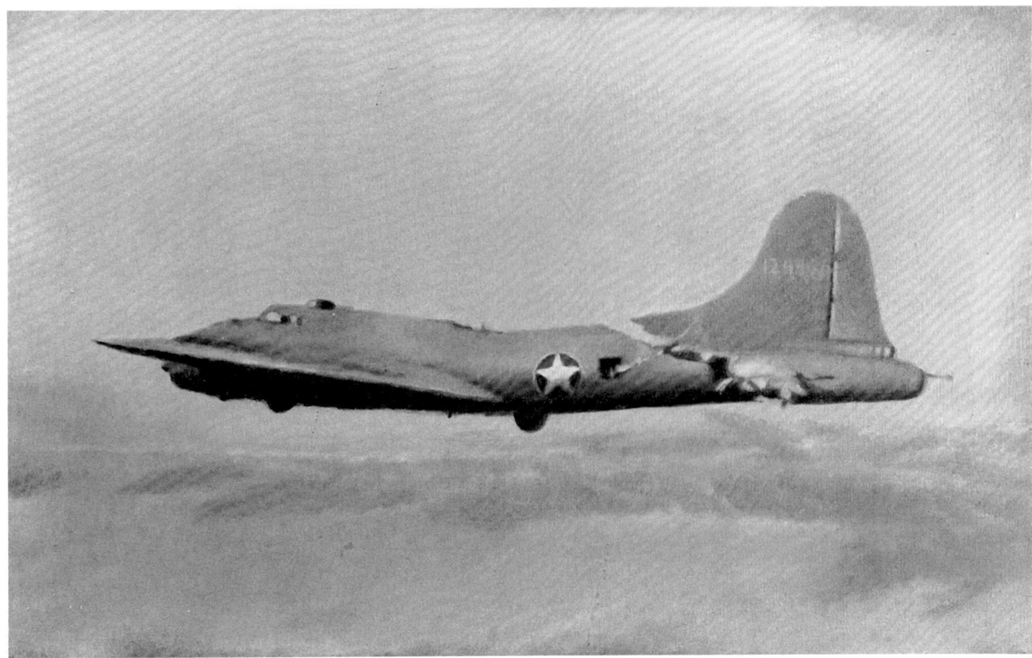

Vija Celmins, *Flying Fortress,* 1966, oil on canvas, 16 x 26 in. The Edward R. Broida Collection.

perceptible but clearly fatal rift between the bomber and its tail, and imagine the emotions of the men whose heads we can just make out at the other end of the plane. Hers was a resurrection project: "I thought of it as putting the images that I found in books and magazines back in the real world—in real time. Because when you look at the work you confront the here and now. It's right there."[12]

In 1966 the twenty-eight-year-old artist was given a show, which was, as she put it, "somewhat successful" and which, she says, scared her.[13] She turned her attention to looking at the world, but through a camera: "What I really liked was looking through the camera lens. I had a job at the University of California, Irvine, and used to drive to it back and forth on the freeway taking photographs by balancing my camera on the steering wheel."[14] For Celmins, the camera was a distancing tool that allowed her to compress complex, three-dimensional reality into a two-dimensional image she could transform into art:

> It occurred to me that if I were to make an image that was solid-looking but still trying to pull you into a picture, there would be a problem. But if I had an image that interlocked with the picture plane, then the problem would be solved. That's when the ocean images evolved. I made a break and the other things opened up: to make it work two-dimensionally, you have to abstract it.[15]

She stopped painting, and for ten years did graphite (pencil) drawings of the surfaces of the moon and of the earth—both sea and desert: "One thing led to another. When I started looking I began to look more at my own work, and I think I made the work more about looking. Essentially, it's very conceptual work—it's about looking."[16]

Celmins was also grappling with personal issues during this time, "several relationships that, unfortunately, [did] not work out."[17] In 1975–76 she moved to Big Sur and took up birdwatching "with great gusto and a sense of discovery. Training for the eyes, that's how I think of it."

> Around this time I also meet a Tibetan Buddhist monk named Chogyam Trungpa Rimpoche. He likes art and artists. . . . I practice sitting. I am attracted to Buddhism and I like the idea of paying attention to what is and letting go of the ego. The final step of becoming a disciple I cannot do. An important book for me is Shunryu Suzuki's *Zen Mind, Beginner's Mind.*[18]

Chogyam Trungpa was a charismatic Tibetan *tulku*—incarnate teacher—who had abandoned his monastic vows in order, he said, to communicate more effectively with Westerners. He settled in the United States in 1970. An artist himself, Trungpa did, indeed, have many artists, musicians, and writers among his students. (He founded the strongly arts-oriented Naropa University in Boulder, Colorado.) In the course of his teachings on meditation, perception, and artistic expression, Trungpa developed a concept that he called "dharma art." The Sanskrit word *dharma* means both "law" and "teachings," but its literal meaning is closer to the idea of "carrying" or "holding."[19] It is not difficult to imagine the appeal of this teaching for Celmins, who feels she missed her childhood, and one of whose deepest regrets is not having had a homeland: "I imagine that would have been very comforting to me and would have given me a different kind of strength."[20] For Trungpa, dharma, in the context of art, was "the state before you lay your hand on your brush, your clay, your canvas—very basic, peaceful, and cool, free from neurosis";[21] in Celmins's words, "letting go of the ego."

In his teachings about art, Trungpa worked with the Tibetan Buddhist concept of *yün,* or inherent richness. He organized a study group called the Explorers of the Richness of the Phenomenal World. Like Celmins, Trungpa used the camera as a tool for seeing—for framing—the world. His photographs from the early seventies are about emptiness, or, as he put it, the "empty gap of mind."[22] One, entitled *Beam* (1974), has as its ostensible subject a "moonset" over a crevice in distant hills. An elongated, shadowy form—the beam?—intrudes from the upper right into a horizon otherwise empty of anything but light. *Lichen* (1974), on the other hand, bears an uncanny resemblance to Celmins's desertscapes. Trungpa said of it, "It's another overcrowded *ratna* situation, which provides some kind of

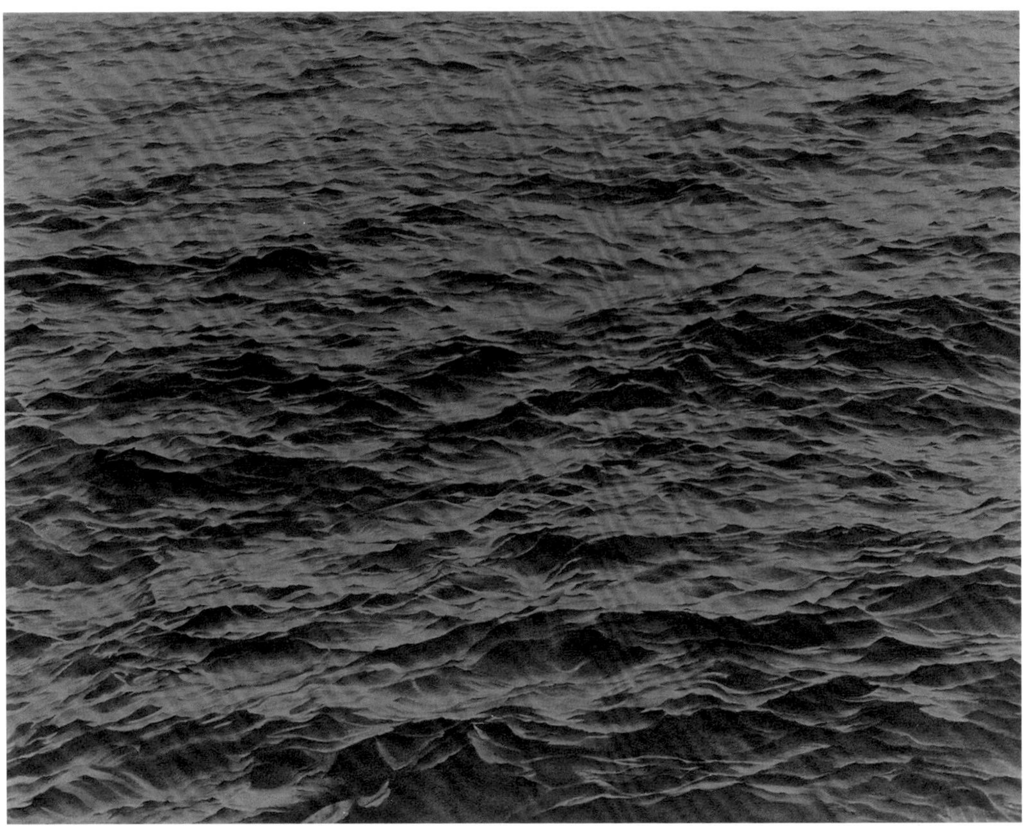

Vija Celmins, *Untitled (Big Sea #2)*, 1969, graphite on acrylic ground on paper, 34 x 45 in. Private collection. Courtesy McKee Gallery, New York.

the mind."[35] Just as Trungpa's teachings attracted her, a chapter in Suzuki's book entitled "Mind Waves," about maintaining "imperturbable composure," might also have seemed preternaturally right:

> When you try to stop your thinking, it means you are bothered by it. Do not be bothered by anything. It appears as if something comes from outside your mind, but actually it is only the waves of your mind, and if you are not bothered by the waves, gradually they will become calmer and calmer. . . . Even though waves arise, the essence of your mind is pure; it is just like clear water with a few waves. Actually water always has waves. Waves are the practice of the water.[36]

"Waves are the practice of water"; art is the practice of artists.

Celmins has said she practiced meditation, but she never took the "final step" of becoming a "disciple" of Trungpa or anyone else. Instead, like Ad Reinhardt, Vija Celmins chose an-

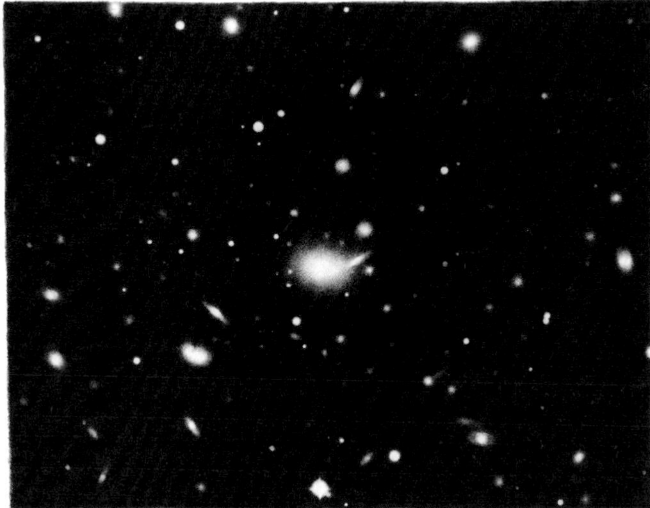

Vija Celmins, *Galaxy #4 (Coma Bernices)*, 1973, graphite on acrylic ground on paper, 12⅛ x 15 in. Collection Paine Webber Group Inc., New York. Photo: Richard Nicol. Courtesy McKee Gallery, New York.

other way. Already in the mid-1960s, her notes, which seem inspired by Reinhardt's Zen-influenced "Twelve Rules for a New Academy," outline her path.

> no composition
> no gestures
> no artificial color
> no distortion
> no angst or effort showing
> no ego
> (dead-pan paintings)[37]

But unlike Reinhardt's set of vows for truly abstract painting (the only truly realistic painting, according to Yves Klein), Celmins's list seems more a set of operating instructions for packing nonverbal content into a highly controlled art of representation. Highly attended to might be a better way of putting it, for her art has evolved from the representation of studied emotion to a sustained practice of focus on the phenomenal world, its surfaces and its depth, a representation that is so tightly focused it becomes abstract.

The power of Celmins's *Webs* devolves from their inheritance of both these themes. Like life, they are beautiful death-traps. But they are also places to "feel free," for they evoke the Chinese Buddhist patriarch Fe-tsang's metaphor of the bejeweled fishing net of Indra. Just as every jewel of Indra's net reflects the light of all the others, so all phenomena are one, yet there is no reality apart from individual phenomena. "What would a non-hierarchical order look like?" Robert Irwin asks. The *Webs* of Vija Celmins intimate an answer.

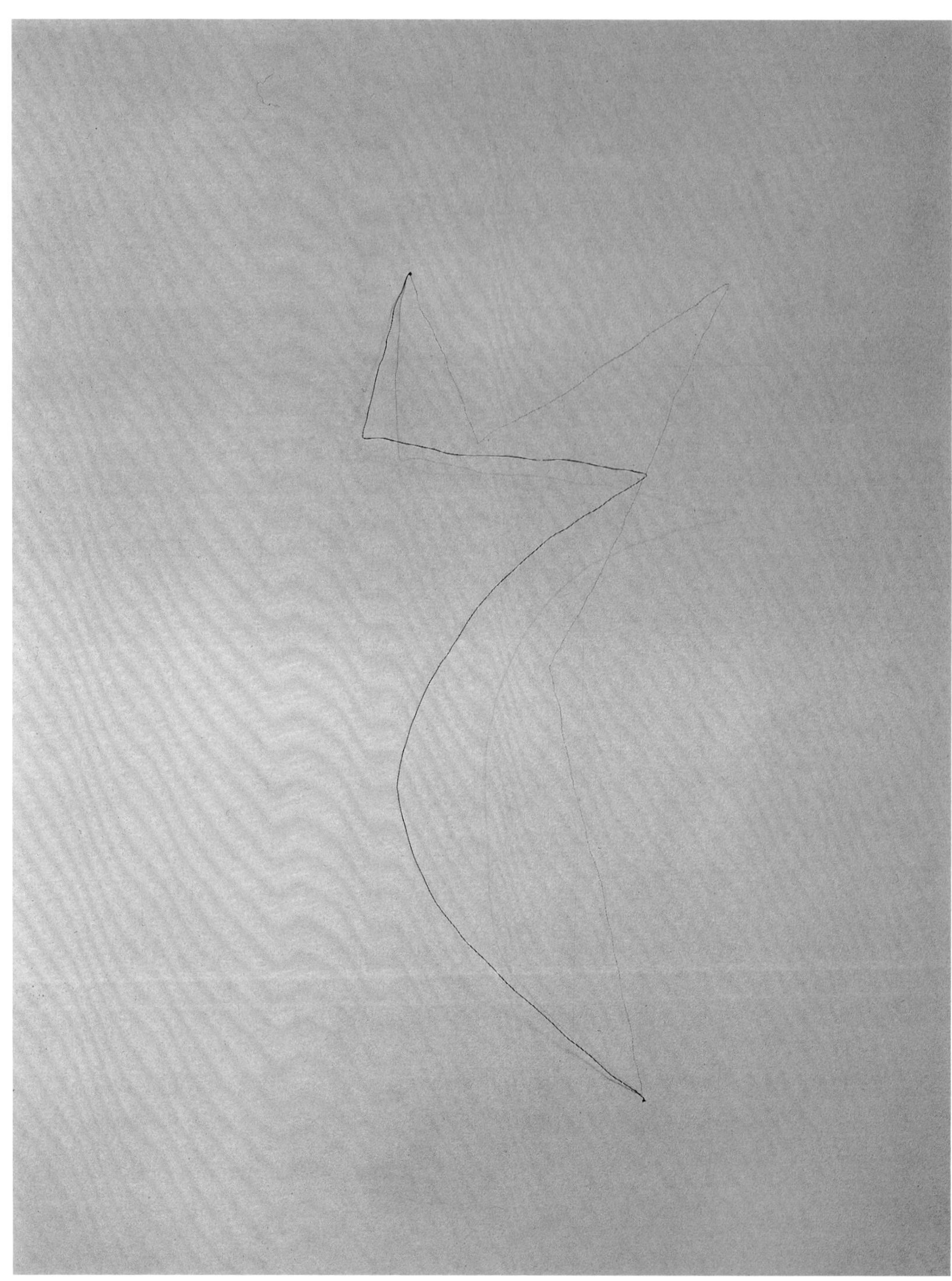

Richard Tuttle, *20th Wire Piece,* 1972, pencil, wire, and nails, 23 x 26 in. Collection Judith Neisser, Chicago. Courtesy Sperone Westwater, New York.

My ambition is someday to be able to stand face-to-face with life itself and be completely unafraid... that is what in fact we are supposed to do in our lives.... I try extremely hard to face all of life, as much as I possibly can. And that's also what the drawings are about.

RICHARD TUTTLE

RICHARD TUTTLE 1941–

MANY COMMENTATORS HAVE POINTED OUT the difficulty of describing the work of Richard Tuttle in more than the most superficial terms. A piece by Tuttle can be made of almost anything, often several anythings combined—florists' wire, broken Styrofoam, light bulbs, the painted wooden ends of coffee stirrers. The scale of his work is usually modest, though it can range from tiny to building-filling. His placement can be quirky, so the work is easy to overlook. Once spotted, it tends to be hard to forget.

Tuttle's work shows very little of what art historians call "development." Unlike Robert Irwin, for example, who has moved in rational stages from painting into environmental work of increasing complexity, Tuttle's pieces have remained neither painting nor sculpture but somehow both. His early shaped, painted canvas *Space* is a good example. What connects Tuttle with Irwin is a shared valuing of the space within which their work exists; what separates them is Tuttle's passionately reciprocal relationship with his objects. Tuttle's goal is "to make something that looks like itself," that looks like life.[1] Nevertheless, as curator Marcia Tucker pointed out in 1975, the bits and pieces that comprise Tuttle's works often "do not look like anything at all . . . are not even visible as potential art before installation"—installation by Tuttle, that is.[2] Once that happens, they couldn't be anything else, so strong is their presence.

Richard Tuttle, *Space,* 1964, acrylic on linen on wood construction, 20¼ x 20¼ x 5⅛ in. Collection Donald L. Bryant Jr. Family Art Trust. Courtesy Sperone Westwater, New York.

Just as Yves Klein insisted on describing his protean art as "painting," Richard Tuttle likes to think of his medium as "drawing." His terminology is perhaps best understood as "drawing" a bow, in the sense of Eugen Herrigel's *Zen in the Art of Archery.* Tuttle pulls his works out of some other dimension and turns them loose in our space and our time. His *Wire Pieces,* created between 1971 and 1974, were made in three different ways. Some were strung along nails placed in the wall according to a paper template. Others were made "by drawing the wire between two graphite lines and cutting it at the center."[3] The most complex are the ones comprising three interrelated lines: a pencil line, a wire that has been stretched along it and then fastened down at one or more points, and the shadow of that wire.

Tuttle's art-making process is, like Agnes Martin's, the product of a meditative mind. As one observer describes the first stage in making a wire piece:

> [It] begins when the artist, pencil in hand, stands parallel and in close proximity to the white wall for the first time, erect yet not tense, his body relaxing around its own axis. His feet, never clad in shoes, are in contact with the floor. . . . The pencil is not applied

> until after a phase of acclimation and orientation: the available space is "measured" with outspread arms, the shoulders and arms loosened up; then comes a moment of calm in which the artist bows his head, coming to dwell "within himself." When he finally raises his head the drawing phase begins.[4]

From another account, the next stage in the process:

> With deliberate, peaceful whole-arm movements, each line is completed in the one attempt; they always seem to be personally proportioned, fitting the limits of his hands or arms. Small bumps in the lines reflect Tuttle's pulse, and on that particular day, the rhythms of the street-drilling machinery on Eleventh Avenue below.[5]

The apprehension of Tuttle's works induces a similar state of heightened consciousness in the mind of the viewer who takes the time to notice—to see—three lines made of graphite, wire, and shadow. Says Tuttle: "I find that seeing a work is a kind of energy, whether I see that drawing and make it or a viewer sees it and comprehends it; there's really no difference. In a way I'm drawing to comprehend a viewer."[6]

Richard Tuttle was born in Rahway, New Jersey, in 1941. His uncle, stationed in Japan after World War II, sent gifts home packed in boxes made of fragrant Kiri wood. Six-year-old Richard's reaction to this fragrance and to the colors and textures contained in these boxes was a kind of aesthetic intoxication: "The sensuality, the smell, the presence, the silk, the sense of faraway opened me to further interest. I've compared it with what I'm told happens to an alcoholic when they take their first drink. They know it's different for them than it is for other people. Right from the first drink, they know." The experience was, he says, intense: "the excitement, I can remember it to this day."[7]

These products of Japanese culture evoked something Tuttle had glimpsed earlier, in a vision he had had when he was about four. There was tension between his parents. In his anxiety during one such confrontation, Richard hid and withdrew into himself: "[I] looked to the left and saw white—a white tree; looked to the right and saw black, darkness, which I didn't like; looked straight ahead and saw grayness, a texture, which was frightening."[8] Then he looked down, and what he saw, which he can't describe, gave him a feeling of happiness and hope.

Tuttle's account of this early childhood experience has qualities in common with John Cage's description of the nine "permanent emotions" of Indian aesthetics—the *rasas:* "The four black: sorrow, fear, anger, disgust. The four white: the heroic, the wondrous, mirth, and the erotic. Finally, the one without color, in the center, toward which any work of art should conduce, tranquility."[9]

Whatever the source—some collective unconscious or just an unusually visual turn of mind—Tuttle's childhood vision produced an artist, a person who draws into the concrete

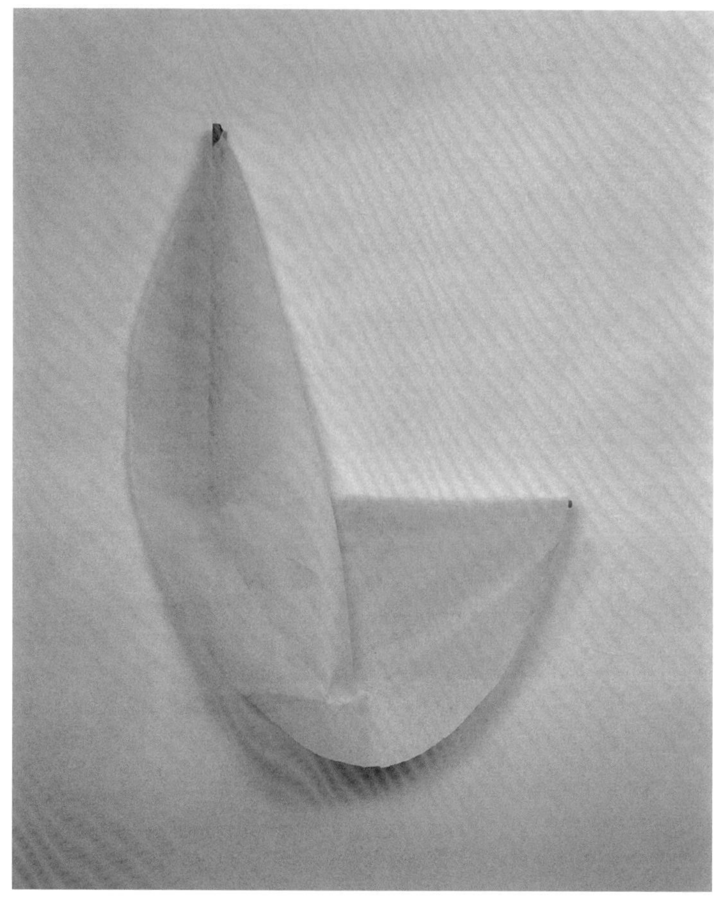

Richard Tuttle, *4th Summer Wood Piece,* 1974, cloth, wood, and staples, 30 x 20 x 1 in. Dorothy and Herbert Vogel Collection. Courtesy Sperone Westwater, New York.

world the invisible reality he has experienced—a reality that has affinities with Duchamp's fourth dimension. The adult Richard Tuttle says of his experience: "To the left is spiritualism, the spiritual—it's not that. To the right it's the world—it's not that. In the front it's like chaos—polarities, strife. And what I saw next—I can't say exactly what it is, but I'm certainly living as if it were art."[10]

Tuttle became a fine arts major at Trinity College in Hartford, Connecticut—home of the Wadsworth Atheneum. In his junior year, the legendary contemporary curator Samuel Wagstaff Jr. arrived at the Atheneum and became a mentor. After graduation Tuttle moved to New York, where he attended Cooper Union art school. In 1964 he worked for Agnes Martin, whose philosophy of life and art was in deep accord with his own. (Tuttle's characterization of Martin's drawing as "the loved line" could serve as a description of his as well.[11]) The two artists became lifelong friends; like Martin, Tuttle would come to build a home and studio in New Mexico.

Richard Tuttle's first show was in 1965, at Betty Parsons's gallery. (Parsons was Agnes Martin's and Ad Reinhardt's dealer at the time.) For the next two years, Tuttle worked to make ends meet as an exhibition installer at Asia House Gallery. He has said, "I learned as much or more from that experience as I did going to galleries."[12] In 1968 Tuttle received a grant from the National Endowment for the Arts to travel to Japan. He spent six months there, returning again in 1972 and 1975. His trips to Japan were interspersed with travel to Greece, birthplace of Western culture, and Turkey, where Europe and Asia meet.

Tuttle notes that his research in the realm of art covers some of the same territory as the philosophy of Kitaro Nishida, founder of the Kyoto School, who in the early twentieth century attempted to reconcile Buddhist perspectives and Western philosophy. One of Nishida's principles was his belief in a universal plane of consciousness. Nishida's idea parallels Tuttle's own conception of the two-dimensional, abstract picture plane of traditional Western painting as a plane of consciousness whose boundaries he aspires to release. But Tuttle had a harder time relating to the writings of Nishida's friend D. T. Suzuki, and his understanding of Zen became not much clearer once he got to Japan:

> The whole Zen thing, I really couldn't swallow that, right from the get-go. But I was interested, and as soon as I got to Japan I tried to ask questions and find people who knew, and I was immediately told that it's a meaningless term, because there's not one Zen, there are ten different Zens. . . . I actually respond more to Chinese Zen, of which there are a couple of schools as well.[13]

About Buddhism in general, however, he says: "I must say it feels very comfortable, it fits like a glove. For example, I take enormous pleasure in my mind to see myself in the hand of Buddha. And I can do that anytime I want."[14]

Clearly, Buddhism is only one piece of Tuttle's larger life-project:

> There's this tremendous urge to figure it out, and to use the creative dimensions, possibilities, the idea that—like Beuys said—we have the entire history of the world in us. And so the truth, the creativity can touch that history of the world inside of us. And what we read about or get to know in this book or that book, all of that gets piled together, in the hope that one can figure it out.[15]

One of Tuttle's heroes in utilizing the "creative dimensions" to engage life is the legendary sixteenth-century Japanese tea-master, Sen no Rikyu. Rikyu served as tea-master to the military ruler Toyotomi Hideyoshi, who had so little appreciation for Rikyu's radical innovations in the art of tea that he ordered Rikyu's ritual suicide at the age of sixty-nine. Hideyoshi came from a peasant background, and the elegant, expensive, imported Chinese tea ware then in vogue was more in keeping with the self-image he wanted to maintain than the clumsy

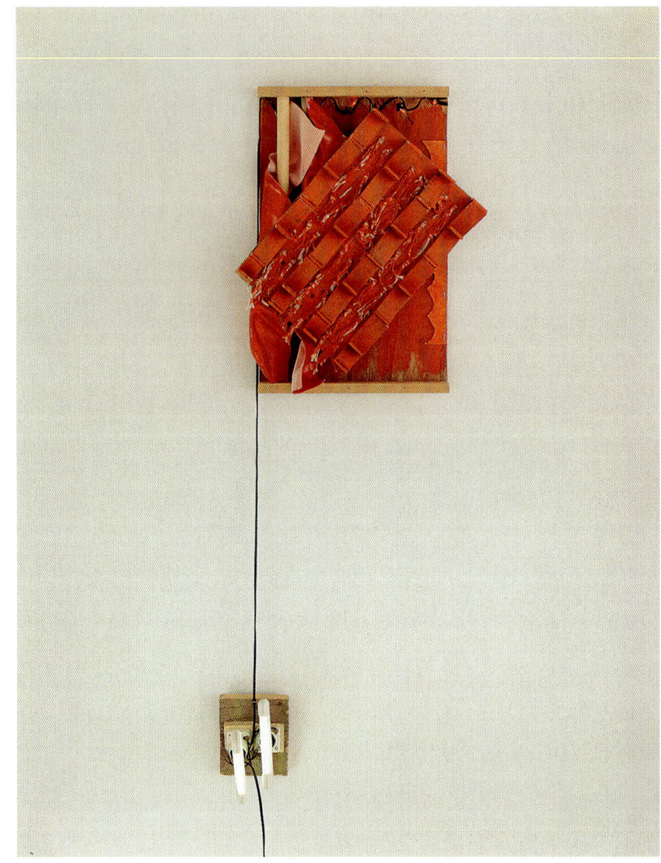

Richard Tuttle, *The Last Light Work*, 1991, acrylic, electric lights, vinyl/cardboard, and wood, 55 x 20 x 7 in. Collection Howard and Donna Stone, Chicago. Courtesy Sperone Westwater, New York.

local wares, natural materials, and rustic, small-scale spaces that Rikyu introduced. Rikyu transformed the ritual tea ceremony into an art form that exemplified the Japanese aesthetic of *wabi-sabi:* the "beauty of things imperfect, impermanent, and incomplete."[16] Rikyu's ephemeral aesthetic made the tea ceremony a ritual that was at once both modest and profound.

What Rikyu accomplished for the tea ceremony, Richard Tuttle has accomplished for modern art. His materials, too, are modest, often local; and his installations tend toward the impermanent. Their beauty resides in their ephemeral sense of perfect rightness. It is this sense of momentary rightness, of shabby perfection, that most closely connects Tuttle's work with that of Agnes Martin. Even as a child, he was vividly aware of noumenal reality: "as an entity, as a complex human entity, I resolved around certainties that were not demonstrated by the concrete world."[17] His goal became accessing it. For Tuttle, the "crossover" point is art:

> Whatever is abstract is not in the world, but when it comes together as art it is in the world. When it comes together in the ultimate degree then you have a great moment in

> the history of art. It's a cat and mouse game. You can see canvas. You can see paint. But you can't see the crossover. You need enough of a suggestion to awaken the mind to the crossover so it can see it, the invisible.[18]

An ancestor of Richard Tuttle on his father's side is the American nineteenth-century Luminist painter John Frederick Kensett. Richard Tuttle could have had Kensett's paintings of light-infused landscapes in mind when he said, "You can see canvas. You can see paint. But you can't see the crossover." The crossover into the light, into that place of heightened energy, takes place in the mind. Like Kensett, like Irwin, Tuttle incorporates light into his work. Robert Irwin once commented, "What I want is the quality of light, its energy, its existence as matter. I don't want the light bulb."[19] For Tuttle, on the other hand, the light bulb is a mechanism for turning invisible energy into visible energy. In 1991 he made a wall piece entitled *The Last Light Work*. "To find an energy equal to electricity, to define electricity, was one of the goals in the light-bulb work," he explains. The piece had small orange bulbs under its top edge, but then, "coming back from Europe, the work I thought was complete was suddenly finished with the fluorescent, which looked like 'electricity' to me."[20] Tuttle is not interested in abstraction; he is interested in making the invisible visible. Electricity is "defined" by the light bulb because the light bulb allows you to see it, to see the invisible, which turns out to look exactly like itself.

This ephemeral experience is, of course, impossible to get from a reproduction of the piece, where light doesn't register. That's just fine with Tuttle: "People like something that lasts," he says; "I like something that vanishes."[21] Words can't convey its proffered experience either. In this, as in the work of all the artists discussed, the most satisfactory surrogate for the art object may be the flower held up by the Buddha in his wordless Flower Sermon, consisting only of this simple gesture. One disciple smiled.

NOTES

All translations from French are by the author unless otherwise noted. The epigraphs at the beginning of this book are from Huston Smith and Philip Novak, Buddhism: A Concise Introduction *(San Francisco: Harper San Francisco, 2003), 89, and Jacques Bacot,* Le poète tibétain Milarépa: Ses crimes–ses épreuves–son nirvana *(Paris: Brossard, 1925), 20.*

FOREWORD

1 From the Sanskrit, *Divyāvadāna,* ed. P. L. Vaidya (Darbhanga: Mithila Institute, 1959). Compare John S. Strong, *The Legend of King Asoka: A Study and Translation of the Asokavadana* (Princeton, N.J.: Princeton University Press, 1983).

INTRODUCTION

The epigraphs are from Kakuzo Okakura, *The Ideals of the East with Special Reference to the Art of Japan* (New York: Dutton, 1920 [1903]), 60–61, and Thich Nhat Hanh, *Vietnam: Lotus in a Sea of Fire* (New York: Hill and Wang, 1967), 94.

1 Arthur C. Danto, *Mysticism and Morality: Oriental Thought and Moral Philosophy* (New York: Basic Books, 1972), 18.

2 Henri-Pierre Roché, "Souvenirs sur Marcel Duchamp," *La nouvelle N.R..F.* 1, no. 6 (June 1953): 1136. See also the translation by William N. Copley in Robert Lebel, *Marcel Duchamp,* trans. George Heard Hamilton (New York: Paragraphic Books, 1959), 85.

3 Stephen Batchelor, *Buddhism Without Beliefs* (New York: Riverhead Books, 1997), 11.

4 Christmas Humphreys, *Buddhism,* rev. ed. (London: Cassell, 1962).

5 Translation from Jan Nattier, "The *Heart Sutra:* A Chinese Apocryphal Text?" *Journal of the International Association of Buddhist Studies* 15, no. 2 (1992): 218 n103.

6 Ibid., 219.

7 A. C. Moule and Paul Pelliot, *Marco Polo: The Description of the World,* vol. 1 (London: Routledge, 1938), 410. The nineteenth-century scholars were Edouard de Laboulaye, "'Barlaam et Josaphat' et le 'Lalitavistara,'" *Journal des Debats,* 26 July 1859; and Felix Liebrecht, "Die Quellen des 'Barlaam und Josaphat,'" *Jahrbuch für romanische und englische Philologie* 2 (1860): 314–34 (from Salvatore Calomino, *From Verse to Prose: The Barlaam and Josaphat Legend in Fifteenth-Century Germany* [Potomac, Md.: Scripta Humanistica (no. 63), 1990], 1 n1).

8 From Colonel Henry Yule's annotated English version, *The Book of Ser Marco Polo, The Venetian, Concerning the Kingdoms and Marvels of the East,* vol. 1 (London: John Murray, 1871), 404–5.

9 Stephen Batchelor, *The Awakening of the West: The Encounter of Buddhism and Western Culture* (Berkeley, Calif.: Parallax Press, 1994), 175.

10 Brian Houghton Hodgson, *Essays on the Languages, Literature and Religion of Nepal and Tibet* (London: Trübner, 1874), 98–99; quoted in Guy Richard Welbon, *The Buddhist Nirvana and Its Western Interpreters* (Chicago: University of Chicago Press, 1968), 36–37.

11 R. Spence Hardy, *A Manual of Budhism, in Its Modern Development; Translated from Singhalese Mss,* 2d ed. (London: Williams and Norgate, 1880), vii.

12 From Paul Gauguin, "Diverses choses," later additions to the manuscript *Noa Noa* (Cabinete des Dessins, Louvre, 1896–98), 272; cited by Bogomila Welsch-Ovcharov, "Paul Gauguin's Third Visit to Brittany," in *Gauguin's Nirvana: Painters at Le Pouldu 1889–90* (Hartford, Conn.: Wadsworth Atheneum in association with Yale University Press, 2001), 162 n158 (my translation).

13 Bernard Frank, *Le panthéon bouddhique au Japon: Collections d'Emile Guimet* (Paris: Musée National des Arts Asiatiques Guimet, Réunion des Musées Nationaux, 1991), 33.

14 J. J. Clarke, *Oriental Enlightenment: The Encounter between Asian and Western Thought* (New York: Routledge, 1997), 20.

15 Eve Kosofsky Sedgwick, "Pedagogy of Buddhism," in *Touching Feeling: Affect, Pedagogy, Performativity* (Durham, N.C.: Duke University Press, 2003), 166–67.

16 Ad Reinhardt, "Twelve Rules for a New Academy," *Art-as-Art: The Selected Writings of Ad Reinhardt,* ed. Barbara Rose (New York: Viking, 1975), 203–7.

I. THE INFINITE MOMENT

1 Sir William Temple, "Upon the Gardens of Epicurus and of Gardening in the Year 1685," *Essays,* vol. 2; quoted in Arthur O. Lovejoy, "The Chinese Origin of a Romanticism," in *Essays in the History of Ideas* (Baltimore: John Hopkins University Press, 1948), 111.

2 Lovejoy, "Chinese Origin," 111 n29. Some additional guesses are given by Osvald Sirén in *China and the Gardens of Europe in the Eighteenth Century,* with intro. by High Honor (Washington, D.C.: Dumbarton Oaks, 1990), 15 n1.

3 Sir William Chambers, *Designs of Chinese buildings, furniture, dresses, machines and utensils, engraved by the best hands from the originals drawn in China by Mr. Chambers. . . . To which is annexed a description of their temples, houses, gardens, &c.* (London, 1757), 15.

4 Sir William Chambers, *A Dissertation on Oriental Gardening* (London, 1772); reprinted with an introduction by John Harris (Farnborough, England: Gregg International Publishers, 1972), 33–35.

5 The "Forty Scenes" were reproduced in G. L. le Rouge, *Détails de nouveau jardins à la mode: Jardins anglo-chinois* (Paris, 1786).

6 From Henri de Lubac, *La rencontre du bouddisme et de l'Occident* (Paris: Aubier, 1952), 152 n4; translated in Stephen Batchelor, *The Awakening of the West: The Encounter of Buddhism and Western Culture* (Berkeley, Calif.: Parallax Press, 1994), 243–44.

7 Emile-Louis Burnouf, "Le Bouddhisme en Occident," *Revue des deux mondes,* 15 July 1888, 372.

8 Paul Carus, *The Gospel of Buddha According to Old Records* (Chicago: Open Court, 1895 [1st ed. 1894]), 25–26. Odilon Redon had the French edition of this book in his library.

9 Burnouf, "Le Bouddhisme en Occident," 356.

CLAUDE MONET

1 Claude Roger-Marx, "M. Claude Monet's 'Water Lilies,'" *Gazette des beaux-arts,* June 1909; cited in Charles F. Stuckey, ed., *Monet: A Retrospective* (New York: Scribner, 1985), 266–67.

2 Quoted in Geneviève Aitken and Marianne Delafond, *La collection d'estampes japonaises de Claude Monet à Giverny* (Giverny: Maison de Monet, 1983), 26.

3 The interviewer was Marc Elder; quoted in Virginia Spate et al., *Monet and Japan* (Canberra: National Gallery of Australia, 2001), 209.

4 Arsène Alexandre, *Claude Monet* (Paris: Bernheim Jeune, 1921), 53. The longer, somewhat convoluted original version goes: "La plus importante des circonstances qui amenèrent Monet à faire un retour sur lui-même et à chercher autre chose (bien entendu dans le sens de sa propre nature) fut le voyage à Londres auquel le contraignit la guerre de 1870."

5 Henry Yule, *Concerning the Kingdoms and Marvels of the East,* vol. 1 (London, 1871), 407 n3.

6 From a manuscript in the Fondation Custodia, Paris (1978-A-20), cited by Shigemi Inaga in Spate et al., *Monet and Japan,* 65.

7 Théodore Duret, *Voyage en Asie* (Paris: Michel Lévy Frères, 1874), 23.

8 Hippolyte Adolphe Taine, "Le bouddhisme: *Die Religion des Buddha und ihre Enstehung,* par M. Koeppen," in *Nouveaux essais de critique et d'histoire,* 4th ed. (Paris: Hachette, 1886 [1865]), 291.

9 Ibid., 302.

10 Raymond Koechlin, "T. Hayashi," *Bulletin de la société franco-japonaise,* December 1906, 2–6, 9; quoted in Spate et al., *Monet and Japan,* 36.

11 Jules Bois, *Les petites religions de Paris,* 2 vols., rev. ed. (Paris: Flammarion, [1894]), 1: 41–42.

12 Georges Clemenceau, *Claude Monet: Les Nymphéas* (Paris: Plon, 1928), 101–2.

13 Georges Clemenceau, *In the Evening of My Thought,* 2 vols., trans. Charles Miner Thompson and John Heard, Jr. (Boston: Houghton Mifflin, 1929), 2: 524.

14 Gustave Geffroy, *Claude Monet: Sa vie, son temps, son oeuvre* (Paris: Crès, 1922), 5.

15 Ibid., 335.

16 Quoted in Steven Z. Levine, *Monet, Narcissus, and Self-Reflection: The Modernist Myth of the Self* (Chicago: University of Chicago Press, 1994), 260.

17 Louis Gillet, *Trois variations sur Claude Monet* (Paris, 1927), 110–11; quoted in ibid., 272.

VINCENT VAN GOGH

1 Vincent van Gogh, *The Complete Letters of Vincent van Gogh,* vol. 3 (Boston: Little, Brown, 2000), 64–65 (letter 544a).

2 Ibid., 429 (letter W2).

3 Ibid., 500 (letter B9 [12]).

4 Ibid., 497 (letter B8 [11]).

5 "Frederik van Eeden, *The Quest* [*Little Johannes* plus two subsequent installments translated by Laura Ward Cole] (New York: Mitchell Kennerley, 1911), 129; cited by Douglas W. Druick and Peter Kort Zegers, *Van Gogh and Gauguin: The Studio of the South,* exh. cat. (Chicago: Art Institute of Chicago with Thames and Hudson, 2001), 104. Van Eeden published an appreciation of van Gogh and his work in his journal *De Nieuwe Gids* after the artist's death; it is available in: Susan Alyson Stein, *Van Gogh: A Retrospective* (New York: Park Lane, 1986), 241–46. In addition to being a writer, van Eeden was a physician and psychiatrist who cared for Theo van Gogh before his death in Amsterdam. Van Eeden later developed the concept of lucid dreaming.

6 Van Gogh, *Complete Letters,* vol. 3: 54–55 (letter 542).

7 Evidence for van Gogh's reading of Burnouf's essay was noted by Victor Merlhès in 1984. For greater elaboration, see Merlhès, *Paul Gauguin et Vincent van Gogh 1887–1888: Lettres retrouvées, sources ignorées* (Taravao, Tahiti: Avant et Après, 1989), 113–18.

8 For an analysis of Schuré's review, see my essay on Redon. The books discussed are Edwin Arnold's *The Light of Asia* (first published in 1871), William Woodville Rockhill's *The Life of the Buddha, and the Early History of His Order* (1884), volume 2 of Louis Leblois's *Les Bibles et les initiateurs religieux de l'humanité* (1884), E. Senart's *Essai sur la légende du Buddha* (2nd ed., 1882), Heinrich Kern's *Der Buddhismus und seine Geschichte in Indien* (1882), A. Barth's *Les religions de l'Inde* (1879), and Jules Barthélemy Saint-Hilaire's *Le Buddha et sa religion* (1866). Other potential sources of information for van Gogh, who read English, include the second edition of R. Spence Hardy's *Manual of Buddhism* (1880), Friedrich Max Müller's *Selected Essays on Language, Mythology, and Religion* (1881), and Hermann Oldenberg's *The Buddha: His Life, His Doctrine, His Order* (1882; rev. ed. 1888).

9 Van Gogh, *Complete Letters,* vol. 3: 496 (letter B8 [11]).

10 Hippolyte Adolphe Taine, "Le bouddhisme: *Die Religion des Buddha und ihre Enstehung,* par M. Koeppen," in *Nouveaus essais de critique et d'histoire,* 4th ed. (Paris: Hachette, 1886 [1865]), 291, 296.

11 Ibid., 286.

12 Ernest Renan, Preface, *Nouvelles études d'histoire religieuse* [1884], in Henriette Psichari, ed., *Oeuvres complètes de Ernest Renan,* vol. 7 (Paris: Calmann-Lévy, 1947), 705.

13 Ernest Renan, *The Life of Jesus,* trans. Charles Edwin Wilbour (New York: Carleton, 1864 [1857]), 221.

14 Renan, "Premiers travaux sur le bouddhisme," *Nouvelles études,* 764.

15 Ibid., 771–72.

16 Van Gogh, *Complete Letters,* vol. 3: 55 (letter 542).

17 Ibid., 516 (letter to Bernard, B18 [15], from late September 1888).

18 Ibid., 64–65 (letter 544a).

19 The fate of this painting—that is, how it was damaged and by whom—is far from clear. See Vojtech Jirat-Wasiutynski and H. Travers Newton, "The Historical Significance of Early Damage and Repair to Vincent van Gogh's *Self-Portrait Dedicated to Paul Gauguin,*" *Center for Conservation and Technical Studies* (Cambridge, Mass.: Harvard University Art Museums, 1984), 3–27; and Merlhès, *Gauguin et van Gogh,* 117–18.

20 Van Gogh, *Complete Letters,* vol. 3: 159 (letter 588).

21 Paul Gauguin, *The Writings of a Savage: Paul Gauguin,* ed. Daniel Guérin, trans. Eleanor Levieux (New York: Da Capo Press, 1996 [1978]), 42.

PAUL GAUGUIN

1 See Douglas W. Druick and Peter Kort Zegers, "Le kampong et la pagode Gauguin à l'exposition universelle de 1889," in *Gauguin: Actes du colloque Gauguin* (Paris: Musée d'Orsay, 1991), 121 (fig. 11c); idem, *Van Gogh and Gauguin: The Studio of the South,* exh. cat. (Chicago: Art Institute of Chicago with Thames and Hudson, 2001), 281 (fig. 36).

2 Quoted by Françoise Cachin in Richard Brettell et al., *The Art of Paul Gauguin* (Washington, D.C.: National Gallery of Art, 1988), 106.

3 Paul Gauguin, *The Writings of a Savage: Paul Gauguin,* ed. Daniel Guérin (New York: Da Capo Press, 1996 [1978]), 25.

4 "Lettres inédites d'Emile Schuffenecker, réunies et présentées par Auriant," *Maintenant,* no. 8 (1948): 250.

5 *Dhammapada: The Sayings of Buddha,* trans. with commentary by Thomas Cleary (New York: Bantam, 1995), 108.

6 *Noa Noa par Paul Gauguin,* ed. Jean Loize (Paris: André Balland, 1966), 29.

7 Douglas Cooper, ed., *Paul Gauguin: 45 lettres à Vincent, Théo et Jo van Gogh* (s' Gravenhage, Netherlands: Staatuitgeverij, Lausanne: Bibliothèque des Arts, 1983), 283.

8 *Livre d'or de l'Exposition Universelle,* no. 30 (1 October 1889); reproduced and quoted by Victor Merlhès, "LABOR. Painters at Play in Le Pouldu," in Eric M. Zafran et al., *Gauguin's Nirvana: Painters at Le Pouldu 1889–90,* exh. cat. (Hartford and New Haven: Wadsworth Atheneum with Yale University Press, 2000), 98.

9 J. E. Cirlot, *A Dictionary of Symbols,* trans. Jack Sage (New York: Philosophical Library, 1962), 272.

10 Vincent van Gogh, *The Complete Letters of Vincent van Gogh,* vol. 3 (Boston: Little, Brown, 2000), 64 (letter 544a).

11 Quoted in French in Bogomila Welsh-Ovcharov, "Paul Gauguin's Third Visit to Brittany," in *Gauguin's Nirvana,* 58. The manuscript is in the Cabinet des Dessins, Louvre.

12 Gauguin, *Writings of a Savage,* 41.

13 Van Gogh, *Complete Letters,* vol. 3: 64 (letter 544a).

14 Stephen F. Eisenman, *Gauguin's Skirt* (London: Thames and Hudson, 1997), 189. The Vietnamese Buddhist friend was Nguyen van Cam.

ODILON REDON

1 From Kay Larson, "Shaping the Unbounded: One Life, One Art," in *Buddha Mind in Contemporary Art,* ed. Jacquelynn Baas and Mary Jane Jacob (Berkeley: University of California Press, 2004), 61.

2 Odilon Redon, *A soi-même: Notes sur la vie, l'art et les artistes* (Paris: Corti, 1979 [1922]), 11.

3 Ibid., 121; trans. and quoted in Douglas W. Druick et al., *Odilon Redon, 1840–1916* (Chicago and New York: Art Institute of Chicago with Abrams, 1994), 18.

4 Douglas W. Druick and Peter Kort Zegers, "Painful Origins," in Druick et al., *Redon,* 18.

5 Gustave Flaubert, *The Temptation of St. Antony, or, A Revelation of the Soul* (New York: Howard Fertig, 1978 [1904]), 105. The print is number 132 in André Mellerio's catalog *Odilon Redon* (Paris: Société pour l'Etude de la Gravure Français, 1913), 113.

6 Flaubert, *St. Anthony,* 104; Mellario, *Redon,* 115 (no. 145).

7 Flaubert, *St. Anthony,* 108.

8 Roseline Bacou, "La bibliothèque d'Odilon Redon," in *Festschrift to Eric Fischer: European Drawings from Six Centuries* (Copenhagen: Royal Museum of Fine Arts, 1990), 36. The friend was Maurice Fabre; the exact quote: "J'ai des livres sur le bouddhisme que je n'ai point encore lus. Il me faut reprendre cette vieille *Tentation* de Flaubert."

9 Edouard Schuré, "Le Bouddha et sa légende: Une résurrection de Bouddha," *Revue des deux mondes,* 1 July 1885, 620.

10 Ibid., 621.

11 Redon, *A soi-même,* 18. Clavaud's first treatise, from around the time he met Redon, was on green algae (see Stephen F. Eisenman, *The Temptation of Saint Redon: Biography, Ideology, and Style in the Noirs of Odilon Redon* [Chicago: University of Chicago Press, 1992], 20).

12 Redon, *A soi-même,* 17–18.

13 Bacou, "La bibliothèque d'Odilon Redon," 36.

14 Paul Carus, *The Gospel of Buddha According to Old Records* (Chicago: Open Court, 1895), viii.

15 Sadakichi Hartmann, *Buddha: A Drama in Twelve Scenes* (New York: Author's ed., 1897), 43.

16 Ibid., 44–45.

17 Alec Wildenstein, *Odilon Redon: Catalogue raisonné de l'oeuvre peint et dessiné* (Paris: Wildenstein Institute, 1992), vol. 1, no. 682. This pastel appears to have been inspired by a painted wooden sculpture in the Musée Guimet: *Jizo in Red Robes* (MG 577; ill. in Bernard Frank, *Le panthéon bouddhique au Japon: Collections d'Emile Guimet* [Paris: Réunion des Musées Nationaux, 1991], no. 65).

18 Odilon Redon, *To Myself: Notes on Life, Art and Artists,* trans. Mira Jacob and Jeanne L. Wasserman (New York: Braziller, 1986), 11.

19 Flaubert, *St. Antony,* 105.

II. OTHER DIMENSIONS

The epigraph is from Kakuzo Okakura, *The Book of Tea* (London: Putnam's, 1906), 65–66. Yeno's name in Chinese is Hui-neng.

1 Will Grohmann, *Wassily Kandinsky: Life and Work* (New York: Abrams, 1958), 85.

2 Wassily Kandinsky, *Kandinsky: Complete Writings on Art,* ed. Kenneth C. Lindsay and Peter Vergo (New York: Da Capo Press, 1994), 210.

3 Maria Carlson, "Fashionable Occultism: The World of Russian Composer Aleksandr Scriabin," *Journal of the International Institute* 7, no. 3 (summer 2000): 6.

4 Kandinsky, *Complete Writings,* 145.

5 Ibid., 242.

6 Marcel Duchamp, *The Writings of Marcel Duchamp,* ed. Michel Sanouillet and Elmer Peterson (1973; repr. New York: Da Capo Press, 1989), 151. Written in 1943, this statement was published in the catalog *Collection of the Société Anonyme* (New Haven: Associates of Fine Arts at Yale University, 1950).

7 Quoted in Duchamp, *Writings,* 140.

8 Arturo Schwarz, *The Complete Works of Marcel Duchamp* (New York: Abrams, 1970 [1969]), 197.

9 Marcel Duchamp in "Interview by Dorothy Norman," *Art in America* 57, no. 4 (July–August 1969): 38 [original interview 1953].

10 Duchamp in Pierre Cabanne, *Dialogues with Marcel Duchamp,* trans. Rod Padgett (1971, repr. New York: Da Capo Press, 1987), 16.

11 See Arturo Schwarz, *The Complete Works of Marcel Duchamp,* rev. ed. (New York: Delano Greenidge, 2000), 779, no. 508. The back cover of the magazine reads: "when / the tobacco smoke / also smells / of the mouth / that exhales it / the two odors / are married / by infra-thin." Duchamp's made-up term "infra-thin" implies a quality of thinness below the threshold of thinness. Something, perhaps, more like interpenetration, the marriage of subject and object, "you" not separate from "me."

12 Bonnie Clearwater, ed., *West Coast Duchamp* (Miami Beach: Grassfield Press, 1991), 107.

13 Donald S. Lopez Jr., "The Heart Sutra as Tantra," in *Elaborations on Emptiness: Uses of the Heart Sutra* (Princeton, N.J.: Princeton University Press, 1996), 90–91.

14 *Mahayana-Sutralamkara, exposé de la doctrine du Grand Véhicule selon le système Yogacara,* 2 vols., ed. and tr. from Nepal manuscript by Sylvain Levi (Paris: H. Champion, 1907–11).

15 Gilles Bégin, *Les peintures du Bouddhisme tibétain* (Paris: Musée National des Arts Asiatiques-Guimet, 1996), 16.

16 The first documented visit to an exhibition that Duchamp and Brancusi made together was in October 1912, when they went with Fernand Léger to the Grand Palais to see a show of airplanes (Pontus Hulton, Natalie Dumitresco, and Alexandre Istrati, *Brancusi* [London: Faber and Faber, 1988], 92).

17 Lanier Graham, "Duchamp & Androgyny: The Concept and its Context," *tout-fait: The Marcel Duchamp Studies Online Journal* 2, no. 4, January 2002 (www.toutfait.com/issues/volume2/issue_4/articles/graham/graham1.html); also in Graham, *Duchamp & Androgyny: Art, Gender, and Metaphysics* (Berkeley: No-Thing Press, 2003).

18 William James, "Philosophical Conceptions and Practical Results," in *Pragmatism,* ed. Frederick H. Burkhardt (Cambridge, Mass.: Harvard University Press, 1975), 259; quoted in Louis Menand, ed., *Pragmatism: A Reader* (New York: Vintage Books, 1997), xiii.

19 See Robert H. Sharf, "The Zen of Japanese Nationalism," in *Curators of the Buddha,* ed. Donald S. Lopez Jr. (Chicago: University of Chicago Press, 1995), 107–60.

20 John Dewey, *Art as Experience* (New York: Perigee Books, 1980 [1934]), 3.

21 Pam Ecker, "John Dewey, 1959–1952" (spring 1997), www.bgsu.edu/departments/acs/1890s/dewey/dewey .html, p. 1.

WASSILY KANDINSKY

The epigraph is from Wassily Kandinsky, *Kandinsky: Complete Writings on Art,* ed. Kenneth C. Lindsay and Peter Vergo (New York: Da Capo Press, 1994), 289.

1 Quoted in Peg Weiss, *Kandinsky in Munich: The Formative Jugenstil Years* (Princeton, N.J.: Princeton University Press, 1979), 129.

2 Peg Weiss, *Kandinsky and Old Russia: The Artist as Ethnographer and Shaman* (New Haven: Yale University Press, 1995), 87–92.

3 Wassily Kandinsky, "Empty Canvas, etc.," in *The Painter's Object,* ed. Myfanwy Evans (London: Gerald Howe, 1937), 54.

4 Will Grohmann, *Wassily Kandinsky: Life and Work* (New York: Abrams, 1958), 13.

5 Michael Sadleir *[sic], Michael Ernest Sadler: A Memoir By His Son* (London: Constable, 1949), 238. Sadler gave Kandinsky's book the English title *The Art of Spiritual Harmony.* Published in 1914, this translation was read by Georgia O'Keeffe.

6 Kandinsky, *Complete Writings,* 358 (from "Reminiscences").

7 Ibid., 382.

8 Ibid.

9 Ibid., 368.

10 Ibid., 364–65.

11 Quoted in Vivian Endicott Barnett, *Vasily Kandinsky: A Colorful Life* (Munich: Lenbachhaus, 1995), 160.

12 Kandinsky, *Complete Writings,* 363.

13 Ibid., 364.

14 For this important passage I have used the translation given in Robert L. Herbert, ed., *Modern Artists on Art: Ten Unabridged Essays* (Englewood Cliffs, N.J.: Prentice-Hall, 1964), 26.

15 Kandinsky, *Complete Writings,* 364.

16 Ibid., 360.

17 Ibid., 361.

18 Ibid., 380.

19 Ibid., 59. The 1908 Munich Exhibition is discussed by Helen Westgeest in *Zen in the Fifties: Interaction in Art Between East and West* (Amstelveen, Netherlands: Cobra Museum Voor Moderne Kunst, 1996), 40 n18.

20 Michael Sullivan, *The Meeting of Eastern and Western Art* (Berkeley: University of California Press, 1989), 248.

21 Thich Nhat Hanh, *The Heart of Understanding* (Berkeley, Calif.: Parallax Press, 1988), 1.

22 Wassily Kandinsky, *Sounds,* trans. with an introduction by Elizabeth R. Napier (New Haven: Yale University Press, 1981), 42.

23 *The Vimalakirti Sutra,* trans. from Kumarajiva's Chinese version by Burton Watson (New York: Columbia University Press, 1997), 110.

24 *The Holy Teaching of Vimalakirti: A Mahayana Scripture,* trans. from Tibetan by Robert A. F. Thurman (University Park: Pennsylvania State University Press, 1976), 77.

CONSTANTIN BRANCUSI

The epigraph is quoted in Petre Pandrea, *Portrete si controverse,* vol. 1 (Bucharest, 1945), 170–71; cited in Roger Lipsey, *An Art of Our Own: The Spiritual in Twentieth-Century Art* (Boston: Shambhala, 1988), 237.

1 Quinn Collection, New York Public Library; quoted in Friedrich Teja Bach, Margit Rowell, and Ann Temkin,

Constantin Brancusi, 1876–1957, exh. cat. (Philadelphia and Cambridge: Philadelphia Museum of Art with MIT Press, 1995), 178.

2 Anna C. Chave has written about the Tantric content of Brancusi's sculpture in *Constantin Brancusi: Shifting the Bases of Art* (New Haven: Yale University Press, 1993), 119–23.

3 Note reproduced and translated in Pontus Hulton, Natalie Dumitresco, and Alexandre Istrati, *Brancusi* (London: Faber and Faber, 1988), 222, 269.

4 See epigraph above.

5 Sanda Miller, *Constantin Brancusi: A Survey of His Work* (Oxford: Clarendon Press, 1995), 69–72. Miller expands upon the argument made by Athena T. Spear in "A Contribution to Brancusi Chronology," *Art Bulletin* 48 (March 1966): 45–49.

6 Quoted in Bogdan Urbhanowicz, "Visita mea la Brâncuşi: Decembrie, 1956," in *Colocviul Brâncuşi, 13–15 October 1967, Bucharest* (Bucharest, 1968), 108–10; cited in Miller, *Brancusi,* 79.

7 Henri-Pierre Roché, "L'enterrement de Brancusi," in *Hommage de la sculpture à Brancusi,* ed. Suzanne de Coninck (Paris, 1957), 29; cited in Alexandra Parigoris, "The Road to Damascus," in *Constantin Brancusi: The Essence of Things,* ed. Carmen Giménez and Mathew Gale (London: Tate, 2004), 51.

8 L. de Milloué, *Petit guide illustré au Musée Guimet* (Paris: Leroux, 1900), 137. The image thus described is Yamantaka, the ferocious manifestation that, according to Tibetan tradition, Manjusri (Wisdom) assumed to conquer Yama, the embodiment of death.

9 Quoted in Carola Giedion-Welcker, *Constantin Brancusi,* trans. Maria Jolas and Anne Leroy (New York: Braziller, 1959), 219, 220.

10 Quoted in Pandrea, *Portrete si controverse,* 1: 164; cited in Radu Varia, *Brancusi* (New York: Rizzoli, 1986), 300 n18.

11 Margit Rowell, "Brancusi: Timelessness in a Modern Mode," in Bach et al., *Brancusi,* 42–43.

12 Cecilia Cutescu-Storck, unpublished ms., 1961; quoted in Barbu Brezianu, "Pages inédites de la correspondance de Brancusi," *Revue roumaine d'histoire de l'art* 1, no. 2 (1964): 398 n. 18; cited in ibid., 42.

13 Hulton et al., *Brancusi,* 243. An entire book has been devoted to this subject: Varia's *Brancusi.*

14 Gilles Bégin, *Les peintures du Bouddhisme tibétain* (Paris: Musée National des Arts Asiatiques-Guimet, 1996), 16.

15 Jacques Bacot, "Pèlerinage du Dokerla (Tibet Sud-Oriental)," *Annales du Musée Guimet, Bibliothèque de Vulgarisation,* vol. 32: *Conférences faites au Musée Guimet* (Paris: Leroux, 1909), 195–218. *The Prayer* was the title of the 1907 sculpture Brancusi showed at the 1910 Salon des Indépendants.

16 Jacques Bacot, "L'art tibétain," *Annales du Musée Guimet, Bibliothèque de Vulgarisation,* vol. 36: *Conférences faites au Musée Guimet* (Paris: Hachette, 1912), 191–220.

17 Ibid., 195.

18 Jacques Bacot, Introduction, *Le poète tibétain Milarépa: Ses crimes—ses épreuves—son nirvana* (Paris: Bossard, 1925), 20.

19 Ibid., 19.

20 R. Pollack, "Brancusi's Sculpture versus His Homemade Legend," *Art News,* February 1960, 63.

21 Bacot, Introduction, *Milarépa,* 19–20.

22 Quoted in Giedion-Welcker, *Brancusi,* 220.

23 From a letter to Marie-Louise Gravier, late January 1919, quoted in Hulton et al., *Brancusi,* 121.

24 Hulton et al., *Brancusi,* 56.

25 Christian Zervos, *Constantin Brancusi: Sculptures, peintures, fresques, dessins* (Paris: Cahiers d'art, 1957), 103.

26 Hulton et al., *Brancusi,* 212.

MARCEL DUCHAMP

The epigraphs are from Pierre Cabanne, *Dialogues with Marcel Duchamp,* trans. Rod Padgett (1971; repr. New York: Da Capo Press, 1987), 72; Calvin Tomkins, *Duchamp: A Biography* (New York: Henry Holt, 1996), 408.

1 Originally published in *Artforum* 7, no. 3 (November 1968): 6, Johns's note is reprinted in *Jasper Johns: Writings, Sketchbook Notes, Interviews,* ed. Kirk Varnedoe, comp. Christel Hollevoet (New York: Museum of Modern Art, 1996).

2 Marcel Duchamp, *The Writings of Marcel Duchamp,* ed. Michel Sanouillet and Elmer Peterson (1973; repr. New York: Da Capo Press, 1989), 27, 23. Duchamp's original French reads "Etant donné que . . . ; si je suppose que je sois souffrant beaucoup . . . " (Michel Sanouillet, *Marchand du sel* [Paris: Le Terrain Vague, 1958], p. 31).

3 Henri-Pierre Roché, "Souvenirs sur Marcel Duchamp," *La nouvelle N.R.F.* I, no. 6 (June 1953): 1136; a translation of this essay by William N. Copley was published in Robert Lebel, *Marcel Duchamp* (New York: Paragraphic Books, 1959), 79–87.

4 Lebel, *Duchamp,* 2.

5 Roché in ibid., 79.

6 The single notable exception is the Taiwanese art historian Tosi Lee, author of an unpublished 1993 doctoral dissertation and a recent essay on Duchamp and Buddhism (see references). Several authors—for example, Robert Lebel (*Duchamp,* 97) and Arturo Schwarz (*The Complete Works of Marcel Duchamp,* rev. ed. [New York: Delano Greenidge, 2000], 33)—have pointed out parallels between Duchamp's thinking and Zen Buddhism. See also Kay Larson, "Shaping the Unbounded: One Life, One Art," in *Buddha Mind in Contemporary Art,* ed. Jacquelynn Baas and Mary Jane Jacob (Berkeley: University of California Press, 2004), 62–63.

7 Linda Dalrymple Henderson, *Duchamp in Context: Science and Technology in the Large Glass and Related Works* (Princeton, N.J.: Princeton University Press, 1998), 236 n4.

8 For example, in 1913 Duchamp stated: "If I am to tell what my own point of departure has been, I should say that it was the art of Odilon Redon" (quoted in Jacques Caumont, "Biography," in *Marcel Duchamp,* ed. Museum Jean Tinguely, Basel [Ostfildern-Ruit: Hatje Cantz, 2002], 187).

9 For more on this subject, see Linda Dalrymple Henderson, *The Fourth Dimension and Non-Euclidean Geometry in Modern Art* (Princeton, N.J.: Princeton University Press, 1983). On Kupka's importance for Duchamp, see Henderson's *Duchamp in Context.*

10 Cabanne, *Dialogues with Duchamp,* 38.

11 Ibid., 39–40.

12 Jennifer Gough-Cooper and Jacques Caumont, "Ephemerides on and about Marcel Duchamp and Rrose Sélavy, 1887–1968," in *Marcel Duchamp,* exh. cat. (Milan: Bompiani, 1993), *Ephemerides,* June 21, 1967.

13 Tosi Lee, "Watering, That's My Life: The Symbolism and Self-Imaging of Marcel Duchamp" (Ph.D. thesis, University of Illinois at Urbana-Champaign, 1993), 287.

14 *Writings of Duchamp,* ed. Sanouillet and Peterson, 32.

15 Gough-Cooper and Caumont, "Ephemerides," June 16, 1918.

16 Translated from the Sanskrit by Louis de la Vallée Poussin, *Bodhicaryavatara: Introduction à la pratique des futurs bouddhas, poème de Çantideva* (Paris: Librairie Bloud, 1907), 20 (3.27). Chinese and Tibetan versions of this Sanskrit text were discovered at Tun-huang in 1906–8.

17 Ibid., 101–2 (8.120).

18 Alfred Jarry, *Exploits and Opinions of Doctor Faustroll, Pataphysician,* trans. Simon Watson Taylor (Boston: Exact Change, 1996), 21. In this book, published posthumously in 1911, Jarry mentions a "painting machine" (86).

19 Cabanne, *Dialogues with Duchamp,* 31.

20 Lebel, *Duchamp,* 74.

21 Cabanne, *Dialogues with Duchamp,* 17.

22 Tomkins, *Duchamp,* 99 (from Duchamp's unpublished notes for a lecture, 1964).

23 Cabanne, *Dialogues with Duchamp,* 67.

24 From a 1968 interview with John Russell, quoted in Alice Goldfarb Marquis, *Marcel Duchamp: Eros, c'est la vie* (Troy, N.Y.: Whitston, 1981), 86.

15 Kakuzo Okakura, *The Book of Tea* (London: Putnam's, 1906), 59–61.

16 Ibid., 65.

17 Ibid., 68–69.

18 Ibid., 67.

19 From a letter of October 25, 1915, in Pollitzer, *Woman on Paper,* 33.

20 Ernest F. Fenollosa, *Epochs of Chinese and Japanese Art,* vol. 2 (New York: Frederick A. Stokes, 1912), 18.

21 Okakura, *Book of Tea,* 126.

22 Pollitzer, *Woman on Paper,* 28.

23 Cowart et al., *O'Keeffe,* 176.

24 Pollitzer, *Woman on Paper,* 226.

25 Cowart et al., *O'Keeffe,* 10.

26 *The Secret of the Golden Flower: A Chinese Book of Life,* trans. Richard Wilhelm with foreword and commentary by C. G. Jung (New York: Harcourt, Brace, 1962 [1931]), xiv.

27 Ibid., 25, 55, 21.

28 Ibid., 59.

29 Ibid., 53.

III. THE SPACE OF ART

The epigraphs are from Isamu Noguchi, "The Complete Artist," in *Isamu Noguchi: Essays and Conversations,* ed. Diane Apostolos-Cappadona and Bruce Altshuler (New York: Abrams, 1994), 47–48; Jasper Johns, transcribed notebook page, in *Jasper Johns: Writings, Sketchbook Notes, Interviews,* ed. Kirk Varnedoe, comp. Christel Hollevoet (New York: Museum of Modern Art, 1996), 76.

1 Groundbreaking work on the stylistic influence of Japanese art in the West during the nineteenth century was done by Gabriel Weisberg and Philip Dennis Cate (Gabriel P. Weisberg et al., *Japonisme: Japanese Influence on French Art, 1854-1910,* exh. cat. [Cleveland: Cleveland Museum of Art, 1974]), Colta Feller Ives (*The Great Wave: The Influence of Japanese Woodcuts on French Prints,* exh. cat. [New York: Metropolitan Museum of Art, 1973]), and Phylis Anne Floyd ("Japonisme in Context: Documentation, Criticism, Aesthetic Reactions" [Ph.D. thesis, University of Michigan, 1983]). For more recent research, see Virginia Spate et al., *Monet and Japan* (Canberra: National Gallery of Australia, 2001).

2 For a personal account of Suzuki and his teaching, see Arthur C. Danto, "Upper West Side Buddhismn," in *Buddha Mind in Contemporary Art,* ed. Jacquelynn Baas and Mary Jane Jacob (Berkeley: University of California Press, 2004), 49–59.

3 Eugen Herrigel, *Zen in the Art of Archery,* trans. R. R. C. Hull, introduction by D. T. Suzuki (New York: Pantheon, 1953), 18.

4 Noguchi, "The Complete Artist," 48.

5 Katharine Kuh, *The Artist's Voice: Talks with Seventeen Artists* (New York: Harper and Row, 1962), 144.

6 Herrigel, *Zen in the Art of Archery,* 51.

7 In Alan R. Solomon and John Cage, *Jasper Johns,* exh. cat. (New York: Jewish Museum, 1964), 5.

8 Ibid.

9 Duchamp talked about the fourth dimension in a 1959 interview with Richard Hamilton: "Anything that has a three-dimensional form is the projection in our world from a fourth-dimensional world" (on CD *Marcel Duchamp: The Creative Act*). He described the role of the artist as a "mediumistic being" in a paper delivered at a 1957 meeting of the American Federation of Arts in Houston; see Duchamp, "The Creative Act," reprinted in *The Writings of Marcel Duchamp,* ed. Michel Sanouillet and Elmer Peterson (New York: Da Capo Press, 1989), 138.

10 Thomas McEvilley, "Yves Klein, Messenger of the Age of Space," *Artforum* 20, no. 5 (January 1982): 38.

ISAMU NOGUCHI

The epigraph is from Roger Lipsey's April 1987 interview with the artist, quoted in Lipsey's *An Art of Our Own: The Spiritual in Twentieth-Century Art* (Boston: Shambhala, 1988), 355.

1 Isamu Noguchi, *Isamu Noguchi: A Sculptor's World* (New York: Harper and Row, 1968), 40.

2 Ibid., 38.

3 Constantin Brancusci, in *This Quarter* 1, suppl. (1925): 236; Isamu Noguchi, *Isamu Noguchi: Essays and Conversations,* ed. Diane Apostolos-Cappadona and Bruce Altshuler (New York: Abrams, 1994), 115.

4 Yone Noguchi, *The Story of Yone Noguchi, Told by Himself* (Philadephia: Jacobs, 1915), 192–93.

5 Noguchi, *Noguchi: A Sculptor's World,* 11.

6 Ibid., 13.

7 Ibid., 14.

8 Ibid.

9 Ibid.

10 Ibid., 15.

11 Ibid. Bonnie Rychlak attributes the change to Isamu's wish to capitalize on his father's fame in Europe, to which he traveled on a Guggenheim fellowship in 1927. But the change of name occurred in 1923—hardly "shortly before leaving for Paris," as Rychlak characterizes it (*Zen No Zen: Aspects of Noguchi's Sculptural Vision* [New York: Isamu Noguchi Foundation, 2002], 11).

12 Noguchi, *Noguchi: A Sculptor's World,* 17.

13 Ibid., 16.

14 Ibid., 17.

15 Ibid., 18. ("I read everything pertaining to sculpture and the Orient, from Coomaraswami to Max Müller.")

16 Ibid., 19.

17 Ibid., 20.

18 Interview with Dore Ashton around 1984, in Ashton, *Noguchi East and West* (Berkeley: University of California Press, 1992), 42.

19 Noguchi, *Noguchi: Essays and Conversations,* 20.

20 Isamu Noguchi, "Towards a Reintegration of the Arts," *College Art Journal* 9, no. 1 (Autumn 1949): 59.

21 Noguchi, *Noguchi: A Sculptor's World,* 33.

22 Ibid., 13 (Yone Noguchi, *Seen and Unseen or, Monologues of a Homeless Snail* [San Francisco: Burgess and Garnett, 1897]).

23 Noguchi, *Noguchi: A Sculptor's World,* 25.

24 Ibid., 28.

25 Ibid., 31.

26 Ibid., 29.

27 Ibid., 30.

28 Ibid.

29 Ibid., 19.

30 Yoshida Kenko, *The Harvest of Leisure,* trans. Ryukichi Kurata, introduction by L. Adams Beck (London: Murray, 1948 [1931]), 17.

31 "Noguchi: The Bollingen Journey," an exhibition brochure for the Noguchi Museum, Queens, New York, 2003.

32 In Kenko, *The Harvest of Leisure,* 7, 9–10.

33 From a 1953 essay for the Museum of Modern Art in Kamakura, reprinted in Noguchi, *Noguchi: Essays and Conversations,* 101.

34 Noguchi, *Noguchi: A Sculptor's World,* 31.

35 Ibid., 40.

36 Ibid., 31–32.

37 Daisetz Teitaro Suzuki, *An Introduction to Zen Buddhism* (New York: Philosophical Library, 1949), 54–55.

38 Noguchi, *Noguchi: A Sculptor's World*, 168.

39 Ibid.

40 Ibid.

41 Ibid., 14.

42 Ibid., 35.

AD REINHARDT

The epigraph is from Ad Reinhardt, "Art-as-Art," in *Art-as-Art: The Selected Writings of Ad Reinhardt*, ed. Barbara Rose (New York: Viking, 1975), 56; it was originally published in *Art International* in December 1962.

1 Lawrence Alloway, "Artists as Writers, Part Two: The Realm of Language," *Artforum* 12 (April 1974): 30.

2 Quoted in David J. Clarke, *The Influence of Oriental Thought on Postwar American Painting and Sculpture* (New York: Garland, 1988), 147.

3 Quoted in Thomas B. Hess, "Editorial: Ad (Adolph Dietrich Friedrich) Reinhardt," *Art News* 66, no. 6 (October 1967): 23.

4 It was reprinted verbatim in the 1991 catalog to the retrospective at the Museum of Modern Art, which doesn't even give the cause of his death at age fifty-three. (He died of a heart attack.) See Ad Reinhardt, "Chronology," in Lucy Lippard, *Ad Reinhardt Paintings*, exh. cat. (New York: Jewish Museum, 1966), 30–34.

5 Ibid., 34.

6 Ibid., 36.

7 Ad Reinhardt, "Timeless in Asia," *Art News* 58, no. 9 (January 1960): 34.

8 Ibid., 34.

9 Ibid.

10 Hess, "Editorial," 23.

11 In *Ad Reinhardt*, exh. cat. (New York: Rizzoli with Museum of Modern Art, 1991), 28.

12 Quoted in Clarke, *Influence of Oriental Thought*, 69.

13 Ad Reinhardt, "Autointerview," *Art News*, March 1965; reprinted in Reinhardt, *Art-as-Art*, 11–12.

14 Lin-chi, quoted in Alan W. Watts, *The Spirit of Zen: A Way of Life, Work and Art in the Far East* (London: John Murray, 1948 [1936]), 49.

15 Ad Reinhardt, "Seven Quotes by Ad Reinhardt," *It Is*, no. 4 (Fall 1959): 25.

16 Watts, *The Spirit of Zen*, 49–50.

17 From Ad Reinhardt, "The Artist in Search of a Code of Ethics," 1960; reprinted in Reinhardt, *Art-as-Art*, 162.

18 Hess, "Editorial," 23.

19 Yve-Alain Bois, "The Limit of Almost," in *Ad Reinhardt* (1991), 28.

20 Lippard, *Reinhardt Paintings*, 9.

21 Reinhardt, *Art-as-Art*, 203–7.

YVES KLEIN

The epigraph is from Yves Klein Archives, T16.6; quoted in Nicholas Charlet, *Yves Klein* (Paris: Adam Biro, 2000), 9.

1 Thomas McEvilley, Nan Rosenthal, et al., *Yves Klein 1928–1962: A Retrospective*, exh. cat. (Houston: Rice University, 1982), 46.

2 Ibid., 218–19; translation Thomas McEvilley.

3 Ibid., 218.
4 Sidra Stich, *Yves Klein* (Stuttgart: Cantz, 1994), 15.
5 Jigoro Kano, *Judo (Jujutsu)* (Tokyo: Maruzen [Tourist Library 16], 1937), 11.
6 Stich, *Klein,* 17.
7 Ibid.
8 McEvilley, Rosenthal, et al., *Klein,* 243.
9 Photo of Klein: Gilbert Perlein, Bruno Corà, et al., *Yves Klein: Long Live the Immaterial!* (New York: Delano Greenidge Editions, 2000), 212; for Musée Guimet paintings, see *Rituels tibétains: Visions secrètes du Ve Dalaï Lama,* exh. cat. (Paris: Musée National des Arts Asiatiques-Guimet, Réunion des Musées Nationaux, 2002), 32.
10 Max Heindel, *Rosicrucian Cosmo-Conception, or Mystic Christianity an Elementary Treatise upon Man's Past Evolution, Present Constitution and Future Development* (Oceanside, Calif.: Rosicrucian Fellowship, 1920 [1911]), 515. (Heindel's "elementary treatise" runs to almost 600 pages.)
11 From "The Monochrome Adventure," Perlein, Corà, et al., *Klein,* 80; I have modified the translation very slightly based on the French text given in McEvilley, Rosenthal, et al., *Klein,* 254 n. 102.
12 Perlein, Corà, et al., *Klein,* 214.
13 Stich, *Klein,* 35.
14 Kano, *Judo,* 19.
15 Stich, *Klein,* 67.
16 McEvilley, Rosenthal, et al., *Klein,* 105.
17 From Jasper Johns's artist's statement in Dorothy C. Miller, *Sixteen Americans,* exh. cat. (New York: Museum of Modern Art, 1959), 22; reprinted in Johns, *Jasper Johns: Writings, Sketchbook Notes, Interviews,* ed. Kirk Varnedoe, comp. Christel Hollevoet (New York: Museum of Modern Art, 1996), 20.
18 Perlein, Corà, et al., *Klein,* 221.
19 Alan W. Watts, *The Spirit of Zen: A Way of Life, Work and Art in the Far East* (London: John Murray, 1948 [1936]), 39–40.
20 Quoted in Stich, *Klein,* 29.
21 From *Dépassement de la problématique de l'art,* regarding his two Paris exhibitions of 1957; in Perlein, Corà, et al., *Klein,* 218.
22 From Klein's lecture at the Sorbonne, June 3, 1959; in ibid., 220.
23 Quoted by Thomas McEvilley, "Yves Klein: Conquistador of the Void," in McEvilley, Rosenthal, et al., *Klein,* 51.

JASPER JOHNS

The epigraph is from an interview by Gunnar Jespersen, February 1969; reprinted in Jasper Johns, *Jasper Johns: Writings, Sketchbook Notes, Interviews,* ed. Kirk Varnedoe, comp. Christel Hollevoet (New York: Museum of Modern Art, 1996), 134–36.

1 From an interview by Yoshiaki Tono, 1975; reprinted in ibid., 147–48.
2 Eugen Herrigel, *Zen in the Art of Archery,* trans. R. R. C. Hull, introduction by D. T. Suzuki (New York: Pantheon, 1953), 20.
3 Ibid., 56.
4 Daisetz T. Suzuki, *The Essentials of Zen Buddhism* (London: Luzac, 1933), 293.
5 From an interview by Annelie Pohlen, 1978; reprinted in Johns, *Johns: Writings,* 170–71.
6 Herrigel, *Zen in the Art of Archery,* 49.
7 Interview by Pohlen, 171.
8 Daisetz Teitaro Suzuki, *The Zen Doctrine of No-Mind: The Significance of the Sutra of Hui-neng (Wei-lang),* ed. Christmas Humphreys (London: Century Hutchinson, [1949] 1986), 25–26.

9 From a notebook page reproduced in Johns, *Johns: Writings*, 37.

10 Jonathan D. Katz, "John Cage's Queer Silence; or, How to Avoid Making Matters Worse," in *Writings through John Cage's Music, Poetry, and Art*, ed. David W. Bernstein and Christopher Hatch (Chicago: University of Chicago Press, 2001), 45.

11 From an interview by Yoshiaki Tono, spring 1964; reprinted in Johns, *Johns: Writings*, 98.

12 Arturo Schwarz, *The Complete Works of Marcel Duchamp* (New York: Abrams, 1970), 442.

13 Kirk Varnedoe, *Jasper Johns: A Retrospective*, exh. cat. (New York: Museum of Modern Art, 1996), 166.

14 Ibid., 387 n23.

15 Alan W. Watts, *The Way of Zen* (New York: Vintage Books, 1989 [1957]), 66.

16 I am indebted to Tosi Lee for this perspective on Duchamp's *Trap;* see Lee, "Watering, That's My Life: The Symbolism and Self-Imaging of Marcel Duchamp" (Ph.D. thesis, University of Illinois at Urbana-Champaign, 1993), 98.

17 Michael Crichton, *Jasper Johns* (New York: Abrams, 1994), 49.

18 Richard S. Field, *Jasper Johns: Prints 1970–1977* (Middletown, Conn.: Wesleyan University, 1978), 72.

19 From *Artforum* 7, no. 3 (November 1968): 6; reprinted in Johns, *Johns: Writings*, 22.

20 Field, *Johns*, 16.

21 From a 1960 review of Richard Hamilton's typographic version of the contents of Marcel Duchamp's *Green Box;* reprinted in Johns, *Johns: Writings*, 20.

22 From an interview by John Coplans in *The Print Collector's Newsletter* 3, no. 2 (May–June 1972); reprinted in Johns, *Johns: Writings*, 138.

23 Note by Jasper Johns regarding *White Flag* ("This Week's Cover") in *Asahi Magazine* (Tokyo) 8, no. 46 (November 6, 1966); reprinted in Johns, *Johns: Writings*, 21–22.

24 Bryan Robertson and Tim Marlow, "The Private World of Jasper Johns," *Tate: The Art Magazine*, no. 1 (Winter 1993): 42; quoted by Bernstein in Varnedoe, *Johns*, 46.

25 Duchamp's words are in Calvin Tomkins, *Duchamp: A Biography* (New York: Henry Holt, 1996), 408; Johns's come from a notebook page a year or so after Johns met Duchamp (1961), reproduced in Johns, *Johns: Writings*, 27.

26 See Schwarz, *Complete Works of Duchamp*, 585, no. 301.

27 From interview by Pohlen; reprinted in Johns, *Johns: Writings*, 173.

28 From a conversation with David Vaughn in Susan Sontag, Richard Francis, et al., *Cage-Cunningham-Johns: Dancers on a Plane: In Memory of Their Feelings* (New York: Knopf in association with Antony d'Offay Gallery, 1989), 141.

IV. THE SOUND OF THE MIND

The epigraphs are from John Cage, *Silence* (Hanover, N.H.: Wesleyan University Press, 1973 [1961]), 143; Nam June Paik in a 1991 "conversation" with David Ross, in *Nam June Paik: Video Time—Video Space*, ed. Toni Stooss and Thomas Kellien (New York: Abrams, 1993), 62; Yoko Ono, "To the Wesleyan People" (1966), in Alexandra Munroe with Jon Hendricks et al., *Yes: Yoko Ono*, exh. cat. (New York: Japan Society and Abrams, 2001), 288.

1 Cage was fond of repeating this phrase, and it appears often in the many published interviews with him. This particular version is from Kathan Brown, *John Cage Visual Art: To Sober and Quiet the Mind* (San Francisco: Crown Point Press, 2000), 45.

2 From a 1982 interview with Stephen Montague excerpted in Richard Kostelanetz, ed., *Conversing with Cage* (New York: Routledge, 2003 [1987]), 33.

3 From the 1963 "Fluxus Manifesto" by George Maciunas, reproduced in Jon Hendricks, *Fluxus Codex* (New York: Abrams, 1988), 24.

4 From a 1963 letter to Tomas Schmit, excerpted in Clive Phillpot and Jon Hendricks, *Fluxus: Selections from the Gilbert and Lila Silverman Collection* (New York: Museum of Modern Art, 1988), 24.

5 Ken Friedman, "Fluxus Performance," in *The Art of Performance: A Critical Anthology,* ed.Gregory Battcock and Robert Nickas (New York: Dutton, 1984), 59; Maciunas's remark is from a 1973 foldout diagram, a reproduction of which is inserted inside the front cover of Charles Dreyfus, *Happenings and Fluxus,* exh. cat. (Paris: Galerie 1900–2000, 1989).

6 Hendricks, *Fluxus Codex,* 24.

7 From a 1992 interview with David T. Doris, in Doris, "Zen Vaudeville: A Medi(t)ation in the Margins of Fluxus," in *The Fluxus Reader,* ed. Ken Friedman (West Sussex: Academy Editions, 1998), 114.

8 From the article "Afterlude to the Exposition of Experimental Television," excerpted in Doris, "Zen Vaudeville," 127.

9 Ibid., 126–27.

10 Ibid., 127.

11 *For the Birds: John Cage, in Conversation with Daniel Charles* (Boston: Marion Boyars, 1981), 56.

12 From Ono,"To the Wesleyan People," 291.

13 Ibid.

14 For Maciunas's claim, see Hendricks, *Fluxus Codex,* 21; for Paik's self-description, see a 1991 letter to Kate Millett, quoted in Kate Millett, "Bonyari," in *Nam June Paik,* ed. Stooss and Kellein, 112.

15 From a 1978 interview with Robin White, quoted in Constance Lewallen, "Cage and the Structure of Chance," in *Writings through John Cage's Music, Poetry, and Art,* ed. David W. Bernstein and Christopher Hatch (Chicago: University of Chicago Press, 2001), 234.

JOHN CAGE

The epigraph is from Thomas McEvilley, "In the Form of a Thistle: A Conversation with John Cage," *Artforum* 31, no. 4 (October 1992): 97.

1 John Cage, *Silence* (Hanover, N.H.: Wesleyan University Press, 1973 [1961]), 109.

2 Ibid., ix.

3 Ibid., x.

4 Kathan Brown, *John Cage Visual Art: To Sober and Quiet the Mind* (San Francisco: Crown Point Press, 2000), 45.

5 Calvin Tomkins, *The Bride and the Bachelors: Five Masters of the Avant-Garde* (New York: Viking, 1968 [1965]), 99.

6 "Taking Chances: Laurie Anderson and John Cage," *Tricycle: The Buddhist Review* 4, no. 4 (Summer 1992): 54.

7 Cage remembered attending Suzuki's lectures "for three years, up until 1951" (from a 1974 interview by Paul Cummings, in Jonathan D. Katz, "John Cage's Queer Silence; or, How to Avoid Making Matters Worse," in *Writings through John Cage's Music, Poetry, and Art,* ed. David W. Bernstein and Christopher Hatch [Chicago: University of Chicago Press, 2001], 45). But Suzuki only returned to the United States in 1949, and he didn't begin teaching at Columbia until 1951, although he may have given a lecture or two in New York before then. Cage may have intended to say "*after* 1951," or he may have confused his study with Suzuki the person with his study of Suzuki's books.

8 From a 1966 interview with Irving Sandler, excerpted in Richard Kostelanetz, ed., *Conversing with Cage* (New York: Routledge, 2003 [1987]), 13. Nancy Wilson Ross was a significant agent in the spread of information about Buddhism through her friendships and her writings. This lecture, entitled "The Symbols of Modern Art," took place in 1938. In her lecture notes, Ross simply mentions the similarity between Dada and Zen. (Thanks to Hilary Rand for obtaining a photocopy of this lecture from the Ranson Humanities Center at the University of Texas.)

9 Tomkins, *The Bride and the Bachelors,* 97.

9 From a 1992 quote in Munroe et al., *Yes: Yoko Ono,* 132.

10 Munroe et al., *Yes: Yoko Ono,* 18.

11 Ono, *Grapefruit,* n.p. (section 1, piece 2).

12 Ibid. (section 1, piece 13).

13 Ibid. (section 3, piece 17).

14 Ibid. (piece 15).

15 Ibid. (piece 30).

16 Ibid. (piece 5).

17 Ibid. ("Record of 13 Concert Piece Performances," piece 3).

18 Ono, *Instruction Paintings,* 5.

19 Ibid., 10.

20 Ibid., 25.

21 Ono, *Grapefruit,* n.p. (first item in the last section). Also Munroe et al., *Yes: Yoko Ono,* 286.

22 Munroe et al., *Yes: Yoko Ono,* 287.

23 From Yoko Ono, "To the Wesleyan People" (1966), in ibid., 288.

24 Joan Retallack, ed., *Musicage: Cage Muses on Words, Art, Music* (Hanover, N.H.: Wesleyan University Press, 1996), 75.

LAURIE ANDERSON

The epigraphs are from Laurie Anderson, "Time and Beauty," in *Buddha Mind in Contemporary Art,* ed. Jacquelynn Baas and Mary Jane Jacob (Berkeley: University of California Press, 2004), 115–16, and her remarks at the eighth meeting of the consortium "Awake: Art, Buddhism, and the Dimension of Consciousness," February 7, 2003, Green Gulch Farm Zen Center, Sausalito (author's transcription).

1 RoseLee Goldberg, *Laurie Anderson* (New York: Abrams, 2000), 125.

2 Anderson, "Time and Beauty," 121.

3 Laurie Anderson, *Stories from the Nerve Bible: A Retrospective 1972–1992* (New York: HarperCollins, 1994), 13.

4 In Thierry Raspail and Laurie Anderson. *Laurie Anderson: The Record of the Time,* exh. cat. (Lyon: Musée d'Art Contemporain, 2002), 24–25.

5 Goldberg, *Anderson,* 74.

6 Anderson, "Time and Beauty," 121.

7 Ibid.

8 In Thomas Merton, *Mystics and Zen Masters* (New York: Farrar, Straus and Giroux, 1967), 236.

9 Laurie Anderson, "A Short Biography," in Raspail and Anderson, *Anderson,* 16.

10 Ibid., 16–17.

11 Goldberg, *Anderson,* 58.

12 Anderson, *Stories from the Nerve Bible,* 14.

13 Goldberg, *Anderson,* 48.

14 Ibid.

15 Ibid.

16 From a discussion with the author, February 8, 2003.

17 Anderson, *Stories from the Nerve Bible,* 40.

18 "Walking & Falling" from *United States,* 1983; Goldberg, *Anderson,* 96.

19 Ibid.

20 Shunryu Suzuki, *Zen Mind, Beginner's Mind: Informal Talks on Zen Meditation and Practice,* ed. Trudy Dixon (New York: Weatherhill, 1999 [1970]), 31–32.

21 Anderson, "Time and Beauty," 121.

V. LIGHT AND INSIGHT

The epigraph is from Daisetz Teitaro Suzuki, *Manual of Zen Buddhism* (New York: Grove Press, 1960), 132. Kakuan Shien (Kuo-an Shih-yuan) was a twelfth-century Ch'an master.

1 Ibid., 11.

2 Ibid., 128.

3 Translated in ibid., 144.

4 From an interview with Joan Simon in *Landmarks: Sculpture Commissions for the Stuart Collection at the University of California, San Diego* (New York: Rizzoli, 2001), 71.

5 Quoted in Lawrence Weschler, *Seeing Is Forgetting the Name of the Thing One Sees: A Life of Contemporary Artist Robert Irwin* (Berkeley: University of California Press, 1982), 148.

6 Shunryu Suzuki, *Zen Mind, Beginner's Mind: Informal Talks on Zen Meditation and Practice,* ed. Trudy Dixon (New York: Weatherhill, 1999 [1970]), 32.

7 From an interview with Paul Nesbitt, in *Richard Tuttle: Grey Walls Work,* exh. cat. (London: Camden Arts Centre, 1997), 50, 47.

8 From the cover of the brochure for the exhibitions *North-South Axis* and *The Poetry of Form,* Museum of Fine Arts, Santa Fe, 1995.

9 Robert A. F. Thurman, "The Buddha's Smile: Enlightenment and the Pursuit of Happiness," in *In Pursuit of Happiness,* ed. Leroy S. Rouner (Notre Dame, Ind.: University of Notre Dame Press, 1995), 89–90.

AGNES MARTIN

The epigraph is from Agnes Martin, *Writings* (Ostfildern, Germany: Cantz, 1991), 15.

1 Shunryu Suzuki, *Zen Mind, Beginner's Mind: Informal Talks on Zen Meditation and Practice,* ed. Trudy Dixon (New York: Weatherhill, 1999 [1970]), 32 (see also the section on Laurie Anderson, p. 205).

2 Martin, "The Untroubled Mind," *Writings,* 40.

3 Shunryu Suzuki, *Zen Mind, Beginner's Mind,* 32.

4 Martin, "The Still and the Silent in Art," *Writings,* 89.

5 Martin, "The Untroubled Mind," 41.

6 Barbara Haskell, *Agnes Martin,* exh. cat. (New York: Whitney Museum of American Art with Abrams, 1992), 96.

7 From a letter to David J. Clarke, published in Clarke's *The Influence of Oriental Thought on Postwar American Painting and Sculpture* (New York: Garland, 1988), 231.

8 Martin, "What We Do Not See If We Do Not See," *Writings,* 117.

9 Daisetz Teitaro Suzuki, *Manual of Zen Buddhism* (New York: Grove Press, 1960), 144.

10 Martin, "The Untroubled Mind," 36, 42, 44. Wilson recorded these statements in 1972.

11 Ibid., 37.

12 Ad Reinhardt, quoted in Thomas B. Hess, "Editorial," *Art News* 66, no. 6 (October 1967): 23.

13 From the transcript of a 1989 interview with Suzan Campbell in the Archives of American Art; quoted in Anna C. Chave, "Agnes Martin: 'Humility, the Beautiful Daughter . . . ,'" in Haskell, *Agnes Martin,* 131.

14 *Agnes Martin, Richard Tuttle,* exh. cat. (Fort Worth: Modern Art Museum, 1998), 10.

15 Ibid., 82.

16 Martin, "What Is Real?" *Writings,* 95.

ROBERT IRWIN

The epigraph is quoted in Lawrence Weschler, "Playing It As It Lays and Keeping It in Play," in *Robert Irwin,* exh. cat. (Los Angeles: Museum of Contemporary Art, 1993), 173.

1 Robert Irwin, *Being and Circumstance: Notes toward a Conditional Art* (Larkspur Landing, Calif.: Lapis Press with Pace Gallery and San Francisco Museum of Modern Art, 1985), 145.

2 From Robert Irwin, "The Hidden Structures of Art," in *Robert Irwin* (Museum of Contemporary Art), 35.

3 Weschler, "Playing It As It Lays," 174.

4 Quoted in Lawrence Weschler, *Seeing Is Forgetting the Name of the Thing One Sees: A Life of Contemporary Artist Robert Irwin* (Berkeley: University of California Press, 1982), 36–37.

5 Quoted in ibid., 37.

6 From John Hallmark Neff, "Hands-on: Irwin and Abstract Expressionism," in *Robert Irwin* (Museum of Contemporary Art), 80.

7 Quoted in Weschler, *Seeing Is Forgetting,* 58.

8 Quoted in ibid.

9 Quoted in ibid., 59.

10 Quoted in ibid., 61.

11 Quoted in ibid., 67.

12 Quoted in ibid., 68.

13 Quoted in ibid.

14 Quoted in ibid., 76.

15 Philip Leider, "Robert Irwin," in *Robert Irwin, Kenneth Price,* exh. cat. (Los Angeles: Los Angeles County Museum of Art, 1966), n.p.

16 Ibid.

17 Ibid.

18 Quoted in Weschler, *Seeing Is Forgetting,* 104.

19 Quoted in ibid., 151.

20 Quoted in ibid.

21 Quoted in ibid., 152.

22 Quoted in ibid.

23 Quoted in ibid., 183.

24 Quoted in ibid.

25 Quoted in ibid., 160.

26 Ibid, 162.

27 Quoted in ibid., 163.

28 Quoted in ibid., 164.

29 Daisetz Teitaro Suzuki, *Manual of Zen Buddhism* (New York: Grove Press, 1960), plates 9–11.

30 From an interview with Frederick S. Wight in *Transparency, Reflection, Light, Space: Four Artists,* exh. cat. (Los Angeles: UCLA Art Galleries, 1971), 98.

31 From Robert Irwin, "The Hidden Structures of Art," in *Robert Irwin* (Museum of Contemporary Art), 28.

VIJA CELMINS

The epigraph is from an interview with Jeanne Silverthorne in *Parkett,* no. 44 (July 1995): 42.

1 Ibid., 41.

2 From an interview with Chuck Close in *Vija Celmins,* ed. William S. Bartman (New York: A.R.T. Press, 1992), 20.

3 From "chronology" by Vija Celmins, in *Vija Celmins,* 61.

4 Ibid.
5 Ibid.
6 Ibid.
7 Chuck Close, quoting from Celmins's notebook, in *Vija Celmins,* 46.
8 From interview with Silverthorne, 41.
9 Ibid.
10 Vija Celmins in *Vija Celmins* 61.
11 Ibid.
12 From interview with Close, 12.
13 Celmins in *Vija Celmins,* 61.
14 From interview with Close, 16.
15 From an interview with Jeff Rian in *Flash Art,* no. 189 (Summer 1996): 108.
16 From interview with Close, 26.
17 *Vija Celmins,* 61.
18 Ibid., 62.
19 *The Shambhala Dictionary of Buddhism and Zen* (Boston: Shambhala, 1991), 54.
20 From interview with Close, 23.
21 Chogyam Trungpa, *Dharma Art,* ed. Judith L. Lief (Boston: Shambhala, 1996), viii.
22 Ibid., 37.
23 Ibid., illustration 16. *Beam* is illustration 6.
24 Ibid., 84.
25 Fom interview with Close, 53–54.
26 From interview with Rian, 110.
27 Ibid., 42.
28 Trungpa, *Dharma Art,* 15.
29 From interview with Close, 23.
30 From interview with Silverthorne, 42.
31 Ibid.
32 From interview with Close, 17.
33 Ibid.
34 Ibid., 14.
35 Ibid., 49.
36 Shunryu Suzuki, *Zen Mind, Beginner's Mind: Informal Talks on Zen Meditation and Practice,* ed. Trudy Dixon (New York: Weatherhill, 1999 [1970]), 34–35.
37 From Celmins's unpublished notes, quoted in James Lingwood, "Pictures of Facts: Vija Celmins's Work from the 60s," in Lingwood, ed., *Vija Celmins, Works 1964–96,* exh. cat. (London: Institute of Contemporary Art, 1996), 22.

RICHARD TUTTLE

The epigraph is from an interview with Jürgen Glaesemer, in *Richard Tuttle: Wire Pieces,* exh. cat. (Bordeaux: Musée d'Art Contemporain, 1986), 33.

1 Tuttle quoted in Marcia Tucker, *Richard Tuttle,* exh. cat. (New York: Whitney Museum of American Art, 1975), 5.
2 Ibid., 9.

3 Ibid., 6.

4 Margrit Franziska Brehm in Jochen Poetter, *Richard Tuttle: Chaos, die/the Form,* exh. cat. (Stuttgart: Staatliche Kunsthalle Baden-Baden, 1993), 18.

5 Ellen Lubell, in *Arts Magazine* (November 1972); reprinted in *Richard Tuttle: Wire Pieces,* 27.

6 From interview with Glaesemer, 33.

7 From a discussion with the author, March 1, 2003.

8 From a discussion with the author, April 8, 1999.

9 Quoted in Toni Stooss and Thomas Kellein, eds., *Nam June Paik: Video Time, Video Space* (New York: Abrams, 1993), 22.

10 From a discussion with the author, March 1, 2003.

11 From an interview with Michael Auping, excerpted in *Agnes Martin, Richard Tuttle,* exh. cat. (Fort Worth: Modern Art Museum, 1998), 10.

12 Quoted by Michael Auping, "On Relationships," in ibid., 82.

13 From a discussion with the author, March 1, 2003.

14 Ibid.

15 Ibid.

16 Leonard Koren, *Wabi-Sabi for Artists, Designers, Poets and Philosophers* (Berkeley, Calif.: Stone Bridge Press, 1994), 7.

17 From a discussion with the author, March 1, 2003.

18 From Kathan Brown, *Richard Tuttle: Any Two Points* (San Francisco: Crown Point Press, 1999), n.p.

19 From an interview with Frederick S. Wight, in *Transparency, Reflection, Light, Space: Four Artists,* exh. cat. (Los Angeles: UCLA Art Galleries, 1971), 96.

20 *Richard Tuttle: Community* (Chicago: Arts Club, 1999), 26.

21 From Richard Tuttle, *Richard Tuttle Portland Works 1976,* exh. cat. (Cologne: Galerie Karsten Greve, and Boston: Tomas Segal Gallery, 1988), quoted in ibid.

SELECTED BIBLIOGRAPHY

INTRODUCTION

A good general survey of Buddhism is Peter Harvey's *An Introduction to Buddhism: Teachings, History and Practices* (Cambridge: Cambridge University Press, 1990). An impressive and revealing chronological bibliography of European and American books and essays on Buddhism published between 1800 and 1890 is provided by Roger-Pol Droit in his *Le culte du néant: Les philosophes et le Bouddha* (Paris: Editions du Seuil, 1997), 243–345.

Almond, Philip C. *The British Discovery of Buddhism*. Cambridge: Cambridge University Press, 1988.

Batchelor, Stephen. *The Awakening of the West: The Encounter of Buddhism and Western Culture*. Berkeley, Calif.: Parallax Press, 1994.

Bowie, Theodore. *East-West in Art: Patterns of Cultural and Aesthetic Relationships*. Bloomington: Indiana University Press, 1966.

Clarke, J. J. *Oriental Enlightenment: The Encounter between Asian and Western Thought*. New York: Routledge, 1997.

de Jong, J. W. *A Brief History of Buddhist Studies in Europe and America*. Tokyo: Kosei, 1997.

Hamilton, Sue. *Indian Philosophy: A Very Short Introduction*. Oxford: Oxford University Press, 2001.

Lopez, Donald S., Jr., ed. *Curators of the Buddha: The Study of Buddhism under Colonialism*. Chicago: University of Chicago Press, 1995.

Magee, Bryan. *The Philosophy of Schopenhauer*, rev. ed. Oxford: Oxford University Press, 1997.

Prebish, Charles S. *Luminous Passage: The Practice and Study of Buddhism in America*. Berkeley: University of California Press, 1999.

Prebish, Charles S., and Martin Baumann, eds. *Westward Dharma: Buddhism Beyond Asia*. Berkeley: University of California Press, 2002.

Prebish, Charles S., and Kenneth K. Tanaka, eds. *The Faces of Buddhism in America*. Berkeley: University of California Press, 1998.

Seager, Richard Hughes. *Buddhism in America*. New York: Columbia University Press, 1999.

Sedgwick, Eve Kosofsky. "Pedagogy of Buddhism." In *Touching Feeling: Affect, Pedagogy, Performativity*, 153–81. Durham, N.C.: Duke University Press, 2003.

Sullivan, Michael. *The Meeting of Eastern and Western Art*. Berkeley: University of California Press, 1989.

Trainor, Kevin, ed. *Buddhism: The Illustrated Guide*. Oxford: Oxford University Press, 2001.

Tweed, Thomas A. *The American Encounter with Buddhism, 1844–1912: Victorian Culture and the Limits of Dissent*. Chapel Hill: University of North Carolina Press, 2000 [1992].

Tweed, Thomas A., and Stephen R. Prothero, eds. *Asian Religions in America: A Documentary History*. Oxford: Oxford University Press, 1999.

Welbon, Guy Richard. *The Buddhist Nirvana and Its Western Interpreters*. Chicago: University of Chicago Press, 1968.

I. THE INFINITE MOMENT

Burnouf, Emile-Louis. "Le Bouddhism en Occident." *Revue des deux mondes*, 15 July 1888, 340–72.

Carus, Paul. *The Gospel of Buddha Compiled from Ancient Records*. Chicago: Open Court Publishing Company, 1894 [French ed. 1895].

Lovejoy, Arthur O. "The Chinese Origin of a Romanticism." In *Essays in the History of Ideas*, 99–135. Baltimore: John Hopkins University Press, 1948.

Renan, Ernest. "Premiers travaux sur le Bouddhism." *Nouvelles études d'histoire religieuse* [1884]. In *Oeuvres complètes de Ernest Renan*, ed. Henriette Psichari, 746–820. Paris: Calmann-Lévy, 1947.

Sirén, Osvald. *China and the Gardens of Europe in the Eighteenth Century*, with introduction by Hugh Honor. Washington, D.C.: Dumbarton Oaks, 1990.

Taine, Hippolyte Adolphe. "Le Bouddhisme: *Die Religion des Buddha und ihre Enstehung*, par M. Koeppen." *Nouveaus essais de critique et d'histoire*, 4th ed., 263–316. Paris: Hachette, 1886 [1st ed. 1865].

Thacker, Christopher. *The History of Gardens*. Berkeley: University of California Press, 1979.

CLAUDE MONET

Aitken, Geneviève, and Marianne Delafond. *La collection d'estampes japonaises de Claude Monet à Giverny*. Giverny: Maison de Monet, 1983.

Alexandre, Arsène. *Claude Monet*. Paris: Bernheim Jeune, 1921.

Clemenceau, Georges. *Claude Monet: Les Nymphéas*. Paris: Plon, 1928.

Geffroy, Gustave. *Claude Monet: Sa vie, son temps, son oeuvre*. Paris: G. Crès, 1922.

Levine, Steven Z. *Monet, Narcissus, and Self-Reflection: The Modernist Myth of the Self*. Chicago: University of Chicago Press, 1994.

Russell, Vivian. *Monet's Water Lilies*. London: Frances Lincoln, 1998.

Spate, Virginia, et al. *Monet and Japan*, exh. cat. Canberra: National Gallery of Australia, 2001.

Stuckey, Charles F., ed. *Monet: A Retrospective*. New York: Scribner, 1985.

VINCENT VAN GOGH

Druick, Douglas W., and Peter Kort Zegers. *Van Gogh and Gauguin: The Studio of the South*, exh. cat. Chicago: Art Institute of Chicago with Thames and Hudson, 2001.

Maurer, Naomi Margolis. *The Pursuit of Spiritual Wisdom: The Thought and Art of Vincent van Gogh and Paul Gauguin.* Madison, N.J.: Fairleigh Dickinson University Press; London: Associated University Presses, 1998.

Merlhès, Victor. *Paul Gauguin et Vincent van Gogh 1887–1888: Lettres retrouvées, sources ignorées.* Taravao, Tahiti: Avant et Après, 1989.

Silverman, Deborah. *Van Gogh and Gauguin: The Search for Sacred Art.* New York: Farrar, Straus and Giroux, 2000.

Van Gogh, Vincent. *The Complete Letters of Vincent van Gogh,* 3rd ed. Boston: Bulfinch Press/Little, Brown, 2000.

PAUL GAUGUIN

See also listings under Vincent van Gogh.

Amishai-Maisels, Ziva. *Gauguin's Religious Themes.* Ph.D. thesis, Hebrew University, 1969. In *Outstanding Dissertations in the Fine Arts.* New York, 1985.

Brettell, Richard, et al. *The Art of Paul Gauguin,* exh. cat. Washington, D.C.: National Gallery of Art, 1988.

Druick, Douglas W., and Peter Kort Zegers. "Le kampong et la pagode Gauguin à l'Exposition Universelle de 1889." In *Gauguin: Actes du colloque Gauguin,* 101–42. Paris: Musée d'Orsay, 1991.

Eisenman, Stephen F. *Gauguin's Skirt.* London: Thames and Hudson, 1997.

Gauguin, Paul. *The Writings of a Savage: Paul Gauguin,* ed. Daniel Guérin, intro. Wayne Anderson, trans. Eleanor Levieux. New York: Da Capo Press, 1996 [1978].

Jirat-Wasiutynski, Vojtech, and H. Travers Newton Jr. *Technique and Meaning in the Paintings of Paul Gauguin.* Cambridge: Cambridge University Press, 2000.

Merlhès, Victor, ed. *Correspondance de Paul Gauguin: Documents, témoinages.* Paris: Fondation Singer-Polignac, 1984.

Zafran, Eric M., et al. *Gauguin's Nirvana: Painters at Le Pouldu 1889–90,* exh. cat. Hartford and New Haven: Wadsworth Atheneum with Yale University Press, 2001.

ODILON REDON

Bacou, Roseline. "La bibliothèque d'Odilon Redon." In *Festschrift to Eric Fischer: European Drawings from Six Centuries,* 29–37. Copenhagen: Royal Museum of Fine Arts, 1990.

———. *Lettres de Gauguin, Gide, Huysmans, Jammes, Mallarmé, Verhaeren . . . à Odilon Redon.* Introduction by Arï Redon. Paris: Corti, 1960.

Druick, Douglas W., et al. *Odilon Redon, 1840–1916,* exh cat. Chicago and New York: Art Institute of Chicago with Abrams, 1994.

Eisenman, Stephen F. *The Temptation of Saint Redon: Biography, Ideology, and Style in the Noirs of Odilon Redon.* Chicago: University of Chicago Press, 1992.

Mellerio, André. *Odilon Redon: Peintre, Dessinateur et Graveur.* Paris: Floury, 1923.

Redon, Odilon. *A soi-même: Journal (1867–1915), notes sur la vie, l'art et les artistes.* Paris: Corti, 1979 [1961]. In English: *To Myself: Notes on Life, Art and Artists,* trans. Mira Jacob and Jeanne L. Wasserman. New York: Braziller, 1986.

Sandström, Sven. *Le monde imaginaire d'Odilon Redon: Etude iconologique.* Lund, Sweden: CWK Gleerup, 1955.

II. OTHER DIMENSIONS

Bacot, Jacques. "L'art tibétain." In *Annales du Musée Guimet, Bibliothèque de Vulgarisation,* vol. 36: *Conférences faites au Musée Guimet en 1911,* 191–220. Paris: Hachette, 1912.

———. "Pèlerinage du Dokerla (Tibet Sud-Oriental)." In *Annales du Musée Guimet, Bibliothèque de Vulgarisation,* vol. 32: *Conférences faites au Musée Guimet,* 195–218. Paris: Leroux, 1909.

Bharati, Agehandanda. *The Tantric Tradition.* London: Rider, 1965.

Cozort, Daniel. *Highest Yoga Tantra: An Introduction to the Esoteric Buddhism of Tibet.* Ithaca, N.Y.: Snow Lion, 1986.

Dewey, John. *Art as Experience.* New York: Perigee Books, 1980 [1934].

English, Elizabeth. *Vajrayogini: Her Visualizations, Rituals, and Forms.* Boston: Wisdom Publications, 2000.

Fenollosa, Ernest Francisco. *Epochs of Chinese and Japanese Art: An Outline History of East Asiatic Design,* 2 vols., ed. Mary McNeil Fenollosa. London: Heinemann, 1912.

Fields, Rick. *How the Swans Came to the Lake: A Narrative History of Buddhism in America,* 3rd ed. Boston: Shambhala, 1992.

Frank, Bernard. *Le panthéon bouddhique au Japon: Collections d'Emile Guimet.* Paris: Réunion des Musées Nationaux, 1991.

Grünwedel, Albert. *Mythologie du Buddhisme au Tibet et en Mongolie,* trans. from German by Ivan Goldschmidt. Leipzig: Brockhaus, 1900.

Gyatso, Geshe Kelsang. *Clear Light of Bliss: The Practice of Mahamudra in Vajrayana Buddhism.* (Ulverston, England: Tharpa Publications, 2002.

Hackin, J. *Guide-catalogue du Musée Guimet: Les collectionis bouddhiques.* Paris: G. Van Oest, 1923.

Huntington, John C., and Dina Bangdel. *The Circle of Bliss: Buddhist Meditational Art,* exh. cat. Columbus, Ohio: Columbus Museum of Art, 2003.

Kuh, Katharine. *The Artist's Voice: Talks with Seventeen Artists.* New York: Harper and Row, 1962.

Lancaster, Clay. *The Incredible World's Parliament of Religions at the Chicago Columbian Exposition of 1893.* Fontwell, Sussex: Centaur Press, 1987.

Lipsey, Roger. *An Art of Our Own: The Spiritual in Twentieth-Century Art.* Boston: Shambhala, 1988.

Lopez, Donald S., Jr. "The Heart Sutra as Tantra." In *Elaborations on Emptiness: Uses of the Heart Sutra,* 83–109. Princeton, N.J.: Princeton University Press, 1996.

Menand, Louis, ed. *Pragmatism: A Reader.* New York: Vintage Books, 1997.

Milloué, L. de. "Bouddhisme." In *Annales du Musée Guimet,* vol. 22. Paris: Leroux, 1907.

———. *Petit guide illustré au Musée Guimet,* 4th rev. ed. Paris: Leroux, 1900.

Mullin, Glenn H., with Jeff J. Watt. *Female Buddhas: Women of Enlightenment in Tibetan Mystical Art.* Santa Fe: Clear Light, 2003.

Okakura, Kakuzo. *The Book of Tea.* London: Putnam's; New York: Fox, Duffield, 1906.

Rawson, Philip. *Tantra: Indian Cult of Ecstasy.* London: Thames and Hudson, 1973.

Sharf, Robert H. "The Zen of Japanese Nationalism." In *Curators of the Buddha,* ed. Donald S. Lopez Jr., 107–60. Chicago: University of Chicago Press, 1995.

Snellgrove, David L. *Indian Buddhists and Their Tibetan Successors.* London: Serindia, 1987.

Tuchman, Maurice, ed. *The Spiritual in Art: Abstract Painting 1890–1985,* exh. cat. Los Angeles and New York: Los Angeles County Museum of Art with Abbeville Press, 1986.

White, David Gordon, ed. *Tantra in Practice.* Princeton, N.J.: Princeton University Press, 2000.

WASSILY KANDINSKY

Barnett, Vivian Endicott. *Vasily Kandinsky: A Colorful Life.* Munich: Lenbachhaus, 1995 (distrib., New York: Abrams, 1996).

Grohmann, Will. *Wassily Kandinsky: Life and Work.* New York: Abrams, 1958.

Kandinsky, Wassily. *Kandinsky: Complete Writings on Art,* ed. Kenneth C. Lindsay and Peter Vergo. New York: Da Capo Press, 1994.

Ringbom, Sixten. "Art in 'The Epoch of the Great Spiritual': Occult Elements in the Early Theory of Abstract Painting." *Journal of the Warburg and Courtauld Institutes* 29 (1966): 386–418.

———. *The Sounding Cosmos: A Study in the Spiritualism of Kandinsky and the Genesis of Abstract Painting.* Turku, Finland: Abo Akademi University (Acta Academiae Aboensis, Ser. A, Vol. 38, No. 2), 1970.

Weiss, Peg. *Kandinsky and Old Russia: The Artist as Ethnographer and Shaman.* New Haven: Yale University Press, 1995.

———. *Kandinsky in Munich: The Formative Jugenstil Years.* Princeton, N.J.: Princeton University Press, 1979.

CONSTANTIN BRANCUSI

Bach, Friedrich Teja; Margit Rowell; and Ann Temkin. *Constantin Brancusi, 1876–1957,* exh. cat. Philadelphia and Cambridge: Philadelphia Museum of Art with MIT Press, 1995.

Bazin, Nathalie. "Jacques Bacot, des monastères du Tibet aux salles de la Sorbonne." In *Âges et visages de l'Asie: Un Siècle d'exploration à travers les collections du musée Guimet,* 141–54. Dijon: Musée des Beaux-Arts de Dijon, 1996.

Brancusi et Duchamp: Regards historiques. Paris: Centre Pompidou, Les carnets de l'Atelier Brancusi, 2000.

Chave, Anna C. *Constantin Brancusi: Shifting the Bases of Art.* New Haven: Yale University Press, 1993.

Giedion-Welcker, Carola. *Constantin Brancusi,* trans. Maria Jolas and Anne Leroy. New York: Braziller, 1959.

Giménez, Carmen; Matthew Gale; et al. *Constantin Brancusi: The Essence of Things.* London: Tate; New York: Guggenheim, 2004.

Hulton, Pontus; Natalie Dumitresco; and Alexandre Istrati. *Brancusi.* Paris: Flammarion, 1986; London: Faber and Faber, 1988.

Miller, Sanda. *Constantin Brancusi: A Survey of His Work.* Oxford: Clarendon Press, 1995.

Le poète tibétain Milarépa: Ses crimes—ses épreuves—son nirvana, trans. from Tibetan with an introduction by Jacques Bacot. Paris: Bossard, 1925.

Varia, Radu. *Brancusi.* New York: Rizzoli, 1986.

MARCEL DUCHAMP

Cabanne, Pierre. *Dialogues with Marcel Duchamp,* trans. Ron Padgett. New York: Da Capo Press, 1987.

D'Harnoncourt, Anne, and Kynaston McShine, eds. *Marcel Duchamp,* exh. cat. New York: Museum of Modern Art, 1973.

Duchamp, Marcel. *The Writings of Marcel Duchamp,* ed. Michel Sanouillet and Elmer Peterson. New York: Da Capo Press, 1989 [1973].

Gough-Cooper, Jennifer, and Jacques Caumont. "Ephemerides on and about Marcel Duchamp and Rrose Sélavy, 1887–1968." In *Marcel Duchamp,* exh. cat. Milan: Bompiani, 1993.

Henderson, Linda Dalrymple. *Duchamp in Context: Science and Technology in the Large Glass and Related Works.* Princeton, N.J.: Princeton University Press, 1998.

Kuenzli, Rudolf, and Francis M. Naumann, eds. *Marcel Duchamp: Artist of the Century.* Cambridge: MIT Press, 1989.

Lebel, Robert. *Marcel Duchamp,* trans. George Heard Hamilton. New York: Paragraphic Books, 1959.

Lee, Tosi. "Fire Down Below and Watering, That's Life: A Buddhist Reader's Response to Marcel Duchamp." In *Buddha Mind in Contemporary Art,* ed. Jacquelynn Baas and Mary Jane Jacob. Berkeley: University of California Press, 2004.

———. "Watering, That's My Life: The Symbolism and Self-Imaging of Marcel Duchamp." Ph.D. thesis, University of Illinois at Urbana-Champaign, 1993.

Matisse, Paul, ed. *Marcel Duchamp Notes.* Boston: G. K. Hall, 1983.

Museum Jean Tinguely Basel, ed. *Marcel Duchamp*. Ostfildern-Ruit: Hatje Cantz, 2002.

Naumann, Francis M., and Hector Obalk, eds. *Affectionately Marcel: The Selected Correspondence of Marcel Duchamp,* trans. Jill Taylor. Ghent: Ludion Press, 2000.

Schwarz, Arturo. *The Complete Works of Marcel Duchamp*. New York: Abrams, 1970; rev. ed. New York: Delano Greenidge, 2000.

Tomkins, Calvin. *Duchamp: A Biography*. New York: Henry Holt, 1996.

GEORGIA O'KEEFFE

Cowart, Jack; Juan Hamilton; and Sarah Greenough. *Georgia O'Keeffe: Art and Letters,* exh cat. Washington, D.C.: National Gallery of Art, 1987.

Dow, Arthur Wesley. *Composition: A Series of Exercises in Art Structure for the Use of Students and Teachers,* 7th ed. New York: Doubleday, Page, 1913 (1st ed. 1899). (This is the edition O'Keeffe had; to her Texas students she assigned Dow's more condensed and less expensive *Theory and Practice of Teaching Art* published by Teachers College, Columbia University, 1912.)

Green, Nancy E., et al. *Arthur Wesley Dow: His Art and His Influences,* exh. cat. New York: Spanierman Gallery, 2004.

Kuh, Katharine. *The Artist's Voice: Talks with Seventeen Artists*. New York: Harper and Row, 1962.

Moffatt, Frederick C. *Arthur Wesley Dow (1857–1922),* exh. cat. Washington, D.C.: Smithsonian Institution Press, 1977.

O'Keeffe, Georgia. *Georgia O'Keeffe*. New York: Viking Press, 1976.

Pollitzer, Anita. *A Woman on Paper: Georgia O'Keeffe*. New York: Touchstone, 1988.

Richter, Peter-Cornell. *Georgia O'Keeffe and Alfred Stieglitz*. New York: Prestel, 2001.

Rose, Barbara. "Georgia O'Keeffe's Universal Spirital Vision." In *Georgia O'Keeffe,* exh. cat., 98–100. Tokyo: Saibu Museum of Art, 1988.

Turner, Elizabeth Hutton. *Georgia O'Keeffe: The Poetry of Things,* exh. cat. Washington, D.C., and New Haven: Phillips Collection with Yale University Press, 1999.

Udall, Sharyn R. *O'Keeffe and Texas,* exh. cat. San Antonio and New York: Marion Koogler McNay Art Museum with Abrams, 1998.

Wagner, Anne Middleton. *Three Artists (Three Women): Modernism and the Art of Hesse, Krasner, and O'Keeffe*. Berkeley: University of California Press, 1996.

III. THE SPACE OF ART

Clarke, David J. *The Influence of Oriental Thought on Postwar American Painting and Sculpture*. New York: Garland, 1988.

Gelburd, Gail, and Geri De Paoli. *The Transparent Thread: Asian Philosophy in Recent American Art*. Hempstead, New York, and Philadelphia: Hofstra University and Bard College, with the University of Pennsylvania Press, 1990.

Herrigel, Eugen. *Zen in the Art of Archery,* trans. R. R. C. Hull, introduction by D. T. Suzuki. New York: Pantheon, 1953.

Lipsey, Roger. *An Art of Our Own: The Spiritual in Twentieth-Century Art*. Boston: Shambhala, 1988.

Noguchi, Yone. *Selected English Writings of Yone Noguchi: An East-West Literary Assimilation,* 2 vols., ed. Yoshinobu Hakutani. London: Associated University Presses, 1990.

Suzuki, Daisetz Teitaro. *The Essentials of Zen Buddhism*. London: Luzac, 1927, 1933, 1934.

———. *An Introduction to Zen Buddhism,* foreword by C. G. Jung. New York: Philosophical Library, 1949.

———. *The Zen Doctrine of No-Mind: The Significance of the Sutra of Hui-neng (Wei-lang),* ed. Christmas Humphreys. London: Century Hutchinson, 1986 [1949].

Watts, Alan W. *The Spirit of Zen: A Way of Life, Work and Art in the Far East*. London: John Murray, 1948 [1936].

Westgeest, Helen. *Zen in the Fifties: Interaction in Art between East and West.* Zwolle: Waanders; Amstelveen: Cobra Museum voor Moderne Kunst, 1996.

ISAMU NOGUCHI

Altshuler, Bruce. *Isamu Noguchi.* New York: Abbeville, 1994.

Ashton, Dore. *Noguchi East and West.* Berkeley: University of California Press, 1992.

Duus, Masayo. *The Life of Isamu Noguchi: Journey without Borders.* Trans. Peter Duus. Princeton, N.J.: Princeton University Press, 2004.

Hunter, Sam. *Isamu Noguchi.* New York: Abbeville, 1978.

Noguchi, Isamu. *Isamu Noguchi: Essays and Conversations,* ed. Diane Apostolos-Cappadona and Bruce Altshuler. New York: Abrams, 1994.

———. *Isamu Noguchi: A Sculptor's World.* Foreword by R. Buckminster Fuller. New York: Harper and Row, 1968.

Rychlak, Bonnie. *Zen No Zen: Aspects of Noguchi's Sculptural Vision.* New York: Isamu Noguchi Foundation, 2002.

AD REINHARDT

Bois, Yve-Alain. *Ad Reinhardt,* exh. cat. New York: Rizzoli with Museum of Modern Art, 1991.

Hess, Thomas B. "Editorial: Ad (Adolph Dietrich Friedrich) Reinhardt." *Art News* 66, no. 6 (October 1967): 22–23.

Lippard, Lucy R. *Ad Reinhardt Paintings,* exh. cat. With preface by Sam Hunter and chronology by the artist. New York: Jewish Museum, 1966.

McEvilley, Thomas. "Heads It's Form, Tails It's Not Content." *Artforum* 21, no. 3 (November 1982): 50–61.

Reinhardt, Ad. *Art-as-Art: The Selected Writings of Ad Reinhardt,* ed. Barbara Rose. New York: Viking, 1975.

———. "Timeless in Asia." *Art News* 58, no. 9 (January 1960): 32–35.

YVES KLEIN

Charlet, Nicholas. *Yves Klein.* Paris: Adam Biro, 2000.

McEvilley, Thomas. "Yves Klein, Messenger of the Age of Space." *Artforum* 20, no. 5 (January 1982): 38–51.

McEvilley, Thomas; Nan Rosenthal; et al. *Yves Klein 1928–1962: A Retrospective,* exh. cat. Houston: Rice University, 1982.

Perlein, Gilbert; Bruno Corà; et al. *Yves Klein: Long Live the Immaterial!* New York: Delano Greenidge Editions, 2000.

Stich, Sidra. *Yves Klein.* Stuttgart: Cantz, 1994.

JASPER JOHNS

Crichton, Michael. *Jasper Johns.* New York: Abrams, 1994.

Field, Richard S. *Jasper Johns: Prints 1970–1977.* Middletown, Conn.: Wesleyan University, 1978.

Johns, Jasper. *Jasper Johns: Writings, Sketchbook Notes, Interviews,* ed. Kirk Varnedoe, comp. Christel Hollevoet. New York: Museum of Modern Art, 1996.

Rose, Barbara. "Jasper Johns: The Tantric Details." *American Art* 7, no. 4 (Fall 1993): 47–71.

Rosenthal, Nan, and Ruth E. Fine. *The Drawings of Jasper Johns,* exh. cat. Washington, D.C.: National Gallery of Art, 1990.

Solomon, Alan R., and John Cage. *Jasper Johns,* exh. cat. New York: Jewish Museum, 1964.

Sontag, Susan; Richard Francis, et al., *Cage-Cunningham-Johns: Dancers on a Plane: In Memory of Their Feelings.* New York: Knopf in association with Antony d'Offay Gallery, 1989.

Varnedoe, Kirk, with Roberta Bernstein. *Jasper Johns: A Retrospective,* exh. cat. New York: Museum of Modern Art, distributed by Abrams, 1996.

IV. THE SOUND OF THE MIND

Armstrong, Elizabeth, et al. *In the Spirit of Fluxus.* Minneapolis: Walker Art Center, 1993.

Doris, David T. "Zen Vaudeville: A Medi(t)ation in the Margins of Fluxus." In *The Fluxus Reader,* ed. Ken Friedman, 91–135. West Sussex: Academy Editions, 1998.

Hendricks, Jon. *Fluxus Codex.* New York: Abrams, 1988.

Phillpot, Clive, and Jon Hendricks. *Fluxus: Selections from the Gilbert and Lila Silverman Collection,* exh. cat. New York: Museum of Modern Art, 1988.

Schimmel, Paul, et al. *Out of Actions: Between Performance and the Object, 1949–1979,* exh. cat. Los Angeles: Museum of Contemporary Art, 1998.

JOHN CAGE

Bernstein, David W., and Christopher Hatch, eds. *Writings through John Cage's Music, Poetry, and Art.* Chicago: University of Chicago Press, 2001.

Brown, Kathan. *John Cage Visual Art: To Sober and Quiet the Mind.* San Francisco: Crown Point Press, 2000.

Cage, John. *Silence.* Hanover, N.H.: Wesleyan University Press, 1973 [1961].

Kostelanetz, Richard, ed. *Conversing with Cage.* New York: Routledge, 2003 [1987].

Retallack, Joan, ed. *Musicage: Cage Muses on Words, Art, Music.* Hanover, N.H.: Wesleyan University Press, distributed by University Press of New England, 1996.

Tomkins, Calvin. *The Bride and the Bachelors: Five Masters of the Avant-Garde.* New York: Viking, 1968 [1965].

NAM JUNE PAIK

Decker-Phillips, Edith. *Paik Video.* Barrytown, N.Y.: Barrytown, 1998 [1988].

Hanhardt, John G. *The Worlds of Nam June Paik,* exh. cat. New York: Solomon R. Guggenheim Museum, 2000.

Hanhardt, John G., et al. *Nam June Paik, Composer,* exh. cat. New York: Whitney Museum of American Art with W. W. Norton, 1982.

Melencamp, Patricia. "The Old and the New: Nam June Paik." *Art Journal* 54, no. 4 (Winter 1995): 41–47.

Smith, Walter. "Nam June Paik's *TV Buddha* as Buddhist Art," *Religion and the Arts* 4, no. 3 (2000): 359–73.

Stooss,Toni, and Thomas Kellien, eds. *Nam June Paik: Video Time, Video Space.* New York: Abrams, 1993.

YOKO ONO

Munroe, Alexandra, with Jon Hendricks et al. *Yes: Yoko Ono,* exh. cat. New York: Japan Society and Abrams, 2001.

Ono, Yoko. *Grapefruit: A Book of Instructions and Drawings by Yoko Ono.* Introduction by John Lennon. New York: Simon and Schuster, 2000 [1964].

———. *Instruction Paintings.* New York: Weatherhill, 1995.

LAURIE ANDERSON

Anderson, Laurie. *Stories from the Nerve Bible: A Retrospective 1972–1992.* New York: HarperCollins, 1994.

Goldberg, RoseLee. *Laurie Anderson.* New York: Abrams, 2000.

Howell, John. *Laurie Anderson.* New York: Thunder's Mouth Press, 1992.

Kardon, Janet. *Laurie Anderson: Works from 1969 to 1983,* exh. cat. Philadelphia: Institute of Contemporary Art, University of Pennsylvania, 1983.

Laurie Anderson: The Record of the Time, exh. cat. With essays by Thierry Raspail and Laurie Anderson. Lyon: Musée d'Art Contemporain, 2002.

V. LIGHT AND INSIGHT

Mookerjee, Ajit. *Tantra Art: Its Philosophy and Physics.* New Delhi and Paris: Rupa in collaboration with Ravi Kumar, 1994 [1966].

Suzuki, Daisetz Teitaro. *Manual of Zen Buddhism.* New York: Grove Press, 1960.

Suzuki, Shunryu. *Zen Mind, Beginner's Mind: Informal Talks on Zen Meditation and Practice,* ed. Trudy Dixon. New York: Weatherhill, 1999 [1970].

Thurman, Robert A. F. "The Buddha's Smile: Enlightenment and the Pursuit of Happiness." In *In Pursuit of Happiness,* ed. Leroy S. Rouner. Notre Dame, Ind.: University of Notre Dame Press, 1995.

Trungpa, Chogyam. *Dharma Art,* ed. Judith L. Lief. Boston: Shambhala, 1996.

AGNES MARTIN

Agnes Martin, Richard Tuttle, exh. cat. Fort Worth: Modern Art Museum, 1998.

Haskell, Barbara. *Agnes Martin,* exh. cat. New York: Whitney Museum of American Art and Abrams, 1992.

Martin, Agnes. *Writings.* Ostfildern, Germany: Cantz, 1991.

McEvilley, Thomas. "Grey Geese Descending: The Art of Agnes Martin." *Artforum* 25, no. 10 (Summer 1987): 94–99.

Rand, Yvonne. "On Seeing *Untitled #3: Bands of White and Graphite.*" In *Searchlight: Consciousness at the Millennium,* ed. Lawrence Rinder, 108–15. New York: Thames and Hudson, 1999.

Rifkin, Ned. *Agnes Martin: The Nineties and Beyond.* Houston: Menil Foundation and Cantz, 2002.

ROBERT IRWIN

Irwin, Robert. *Being and Circumstance: Notes toward a Conditional Art.* Larkspur Landing, Calif.: Lapis Press with Pace Gallery and San Francisco Museum of Modern Art, 1985.

Leider, Philip. "Robert Irwin." In *Robert Irwin, Kenneth Price,* exh. cat. Los Angeles: Los Angeles County Museum of Art, 1966.

Robert Irwin, exh. cat. Los Angeles: Museum of Contemporary Art, 1993.

Weschler, Lawrence. *Seeing Is Forgetting the Name of the Thing One Sees: A Life of Contemporary Artist Robert Irwin.* Berkeley: University of California Press, 1982.

VIJA CELMINS

Lingwood, James, ed. *Vija Celmins, Works 1964–96,* exh. cat. London: Institute of Contemporary Art, 1996.

Rippner, Samantha. *The Prints of Vija Celmins,* exh. cat. New York and New Haven: Metropolitan Museum of Art with Yale University Press, 2002.

Vija Celmins. Interviewed by Chuck Close, ed. William S. Bartman. New York: A.R.T. Press, 1992.

RICHARD TUTTLE

Agnes Martin, Richard Tuttle, exh. cat. Fort Worth: Modern Art Museum, 1998.

Poetter, Jochen. *Richard Tuttle: Chaos, die/the Form,* exh. cat. Stuttgart: Staatliche Kunsthalle Baden-Baden, 1993.

Richard Tuttle: Community, exh. cat. Chicago: Arts Club, 1999.

Richard Tuttle: Grey Walls Work, exh. cat. London: Camden Arts Centre, 1997.

Richard Tuttle: Replace the Abstract Picture Plane, exh. cat. Zug, Switzerland: Kunsthaus Zug and Cantz, 2001.

Richard Tuttle: Wire Pieces, exh. cat. Bordeaux: Musée d'Art Contemporain, 1986.

Tucker, Marcia. *Richard Tuttle,* exh. cat. New York: Whitney Museum of American Art, 1975.

INDEX

Note: Page numbers in italics indicate illustrations.